Jeanne Eagels: A Life Revealed
Fully Revised and Updated

By Eric Woodard and Tara Hanks

BearManor Media

Albany, Georgia

Jeanne Engels: A Life Revealed (Fully Revised and Updated)
Copyright © 2018 Eric Woodard and Tara Hanks. All Rights Reserved.

No part of this book may be reproduced in any form or by any means, electronic, mechanical, digital, photocopying or recording, except for the inclusion in a review, without permission in writing from the the publisher.

Published in the USA by
BearManor Media
P.O. Box 71426
Albany, GA 31708
www.BearManorMedia.com

Softcover Edition
ISBN-10: 1-62933-375-1
ISBN-13: 978-1-62933-375-5

Cover photo by Strauss-Peyton, New York City

Printed in the United States of America

To Jeanne Eagels
In memory of her talent, beauty and fire

Table of Contents

INTRODUCTION	ix
CHAPTER ONE: LITTLE MISS EAGELS 1890 - 1910	1
CHAPTER TWO: THE GREAT WHITE WAY AUGUST 1910 - MAY 1915	27
CHAPTER THREE: THE WORLD AND THE WOMAN JUNE 1915 - DECEMBER 1916	51
CHAPTER FOUR: FIRES OF YOUTH JANUARY 1917 - APRIL 1918	73
CHAPTER FIVE: DADDIES MAY 1918 - OCTOBER 1919	99
CHAPTER SIX: A WONDERFUL THING NOVEMBER 1919 - SEPTEMBER 1922	125
CHAPTER SEVEN: INTRODUCING SADIE THOMPSON - NOVEMBER 1922	155
CHAPTER EIGHT: HIGH SOCIETY DECEMBER 1922 - DECEMBER 1924	181
CHAPTER NINE: COMFORT, LOVE AND RESPECT JANUARY - DECEMBER 1925	209
CHAPTER TEN: PASSION OF THE HEART JANUARY – DECEMBER 1926	233
CHAPTER ELEVEN: HER CARDBOARD LOVER JANUARY - JULY 1927	257
CHAPTER TWELVE: MAN, WOMAN AND SIN AUGUST - DECEMBER 1927	277
CHAPTER THIRTEEN: THE IMP FROM HELL JANUARY - SEPTEMBER 1928	297
CHAPTER FOURTEEN: KLEIG EYES OCTOBER 1928 - SEPTEMBER 1929	331
CHAPTER FIFTEEN: THE LAST ACT OCTOBER 1929	361

CHRONOLOGY	383
CHAPTER SIXTEEN: A CUMULATIVE TRAGEDY	397
CHAPTER SEVENTEEN: YOU CAN'T LIBEL THE DEAD	415
POSTSCRIPT: THE BALLAD OF SADIE THOMPSON	441
BIBLIOGRAPHY	467
INDEX	475

Introduction

"There's no place like home," says Dorothy Gale, ten-year-old heroine of Frank L. Baum's novel, *The Wonderful Wizard of Oz*. After a cyclone transports Dorothy from her Kansas farm to the enchanted world of Oz, she travels to the Emerald City, encountering several strange, yet familiar, characters along the way to meet the Wizard, whom she hopes can help her find her way back home. Published in 1900, Baum's tale soon became an American classic on stage and film.

In the neighboring state of Missouri, another young girl was also dreaming of far-off places. She was raised not on a rural plain but in a working-class neighborhood of Kansas City, Missouri, the smell of manure that continually drifted over from the nearby stockyards filled her nostrils, and the constant rumble of trains with their belching steam engines and loud whistles rang in her ears. Born in the same year as Dorothy, she may well have sat in her own bedroom reading Baum's book, and pictured herself wearing the witch's silver slippers, heading down her own yellow brick road to the Great White Way.

Kansas City has contributed greatly to the entertainment industry, by way of natives and residents who spent their childhoods or early careers in the Midwestern city: Jean Harlow, Walt Disney, Charlie Parker, William Powell, Count Basie, Joan Crawford and Ginger Rogers to name just a few. But the star who once shone brightest of all so has become a mere footnote to America's theatrical past.

Jeanne Eagels: even her name carries an aura, and like so many myths about her, it was her own design. Born in the Midwest to a large, working-class family in the twilight of the nineteenth century, she was smitten by the theatre at an early age. Raw talent, and beauty, were her spurs to an adventurous career, and by her twenties, she was a seasoned professional and star of stage and screen. Her ambition was bold: she wanted nothing less than to become America's answer to the divine Sarah Bernhardt. And after years of toil, Jeanne Eagels found the role that would raise her to the ranks of the immortals, that of Sadie Thompson in *Rain*. But that success was too strong for Jeanne and within a few tumultuous years, the actress was dead, and her life became a cautionary tale.

On film, Jeanne Eagels was surpassed by others—often playing the same parts. Only a scant handful of her screen performances exist to give us an idea of what she could have achieved.

Younger actresses followed Jeanne's lead, including Bette Davis and Barbara Stanwyck, and they achieved the celluloid immortality Eagels was denied. She also opened the door for "bad girls with good hearts" which allowed Mae West to flourish on stage and Jean Harlow's overt sexuality to sizzle on-screen, paving the way for the most famous blonde of all: Marilyn.

Who led me to Jeanne.

While the names of Jeanne Eagels and Sadie Thompson were not unknown to me, I had paid them very little attention until researching Monroe's attempt to play Thompson on television in the early 1960s. What little information I found on the actress was confusing and contradictory. Once that project was complete, I returned to the elusive Miss Eagels and devoted my time to uncovering all I could about this mysterious woman. In the memoirs of her contemporaries, she rates no more than a page or two; in histories of the theatre, a paragraph or four; and in movie lore, a fleeting reference—much of it hyperbolic, if not outright fantasy. A single volume was dedicated to her life—Edward Doherty's *The Rain Girl*—published in 1931, following a 1930 serialization in *Liberty Magazine*.

After scouring online newspaper and magazine archives, special collections, Google Books, Ebay and other sources, a larger dossier on the actress soon formed. Out of the dusty files emerged a fascinating woman who, although complex and flawed, deserved to have her full story told in a spirit of justice and respect. The only regret is that my curiosity wasn't ignited decades earlier, when there would have been a chance to locate and speak with family and others who knew her, but sadly, that is no longer the case.

With a shared passion for America's theatrical history and an eloquent style I lack, my co-author, Tara Hanks, helped bring this project to life. The further we explored, the more intrigued we were by this extraordinary young woman of great talent, drive, and compassion, driven by demons that ensured both her dramatic ascent to fame, and a chaotic private life seemingly fated to crash and burn.

We also discovered that Miss Eagels herself was not always a reliable source. To say she embroidered the facts would be an understatement. In the early days of mass media, she concocted a romantic version of herself with little thought of detection. Our task has been to utilize our sources, gather data, organize, read between the lines in some places, apply logic in others, until like a jigsaw puzzle of words, we have reassembled her story with all the accuracy we can muster, inspired by the rich materials gathered from the mists of time.

Both of us were struck by the numerous similarities between the life of Jeanne Eagels and Marilyn Monroe, another tragic star whom both Tara and I have long admired. From an early age, both had known poverty and pursued their careers with fierce determination. Each fought typecasting, frequently clashing with their bosses and co-stars. Once famous, their lives were chronicled in microscopic detail by the press, and both came to rely on an ever-growing entourage of doctors, acting coaches and press agents to serve as a barrier from the public. A total of five failed marriages accumulated between them, including one each to a famous sports figure. And finally, both became victims of substance abuse which led to their early deaths by overdose.

Nearly sixty years after her untimely exit, Monroe remains the most talked-about actress of the twentieth century. Scores of documentaries, films, and videos have been dedicated to her. She has been the subject of theatrical productions, television series and even college courses in popular culture and feminism. Scholars debate the import of her journals, letters and poetry; her clothing, costumes, scripts and other items of personal property sell for enormous sums at auctions, while her bombshell image lures steady crowds to cinematic retrospectives and photographic exhibitions.

In her lifetime, Eagels enjoyed the critical acclaim Monroe would achieve all too late. Jeanne Eagels has been unjustly neglected in the years after her death. She was robbed of the chance to bring Sadie Thompson to the big screen, though those who saw her onstage said her greatest performance was never surpassed. Her reputation and talents were trivialized by a steady trickle of malicious gossip, reducing her to that most spectral of beings—a legend without a face. In *Jeanne Eagels: A Life Revealed*, we hope to right some wrongs, fill in some blanks and present the woman behind the enigma, a feisty yet fragile diva who became a genuine phenomenon.

As Monroe once said: "All we demanded was our right to twinkle."

Eric Woodard & Tara Hanks

I would also like to take the opportunity to acknowledge and thank the following people, without whom this book would never have come to

INTRODUCTION

be: James Woodard, Andrew Hanks, Heidi Hanson Freeman, Michelle Morgan, Carlton Stoval, Theresa Schult, and the late Liz Smith.

Much gratitude to David Stenn, Ivan Damiano, John Duel, Jean Cameron-Smith.

All photographs from author's collection unless otherwise noted.

Chapter 1
Little Miss Eagels: 1890-1910

On a bend in the Missouri River where it meets the Kansas River, the town of Kansas, Missouri was incorporated in 1850, with 2,500 residents living within an official city limit of less than a square mile. By the mid-nineteenth century, the towns of Kansas, Westport, and nearby Independence had become critical points in America's westward expansion towards the Pacific Ocean. Three major trails—the Santa Fe, California, and Oregon—all originated in Jackson County, Missouri.

In 1869 the Hannibal & St. Joseph Railroad bridge, stretching across the Missouri River, was built, opening the way in 1871, for the Kansas City Stockyards to open—two-thirds in Kansas and one-third across state lines in the town of Kansas' West Bottoms district. Meatpacking plants owned by Cudahy, Armour, and Swift soon followed bringing jobs and workers with families. The city's population grew to 55,000 by decade's end. Livestock was the area's bread and butter, earning it the lowly nickname of "Cow Town."

To accommodate the twenty-six different railroad systems that now converged at the train yards, Union Depot, second-largest east of New York, was built in 1878. Quickly dubbed the "Jackson County Insane Asylum" (as both were designed by the same architect), the building had arched windows framed in stone and rows of dormers jutting out from the steeply pitched roof. A 125-foot clock tower, the tallest structure in town, greeted all who disembarked from the nearly 200 daily trains.

Nine years later, that tower was one of the first things that Edward W. Eagles, his wife Julia and daughter Edna saw when they arrived in 1887 from Leavenworth, Kansas, forty miles west. One of eight children, Edward was the son of William Henry Eagles, a Pennsylvania Dutch farmer who had relocated the family to Leavenworth in around 1875. His mother Emily Rebecca was raised in Tennessee by Irish parents. Julia Sullivan was one of five daughters and three sons born to Eugene and Hanorah Sullivan, who came to Boston from County Cork, Ireland in 1845. Like the Eagles, the Sullivans had moved to Leavenworth when Julia was still young. The couple met while living in Platte City, Missouri and were married in 1886, before returning to Leavenworth where in July 1887, Edna was born.

After striking out alone in Kansas City, the couple plus one settled into their home at 2134 Summit Street. Edward soon found work as a carpenter, enabling the family to move to 2017 McGee Street in 1888.

A year later the town of Kansas merged with neighboring Westport, renaming themselves Kansas City – now boasting a population of 125,000 residents, twenty-five schools, over sixty-five miles of planked sidewalks, fifteen miles of paved streets, and an extensive thirty-five-mile cable-car system that rivaled San Francisco's.

By then the family was living at 2413 Locust Street and would soon move again to the neighborhood of McGee and Thirtieth Street; where they welcomed a second daughter on June 26, 1890, naming her Amelia Eugenia after Julia's father, Eugene Sullivan. With no birth certificate known to exist, Eugenia's exact birth year is almost impossible to establish. Conflicting census records give a range of 1889-1891. She would later claim 1894 in the press and on passport applications, while her first biographer Eddie Doherty's estimate of 1890 may be closer to the truth and is now accepted as fact.

Each year found the family in a different residence: 1607 Penn Avenue in 1891; 1713 Cherry Street in 1892; and finally, 1319 Grove Street by 1893. With another child on the way, a larger house seemed the only solution.

But no matter their address, the girls were often visited by their maternal grandfather. Doherty described Sullivan as a "strong, heavy-fisted man," who "worked hard all his life and played hard. His only recreations were writing pieces for Irish-American newspapers and playing with his grandchildren." Eugenia and her rag doll, "Judy Punch", would accompany him on errands, and he bragged to anyone who would listen about "... her generosity and the wily way she helped Edna without sacrificing any interest of her own. When Edna was given candy or cookies, she split with Eugenia. When Eugenia received anything she said, 'Edna wants some too.'"

Eugenia's world was shattered when Sullivan died in Leavenworth on December 4, 1893. But though one life had been taken, another was on its way. A son was born in January 1894 whom the couple named Edward. The family's joy was short-lived, as the infant died of unknown causes on March 29. Possibly to rid themselves of sad memories, the family relocated shortly thereafter to 1729 Michigan Street.

Beginning in about 1895, a movement by local officials to transform Kansas City's industrial boom-town image with a municipality-wide program into "The City Beautiful" was implemented. Numerous parks, filled with bubbling fountains and statuary, were created for residents to enjoy. Wide boulevards branching out from the center of town were soon filled with mansions and estates. Construction boomed so rapidly that local offices were opened by architectural firms from Chicago, New York, and Boston. Edward's business grew as fast as the city skyline. The Board of Trade, New York Life and New England Buildings, Exposition Hall, Jackson County Courthouse and Emery, Bird, Thayer & Company department store all reached towards the clouds within months and blocks of each other. In 1897 the Eagles clan moved to 2407 Cherry Street, and then two houses down to 2403.

Growing up, Eugenia (also called Gee-Gee or Jennie by her family), suffered from frequent respiratory illnesses. Some would have labeled her a "frail child," but she didn't allow these limitations to deter her from playing with her sister or the neighborhood children. "My earliest recollection is of quarreling with some children in our street who made fun of us because we used the broad 'a' in 'bath' and in 'laugh,'" she told Ada Patterson in a September 1923 interview for *Theatre Magazine*. "My sister gave up the contest. She consented to flatten her 'a'. I refused. I said I would not be bullied into using a sound that was not right. I loved combat. I love it now."

She could best any boy climbing trees, walking fences, or jumping from porches. At seven, she fell and broke her right arm. As Julia had given birth to daughter Helen in April, a doctor was called to the house to stave off another costly trip to hospital. Set incorrectly, the injury would cause Eugenia pain when damp, a recurring problem throughout her life. Later that year, the family moved again to 2324 South McCoy Street, where brother Leo was born on September 21, 1898.

It was here that Eugenia befriended Ruby Stapp, whose parents Edward and Mollie owned a grocery store at 2424 McCoy. The eight-year-olds would loiter around the candy counter hoping for a sweet and sometimes waited on customers when the elder Stapps were busy elsewhere. They would sit under the huge yellow rose bush in Eugenia's backyard, having a "tea party" with their dolls, or giggling about a certain boy they both liked, and planning their eventual weddings to the unsuspecting groom. It wasn't much of a contest, Ruby admitted to Eddie Doherty: even at that tender age, Eugenia "didn't think men or boys worth fighting for," but she could do no wrong in Stapp's admiring eyes. On one occasion when Ruby had a loose tooth, Eugenia—itching to play dentist—promised to extract it using only a piece of string and a quick jerk. Of course, the "patient" had to fall asleep, which took longer than expected as both girls were in high spirits all evening. Slumber came eventually, and by morning Ruby's tooth was gone. A born storyteller, Eagles later claimed it was her tooth which was pulled out by Stapp: ". . . though only a child, of course, but I was an actress even then, playing all over the Middle West. I could make up as a witch or a hag, thanks to that missing tooth. I could paint my other teeth black—and there was the ugly gap right in the center. It was quite effective."

Stapp also recalled her friend's love of pickles. If she couldn't wheedle a free one from the giant barrel at Mr. Stapp's store, she'd beg a penny from her mother to buy one. Jeanne would later claim "short intervals of school-going," totaling less than two years. In fact, she was a very bright child, who did well at the Morse Public School on Charlotte Avenue (between 20th and 21st Streets), and when family finances allowed, Saint Joseph's Parochial School at 1826 Forest Avenue, where her antics tested the nuns' patience. Sister Alma Cecile told Doherty of one such incident, when the nun noticed a distinct odor in the classroom and summoned the young student up to her desk.

"Eugenia, I smell pickles. Have you one?"

"No ma'am," came the reply.

Pointing to her leg, Sister Cecile asked, "What is that unsightly bulge in your stocking?"

"That's a pickle, Sister. It's in my stocking, but I haven't *got* it."

"*Touché*, Miss Eagles," the nun may have thought, turning away before her dour expression melted into a wry smile.

By 1900, Kansas City was the twenty-second largest city in the country with a population of over 160,000 residents, important enough to host the 1901 Democratic National Convention. The Eagles were now living at 2111 Campbell Street, and the fairy godmother who would set Eugenia on her path to fame had arrived in Kansas City.

With film-making still in its experimental stages, and radio and television decades from reality, live performance was still the mainstay of mass entertainment. Audiences gathered at the one of several Kansas City theatres such as the Auditorium, the Grand, the Gillis, or the Coates and Ninth Street opera houses, all of which imported their performers and shows from New York. Minor and extra roles were filled with semi-professional actors and amateurs, mostly local residents. One of the most reputable troupes, the Kansas City-based Woodward Stock Company, was large enough to have its own acting school, led by Mrs. Georgia Brown.

Born in Quebec, Georgia moved to America at three, making her stage debut at six at Cleveland Academy of Music, where her father worked as manager. After his death when she was twelve, she toured with her mother as The Morrell Sisters, learning melodramatic tear-jerking songs, and such dance steps as the buck-and-wing and double shuffle from fellow vaudevillians. Her mother remarried, to Edwin Brown, and the family settled in Lawrence, Kansas. Georgia took her stepfather's surname professionally, keeping it even after she later married and raised a daughter.

While teaching at the University of Kansas' Drama Department (which she would eventually head), Georgia began visiting Kansas City, to stage youth theatrical productions such as Gilbert and Sullivan's operetta, *Iolanthe*, featuring a cast of 150 children between the ages of four and ten, at the Coates Opera House.

She opened her first dramatic school in 1900, at 3212 Troost Avenue, several miles from the Eagles' 2898 East 18th street home. Brown loved her students and they loved her back. She was firm, but fair. A 1953 *Kansas City Times* profile recounted that in October 1901, Georgia had presented a children's production of Shakespeare's *A Midsummer Night's Dream*. Seven little girls were chosen by Brown to play Puck, the mischievous sprite, in order to circumvent any problems with pre-curtain illnesses, and to give each child an opportunity on stage.

According to the *Times*, local newspaper critics had given favorable notices to those who played the principal parts, and even predicted stage careers for six of the seven young ladies who played Puck. However, they all failed to mention the only one who would later become one of the greatest stars of Broadway. "I tried to discover the reason," Georgia Brown told the *Kansas City Star* in 1925, "but I never could find out whether the critics actually did not like her or just forgot to mention her. Anyway, the six little girls who were promised stage careers in such complimentary terms are housewives, businesswomen, schoolteachers . . . While the seventh—well, the seventh was Jeanne Eagels."[1]

"I played the grave-digger in *Hamlet*[2] . . . They gave me the chance to play Shakespeare because nobody else of the tender age of seven would do so. They wouldn't say the rather amazing words . . . the other kiddies. I took it all quite seriously and said ALL the words without a quiver. Once I had begun I could not be stopped. I was ill when I was not on the stage. It seemed to me I couldn't breathe in any other atmosphere."

Undeterred, Jeanne worked hard, and in 1902, her mentor felt confident enough with the progress to cast her as Little Eva, the plantation owner's dying daughter, in *Uncle Tom's Cabin* at the Willis-Wood Theatre. Her dancing abilities won her spots in the ballets and shows that Georgia supervised for the 1902 to 1904 Priests of Pallas Festivals; an annual October event created by city officials in 1887, featuring elaborate electrical floats, music, and entertainment to rival Mardi Gras.

Ruby and her family had relocated to West Peculiar, the next county south of Kansas City in 1900, when the Eagles moved to 22401 Cherry Street. But Eugenia wasn't lonely, as her brother George was born in July

---

[1] Eddie Doherty names only two other girls, Tessie Marshall and Helen Levenson, in his 1930 serialization for *Liberty* magazine. Marshall was later employed as a clerk at Montgomery Ward & Company, while Levenson's fate is unknown.

[2] *Hamlet* was not produced by either Brown or the Woodward Company in 1901, but that didn't prevent Eagels from making this claim to the press on more than one occasion.

1902, and she had a small circle of friends including Alma Cohen, Mary Marguerite (Margaret) Knowles, Ruth M. Malone, Thecla Tempelman, and Anna Belle Mall. Outside of school, the girls attended church together and played at each other's houses. At the Cohen home, Alma's mother would make them coffee cake. Jeanne would remain life-long friends with the girls and frequently visited with them on her return trips home.

Eugenia thrived on the stage, and knew it was her life's calling. She was more inspired by reading a play than studying religion, history, or any other subject in school. "Once I'd played in front of an audience, it was battle royal to keep me off the stage," she told the *Boston Globe* in 1925. "I did all this in the face of pretty stiff family opposition, for the perfectly natural idea was that I ought to be going to school uninterruptedly."

In the spring of 1903, on the day of Eugenia's confirmation at St. Joseph's, the heavens opened. A sheet of rain stood between the group of girls standing on the porch of the school, and the church a block away. Ignoring the catcalls of "You're gonna get wet, you're gonna get wet," Eugenia folded up her veil and dress, held them under her petticoats and sprinted for the church, pigtails flying as she dodged puddles on the sidewalk. Hurriedly redressing in the vestibule, the slightly damp but victorious pilgrim was ready to face her congregation.

On May 30, torrential rains and severe floods ravaged Kansas City. At Union Station in the low-lying lands of the city, waylaid passengers scrambled to the second floor, watching as up to twenty feet of water submerged vast parts of downtown.

The ensuing damage totaled millions of dollars and brought the city to a standstill for twelve days. Sixteen bridges were destroyed, including those carrying pipes supplying Kansas City with water. Even where electricity was reconnected, streetcars were unable to run as miles of tracks were twisted like pretzels, or fully submerged. Only twenty people lost their lives, but over 16,000 residents, mostly poor, were left homeless. Officials made the decision not to re-open the schools damaged in the deluge, and those surrounding the flood zone became overcrowded with new students.

Believing the tragedy was a sign from above that she should follow her dreams of a life on the stage, Eugenia dropped out of school altogether. Mandatory education was not a priority in the early 1900s, and her natural intelligence and the ability to quickly absorb and learn from those around her would compensate for her lack of formal education. A more immediate benefit to the family was her help around the house with baby George and her other siblings.

Encroaching illness was hampering Edward's carpentry business, and before long the family fortunes declined. At fourteen, Eugenia found employment at the Emery, Bird & Thayer Department Store as a stock clerk. With her first weekly pay-check of $5, she bought her mother a blouse, plus an account book for her father and a couple of theatre tickets. With only 10¢ left, she walked home to save the trolley fare.

Joseph Maloney, the store's long-standing timekeeper, was interviewed by the *Kansas City Star* in 1930. "Miss Eagles was not unusually good-looking," he said. "She was a slender girl and just past the awkward stage. But there was something about her that attracted attention." Her work was "satisfactory," Maloney recalled, "but I think it was just something to be doing while she waited for her chance on the stage."

Eugenia was promoted to cashier, but with most of her salary going towards the family bills and occasional treats of make-up or matinee theatre tickets, there was no money left for acting lessons. Sometimes there wasn't even enough for those other small pleasures, whereupon she resorted to charging 50¢ worth of postage stamps to the family account at the drug store, and then selling them to get the 25¢ admission with a nickel for candy or soda. Eugenia and Margaret Knowles haunted Georgia Brown's classroom at every spare moment, and even if it was closed, just being nearby was enough.

Sitting at the top of the iron steps which ran up outside the Auditorium to the classroom, through the open door, Eugenia listened to and practiced exercises in elocution and other speech techniques, while keeping her eye on the stage door below for her cue as an extra or bit player in the current Woodward Company production.

Mrs. Brown complained that keeping the door open distracted her pupils, but she couldn't deny Eugenia's enthusiasm, or her logic. "If you close the door Mrs. Brown, and I have to stay inside, I'll miss my cues," she protested. "Or else, I'll have to stay outside, and I won't learn anything."

Desperate to stand out from the crowd, she would apply make-up while sitting under the front porch, then proceed to take a walk or trolley ride. "Dear me," the teenager exclaimed haughtily, "I have had to come away from the theatre in such a rush; I didn't have time to take off my make-up." During her October 1924 curtain speech given at the final New York performance of *Rain* before going on tour, she would tell the audience of "the girl who used to ride the streetcar from the Georgia Brown Dramatic School to her home out northeast, her make-up still on to impress people with the fact she was an actress." Throughout her life she would credit Georgia as "My first and only teacher—to whom I owe everything."

In a 1927 brochure advertising Mrs. Brown's school, Jeanne was referred to as ". . . the most famous and most ambitious child of the school's history." In the same year, she remembered her days at the school in an interview with John B. Kennedy of *Collier's Weekly*. "A swarm of little girls and boys competed for places in every play," she told him. "I had one advantage; I could toe-dance." Kennedy reported that "Little Miss Eagels had a greed for industry. Whenever another child was too ill or injured to perform, [she] would play their parts as well as her own. On one occasion, an old-fashioned roll-down curtain collapsed suddenly on an ensemble and injured three youngsters. [She] doubled for two of them in the next act." In her own words, "I prayed for similar misfortunes to put more of them out of commission so that I could do their bits."

As this miniature Eve Harrington would conclude, "It all came under the head of experience."

Little Miss Eagels: 1890-1910

***

By 1907, Eugenia had blossomed into a lovely young woman of five feet and six inches, weighing a slender 115 pounds. She had fine medium brown hair, expressive blue/green eyes, a flawless complexion, dimpled chin, pert nose, and strong jaw-line. Impishly pretty, she was fast becoming a beauty, with an ethereal quality surpassed only by her extraordinary talent and iron will. On July 9, two weeks after her seventeenth birthday, her mother gave birth to the family's last child, a son named Daniel Paul.

Eugenia took a cold, hard look at her likely future if she remained in Kansas City, and it wasn't promising. Her father was in poor health, and she would have to help her mother raise three young boys, along with ten-year-old Helen. She might become the Woodward Company's ingénue, appearing locally and perhaps eventually moving on to Chicago, but she had known from early childhood that she was destined for greater things than life in Missouri had to offer; she wanted the entire United States to know exactly who she was. The only way to achieve that was to get away from Kansas City and its "Cow Town" reputation (no matter how assiduously the city fathers endeavored to beautify it). On Georgia's advice—and with the recommendation of theatrical agent Al Mackensen—she auditioned for and was hired by the Dubinsky Brothers Stock Company.

The three Dubinsky Brothers—Morris (aka Maurice), the eldest at twenty-five; Edward or "Handsome Ed," and Ben, the youngest—jointly headed a well-known and respected traveling repertory company, supposedly won by Maurice in a 1902 card game. By the time Eugenia joined the Dubinsky Brothers Stock in 1907, they were also managers of Wallach's Theatre Companies in Atlanta, Georgia; Rock Island, Illinois; and Salt Lake City, Utah.

In larger cities like Kansas City, audiences had a wealth of venues and theatrical productions to choose from, but in the smaller towns where there was only one venue (or none at all), entertainment was limited to whatever came in by train or wagon. Traveling stock companies, so named because they had a constant supply of performers and plays, worked a circuit comprised of small towns and cities, and often staged one show in a four-week rotation before starting another. This gave the actors experience in playing a wide range of roles, dealing with audiences, constant travel, and often deplorable living conditions. Companies traveled by rail in unheated cars, with actors trying to catch up on sleep while sitting in an uncomfortable seat. Once the train stopped at whichever small town was on the circuit, wagons carried props, scenery, and trunks while most of the cast walked alongside, toting their luggage to the venue in which they were to perform. It might be an opera house with a stage and footlights, or a bare room over the town grocery store with a row of kerosene lamps on the floor. Dressing rooms were rare, and if one was available, it was given to the girls, while the men changed outside in the alley or the nearest saloon. Accommodations were dollar-a-day hotels, meals included, with a shared bath and usually a bed-mate.

Their current production was *Pickings from Puck*, a selection of commentaries, stories, and cartoons from the satirical publication, *Puck*, a magazine filled with poems, ballads, character sketches, short stories, dialogue, and lithographs. Echoing Shakespeare's words, "What fools these mortals be," *Pickings From Puck* poked fun at human nature. The two-hour show was billed as "a melodious masterpiece punctuated with spicy sparkling dialogue and clean effervescent fun. Ringing, swinging, laughing, singing, musical tomfoolery, the best of all musical comedies. Pretty girls—laughing comedians—the liveliest and best drilled chorus in America, including the original and famous American Pony Ballet." Eugenia was one of the "twelve glorious lilies and roses of young womanhood, each gifted with sweet-toned throats that blend harmoniously in entrancing melodies." She joined a cast of twenty-two, passing through Iowa, Nebraska, Montana, Kansas, and Missouri. The schedule never altered, regardless of the foulest weather. January 20, 1908 found the Dubinskys in the first of ten cities over the next eleven days.

While grateful small-town audiences frequently showered visiting entertainers with applause, there would always be a smattering of catcalls and boos. Matters could sometimes even turn physical, as occurred during the November 6 performance in Mound City, Missouri.

As retold by the *Holt County Sentinel*, audience member Mister Carl Johnson had jumped on the stage in the middle of the show and attacked Maurice, causing the other players to scatter into the wings. Johnson pursued Dubinsky's leading lady, Helen Bates, into her dressing room where he attempted to strangle her. The lone police officer who followed them backstage was overpowered by the large assailant, and Johnson ran to center-stage, where he was apprehended by a group of men. He was then carried up the aisle out of the theatre and placed into the police caboose, which was engulfed in flames after Johnson set his bedding on fire. The audience was totally unaware of the commotion outside, as the stage had been reset; and though injured with cuts and bruises, Dubinsky and Bates resumed their performance, following the age-old dictum that "the show must go on."

Eugenia was not mentioned in published reports of the incident, presumably safe in her own dressing room during the melee, but she was subjected to a frightening ordeal later that month. During the Dubinskys' presentation of the Greek myth, *Pygmalion*, she stood inside a large picture frame, frozen in place until her cue to come alive, inspiring the artist to paint his masterpiece.

From her perch on stage in Grand Island, Nebraska, she overheard two men angrily debating whether or not she was a living being, or just a work of art. Pulling out his revolver, one told the other, "I'll find out!" He promptly fired a shot into the ceiling; which not only startled the audience, but also caused the young actress to fall out of the frame and onto the stage, proving one man's point at least.

Eugenia quickly worked her way up from clumsy set dressing. "She began in the chorus but within three months had taken over the lead role in a musical," Ed Dubinsky told the *Kansas City Star* in 1930. "That's the kind of girl she was. Beautiful but clever. I never saw anyone quite like her ... a remarkable actress and she won her success after a hard struggle."

Later in her career, she would liberally embellish stories of her time with the Dubinskys, often pretending to have been much younger than she really was when she joined the company. She once claimed that the company had traveled with only one pony, with the remaining mounts purloined from local livery stables or farmers. When angry residents saw their horses onstage, the troupe would be chased out of town. With each retelling, the show and number of mounts would change, but always ended with the same result. "That set my horse into a gallop, and it never stopped until I arrived at the next town, nine miles distant," she told *Goodwin's Weekly*. "There I found myself alone, clothed in a white leather riding suit (which was my costume for the play) without a cent of money and so scared I couldn't even remember our next booking. It took the company man three days to locate me and to again get his show together. My only subsistence was an ice-cream soda, which I begged from a druggist. I was a terrifically frightened little girl of thirteen summers who felt that her destiny had been forever sealed by such an experience."

"Those earlier years when I was trooping around through this territory we played in theatres that were upstairs over the village grocery store and they had lamps for footlights," she told the *Kansas City Star* in 1916. "There was usually a post in the center of the stage, and you either had to stand in front of it or stand behind and duck your head around it. I played everything from Little Eva to Camille. Oh yes, I was a leading woman at fifteen. Then, between acts I'd go out and sing and dance, but my great specialty was imitations. I used to imitate Eva Tanguay, Anna Held, Harry Lauder and all the rest of them. As a matter of fact, I had never seen any of the celebrities I was mimicking, but neither had the audience. They didn't know the difference and neither did I. I imitated them so often I got thinking myself that I had seen them. The plays were thrillers. My big speech used to end up, 'Stand back, you cur, or I'll shoot.' We used to play that all over the boards and we made them like it too."

"Those two years taught me little about acting, but they taught me a lot about myself," Jeanne admitted. "I learned to know myself and I learned a lot about other people... I have tried to keep my head level and not be carried away with success. I realize that at twenty-one I cannot be as good as I will be later if I keep on working to improve. My start, now that I have it, is beautiful, but it seems perfectly natural to me. I always knew I was going to do something worthwhile. Others may have doubted it, but I never did. It came to me because I got out and worked for it..."

According to Eddie Doherty, she not only had an affair with Maurice Dubinsky, but also married him, and may even have given birth to a child who either died or was adopted by a non-theatrical family. "I have no records either of the marriage or of the annulment that is supposed to have ended it," Doherty admitted. "I have no record to prove that a child was born." Yet he did claim that Julia Eagles received a telegram from her daughter in Excelsior Springs during the couple's honeymoon, with Eugenia declaring "I am now Mrs. Dubinsky." The new bride opened department store charge accounts in her husband's name and told a slumber party of her girlfriends about the marriage, and how Maurice's mother "hates me... because I am a Catholic and she is a Jew. I know how my mother must feel about it. But—I love him. And that's all that matters."

While Doherty was unable to prove these allegations, there is evidence of a possible marriage from various sources. On March 19, 1908, the *Iowa Atlantic Evening News* noted a "Mr. and Mrs. Dubinsky from the *Pickings from Puck* company arriving at the Pullman Hotel" for that night's performance. However, a couple registering as husband and wife may have done so merely for appearance's sake. The same article mentions an E. Engall (possibly a misspelling), also from *Puck*, checking into a separate establishment, the Cardio, where Ben Dubinsky, youngest of the brothers, was also staying.

In his autobiography, *Sitting Pretty*, actor Clifton Webb—who would later become one of Jeanne's closest friends—teased the old rumor, albeit in jest. "She called me 'Cliffy' and I called her 'Mrs. Dubinsky' which used to burn her up," Webb remembered. "'Son of a bitch, don't call me that,' she'd tell me."

Jeanne's only public acknowledgment of a prior marriage came in her 1923 interview with Ada Patterson for *Theatre Magazine*. "I played in a stock company in Kansas City; I played in repertoire companies in the Middle West; in tent shows," she said, recalling her time with the Dubinskys. "I played all kinds of parts—old women without teeth."

Patterson inquired, "Who cast a pretty girl for an old woman?"

She replied, "My husband." With a steely grin she continued, "But we will forget him. Marriage I have put behind me with other unsuccessful experiments."

Eugenia was probably too young, and certainly too ambitious for marriage. Her mother Julia never mentioned a wedding and would tell the press no more than this: "Jeanne did like him. He was a fine man and she naturally appreciated his kindness and admired his good character."

True or not, the relationship was eloquently described by his brother, Ed Dubinsky, who recalled that Maurice had "nourished her talent" with his charm and knowledge of literature. "The love [she] had for Maurice I think was a beautiful thing," Ed mused. "I believe it was the mainspring of her entire career. She left him and went away to New York, but I am certain she never shook off his influence."

"He was my brother, and I cared for him tremendously," Ed told the *Kansas City Star* in 1930, but he never meddled in Maurice's private affairs. "He and I cared so much for each other we knew when to be silent, when to let each other alone. I had no desire to pry into what might be a painful secret. What he didn't wish to tell he didn't need to."

"Only I know that she loved him and that she never stopped loving him," Ed insisted, adding that theirs was no "counterfeit love" to be cast off lightly, and that Maurice never treated his marriage to the future star as a "marketable commodity." Nonetheless, Ed would use a theatrical analogy to describe the couple, recalling "a sort of Camille-Armand quality in their relationship."

Ed Dubinsky was in the audience when Jeanne returned to the Kansas City stage in 1925 with her greatest success, *Rain*. It seems probable that Maurice—by then remarried and a father—accompanied Ed that evening. "She never looked at Maurice but there was pain in her eyes," Ed claimed. "She never spoke of him, but with a wistful tone ... I believe this explains her irony, her cynicism. It was her inner tragedy."

If the marriage was a distinct possibility, the rumor of a child is more nebulous—and a free-wheeling life on the road would have been incompatible with the responsibilities of motherhood. The allegation was denied by both Jeanne's family and friends, and she never talked about it in public, although she would sometimes confide in friends. Doherty noted that she mentioned the incident years later to director Sam Forrest, while starring in *A Gentleman's Mother*, a play about maternal sacrifice. "I let people take him from me," she lamented. "I don't know whether he's dead or alive. I don't know whether he's a gentleman or a burglar. He may be a tramp and I would see him somewhere and would not recognize him." This may have been a product of Jeanne's vivid imagination, and identification with the role. In any case, the story has never been verified.

Doherty also claimed that the mother of actress Ina Claire, who met Jeanne in 1911, knew of the baby's existence. A distraught Eagels had come to her one night, clutching a telegram from Kansas City, and sobbed, "My baby is dead. My poor little baby!"

Cecil Cunningham, another actress who befriended Jeanne in 1912, believed the baby was real, but had died. In a 1930 interview with Elizabeth Goldbeck for *Photoplay* magazine, Cunningham recalled Jeanne's drunken confession one night in Chicago, at a cast party for *The Pink Lady*. Jeanne claimed she had become pregnant by a fellow actor while touring with a theatrical company, but he abandoned her for another girl. She was so heartbroken that she fell ill and was confined to a sanatorium. After the boy was born, she left him in her mother's care and returned to the troupe, but on the same night she was reunited with her lover, her son died. She suffered a nervous breakdown and was "put on a nut farm... She recovered eventually, but the shock never really left her."

"It has been said that [her] baby is not dead, but I don't believe it," Cunningham added. "She never departed from that story. And I'm sure if her son had lived, her mother would have been proud to let the boy and the world know that he was [her] child."

Pickings From Puck ended a nine-month tour in March 1909, and Eugenia took the opportunity to spend time with her family, who had relocated from 1610 Tracy Avenue to 1405 Garfield Avenue. With Edward's rheumatism now worsening, she spent several weeks helping Julia around the house and taking care of her siblings, before returning to the Dubinskys for their Summer season tour. The money sent home by Eugenia, combined with Edna's working wage, was all that kept the family from being thrown out into the street.

Under the large canvas tent set up on an empty lot, Eugenia appeared in several one-night shows: *When Women Love*, *A Slave Girl*, *The Newsboy*. On June 16, the *Chillicothe Constitution* remarked that *Newsboy* was "full of humor and splendid climaxes... the specialties were very entertaining... the audience was well pleased." So pleased, in fact, that the company extended their stay in the Ohio town, giving one cast member the opportunity to fall in love and propose to a local girl. The *Constitution* reported on July 17 that a flood had nearly torn the young couple apart, but courageous actions by the groom enabled the nuptials to take place in the neighboring town of Brookfield. All of the cast, including Eugenia, attended the reception, which lasted "well into the night."

Variety's August 22 edition announced that a revised *Pickings From Puck* would began its latest tour under the management of Maurice, opening on October 1 in Kansas City, before "taking off to parts unknown."

Just over four months into the next tour, Eugenia was called back to Kansas City. Edward had succumbed to arterial insufficiency on the morning of February 14, 1910, at the family's 3016 Euclid Street residence.

The next few days were a blur as relatives came from Leavenworth to attend services at St Vincent's Church on Flora Street, with his burial at Saint Mary's Cemetery two days later.

As ardently as Eugenia craved a life on the stage, her familial ties were more pressing. Her mother now headed a household that numbered six children—aged three to twenty-two.

Whatever had passed between them, Maurice and Eugenia's life together was now over, both personally and professionally. The April 1910 Census recorded Maurice as single, living in Rock Island, Iowa with his parents and brothers; Eugenia was also listed as single and living with her mother, siblings and two boarders, Mylo and Lucinda Massie. Maurice married again in 1916 and fathered a daughter three years later. He spent the next decade living in Kansas City, and died there in 1929. The brothers founded American Multi-Cinema Theaters (AMC) in 1920, rebranding as Durwood Theaters in the 1930s. Since reverting to its original name in the 1960s, AMC has grown exponentially, and is currently the world's largest theater chain.

Eugenia had described her occupation as "actress," but at this point it was in name only. New York with its proliferation of venues was the only city where an actor could become a star. The only question on her mind was how to get there. Money was tighter than ever, but regular jobs weren't for her. Among her friends, Ruth Malone was working at the Auditorium Confectionery Company; Thecla Tempelman was a stenographer; and Anna Bell Mall would soon be marrying Frederick Kretchmar. With no beau, and no employment on the horizon for Eugenia, there was no chance of escape. It would take a miracle, and eventually a miracle-worker rode into town on a cold November night—November 11, to be exact.

A major name in musical comedy for the past decade, Richard Carle had embarked on a pre-Broadway tour for *Jumping Jupiter*, overseeing every aspect of the show as its author, producer, director, lyricist, and leading man. Carle starred as Professor Jupiter Goodwillie, who attempts to save a good friend's reputation from the threats of a spurned Parisian coquette. Goodwillie pretends the *mademoiselle* is his wife, a well-meaning ruse that falls flat when his own spouse appears. Escapades and shenanigans ensue, until all is resolved by the final curtain. The extremely thin plot was fattened up with fifteen musical numbers with titles including "Mississippi Dip" and "Possum Rag", and a series of comic turns featuring Carle and a chorus of twelve lovely young ladies, each named after popular automobiles of the time: Buick, Packard, Cadillac, Pierce, etc.

Eugenia auditioned and was hired to appear in the show as Miss Renault, but it could have been worse; poor Margaret Strassel was stuck with Miss Locomobile. Aside from performing "The Wedding Song" with Carle, she was given just one line in a skit, which Jeanne recalled years later was "My face is hot!" Carle's retort escaped her memory.

Finally, she had the means to walk away from the town she had called home for twenty years, a place she felt "wasn't even aware of my existence." Of course, she would miss her mother and siblings, friends and Mrs. Brown; but a life on the stage was all she had ever wanted, and the extra money would help to support her large family.

Even as her train pulled out of Union Depot, its clock tower getting smaller with each minute, the "Sarah Bernhardt of the sticks" had already begun plotting her triumphant return, hoping to "stand on its front doorstep someday and say to the old town: 'Well! See who's here! Little Eugenia Eagles has come back home to show you what she can do.'"

LITTLE MISS EAGELS: 1890-1910

Top left - Eugenia Eagles age five (1895); *Photograph courtesy of the David Stenn Collection.* Right - Eugenia with her youngest brother Leo (circa 1900) Lower left - Jeanne's first dramatic teacher, Georgia Brown.

Left - Eugenia aged twelve (1902); *Photograph courtesy of the Ivan Damiano Collection.* Right - Eugenia in Native American costume, from an unknown production (circa 1913).

Top - The Union Depot in Kansas City, MO. (1878-1914)
Bottom – Flood view (1903)

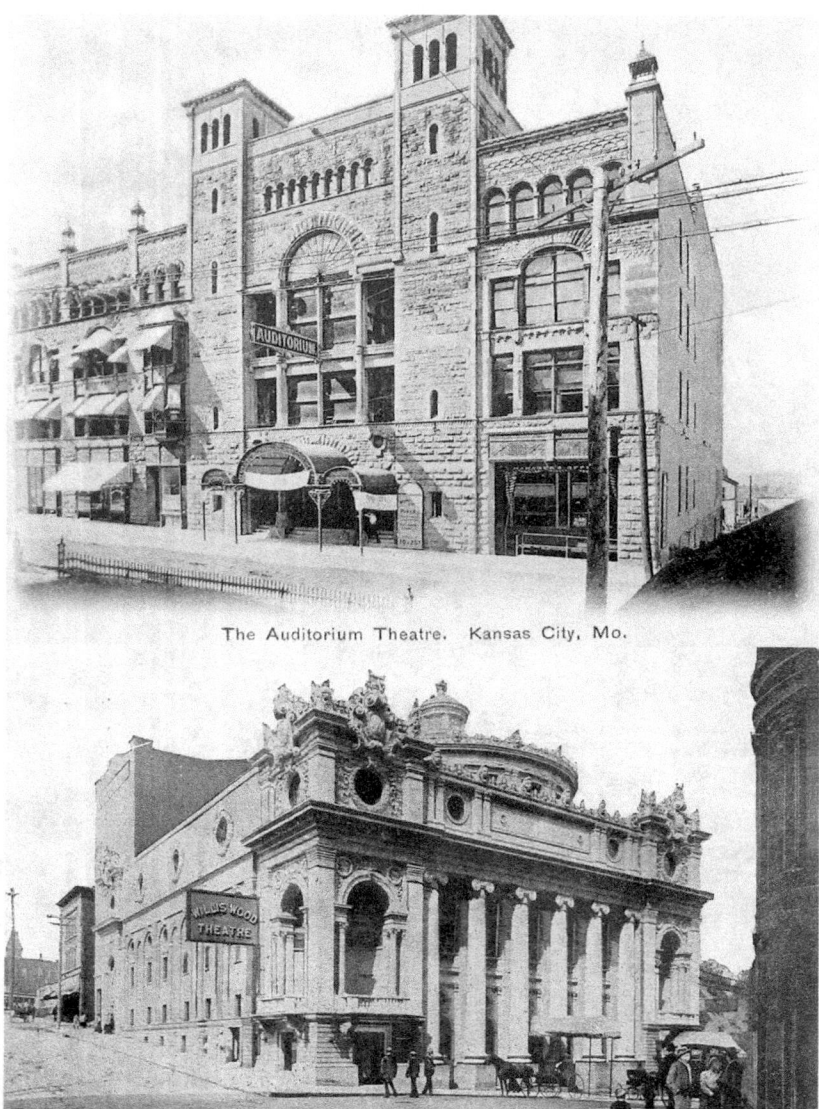

Top - The Auditorium Theatre (1887-1960), located at the Northeast corner of 9th and Holmes, Kansas City; Georgia Brown's Dramatic School was up the stairs at the rear of the building. Bottom - The Willis-Wood Theatre (1902-1917), located at 118 West 11th Street, where Richard Carle would give Eugenia her first big break.

Clockwise from left - Advertisement for *Pickings From Puck* (1908); Morris "Maurice" Dubinsky; "Handsome Ed"; Dubinsky tent show (circa 1917); Ben, the youngest Dubinsky brother; Morris with Miss Irene Daniel in *Pickings from Puck* (1908); Advertisement (1910.)

Chapter 2
The Great White Way: August 1910 – May 1915

With Kansas City and the Dubinskys now in her past, it was time for Eugenia to prepare herself for a change of scene; a different world, in fact, with none of her old life's certainties. By the end of 1910, her name, age, background, and even hair color would all be transformed. Long before reinvention became a cliché, she and many other aspiring performers would cast aside humble origins to carve out new identities, and seek their fortunes.

An actor's name needed marquee appeal, and Eugenia lacked glamour. "Jennie," her childhood nickname, was strongly associated with the late Jenny Lind, an opera singer known as the Swedish Nightingale, and Jean was rather plain, so instead she adopted the French Jeanne, perhaps in tribute to Georgia (nee Georgianne) Brown. Jeanne kept her family surname, but (possibly to avoid irksome bird puns) altered the spelling. Looking much younger than her actual age, Jeanne now claimed she was born in 1894, not 1890, and in Boston, not Kansas City.

Jeanne joined *Jumping Jupiter* in mid-tour after its four-month run in Chicago, crisscrossing the Midwest in towns and cities much larger than those preferred by the Dubinskys, finally reaching Manhattan in March 1911.

When Jeanne arrived in New York, a letter addressed to "Jean Eagels" awaited her at the offices of a trade publication, the *New York Dramatic Mirror*. In their January 25 Letter List, hers was one of many missives sent by hopeful fans.

New York City had a population of over four million people spread out among five boroughs, with 2,500,000 in Manhattan alone. As in the smaller cities, many desired nightly entertainments. By 1910, venues stretched from Greenwich Village to the Upper West Side, but most could be found between Sixth and Seventh Avenues from Thirty-Ninth to Forty-Eighth Streets, in what was now known as the Theatre District. Over forty theatres were clustered around the former Longacre Square, renamed Times Square after the *New York Times* building opened there in 1904.

Jeanne had become particularly close with two of the cast, and they would remain friends for life— Ina Claire, who played *Jumping Jupiter*'s ingénue, Molly Pebbleford, and fellow chorine Helen Broderick (Miss Winton.) Broderick was a year younger than Jeanne and had danced in the first Ziegfeld Follies. She also doubled as Ina Claire's understudy.

Jeanne had more in common with Ina Claire. Born in 1893, Ina had begun performing impersonations at the age of four and after finishing school persuaded her mother to allow a career in Vaudeville, where she was spotted by the producer of *Jumping Jupiter*.

Eagels and Broderick found a room at the Claridge Hotel and settled in for what they hoped (as did Claire), was a long and successful run.

Unfortunately for the cast and crew of *Jumping Jupiter*, what had played well in Chicago and smaller towns was deemed too low-brow for a more sophisticated audience. The show was savaged in the New York press.

"It was deadly" (*New York Evening World*); "Seems out of place on Broadway" (*New York Evening Post*); "Does not jump. It limps" (*New York Herald*); "Nothing drearier has been seen even in the line of musical comedy. . ." (*New York Tribune*); "Offensively stupid and tedious." (*New York Press*)

Jumping Jupiter lasted a meager twenty-four performances before folding on March 24. *Variety* reported a week later that the show would re-open in Atlantic City on July 31 for two weeks, ahead of a Pacific Coast tour starting in Los Angeles.

***

Helen Broderick had nothing to worry about. She had recently married Lester Crawford Pendergast, another cast member. Lester would guide Broderick to success in both stage and film. Their son, Broderick Crawford, born in December 1911, would later become one of the leading character actors of the 1940s and 1950s.

Ina Claire had been offered a role in another musical, *The Quaker Girl*, which she would play for more than a year. This was followed by a stint with the Ziegfeld Follies. Like Broderick, Ina Claire would forge a second career in Hollywood comedies, such as *Ninotchka* (1939), but this was all far in the future.

Jeanne was faced with a tortuous decision: whether to stay with *Jumping Jupiter* as a chorus girl, or to leave and take her chances on finding a better role. With time on her side, she headed back to Kansas City for several weeks, resting at her family's current home on 2304 East Eighth Street, and seeking advice from both her mother, Julia, and her mentor, Georgia Brown.

Having only one show under her belt, and without representation, it was going to be a steep climb up the ladder of success. Jeanne certainly had experience, but little formal training, and lacked powerful connections, in a business where word-of-mouth could make or break a career. However, in an era when acting was still considered a disreputable profession, Jeanne did have one advantage: the support of her family, which bolstered her confidence and may explain her willingness to take risks. After all, she had only her pride to lose.

Broadway, the hub of New York's theatre district since the 1860s, was monopolized by the Theatrical Syndicate by the early 1900s. The Syndicate had been formed to connect all theatres controlled by its six founding members[3] into a national chain. By dealing with individual theatre managers, the Syndicate would arrange *Jupiter*'s tour. This standardized the booking process and side-stepped conflicts between dual shows playing the same territories due to lack of communication. The drawbacks were mostly felt by actors, agents, and managers obliged to present second-rate material.

Starting from about 1910, the Syndicate's iron grip was loosened by the Shuberts, three brothers who ran a chain of theatres in upstate New York. Starting with one leased venue in Manhattan, they were soon building more while purchasing numerous theatres nationwide. Dissatisfied actors defected to the Shuberts in droves, and the Big Six soon found themselves lacking performers. Hot on their trail, the Shuberts acquired similar works of superior quality, cutting into the profits of the Syndicate's contracted theatres. Eventually, 1,200 small-town venues merged with the Shuberts and several other independent producers to form the National Theatre Owners Association.

Producers like Belasco, Frohman, and Klaw & Erlanger were Broadway's titans, the precursors of 20th Century Fox, Metro-Goldwyn-Mayer, and Paramount in 1930s Hollywood. With investors' support, they raised funds to produce one or more shows at various theatres in Manhattan

---

3   Broadway's 'Big Six' was comprised of producers Charles Frohman, Al Hayman, Samuel F. Nirdlinger, Frederick Zimmerman, A. L. Erlanger, and Marc Klaw.

and the outlying boroughs. Some built up a roster of performers, signing them to exclusive personal contracts that paid a weekly wage whether the actor was currently working or not. Secure employment was Jeanne's goal as she visited the offices of many an agent and producer, embellishing her past experience to no avail.

A young woman as beautiful as Jeanne was never short of company in Manhattan. She dressed up to visit a restaurant, nursing her cup of coffee while waiting to make conversation with a wealthy older gentleman in need of a pretty young companion for dinner or the theatre. Gifts appeared unbidden, such as hats, clothing, jewelry, flowers, or candy. While some men may have expected more, she insisted that most settled for a kiss on the cheek. If anyone crossed the line or was given the wrong impression, Jeanne quickly set them straight. Romance was not on the cards, just the pleasure of her company. In 1917, she told one producer, "I have played in tent shows, in wagon shows, in circuses, in burlesque, in choruses. I have played all the parts an actress can play. I have stayed outside the theatres all night, freezing, soaking wet, trying to get a part to play, or a job as a chorus girl. I have gone hungry and ragged. I have been sick and unable to go to a doctor. I have fought all kinds of men—and women too—to be an actress in New York. And all—I still have my ambition—and my virtue."

Was this the whole truth, or a case of smoke and mirrors? Jeanne was adept at remaking her past, and would have been aware that however liberal attitudes were within her bohemian set, the wider public was more traditional. Theatrical history is littered with tales of stage-door Johnnies, sugar daddies, and chorus girls, who were all too eager for money and fame. Nonetheless, after her alleged secret marriage to Maurice Dubinsky, Jeanne was in no hurry to settle down. At twenty-one, her career came first and she wasn't content to be a good-time girl. Where lesser talents might have succumbed to temptation, she kept her eye on the prize.

"I am timid and afraid of men and far too busy to become well acquainted with them," she told the *New York Sun* in 1917, but it was marriage, not men, that she feared most. "My work fills my life, and I should not care to fall in love or marry before I am very, very old—about thirty-five—because a woman gives too much of herself when she loves, and that would interfere with her career."

***

Through her friends' generosity, Jeanne was able to survive until her next lucky break. *The Pink Lady* was a musical comedy that was produced by entrepreneur A. L. Erlanger, and his lawyer partner, Marcus Klaw. *The Pink Lady* ran from March 13 to December 9 at the New Amsterdam Theatre, and was then set to tour. Jeanne replaced Eunice Mackey as Gabrielle, one of several chorus girls providing back-up vocals for such musical numbers as "On the Saskatchewan," "My Beautiful Lady," and "Donny Did, Donny Didn't," as performed by leading lady Hazel Dawn. Another duty was as background for elaborate group scenes throughout the production.

The producers spared no expense, importing costumes from Paris. A photo spread in the January 28 *Buffalo Courier* showed "Miss Jean Eagels [sic] modeling a gown of pale green faille Francaise, veiled in flesh mousseline de soie (silk muslin), overgrown of white net embroidered in pale green and coral stones. The bodice is empire effect with round neck and sleeves to match. The bottom of the overdress is handsomely embroidered in a deep border of coral and green silk embroidery."

The Pink Lady opened on February 18, 1912, at Chicago's Colonial Theatre. *Billboard* commended it as "a smart and somewhat racy entertainment containing considerable humor and tuneful songs. Klaw and Erlanger have furnished an entirely new production vast and rich in scenic and costume equipment."

During the tour, Jeanne shared a dressing room with fellow chorine Cecil Cunningham. The pair quickly bonded and were inseparable, spending "every waking moment" together. For that reason, Cunningham was suspicious of the fiery reputation that Jeanne later acquired. "In that time, a woman must reveal her real self," Cunningham said. "She may lie and pretend for a while, but with those who live with her she must eventually slip, forget, let the truth slip out. Jeanne's stories to me were always the same. Her dates were always right."

Cunningham remembered Jeanne as loyal and generous, a true "lady" who never cursed or gossiped. She was quiet and reserved, with a "youthful indifference" that set her apart from the other chorus girls. Behind her good-natured reserve, Cunningham believed, Jeanne was "always acting. Not for effect or to deceive, but she never quite let down the bars and admitted people."

While *The Pink Lady* was playing in Indianapolis, Cecil caught the eye of novelist and playwright Booth Tarkington, and brought Jeanne along to a party at his home. The author was charmed as she "walked around softly, appreciating his books and authentic artworks."

Jeanne also amused Cecil with her backstage impersonations, including an uproarious Camille that made her friend "howl with laughter." There was no doubt in Cunningham's mind that Jeanne would become a "great dramatic actress," and that she was merely "awaiting the time when her opportunity would come." After six months on tour with *The Pink Lady*, Jeanne's role was recast with Teddy Hudson, and she returned to Manhattan. Something better had indeed come along.

On August 23, it was announced that Jeanne had joined the cast of *The Mind-the-Paint Girl*, produced by Charles Frohman, another member of the Syndicate. Written by Sir Arthur Wing Pinero, the four-act comedy was of the "play-within-a-play" variety. The heroine is the leading actress at a musical comedy theatre in London, with the title derived from the name of a song that brought her into prominence. One in a cast of thirty, as Olga Cook, Jeanne had eight lines opposite Billie Burke's Lily Parradell.

Recounting to *Collier's Weekly* in 1927 how she had appeared at the theatre for her first rehearsal, Jeanne explained that a stage director handed her a small sheet of typewritten paper.

"My call sheet?" she asked him.

"Nope," he replied. "Your part."

After a week at Atlantic City's Apollo, *The Mind-the-Paint Girl* opened at the Lyceum Theatre on September 9 to a warm reaction from audiences and critics. Attendance began to wane shortly before the Christmas holidays, and with expenses exceeding box office profits, Frohman decided to close the show on January 4. The show then went on tour, closing early March in Chicago. Jeanne's only review from an unknown critic proclaimed, "The girl with the red heels on her shoes has personality!"

The Amazons, Frohman's next production, was a smaller and cheaper affair, also starring Billie Burke. Six year's Jeanne's senior, Burke would later play one of the most beloved characters in Hollywood history, Glinda the Good Witch in *The Wizard of Oz*.

In her 1949 memoir, *With a Feather in my Nose*, Burke recalled, "One of the pretty young actresses in my play was Jeanne Eagels, to whom no one paid much attention then except to observe that she was lovely to look at and pleasant to have around." That is why legend has it that Burke's husband, producer and owner of his own theatre, Florenz Ziegfeld, offered her a weekly salary of $100 or $150 to join his Ziegfeld Follies.[4] As financially tempting as the offer must have been, she boldly rejected it, proclaiming, "I am a dramatic actress."

Determined to become that actress, Jeanne was not swayed by the lure of rhinestones, beads, feathers, and elaborate headdresses. However, almost four months would pass before she found work—not on the stage, but in motion pictures.

***

From 1895 to 1915, many American films were produced in New York, and the city was a hub of film distribution. With the birth of the film

---

4   Despite Jeanne's name never appearing in any Follies rosters, she is still mistakenly credited as being a "Ziegfeld Girl" by some authors.

camera at Thomas Edison's New Jersey laboratory, production companies were built in Fort Lee and across the Hudson River on Long Island and Manhattan. Many early film companies, such as Thanhouser, Biograph, Patheplay, Edison, and Essanay, lasted only a few years before filing for bankruptcy or merging with another studio.

The Ryno Film Company's only claim to fame may be introducing Jeanne to the screen in *The Ace of Hearts*. Released under its Dragon Pictures banner on June 9, the roughly twelve-minute short featured Jeanne as one of two girls, who play a prank on a soldier who is asleep at his post. They thrust a card—the ace of hearts—into the collar of his jacket. Unfortunately, the card later protrudes from his sleeve during a game, and his buddies accuse him of cheating. Falling asleep, the soldier dreams of being court-martialed and jumping from a dock. Upon awakening, he decides to commit suicide. As he points the gun to his head and finger on the trigger, his friends burst through the door with Jeanne in tow. After hearing her confess, the young officer forgives her and—somewhat improbably—they fall in love.

In their June 15 review, the *Dramatic Mirror* commented that "after an original start, the picture develops into a conventional 'dream melodrama.' However, it introduces a young actress of promise and prettiness, Jeanne Eagels, who suggests a young Billie Burke. Outside of Miss Eagels, the acting is fair." A reviewer for *Moving Picture World* was unconvinced: "Several incidents in this drama of barracks life tend to weaken it. A picture of military life should have some regard for customs and regulations."

The limited budget for Jeanne's second Ryno picture, *The Bride of the Sea*, had director John Noble staying up nights with worry. The film's plot concerned a love triangle, which through the deception of one man, results in the death of all three characters by the picture's finish. Most of the sets, such as a working telegraph operator's office, were easily constructed on the studio's Long Island lot. But one scene required a half-sunken steamer, which would cost the cash-strapped studio nearly $100,000. However, fate played a part in solving his dilemma.

What should have been a normal journey for the steamer *John P. Wilson* from Brooklyn's Pier 33 to Stamford Connecticut—a voyage sailed many times before by Captain Harcourt —took a turn for the worse on July 5.

Shortly after 6:00 p.m., the vessel developed a leak while in the Long Island Sound. Harcourt was able to guide the vessel for another mile to Belden's Point on City Island before notifying the passengers of the issue. Fortunately for those on board, the ship stayed afloat a good while. The crew managed to anchor next to the dock, and it wasn't until all forty passengers and seven crew members had disembarked safely that the vessel slowly sank until only the pilot house and smokestack remained above the water line.

With the studio less than a mile from where the *Wilson* now sat, Noble and his entourage visited the site as the sun was setting. Long after others had given up hope, the resourceful director negotiated with the Merchants Steamship Company to postpone salvage efforts until the next afternoon. This allowed a few hours for filming, and Noble instructed his cast and crew to meet at the dock before sunrise.

As the morning sun crept over the horizon, Noble's crew set up two cameras on the dock while the director instructed his leading man and lady as to what he wanted to capture on film. "With vain effort our hero raised himself above the window of the pilot house and yelled a lusty shout," *Motion Picture News* reported on July 12. "A launch appeared on the scene. The hero disappeared and soon reappeared at the window with our heroine in his arms. Action then ceased." What wasn't mentioned was that after Jeanne had gamely boarded the mostly-submerged craft and allowed herself to be picked up by her leading man, as she was lifted over the railing (supposedly into the arms of a crew member positioned off-camera), "our hero" lost his grip, and poor Jeanne fell into the cold Atlantic Ocean with a loud squeal. After drying off and changing into a dry costume, the second take went off without a hitch.

Fortunately, *The Bride of the Sea* was completed without further incident. When the film was released on July 28, the *Dramatic Mirror* judged "the photography, acting and settings superior to the story—a conventional melodrama closing with a repentantly horrible scene . . . There is no denying the realism of many of the scenes and Jean [sic] Eagels gives a particularly engaging performance in the role of the heroine." A skeptical *Moving Picture World* countered, ". . . the acting in this picture does not match up with the photographic work. Neither does the direction."

Jeanne stepped before film cameras for the third time in early 1914 for the Reliance Motion Picture Corporation's *A Lesson in Bridge*. She portrayed Mrs. Willis, wife of a Wall Street clerk. Fascinated by the game of bridge, he loses the "bill money" through gambling. Mr. Willis is involved in a scheme to catch a dishonest co-worker, and brings home a large sum of cash for safe-keeping, but his wife finds it, and not realizing the money is marked, uses some of it to pay the household expenses. Her husband is dismissed from his job until another co-worker guides the authorities to the correct criminal.

Advertisements for the film, released on March 4, included such blurbs as "a Reliance drama presenting a tale of trumps and trickery, with a splendid moral and a powerful appeal to women"; "A strong domestic Reliance Drama, that every woman should see"; and "a social drama that is of particular interest to women who play bride." The film was promoted less for its entertainment value than as a cautionary tale for young ladies involved in the card game.

Four days later on March 8, the soon-to-be eminent director, D.W. Griffith, released his first picture in partnership with Reliance, *Judith of Bethulia*. The Biblical heroine was played by Blanche Sweet, and Griffith filled the minor and extra roles with some of the biggest names in the early film industry: Lillian Gish, Dorothy Gish, Lionel Barrymore, and Jeanne (unbilled). Griffith lauded her performance, saying, "She is one of the rare cameos with something behind it."

***

It wasn't all work and no play for Jeanne. On February 18, she was among the theatrical denizens who gathered at Reisenweber's Cafe just off Columbus Circle (just around the corner from her 200 West Fifty-Eighth Street apartment) for "one of the most successful masked balls in many months," according to the *New York Press*.

She was also rehearsing *The Governor's Boss*, a new stage production written by ex-Indiana Senator James S. Barcus, based upon the impeachment of ex-New York governor William Sulzer in 1913. This three-act play's intricate plot involved the political boss of an unnamed state, its newly elected Governor, his daughter, and a young woman who has been the victim of the boss's son. When the Governor refuses to obey orders, the boss has him impeached. The trial of the Executive constitutes the last act of the play; while the untangling of a triple romance, and the fate of the Governor and boss, create an unexpected twist.

Produced by Barcus, with the investment of a rich, non-theatrical friend and a cast of sixteen, *The Governor's Boss* opened February 28 in Washington D.C., reaching New York's Garrick Theatre by April 13. However, the *New York Times* thought it "as poor and uninteresting a play as might possibly be imagined. The one bright spot is the performance of Richard Gordon as the Governor's Secretary. As for the rest of the company, the less said the better." Audiences stayed away, and the show folded after sixteen performances. Barcus would produce a screen adaptation of *The Governor's Boss* in 1915, starring William Sulzer as himself, and also published a novelization of the play.

Jeanne sailed for Europe on May 18, where she made two lifelong friends and confidants: actor Clifton Webb, and his mother, Mabelle. "Cliffy" was born Webb Parmalee Hollenbeck in Indianapolis on November 19, 1889. His parents divorced when he was a boy, and Mabelle brought him to New York City where she remarried in 1900. By 1908, the nineteen-year-old was known as Clifton Webb, a professional ballroom dancer who would appear in over two dozen operettas before making his Broadway debut in 1913's *The Purple Road*.

While Jeanne was still a struggling actress, Webb was already an established star. Nonetheless, both he and Mabelle quickly grew fond of her.

"The great thing about Jeanne was our intense love for one another," Webb wrote in his unfinished memoir, *Sitting Pretty*. "We were too much alike. She had that husky kind of voice combined with her cock-eyed sense of humor and anybody who has a sense of humor endears themselves to me immediately."

"We went to a party [in Paris] given for (actress) Gaby Deslys," Webb continued, "and everybody came dripping jewels, but Jeanne always did the reverse. She came in a beautiful organdy dress . . . having no jewels . . . she loved the reverse scene." This may have been a matter of necessity rather than a bid for the spotlight. On July 6, *Variety* reported that Jeanne's hotel room (shared with fellow actress Miss Molyneux) had been robbed. This misfortune didn't stop her from making a splash at nightspots such as Pre Catalan and the Moulin Rouge.

Jeanne boarded the *Lusitania* at Liverpool, England on July 25 with an unexpected traveling companion. Muriel G. Sanders, wife of famed tenor Paul Draper, claimed that the singer was in London for his concert debut when he ran into Jeanne the day before. "Paul went off with Jeanne Eagels and never came back," she told reporters. The family story is that during the conversation, Draper told Jeanne of his upcoming performance. "You're not singing a concert," she replied. "You're sailing back to New York tomorrow morning with me." If Muriel's story is true, then it seems the romance did not last long after they landed on American shores. The Drapers divorced in 1916, with a Hazel Barnes named by Sanders as co-respondent. Muriel Draper went on to become a leading light of the Harlem Renaissance, and a prominent social activist.

***

Jeanne's next stage role, another Klaw & Erlanger production, found her starring opposite a handsome leading man, who spent much of the show dressed in women's clothing. More "male actress" than female impersonator, Julian Eltinge had first appeared onstage as a girl at the age of ten. He successfully toured both America and Europe, performed before King Edward VII, and performed in a series of musical comedies written specifically for his talents, from *The Fascinating Widow* in 1910, to his latest production, which had opened at the Knickerbocker Theatre on March 16, 1914.

A musical comedy farce, *The Crinoline Girl* was set at the Hotel de Beau Rivage in Lausanne, Switzerland, and followed the romances of two couples, Tom Hale (Eltinge) and Dorothy Ainsley (Helen Luttrell), and Tom's sister Alice paired with Dorothy's cousin Jerry. Both relationships are censured by Dorothy's father, who knows Tom's reputation as a reckless young man, while Alice is deemed guilty by association. At the resort, a jewel thief who calls himself Lord Bromleigh steals the guests' jewels, aided by a female accomplice in a crinoline dress. Tom disguises himself as the young woman and solves the crime, earning $10,000, and Dorothy's hand in marriage.

Critics enjoyed the play, and Eltinge's performance, but Luttrell earned only modest praise. The *Dramatic Mirror* thought her "an effective daughter," while another critic found her role "sweetly played." The *New York Sun* couldn't even get her name right, using the character's name in their review.

The show was flagging, and Eltinge placed much of the blame on his leading lady. On May 8, the *New York Times* noted that Luttrell had missed the previous evening's performance due to illness. Her replacement, Grace Coburn, was hired at 5:30, received her script at 6:00, and was onstage by 8:00. Coburn would remain in the role for all remaining performances at the Knickerbocker, but a new Dorothy wasn't enough to save *The Crinoline Girl*, and it closed after six weeks.

Eltinge set sail for Europe, but not before instructing the show's producer, A.H. Woods, to "find him another leading lady." Jeanne was then committed to *The Governor's Boss*, and was unaware of Eltinge's dilemma.

The question of how Jeanne got the part has two possible answers. On October 25, the *Washington Times* reported that in mid-April, producer A. H. Woods had ducked into the lobby of a movie house to avoid a sudden spring shower. When the auditorium door opened, he caught of glimpse of Jeanne's face on the screen (probably *A Lesson in Bridge*), and immediately knew she would be an ideal replacement for Luttrell. Unable to learn her name from the theater owner, he contacted the film studio and had them send her out from Los Angeles to New York.[5] He signed her to a contract and then dispatched her to Europe to study acting at his expense. She met Eltinge in Paris that July; and when the actor returned, he told Woods that he had found the perfect actress, never knowing it was Woods who had spirited her overseas.

The second scenario, published in *Green Book* magazine, placed both actors in Paris, with Eltinge noticing Jeanne as their paths crossed multiple times. Try as he might, Jeanne's name eluded him. She was just another American girl on summer vacation. Defeated, Julian sailed for New York, waiting at his Long Island home until rehearsals for the revamped show began. On that day, Eltinge met with Woods in his private office before joining the rest of the cast learned that an actress had been found—"Jeanne Eagels. Had stock and musical comedy and moving picture experience, but isn't known in the Broadway drama." Eltinge was shocked when Wood's office boy led Jeanne into the room to meet her new leading man.

Biographer Eddie Doherty offered a third version, claiming that Jeanne was having lunch with actress Edna Wallace Hopper at Ciro's

---

5   In fact, Jeanne would not visit Los Angeles until her celebrated 1926 tour in *Rain*.

Restaurant in Paris, when Edna spotted Eltinge and invited him over. Hopper, who was known as the "eternal flapper" and would outlive Jeanne by thirty years, introduced the actor to Jeanne, to whom he immediately offered the part.

However it came to pass, *Variety* noted the addition of Jeanne and three other new cast members in an announcement that the show would reopen in Atlantic City by mid-September. *The Crinoline Girl* traveled between the Bronx, Washington D.C., Manhattan, and Brooklyn, and the reviews justified Eltinge's faith in Jeanne. "A striking blonde that fits into his 'dream' as if made for the part," cooed the *Washington Times*. "A charming and graceful blonde creature," the *Washington Herald* agreed. "She made us realize that the ten per cent nature and the rest art statement was only talk after all."

Jeanne was interviewed by Edward Harold Crosby for the *Boston Sunday Post*'s November 22 edition. Crosby, a drama critic and novelist, was charmed by her down-to-earth manner. "She is tall and willowy and has sunny hair and blue eyes," he wrote. Describing her as a "remarkable young woman," he added with surprise that "she had no inclination to play emotional roles." This would have been news to many of her friends, who were in no doubt as to Jeanne's dramatic ambitions.

As they talked of the upcoming Christmas holiday, Crosby's expectations were once again jolted when he learned that this young lady took no pleasure in shopping. "And if the truth was known," Jeanne said, "very few women do. They love to spend money, but it is more the idea of getting rid of coin than the actual purchasing. I do not care for either. I buy what I need and finish the job as quickly as possible."

"I am quite convinced," Crosby remarked, "that Miss Eagels' originality will cause her to become a shining light in the profession in the immediate future."

Further west, the *Indianapolis Star* found her role "very cleverly played." The *Indianapolis News* remarked that Jeanne "made a bewitching picture . . . with a charming personality still unspoiled by affectation of any kind. Her simple, frank manner sets off her blond attractions at their highest value." The *Kansas City Star* ran a lengthy article noting the success of various theatrical performers hailing from Kansas City, mentioning Jeanne's $200 weekly salary for *The Crinoline Girl*; that her picture (*A Lesson in Bridge*) was playing at Munsey's this week; and that she'd recently bought her mother a "nice home on the East Side" (at 4209 South Bentley Avenue).

The Crinoline Girl toured between Illinois, Iowa, and Indiana for much of spring, with plans to head to the Pacific Coast. While playing in Chicago, the cast joined others from concurrent productions at parties and after-hours shows to blow off steam. One of these gatherings was held in the Hotel Sherman's Rose Room. A photograph taken that evening shows a solemn-faced Jeanne seated among a large group of performers including Eltinge, Fanny Brice, and future *Rain* co-star Rapley Holmes, among others. Soon afterwards, however, a nautical tragedy brought the merriment to an abrupt halt. On May 9, 1915, the *Washington Post* alluded to "theatrical conditions" that had prompted Eltinge to abruptly close the show.

Two days previously, the Theatre Syndicate had been dealt a major blow. Charles Frohman was named among 1,195 passengers killed when the *Lusitania* was torpedoed and sunk by a German submarine. The "Big Six" producer often visited the Continent to scope out new productions for American audiences. He had been helping other passengers into lifeboats when he was swept overboard by a wave. Once Frohman's body was recovered, a funeral service was arranged for May 25 at the Temple Emanu-El in New York City, attended by hundreds from the theatrical community, including Jeanne. In less than a year, Frohman's empire was dismantled, including his contracts with Maude Adams, John Drew Jr., Ethel Barrymore, and Marie Tempest. What remained was handed to his younger brother, Daniel, who continued producing on Broadway.

With no paid work on the horizon, Jeanne took the opportunity to study acting with former actress Beverley Sitgreaves, who had begun her

Broadway career in the same year of Jeanne's birth. She had appeared on the London stage, and in Paris with Sarah Bernhardt, whose performance in *Hamlet* she had impersonated along with scenes made famous by the great Italian actress, Eleonora Duse, in a 1903 charity performance. Sitgreaves believed that "the art of acting was to reproduce what would be, if the events on the stage were being lived at the moment by the participants." Jeanne has been cited as an early exemplar of the raw emotional intensity later associated with actors such as Marlon Brando and Kim Stanley, so perhaps this interlude with Sitgreaves—her first dramatic mentor since Georgia Brown—propelled her metamorphosis from chorus girl and silent film player to future legend of the stage.

"The first real dramatic training I had was in Paris from Beverly Sitgreaves," Jeanne told the *Kansas City Star*.[6] "She worked with me and taught me a thousand little things about the stage, the way to use my voice and the way to acquire ease," Jeanne said of Sitgreaves. "She always said she wasn't teaching me anything—just bringing out what was in me. But all of the little things she taught me helped wonderfully. I learned stage technique, which after all, is simply a knowledge of the little things. Life itself is just made up of little things. They are the things that count."

During her European travels Jeanne had picked up a slight British accent, lending her an air of prestige. She would often play this to the hilt, to the annoyance of some of her peers. Beatrice Lillie, a Canadian-born actress of the London stage—who would become a real English lady in 1920, after marrying Sir Robert Peel—once teased Jeanne at a party both were attending: "Oh, lah-de-dah, aren't you being just a little bit British tonight?"

"Yes darling," Jeanne replied sweetly. "Aren't we *both*?"

---

6   Jeanne had returned from Europe and was living in New York when she studied with Beverly Sitgreaves.

THE GREAT WHITE WAY: AUGUST 1910-MAY 1915

Top - Richard Carle with the *Jumping Jupiter* dancers in Chicago (1910.)
Bottom - Times Square, New York City (1911.)

Jeanne as Miss Renault in *Jumping Jupiter* (1911). The full list of the chorus line: Locomobile, Packard, Winston, Daimler, Cadillac, Lozier, Pierce (Arrow), Buick, Huppmobile, Chalmers, and Rainier.

Clockwise: Jeanne as "Olga Cook" in *Mind the Paint Girl* (1913); "Gabrielle" in *The Pink Lady* (1912); and "Dorothy Ansley" in *The Crinoline Girl* (1914.)

Eagels' early short film roles: Top - *Bride of the Sea* (1913), with Glen White. Bottom - As "Mrs. Willis" in *A Lesson in Bridge* (1914.)

THE GREAT WHITE WAY: AUGUST 1910-MAY 1915

Theatrical luminaries gathered in the Rose Room at the Hotel Sherman, Chicago. Group includes #4 Fanny Brice, #9 Julian Eltinge, #23 Jeanne Eagels and #39 Rapley Holmes.

Chapter 3
The World and the Woman:
June 1915–December 1916

During the summer of 1915, Jeanne stayed with her friends from *Jumping Jupiter* days, Helen and Lester Crawford, at their 67th Street apartment. While appearing in Vaudeville, the couple were saving for a home on Long Island to raise their son Broderick, currently living with his grandparents. Nights were spent dining on chow mein and ginger ale, or chili con carne and beer, while Jeanne performed impersonations and shared theatrical gossip. On some evenings, Jeanne would dress in a kimono and stick a large chrysanthemum behind each ear and put *Madame Butterfly* on the record player. She would then mime the part of the deserted Japanese girl in Puccini's opera, crying for her lover, tears streaming down her face like rainwater. As Helen explained to Eddie Doherty, Jeanne did this to prove how easily she could cry, a skill that her friend had not mastered. "Hell!

You want to be an actress. I *am* an actress," Jeanne said, not unkindly but with her usual bluntness. "You have something, though, that I haven't, Helen," she added perceptively. "You can pull the deadpan and wisecrack better than anyone I know. People will roar at you some day. You are going to be a marvelous comedienne."

She was correct in her opinions. Throughout the next decade, Helen Broderick (1891-1959) appeared in a series of stage musicals, farcees and revues. After moving to Hollywood. she established herself as a superb comedic sidekick, most memorably with Ginger Rogers in *Top Hat* (1935) and *Swing Time* (1936).

Jeanne's luck soon took an upward turn, as *Billboard* reported on October 9 that she had signed with Pathé Films to appear in *The House of Fear*, the fifth and final installment of the Ashton Kirk detective series, starring Arnold Daly. Jeanne played Grace Cramp, sister to Sheldon Lewis' George Cramp. The siblings' lives are disrupted by a gang of Mexican bandits, who, in cahoots with their estranged aunt, are hunting for forged currency printing plates that were lately manufactured and then hidden by their deceased father. By the final reel, Kirk has foiled the plot, captured the bandits, and destroyed the plates.

Jeanne's role was so forgettable that when *The House of Fear* episode was released in late November, the *Rome Daily Sentinel*'s critic botched her name: "Mr. Daly is supported by Jennie Sagels [sic] and Sheldon Lewis."

Fortunately, the second part of *Billboard*'s October 9 article was more prescient. "Miss Eagels has also been secured for a new speaking stage production to be put on in this city at an early date," a brief statement read. This was clarified on October 18, when the *New York Sun* revealed that Eagels had been hired by Klaw and Erlanger for a third time. The play was *Outcast*, imported from London and currently on Broadway, with Elsie Ferguson in the lead.

Miriam (Ferguson) is a streetwalker who helps to turn around the life of Geoffrey Sherwood, addicted to drink and drugs after his former fiancé, Valentine, deserted him for a man with money. A grateful Sherwood shows kindness to Miriam; but complications arise when she misreads his actions and falls in love with him. Still besotted with the newly-separated Valentine, Geoffrey offers Miriam a sum of money to leave him alone. But she later returns, finding Sherwood and Valentine together. Tossing down the check, Miriam gives a heartfelt speech which persuades Valentine to reconcile with her husband. Seeing Miriam in a new light, Geoffrey vows to marry her. The pair travel to South America, and a brighter future together.

Elsie Ferguson, described at the time as one of "The Most Beautiful Women ever to step foot on the stage," was a Manhattan native who had begun her career at seventeen in the chorus of *Florodora*. By 1909, she was a major Broadway star in shows such as *Pierre of the Plains* and *Such a Little Queen*. Jeanne was sure that *Outcast* could elevate her to equal status. Months before a tour was announced, she plotted to win the part.

One of Klaw and Erlanger's most successful plays, *Outcast* was slated as a roadshow for the Southern circuit before Ferguson embarked on her own Midwest to Pacific Coast tour. On October 18, the *New York Sun* reported that Jeanne, along with the original London cast, would bring *Outcast* to Trenton, New Jersey on October 21.

Landing the role of Miriam was no fluke, but the result of hard work and ingenuity. While Jeanne had earlier been mistaken for Billie Burke, strangers now stopped to ask if she was Elsie Ferguson. Their resemblance was uncanny, especially in profile.

In *Still: American Silent Motion Picture Photography*, David Shields noted that Jeanne exploited the likeness to her advantage. In late spring, Jeanne "went to the New York studio of photographers Underwood & Underwood looking for an image of Ferguson, searching among a large bin filled with photographs until she came up just the right one. Something powerful and adventurous. Armed with this, she made an attack in force on two or three exclusive Fifth Avenue shops, where she purchased duplicates of everything Miss Ferguson wore in this particular photograph. Within a few days, her hair freshly styled exactly like Ferguson's in the photograph,

Jeanne presented herself to *Outcast*'s producer Thomas W. Riley."

No photos are known to exist from the production, fortunately the *Syracuse Journal* published a detailed review of Jeanne's costumes:

"In the first act, as a girl of the streets, she must wear clothes that are mainline tawdry to suggest the character. The hat, in its way, is a work of art, with its cheap red felt and its straggled thin wisp of white feathers. From this time on, Miriam improves in mind and manners and her various gowns, in their beauty and individuality, show the development of her character."

"In the second act, the cunning little frock of dark blue glove-skin cloth ... the high gray glace kid boots, and the little 'tam' of shirred red velvet ... transform her instantly from the Piccadilly creature to a girl any man would have been proud to have been seen with at the Savoy, where she is anxious to go with friends."

"In the third act, she is in wealthy surroundings and the evening toilette of soft rose brocaded in silver harmonized wonderfully with the grays and blues used in the interior decoration of Miriam's maisonette ... In the last act she presents a stunning figure in an ultra-modish street dress ... mink is making its way back to the ranks of *la mode*."

***

As written by the British dramatist, Hubert Henry Davies, Miriam's grand speech in *Outcast* marked the pinnacle of Eagels' career to date. Through the raw emotion of her acting, Jeanne cut through the play's sentimentality; and, at a time when women across America were campaigning for the right to vote, asserted Miriam's humble desire to redeem her life.

"Geoffrey, I have no claims, no rights, but I am a woman in love. Have pity! You're the only man who's ever treated me fair and now you're turning out just like all the rest. Don't lay it on your conscience that you raised me up and made me better and then went and threw me down. Don't send me back to the old life."

"It's so simple for me to slip away and leave no trace. No relatives to think of! No letters to be sent on. Then I thought perhaps it wouldn't be quite fair to you to leave you that way, without giving you the choice, if I really have, as you say I have, been of some use in helping you pull yourself together. But I guess you can get along without me now, so let it be whatever is best for you, and you needn't worry about me. I shall be all right."

"Did you ever read the marriage service? I never did till the other day, it was after the last time I saw you, one afternoon, I was wandering along and I passed a church, I heard singing, so I stood and listened. Then I thought it could do us no harm if I prayed for us both, so I went inside. That was how I happened to come across the marriage service. It seemed as if it opened my eyes. It made me see that whether you think marriage is something religious or only human, it's a solemn business. It's for the protection of good women. It's their reward. I'll cleave to you, Geoffrey, as long as you wish, but I won't marry you."

***

Outcast opened in Trenton, and while those first reviews are now lost, critics from below the Mason-Dixon Line extolled her later performances.

"The *Outcast* of Jeanne Eagels is very real art. Many conditions must be portrayed ranging from grain like suspicion and drab vulgarity to aching pathos and utter despair and Miss Eagels indicates all of them with a sure and delicate conception and execution." – Douglas Gordon, *Richmond Times-Dispatch*

"You laugh with her in her happiness and you cannot but weep with her in her hopelessness later. Her acting is not of that hectic type that seeks to startle you into recognition of it by pricking you eternally with figurative exclamation points, but it is deliberate and finished and as subtle as absinthe." – *Atlanta Constitution*

With Ferguson now touring in *Outcast*, Klaw & Erlanger brought the Eagels production to New York City and the subway circuit, which consisted of theatres in the outlying boroughs of Brooklyn, the Bronx, and Queens. Jeanne's success back in New York was even greater than in the Southern states.

"Something refreshingly and delightfully now . . . there is a wistful charm about her face and voice in moments of pathos which suggests the formative stage of Maude Adams" –*Brooklyn Daily Eagle*

"At the Empire last night she had the trying and difficult situation of not only being judged upon her own ability to put the part over, but also of being contrasted with Elsie Ferguson. She won admirably upon her own resources . . . She has a face that quickly reflects joy, expectancy and the depths of disappointment." – *Syracuse Journal*

"Harrisburg has not for a long time enjoyed a more finished actress. . ." – *Harrisburg Telegraph*

"Eagels is creating talk for her masterful delineation of the principal part" – *Variety*

Jeanne and her company visited Manhattan's Lyceum Theatre for a Christmas Day matinee and evening show before returning Upstate. On December 26, she told the *Buffalo Courier*, "A man's forgiveness doesn't hold much forgetting. While I am playing this girl of the streets, the curtain might fall from the top of the theatre to the floor at the wrong time and I don't believe I'd ever know anything was happening. That's just how much the part absorbs my thoughts and how intensely interested I am in the character. Always there is sound in my ears, the note that if the girl's early life had been different—if her 'luck' had been changed, and I find myself trying to justify her to those out in front. It's what might have been made of a girl like Miriam that keeps throbbing in my heart. Like [Eugéne] Brieux, "I believe the stage should instruct as well as amuse in the phases of life, we need to know about, for our soul's good, as well as the redemption of the poor creatures of Miriam's type. I don't say all girls of the streets have the quality that this girl had, but I do believe some possess the potential."

***

Outcast returned to Brooklyn's Standard Theatre for a limited two-week run, where Jeanne's performance was noticed by several leading producers. Joseph Brooks, had known her since his days with Klaw & Erlanger. Jeanne trusted Brooks, who had produced, written, or directed twenty-two productions since 1899. On February 5, the *New York Dramatic Mirror* revealed his plans to revive C. Haddon Chambers' 1891 play, *The Idler*, at the Shubert Theatre on March 27, 1916.

Jeanne was cast in the ingénue role of Kate Merryweather, a general's daughter. Her search for love provided a comic interlude in an otherwise dramatic story: As a reckless youth in the Wild West, Sir John Harding had killed a man before returning to England. Bruce McRae, as the brother of the deceased, seeks revenge; and Charles Cherry, playing a young Englishman rejected by Sir John's wife, exploits the situation. Brooks filled the main roles with some of the biggest names of the English stage: Phyllis Neilson Terry, Marie Tempest, Montagu Love, and Cynthia Brooke. Jeanne was the only American in the cast.

The producer spared no expense in costuming. Bespoke gowns were designed for the leading ladies, and Jeanne's wardrobe was acquired from upscale department store Bonwit Teller. As reported in *Variety*'s "By the Skirt" column, she wore "a white tulle frock trimmed in tiny red flowers, an evening dress of white net and blue ribbons, and finally a simple bright pink charmeuse dress."

Rehearsals for *The Great Pursuit* (*Idler*'s new title) began on February 18, and the *Dramatic Mirror* announced that it would open in Canada on March 13. On March 2, however, the *Evening Telegram* reported that after an enthusiastic reception at the Royal Alexandra Theatre in Toronto, Brooks had decided to bypass Montreal's Princess Theatre, and so *The Great Pursuit* came to New York earlier than expected, opening at the Shubert Theatre on March 20.

Billboard summarized reviews from several publications in its April 1 edition:

"*The World*'s impression is that 'as an acting piece it offers excellent opportunities since it contains half-dozen characters of almost equal value.' To which is credited its 'attraction of Joseph Brooks.' *The Herald*'s statement that 'the play is overburdened with dialogue' coincides with the view of *The Evening Sun*'s that 'it is just an English drawing room comedy-drama, 1916 pattern'; and this *The Evening World* echoes with emphatic 'Amen—heaven help it!' Added to these is the deeply-drawn sigh of the *Tribune*: 'It is hopelessly aged dramatic material.'"

Fortunately, Jeanne's personal notices were more generous, noting that her physical charms were matched by her ability:

"Jeanne Eagels, whose brilliant performance as Miriam in *Outcast* won her a place in this great cast, scored a success in the role of Kate Merryweather, the pretty, teasing daughter of the old general. This talented young actress has firmly established herself as a Broadway favorite." – *New York Clipper*

"Miss Jeanne Eagels, who made her first important appearance in a big Broadway production playing the general's daughter, Kate with a great deal of knowing charm and looking quite pretty into the barn." – *New York Herald*

"Jeanne Eagels, in spite of her short skirts, was a most sophisticated Kate." – *Auburn Citizen*

"There was a young girl engaged in the pursuit of a lover, delightfully impersonated by Jeanne Eagels, who seemed to confirm earlier impression formed while she was playing in *Outcast* that she is a most promising young actress." – *Brooklyn Daily Eagle*

Nevertheless, the public stayed away from *The Great Pursuit*, with box office receipts peaking at a paltry $500 to $600 per night. After only twenty-nine performances, Brooks abruptly closed the show on April 15, the same day he informed the press and cast. Three weeks later on May 7, he announced that Jeanne would join the cast of another Brooks production, *Somebody's Luggage*. However, by the time it premiered in late August, Jeanne had been replaced.

She had taken the opportunity to return to Kansas City in May. Her family home was a little quieter since Edna had married a year previously and moved out. Jeanne also visited the Georgia Brown Dramatic School at 800 East Armour Boulevard, inspiring students with tales of her theatrical success. A half-page article published in the *Kansas City Star* on May 17, headlined 'Jeanne Eagels' Success is Writ in Electric Letter on Broadway," explained how the local girl's promising career began. Neither Georgia Brown nor the Dubinskys were mentioned, and Jeanne exaggerated much of her professional experience. Stating her age as twenty-one,[7] she told readers that after seeing her in *Outcast*, David Belasco had approached her, asking if she would like to be "starred immediately."

"I don't want to be a star until the public demands it," was her alleged reply. "I am going to try to keep on improving and my growth must come naturally. Still, if I am as good as people say, I want to be paid in proportion."

In Jeanne's account, Belasco advised, "My child, you must not think of money now. You are artistic. Don't get your art confused with business."

"Since I began to get so much publicity I get scores of letters from little girls who want to go on the stage," she told the *Kansas City Star*. "It is my greatest pleasure to answer those letters because I realize what good a little encouragement will do for anyone who is struggling. Success is only a matter of hard work provided the person has ability. Work and plenty of it will turn many a failure into a success. But success will never come without work and struggle; it never did and it never will. Managers don't go around offering fine parts to unknowns on a silver platter. You've got to get out and make good and it takes courage and work."

"I have often wished I could play in my home town, Kansas City," Jeanne confessed. "So far I have never had the opportunity. I wish I could

---

7   In fact, Jeanne was closer to twenty-six.

play *The Outcast* here because it is the best part I probably ever will have. And when I play here I want the home folks to like me."

***

Almost two years before, the assassination of Archduke Franz Ferdinand during a visit to Sarajevo, capital city of Bosnia, had ignited tensions building across Europe since the turn of the century. Britain and Germany were involved in an arms race, while the Balkan region had been at war since 1912. Germany was further threatened by the growing power of Russia and France. By August 1914, Europe was at war.

Under the leadership of President Woodrow Wilson, America had declared a policy of non-intervention, pursuing diplomatic channels instead. Wilson's predecessor, Theodore Roosevelt, condemned this approach and denounced Kaiser Wilhelm's military and naval campaigns as "piracy." After being narrowly re-elected in 1916, Wilson learned that the German foreign minister had invited Mexico to join the war against the United States. On April 6, 1917, the US Congress declared war on Germany.

This was no great surprise to most Americans, who had considered war inevitable for some time. Charities had been devoting their resources towards the allied nations for several years. Many fund-raising events were organized by New York's theatrical community, who donated their time, venues and star power to raise much-needed funds for those affected by the escalating conflict.

One of many benefits that Jeanne would participate in took place on June 26, 1916, when she joined fellow thespians at the Maxine Elliott Theatre in support of the Fund for Hopelessly Crippled French Soldiers. *A Lady's Name,* starring Marie Tempest, was staged for the event. Additional numbers were performed by Marie Dressler, accompanied by Elsa Maxwell on piano, with dance routines by The Dolly Sisters. Jeanne was one of several celebrities selling cigarettes and candy donated by manufacturers, along with flowers and programs to audience members, raising more than $1,000 that afternoon.

***

On June 14, Joseph Brooks had announced he would direct the upcoming production of *What's Your Husband Doing?*, a farcical adventure by George V. Hobart. Charles Pidgeon (Thomas Ross) and John Widgast (Macklyn Arbuckle, cousin of Roscoe "Fatty" Arbuckle) are divorce attorneys and the best of friends, who promise never to keep secrets from each other. On the same night their wives are planning an anniversary dinner at a local restaurant, Beatrice Ridley (Jeanne Eagels), whom Widgast has known since childhood, seeks his advice about her husband's philandering. In strict confidence, Beatrice takes the lawyer to her husband's regular haunt, the same restaurant where the anniversary dinner is to be held. After one sip of alcohol, she falls asleep on Widgast's shoulder. They are discovered by Pidgeon, who stays with Beatrice while Widgast joins their wives downstairs. Running back and forth, Pidgeon and Widgast fail to notice a flirtation between the women and a young cad who turns out to be Beatrice's husband (and Pidgeon's client). Predictably, the men soon realize the error of their ways, and by the final curtain all three couples have reconciled.

Rehearsals for *Husband* began on August 22. The play opened in mid-September at the Valentine Theatre in Toledo, Ohio to capacity crowds, before transferring to Chicago's Blackstone Theatre on September 25. The *Chicago Tribune* hailed the production as "robust, seemly fun . . . acted *con-amore* by the two stars, and with a great deal of filmy charm by Miss Eagels."

Despite sustaining its early success with packed houses every night, notice was given abruptly on October 11 that the show would close in three days. Cast and crew knew the cause, but the public would have to wait until October 19 for an explanation. According to the *Evening World*, an overworked Brooks, on the verge of nervous collapse, had been ordered by his physician to "immediately cease any involvement with his producing plans and to seek absolute rest and quiet." The producer also followed legal advice to close the show, even though it was making a profit. The *Dramatic Mirror* mentioned that leading man Thomas Ross had proposed taking the show on tour minus Arbuckle, who was considering stumping for President Woodrow Wilson's imminent re-election campaign.

While Jeanne must have felt sympathy for Brooks, who had treated her like a daughter, she was not overly worried by the closure. Because she was then able to fully concentrate on her first full-length motion picture. Four days after *Husband's* rehearsals began, the *New Rochelle Pioneer* reported that she had been signed by Edward Thanhouser to star in a special feature production, *The World and the Woman*. Loosely based on the plot of *Outcast*, the script was written by Philip Lonergan and would be directed by W. Eugene Moore. "When she completes her engagement in New Rochelle," the *Pioneer* added, "she is to be featured by Mr. Brooks in a Broadway production."

***

The Thanhouser Company was founded in 1909 and one of the first motion picture studios in America and had produced over a thousand silent shorts and full-length films. When Jeanne joined their stable of stars, the studio had grown to include several pre-sound stages of various size and a three-acre backlot filled with fountains, bridges, and rustic scenery. This was used for filming when weather permitted, and also served as a public park for the residents of New Rochelle. Main Street, which fronted the studio, attracted carloads of tourists, hoping to glimpse a passing movie star. When the company closed in 1918, its inventory was scattered to the winds. If not properly stored, the nitrate film used in early films eventually turned into dust.

As with the majority of silent films, most of Jeanne's work is now lost; only four, possibly five, of her films remain in existence, and two of those date from the early years of sound. A copy of *The World and the Woman* in excellent condition was discovered in the George Eastman Kodak Film Archives, and can be viewed on the Internet. This provides a rare opportunity to see the Jeanne at twenty-six, and appreciate what drew so many thousands of Americans to her stage performances.

In the Lonergan script, Miriam becomes Mary, a down-on-her-luck woman of the streets, hired by spoiled playboy James Palmer as housekeeper for his vacation cabin in the mountains. On the day after her arrival Mary meets the Collins family, who invite her to join them in church. During the service, Mary experiences a cleansing of her soul and returns to the lodge a changed, happier person. Palmer arrives at the lodge with a large party of friends later that afternoon, and when the two are finally alone, he attempts to force himself upon Mary. Rebuffing his advances in front of his guests, she flees to the only sanctuary she knows—the Collins' family home. A humiliated Palmer laughs off the incident, having first vowed his revenge.

Having confessed her wretched past to Mrs. Collins, Mary is taken in as a housekeeper and nanny. One night, while spying on a party below, the Collins' young daughter, Sunny, falls from the second-floor balcony. Mary lays her hands upon the injured girl who is miraculously healed. After helping others in need, Mary is embraced by the local community. Only Jim Bayliss—a bitter man whose wife, Julia, is crippled after being hit by one of Palmer's automobiles—considers her a fraud. Mary fails in her attempt to cure Julia, and the couple storm from the Collins' home just as Palmer arrives.

Asking to speak privately with his former maid, Palmer insists that Mary become his mistress, threatening to reveal her sordid past. She rejects his offer and he attempts to force himself on her. When this fails, Palmer reveals the faith-healer's dark secret to all gathered. As Mary faints to the floor, disillusioned believers file out of the house. Only the Collins family remains along with Palmer's former friend, Harry Bradley, who is in love with Mary. Fearing she no longer has the power to heal, the betrayed woman decides to leave forever.

Meanwhile, Palmer tells Bayliss that it was Bradley who crippled Julia. A vengeful Bayliss lures Bradley up to a mountain peak, and the two men begin a fight to the death. At the same time, Mary arrives at the Bayliss farm, and tries again to heal Julia. From the mountain top, Bayliss sees his wife walking and rushes downhill, leaving Harry battered but alive. Mary hurries to him, and after bandaging his wounds, sets off again—until Bradley begs her to marry him.

One of the last films made by Thanhouser, *The World and the Woman* began production in late August, finishing by the end of October. The studio would begin phasing down operations in early 1917, and by summer's end had leased the lot to the Clara Kimball Young Film Corporation.

The remaining handful of Thanhouser's releases, including *The World and the Woman*, showed how far the film industry had progressed in just a few years: many features ran over an hour; there were advances in camera techniques, editing, and special effects; there were vastly improved production values in costume, sets, and locations.

Director Eugene Moore's desire for realism presented at least one awkward situation for Jeanne. While shooting her early scenes on the streets of Manhattan, she was walking past a restaurant. Suddenly she stopped and grabbed a couple passing by. She spoke briefly before rushing the bewildered pair over to a moving van that was hiding the camera, cameraman, and director.

"Mr. Moore!" she yelled, as he angrily threw back the canvas cover, ready to berate her. Before a word could leave his lips, she told the couple, "See, it's just a moving picture and I'm acting in it. These aren't my regular Broadway clothes." She then explained that the duo were family friends from Kansas City, whom she had spotted staring in astonishment at what they assumed to be her dire financial circumstances, and dubious new occupation.

Mirroring her role in *Outcast*, Jeanne's clothing symbolized her character's spiritual journey. Her initial, startling appearance was set off by an evening outfit, worn in daytime. White stockings rose beneath a near ankle-length black skirt; topped by an ill-fitting silk blouse, also black, and belted at the waist. Pinned to the lapel was a corsage of red flowers. A small cloche hat and mismatched handbag completed the tawdry ensemble.

The scene in which Jean as Mary relates her misfortunes while sitting in the restaurant, anticipates the opening scene in Eugene O'Neill's 1921 play, *Anna Christie*, which was adapted for the screen in 1923 with Blanche Sweet and in 1930 as Greta Garbo's first "talkie." As the redeemed prostitute, Mary, Jeanne was creating an "outcast" heroine; to be replayed by herself, and then others, in various guises for decades to come.

Mary arrives in the Adirondack Mountains wearing a white shirt beneath the same black top, its collar resembling an angel's wings. Her shoes are now covered with spats, and her black straw hat is brimmed to protect her from the sun. Jeanne's third costume is a maid's uniform: a black dress of cotton or linen, high-collared with long sleeves with a simple belt. She will later add a simple white apron tied around her waist. After healing the little girl, Jeanne is seen in a snow-white dress with tiered eyelet appliques, long sleeves, and a high collar tied with a bow at her neck.

Though the money spent on lavish sets was highly visible—from the luxurious restaurant boasting a glamorous floor-show to the well-appointed home of the family who take Mary in—corners had been cut wherever possible during *The World and the Woman's* production. As *Motion Picture* magazine revealed, the awards and loving cups in Palmer's mountain cabin were an assortment of "Best Boss" mugs, dance competition trophies, and commendations from fraternal organizations, found at several Manhattan thrift stores.

Released on November 19 under the Pathé Gold Rooster Play banner, *The World and the Woman* ran over 5,000 feet of film on five reels, a total of sixty-six minutes. Several critics noted the laying of hands—the practice of healing through prayer—thereby implying an association with Christian Science, the religious movement founded by a Bostonian mystic, Mary Baker Eddy, in 1879. Though still considered a cult by traditional churchgoers, and criticized by leading authors including Mark Twain and Willa Cather, Christian Science's popularity continued to grow during the early twentieth century.

A title-card introduces the healing episode, alluding to without identifying Mary's religion as Christian Science: "Some people have a mysterious power of healing, which science acknowledges but cannot explain, and that a powerful church has been built in this day on the faith in this manner of healing." The penitent girl sees Christ bending over the stricken child—superimposed in an early example of cinematic special effects.

Harriet Hold Dey, President of the Women's Press Club of New York City and a prominent Christian Scientist, attended a private screening of *The World and the Woman*. "The memory of *The World and the Woman* clings to me constantly," she wrote afterward. "I am sure you do not fully realize the strength of the work you have done. It is a deeply interesting story, well-acted, well-produced and well-directed. It will hold the attention of everybody, no matter of what belief." While Mrs. Dey didn't credit Jeanne directly, press reviews singled out her performance for praise—and in 1920, the film was re-released to capitalize on her fame.

"One of the biggest reasons for the picture's appeal is Jeanne Eagels ... the sincerity of her acting goes a long way toward making the story convincing." – Agnes Smith, *Morning Telegraph*

"Jeanne Eagels gave us a perfect suggestion of a Broadway streetwalker in the early part of the offering, following it with a very difficult characterization ... suggesting a tremendous mental power without losing appeal of her 'clinging vine' beauty." – *Wid's Film and Film Folk*

"Young, talented and beautiful ... a splendid interpretation" – *Rochester Post-Express*

"Unquestionably her finest performance. . ." – *Auburn Citizen News*

"A real actress, and at the same time a real beauty" – *Motion Picture News*

"Her art lends the proper touch to a delicate and difficult role" – *Bisbee Daily Review*

"Always convincing . . . shows a complete mastery" – *Moving Picture World*

In January 2018, *The World and the Woman* was screened at the Museum of Metropolitan Art in New York as part of 'To Save and Project', an annual retrospective celebrating rare and early film. "*The World and the Woman* takes a turn into faith-healing, a trend at the time, but what's distinctive about the film is the startlingly modern performance by Eagels," Daniel Eagan commented in *Film Journal*. "She grasped before many of her peers the power of silence, of reacting with just her eyes, of limiting movement to focus emotion. She understood how the camera worked, what it picked up and what it lost, and she used that knowledge to advance the craft of acting for everyone who followed . . . *The World and the Woman* ranks with her best filmed performances."

***

On November 27, three days before Thanksgiving, Jeanne—along with the rest of New York City—learned that her employer, Joseph Brooks, had either fallen or jumped to his death from the eighth-floor window of his West Seventy-Ninth Street home. Under severe stress brought on by overwork, Brooks attempted to slash his throat with a razor two months previously. This incident, and his deteriorating mental health, had been concealed from all but a few close friends and immediate family. Jeanne was among many others from the theatrical community, including Daniel Frohman, Marc Klaw, and George M. Cohan, who attended Brooks' funeral at the Twenty-Third Street Masonic Temple on November 28. Less than two years had passed since another great Broadway producer,

Charles Frohman, was drowned. Those congregated must have been bitterly aware of the transient nature of success.

Then on December 13, it was announced that Jeanne would appear in the supporting cast of *Laughter of Fools*, to be produced by Daniel Frohman, and starring Francis Wilson. Two days before Christmas, it was reported that Wilson had left the show; but rehearsals would continue until another lead was found. *Laughter of Fools* was scheduled to open in Atlantic City on January 1, 1917. However, as a suitable replacement proved elusive, the company disbanded and left the actors without their back wages.

"The company was to be a co-star affair," Wilson explained to the *New York Times*. "This idea being abandoned, I did not feel the play strong enough to risk appearing in it, that it would be professional suicide to do so." After Ann Murdock, Wilson's co-star in the comedy, had left Frohman's management for the Shuberts, Wilson offered to continue rehearsing, and agreed to an out-of-town tour. Confident in the tour's success, Jeanne had leased an apartment at 65 West Sixty-Eighth Street from broker Samuel H. Martin three weeks before the show's premiere, but when Wilson's demand to make the final decision regarding a New York run was rejected, he abandoned the project.

The unemployed thespians sent a letter to their former star—who was also the president of Actors Equity—requesting compensation for their rehearsal time. Wilson graciously obliged, but with a stern reprimand: "This appeal to me would have been unnecessary if they had insisted upon Actors Equity contracts, which would have protected and adequately secured them against loss." 1916 had been a roller-coaster year for Jeanne, replete with both success and failure, yet the recognition she yearned for, from audiences and critics, was finally within her grasp.

Early publicity photograph, used to promote *Outcast* (1915.)

Top - Eagels and touring cast members from *The Outcast* (1915.) Bottom - With co-star Arnold Daly in *The House of Fear* (1915.)

Posing for Kansas City photographers Strauss-Peyton (1916.) This portrait best shows Jeanne's resemblance in profile to actress Elsie Ferguson, whom she replaced in *The Outcast*.

Top left - Eagels with W. Graham Brown who played "General Merryweather," father to "Kate" in *The Great Pursuit* (1916). Bottom Right: Publicity photo for *The Great Pursuit*. Bottom - A scene from Jeanne's début feature, *The World and the Woman* (1916), with Wayne Arey as "Jim Bayliss"; Grace de Carlton as "Julia Bayliss"; and Eagels as "Mary."

Chapter 4
Fires of Youth:
January 1917–April 1918

George Arliss was born in London in 1868 and educated at Harrow. He left his father's publishing house at eighteen to pursue an acting career. Within a decade, he was playing supporting roles on the West End stage. Arliss sailed to America in 1901, as part of Mrs. Patrick Campbell's troupe. He would remain there for two decades. Three years after finding fame in *The Devil* (1908), Arliss was cast in what would become his most celebrated role—*Disraeli*—a portrait of the nineteenth century British Prime Minister that had been tailored for Arliss by Louis N. Parker. Having enjoyed a five-year run on Broadway and beyond, by 1917 Arliss was looking for a more light-hearted production with a pretty young love interest.

Professor's Love Story had been scripted by *Peter Pan* author J. M. Barrie, and the play followed the romantic adventures of Professor Goodwillie, a youngish man who has succumbed to old fogeyism. This absent-minded scientist is watched over by his possessive sister and a doctor friend. When a beautiful secretary, Lucy White, enters his life, the scholar finds himself falling in love—and not with the society woman who has her eye on him. A scheme by the sister and doctor to separate the couple fails miserably, and they then marry and live happily ever after. Their fate is sealed with a silhouetted kiss from behind a translucent curtain; however, this touching moment was repeatedly botched by poor technicians using faulty equipment. After two months on tour, Goodwillie was losing his current Lucy White. Actress Margery Maude was leaving to appear in another Klaw & Erlanger production. Arliss was excluded from the decision, except in his choice of replacement.

Arliss had no amorous designs on his potential co-star, as he was happily married. Since their wedding in 1899, actress Florence "Flo" Arliss had often appeared in his plays. Atop the forty-nine-year-old actor's rather thin frame sat a large head with receding hairline, and there was a rather wide space between his nose and upper lip. It was said that Arliss resembled a turtle, minus its shell.

"Have searched all America and nearest suitable approach to your physical requirements is 116. Says she can meet you half way," read a telegram from George C. Tyler to the actor. Arliss was less concerned with acting ability and beauty than the weight of the actress, because in one scene he would have to carry her across the stage. He was not the athletic type, and not a young man either. After stating at her audition that she weighed 117 pounds, Jeanne was asked to jump into the actor's arms to prove it. A contract was signed on January 13, 1917, with *Professor's Love Story* set to open in Philadelphia nine days later.

During the first day of rehearsals, Jeanne expressed strong opinions on how her role was to be played which exasperated the seasoned thespian. He would later speak of Jeanne "displaying unerring artistry" in the part, but for now, he suggested Miss Eagels return to New York. Upon doing so, she duly reported to the producer's office, complaining that Arliss was "too methodical... set in his ways and will not listen to reason." She was curtly reminded who was the novice, and who was Arliss: and Jeanne returned to Philadelphia a humbled actress who listened to her leading man and realized he was right.

After Philadelphia, *Professor's Love Story* moved to Upstate New York, where critics adored her.

"A season or so ago there came to this city a second road company in which one figure stood out... that of Jeanne Eagels, playing the leading role in *Outcast*. It was predicted at that time that Miss Eagels would before long be found with her name in electric lights... It is a matter of gratification to those who have seen her before to learn that Mr. Arliss has chosen her to tread the same boards with him." – *Syracuse Post Standard*

"Miss Eagels... shows herself to be one of the most promising of our young actresses." – *Syracuse Herald*

"Miss Jeanne Eagels possessed a simplicity and winsomeness of acting which was as fresh as the heather of Scotland where her love won out." – *Auburn Citizen*

"Miss Eagels brings a sweetness and charm to the role of Lucy" – *Ithaca Daily News*

***

Professor's Love Story opened at the Knickerbocker Theatre on February 26, and New York critics were on both sides of the fence.

"Prettily played by Miss Jeanne Eagels" (*Brooklyn Daily Eagle*); "A most decorative secretary" (*New York Sun*); "A pleasing Lucy White" (*New York Tribune*); "Rather hard and uninteresting" (*Evening Telegram*); "Her harsh voice and swinging walk would probably horrify Barrie..." (*Evening World*).

On the afternoon of March 12, Jeanne telephoned the theatre and told stage manager George C. Tyler that she was unable to perform that night. Thrown into a panic, Tyler decided that Jeanne's understudy was not up to the job. He bravely phoned Margery Maude, who had first played the role, to fill in for one performance only. "I never shirked my bit yet," Maude told the *New York Sun*, "and besides, I'm so happy this afternoon that I would like to work a little of my surplus good spirits off by playing any kind of a part tonight. I've just read that my cousin Major-General Maude has captured Baghdad," she explained, adding, "I'd play a maid's part tonight if you asked me to—just for a lark." Jeanne's absence was explained to the audience between the first and second act.

Thanhouser-Pathé announced on March 24, that they had signed Jeanne to appear in two films opposite Frederick Warde, another Englishman, whose screen credits included two Shakespearean roles, *Richard III* and *King Lear*. Warde is also credited with the "discovery" of Douglas Fairbanks Sr., having invited the Denver actor to join his New York troupe in 1902.

Jeanne would be pulling double duty over the following weeks: filming in New Jersey by day, and treading the boards at night. *Professor's Love Story* closed on April 7. By then, Jeanne had been cast in Arliss' revival of *Disraeli*, due to open on April 9. She and Arliss performed the last act of *Disraeli* on March 30, during an Anti-Vivisection Benefit held at the Knickerbocker.

Doherty believed that to keep up the duel schedule of film and stage, it's at this time Jeanne had begun using prescribed drugs while living in Mamaroneck, a small village in Westchester County about an hour north of Manhattan. Her home had previously belonged to former Ziegfeld girl Kay Laurell and was later occupied by Ethel Barrymore. "It was in this house that Jeanne first learned of sedatives—to put her tired nerves to sleep, and stimulants—to make her tired body fresh and invigorated, and her weary mind bright and eager."

Arliss' signature piece re-enacted Benjamin Disraeli's attempt to gain control of the Suez Canal through finance. Disraeli sought to defeat a network of Russian spies in their efforts to wreck the transaction, while facing opposition from the House of Commons. Jeanne was to play Lady

Clarissa Pevensey, replacing Elsie Leslie in the original production. Lady Clarissa was one of several fictional characters created to support the leading man. Both the *Brooklyn Daily Eagle* and the *New York Times* found Jeanne "delightful" in her aristocratic role.

On Sunday May 13, Jeanne spent an afternoon volunteering at the Annual Actors' Fund Fair during "Klaw & Erlanger Day," with actors from all of their productions (Arliss included) manning colorful booths stationed on the first floor and mezzanine of the Grand Central Palace. At the previous night's grand opening, over 10,000 spectators had flooded into the neighboring Exposition Hall and witnessed the unfurling of the American and Allied flags by President Woodrow Wilson. This feat was accomplished by clicking a button from the White House hundreds of miles away. However technological miracles would lose out to spiritual as evangelist Billy Sunday would draw an even greater crowd to the Exposition Hall a week later.

***

Disraeli's Broadway run ended in the third week of May. This must have been a great relief to Jeanne, who was now working on her second film for Thanhouser.

The Fires of Youth was directed by Emile Chautard, with a scenario by Agnes Christine Johnston. Frederick Warde played Iron-Hearted Pemberton, an elderly wealthy industrialist returning to his boyhood town to recapture the joy forsaken while amassing his millions. Pemberton is loathed by his employees who endure low wages and unsafe conditions at his steel mill. Discovering his return, a group of them gather to discuss how to confront the "old devil." Overhearing them, young Billy—played by child actress Helen Badgley—visits the old man's mansion to see if he truly does have horns. Mistaking the butler for Pemberton, Billy befriends the tycoon, and wins his affections. After the child tells him about the workers' complaints, Pemberton disguises himself as "Peter Brown" and takes a job at the factory. He then joins Billy's family as a boarder, and meets the boy's older sister, Rose (played by Jeanne).

An infatuated Pemberton declares Rose the "picture of youth," but as the old man discovers, Rose is in love with Jim, another employee. Pemberton retreats to his mansion, vowing to improve standards at the mill. Thinking his friend lost, Billy rushes to the factory and is badly burned in an explosion. As the boy fights for his life, the workers draw lots to decide who should kill their uncaring employer. Discovering that Rose has drawn for Jim, Pemberton takes his place. In despair, he hands Rose his plans for the factory and leaves, intending to commit suicide. Rose realizes Brown's true identity and follows the distraught man as he wanders aimlessly in the countryside, with visions of Billy's accident haunting him at every turn. Just as Pemberton prepares to shoot himself, Rose takes the gun from his hand and begs him to come back. The final scene shows the tycoon with Billy, fully recovered and ditching school to make mischief.

The original five-reel Pathé Exchange version, lasting more than an hour, is now missing. The Imperial Film Company re-released a two-reel, thirty-one-minute version, which is now available to view on the Thanhouser website, a rare opportunity to experience at least some of Jeanne's performance.

With her hair color still naturally brunette, Jeanne's beauty and grace were not diminished by the simple clothes of the impoverished Rose. When she first appears, she wears a coat with contrasting trim. A knit cap covers her head, with her hair spilling out. After she removes her coat and hat, a simple white blouse with long sleeves and wide collar is revealed, tucked into a plain ankle-length, slate-gray skirt. Her sole accessory is a wide cloth belt/sash around the waist. When Rose, Billy, and Pemberton attend the Lilac Cotillion, Jeanne dons a dark patterned dress topped by a small flower-brimmed hat.

Dressing Jeanne all in white had made a strong impact in *The World and the Woman*, so Chautard found another way to convey her character's pure heart. In one scene, Rose turns on an electric light directly above a gang of unhappy workers embroiled in a heated argument. This has the effect of bathing her in brilliant white light and setting her apart from the rest. Numerous exterior locations include the steel-baron's estate; the crowded city streets where Rose and Billy go window-shopping with their new friend, Pemberton; and an authentic smelting factory yard and furnace. Interior sets ranged from the cramped hovel where Rose's family lives, to the parlor used for the Lilac Cotillion, and the cavernous rooms and hallways of Pemberton's mansion.

The Fires of Youth was released on June 17 to good notices. Most critics agreed with *Exhibitor's Trade Review*, which praised Jeanne's "charming" performance as kind-hearted Rose.

"The acting of the entire cast is strong and special credit should go to Jeanne Eagels for the manner in which she raises a conventional role out of the rut. She acts with judgment and makes a charming appearance." – *Dramatic Mirror*

"Natural and pleasing as a pretty and wholesome young factory girl" – Edward Weitzel, *Moving Picture World*

"This little lady has big possibilities..." – *Wid's Film and Film Folk*

"As pretty a piece of girlishness as I have seen in many a day. She is what I would describe as a 'movie find'..." – *Syracuse Daily Journal*

***

Jeanne had spoken frankly to the *Philadelphia Evening Ledger* about her early work in motion pictures a couple of months before *Fires of Youth* was filmed.

"Of course I wasn't featured at that time. I was legitimately with Billie Burke and her company. I used up the daylight hours—four of them—under the Cooper Hewitts. The other members of the cast used to wonder audibly where on earth I put in my spare moments. They wanted me to go to tea and what-not with them. But I was too busy ... Never, never will the movies equal or banish the spoken drama. I mean no disrespect to what is, after all, a tremendously enthralling form of entertainment. I realize what pictures can do, and what they can't. And I am confident that the future will find the cinema a far greater power for art than it has been."

"One reason it hasn't made the headway we'd like it to is the terrible in-consecutiveness of the thing. Let me give you an example. In one film I did, I ran out of a house three weeks before I acted the scene where I left the room to do so. It is this huddled way of piecing together acting bits that I think should be done away with ... Another of my indictments against the screen is the tendency to do every impressive scene (in the sense of setting) on a mammoth scale ... Close-ups carry over the registration of emotion, but not unless they are quietly done. All great human sensation, perception, is calm. It must be played calmly. Nowadays, many times we are given only sensation in the mass—great hordes of men, stupendous crowds of women and children. The fine personal art of the actor suffers."

"I don't think the actor is the pulse of the machine in motion photography," she concluded. "The director is the man. But he has got to give his histrionic material a chance to expand, to grow—and to think."

Jeanne's last comment was judicious. Emile Chautard, director of *The Fires of Youth*, was considered by many to be the "Dean of Modern Motion Pictures." His career had begun in France, where film's essential artistic and production values were first developed. Displaced by war, a large contingency of French directors, cameramen, and other innovators found sanctuary at Thanhouser, augmenting its rapid ascent. Chautard would direct Jeanne in her second feature for Thanhouser, again opposite Frederick Warde in *Under False Colors*.

***

Jeanne was one of many actresses, including Ethel Barrymore, Constance Collier, and Laura Hope Crews, who were recruited for the Actors Fund Automobile Fashion Show, to be held on June 23 at the

Sheepshead Bay Speedway. Jeanne and the others would don their finest outfits and drive a "glittering array of the most up-to-date models from the automobile manufacturers of the world," whereupon the audience would choose a winner. However, reviews and listings of entries from the charity event reveal that Jeanne, by then working on her third Thanhouser film, was not present.

Under False Colors was a timely film, set in Russia prior to the March 1917 dethronement of Czar Nicholas. Warde played John Colton, a millionaire who takes in Vera (Jeanne Eagels), posing as a friend's daughter who is fleeing Poland for America. "Vera" is really the Countess Olga, having assumed the Polish girl's identity when the boat they were traveling on was torpedoed and sank. Colton's son Jack was in Russia working on a financial matter when he helped the Countess escape. Olga grows closer to the family, and finds herself torn when told that Colton is funding the Russian government. The arrival of young Jack and Vera's father exposes her deception, but not before she saves the life of the elder Colton, threatened by a dissident mob under a self-serving leader with greed and murder on his mind. After his real intentions are revealed, all is forgiven and young Olga and Jack decide to marry.

The exteriors of the Colton residence were filmed on location about twenty miles from the studio at Satanstoe, the thirty-acre summer estate of Standard Oil co-founder Henry M. Flagler, near Mamaroneck.

Publicity for *Under False Colors* proclaimed Jeanne "The Most Charming Woman on the American Stage!" Fortunately, this was a sentiment with which critics agreed whole-heartedly, citing her alliance with Warde as one of the "best starring combinations ever seen on the screen."

"A new and refreshing type of ingénue who does not indulge in soubrette tricks to get her effects." – *Dramatic Mirror*

"Her features are expressive and well-adapted to the screen, and she had just the right touch of naive eagerness and wonderment to give strength to certain scenes." – *Moving Picture World*

"Acting of the highest class" – *Schenectady Gazette*

"The comely and capable photoplay artist is remarkably attractive as the Countess Olga, a young girl of the Russian nobility" – *Bemidji Daily Pioneer*

"Jeanne Eagels . . . has never been seen in a role where her pleasing personality was so pronounced" – *Exhibitors Trade Review*

"The work of Jeanne Eagels entitles her to rank with the best leading-women of the screen" – *Motion Picture*

***

On August 5, the *Kansas City Star* reported that Jeanne was staying at the Hotel Muehlebach. "Managers have promised several times I would have an opportunity to appear in Kansas City," she admitted. "But each time something has interfered. I have not despaired, however. I shall not regard my success as complete until I have appeared in Kansas City."

"I was a little girl in Kansas City," she said. "The days at the [Morse] School will never be forgotten. I really started my theatrical career here, too, although it was a humble beginning."

"Miss Eagels is said to be the most photographed woman in New York now," the article concluded—a measure of how far she had risen since those early days.

***

The final Arliss-Eagels collaboration was co-written by Arliss and inspired by the life of Alexander Hamilton, Secretary of the Treasury during George Washington's first Administration. Jeanne was cast as Maria Reynolds, Hamilton's erstwhile mistress, while Florence Arliss played Mrs. Hamilton. Mrs. Reynolds' husband, a former Commissary officer of the American Revolution, blackmailed Hamilton over the affair, which lasted from 1791-1792. A professional conman, James Reynolds was also embroiled in another financial scam, speculating on back wages owed to veterans of the Revolutionary War. Hamilton was cleared of involvement in counterfeiting, but Thomas Jefferson would later expose his adultery. Mrs. Reynolds eventually divorced her roguish husband. In 1804, her attorney, Aaron Burr, would kill Hamilton in a duel, after the hapless politician had helped Burr's rival to become Governor of New York.

Published versions of the play give detailed descriptions of Jeanne's costumes. For her seduction of Hamilton (in Act Two), she wore a "very low coat cream-colored gown of empire style without sleeves and of a very light filmy material with silk petticoat to match; stockings to match and shoes with straps across instep; dark blue cloak of light material with hood, line with emerald green silk." In Act Four, when Mrs. Reynolds begs Mrs. Hamilton not to leave her husband, Jeanne changed into a "long trailing skirt of white messaline (light silk) with polka dot pattern and red stripe; light gray tight fitting bodice with red tulle shawl; light green bonnet with rose in front on long stem; large feather muff."

Hamilton opened in Atlantic City's Apollo Theatre on September 6, transferring to the Knickerbocker Theatre for its Broadway debut eleven days later. Reviewers were unimpressed by the script, but lauded Jeanne's performance.

"As a work of dramatic construction, the play is far from wonderful. Except for Mrs. Arliss and Jeanne Eagels, who serves as the cat's paw of the conspirators, the support is negligible as to known names but serves its purpose. Eagels' beauty alone prevented the scene in which she, as the vampirish Mrs. Reynolds, ensnares Hamilton, from becoming utterly ridiculous." – *Dramatic Mirror*

"As the fair but light and frail Mrs. Reynolds, Jeanne Eagels had by far the best opportunity for fresh characterization and she availed herself of it with great charm and a very considerable subtlety and humor." – *New York Times*

"The art of Jeanne Eagels keeps brazenness from the surface and creates almost a sympathy for a woman who walked deliberately into the life of America's great statesman and financier with a definite plan to ruin his career." – *Billboard*

"Bewitching enough to seduce any aristocrat" – *New York Call*

"An unshadowed delight to the eye . . . she acts a difficult role with taste and exquisite allurement." – *Philadelphia Public Ledger*

"Jeanne Eagels was charming. There is now an ease and sureness in her work that mark her for big things in the future." – *Brooklyn Daily Eagle*

"Curiously appealing . . . altogether the best in the performance." – Arthur Hornblow, *Theatre Magazine*

***

Shortly after opening in *Hamilton*, Jeanne gave an interview to the *New York Sun*, published on September 30, admitting that praise for her looks, rather than her acting from certain critics, could be frustrating. Perhaps by playing a provocative character from American history, Jeanne hoped to finally break out of the ingénue mold.

"Youth and beauty mean absolutely nothing to me on the stage unless they are accompanied by art. And if you wish to please me do not tell me that I looked perfectly lovely in the costume in the last act, as so many people have done, but that my characterization of Mrs. Reynolds is such a complete work of art that if I hadn't been pointed out to you in my dressing room you never would have known me for the same girl. Oh, you must think I am very vain, but I do take my stage career seriously . . . When a friend of mine said 'you ought to be very happy; you are a success,' I answered 'No.' I am not happy, only excited, for how do I know what I will do next season? When one is acting or doing anything else that requires any amount of creative ability, one has the feeling of being on tiptoe all the time—of never really sitting down to rest. There are pauses yes, but there is no suspension of suspense—at least that is the way I feel about it. But perhaps it is because I am young..."

***

Hamilton closed in New York after eighty performances and proceeded to tour until April 1918. When the show opened at Boston's Hollis Street Theatre in February, Jeanne posed for portrait artist Elizabeth Puitti-Barth at her Saint Botolph Studio. Dressed in her second-act attire, with décolletage exposed and hands tucked into a fur muff, Jeanne gazes sensuously ahead. The portrait is now kept at the Smithsonian Archives of American Art.

During her stay in Boston, Jeanne sublet an apartment on Hemingway Street, near Symphony Hall, with cast-mate Marion Barney. It was there that she first met musician Arthur Fiedler, four years her junior, who would later conduct the Boston Pops Orchestra. Fiedler's good friend and fellow musician, Mayo Walder, told biographer Robin Moore how the romance began.

"Opposite Art's apartment in a window across the way, we had become increasingly aware of a couple of god-looking girls watching us fiddle away as we were forever doing," Walder recalled. "We stopped practicing for a smoke and Arthur walked over to the window and smiled back at the girls. They waved and then we communicated with them by pointed sign language, gesturing for them to meet us downstairs—which they did *con brio*."

"One of the girls, an exceptionally pretty, vivacious blonde identified herself as Jeanne Eagels. She was born and had grown up in Kansas City, Missouri. Arthur was immediately attracted to her. She was in her mid-twenties, petite, slender, with long curly, blonde hair, a lovely, vital girl... Jeanne likewise seemed taken with the dark, handsome Fiedler."

The girls invited Arthur and Mayo to see them in *Hamilton* that evening. "Much to our surprise," Walder continued, "when Art and I went to the theatre, we found that Jeanne, whom we had both thought was just another pretty girl with a small part, actually was George Arliss' leading lady! And she was a hell of an actress, too!"

***

Jeanne elaborated on the differences between stage and screen acting in a March 24 interview with the *Boston Herald*:

"Acting for the films is so different from that of the stage that one has to begin from far off to compare them. The mimetic spirit is as great a requisite in one as in the other. But for the films a woman must first of all be possessed of a certain quality of beauty, not mere prettiness or of severe classic feature; but she must have that indefinable something called 'camera beauty'—that is, the camera must register her prettily. Many otherwise beautiful women who have trouble with their photographs will understand."

"She must have ready wit and mobility of feature as well as of mind, for there is this great difference; she acts from the mind of the director, and not from her own understanding, as is the case on the stage, except in rare instances when the actress enjoys singular privileges. Then there is the lack of inspiration in the studio, the psychological influence of the human presence of the audience. It is all hard work."

"But on the stage there is the employment of the mind, the voice, the body, and the sense, the last giving her by far the greater satisfaction. One can translate one's self into the being played and enjoy the sensation of living the character, not once, but any number of times and have the recompense of knowing what and why you are doing it. The screen audience is worldwide, but I love the speaking stage best."

Actress Ruth Gordon met Jeanne for the first time while *Hamilton* was playing at the Klaw & Erlanger Theatre in Cincinnati. Born in 1896, Ruth had been inspired to take up acting after seeing Hazel Dawn in *The Pink Lady*, while Jeanne was in the touring company. The teenaged Ruth wrote letters to her favorite actresses, and Dawn was the first to reply. After appearing as one of the lost boys in a revival of *Peter Pan*, Ruth was cast in Booth Tarkington's *Seventeen*. Her co-star, Gregory Kelly, became her first husband, and they spent the next few years working together in regional theatre.

Ruth was having dinner at the Sinton Hotel in Cincinnati when her company manager Harold Holstein pointed to Jeanne, who was dining alone. "That's the greatest profile in the world," he said admiringly. Ruth later shared an elevator with Jeanne, and even followed her down the hall. But it was the star who struck up a conversation with her young fan.

"In Chicago Mr. Bruce McRae and I came to see you," she told a dumbstruck Ruth. "You're very good. Mr. Bruce McRae thought so, too."[8]

George Arliss had nothing but praise for his co-star. "During this past season, Miss Margery Maude left the company and her place was taken by the amazingly clever Jeanne Eagels," he said. "Miss Eagels continued in the part of the Secretary [in *The Professor's Love Story*] until the end of the run. She then played Clarissa with me in a short revival of *Disraeli*, and afterward Mrs. Reynolds in *Hamilton*. Three distinct parts, each played with unerring judgment and artistry! She has the vital sense of time. Hers was the talent of making a role a character, epitomizing biography and stepping on to the stage as a person, not a part."

"Then there were the members of the cast whom I came to know and like. Jeanne Eagels was a genius," recalled the co-author of *Hamilton*, Mary P. Hamlin, in her memoir. "Mr. Arliss and I both knew it though she had not had a chance to show it ... David Belasco saw her possibility and came backstage the first night of *Hamilton* in New York. He engaged her for the next season and pushed her to stardom."

Jeanne had previously told the *Kansas City Star* that Belasco initially approached her in 1916, after a performance of *Outcast*. On November 21, 1917, the *New York Clipper* reported that "Jeanne Eagels will be a Belasco

---

8   Bruce McRae (1867-1927) had been Jeanne's leading man in *The Great Pursuit* (1916) and would be again in 1918.

star ... it having been stated last week that David Belasco is just about to give her a contract for several seasons." In later years, Belasco would exaggerate his contribution to her fame, casting himself as her Svengali.

***

Fund-raising efforts within the theatrical community had increased ten-fold since the United States entered the war conflict in April. Leading ladies sold Liberty Bonds onstage, on street corners, and from the steps of the New York Public Library on Fifth Avenue. Food drives were established, and dozens of actresses and chorus girls joined the Women's War Relief Association.

For nearly two weeks, Jeanne rehearsed her part in one of the largest benefits yet attempted. Nearly 500 dramatic, musical, and operatic performers volunteered their time for the Rosemary Pageant, in aid of the American Red Cross.

On October 5, 1917, nearly 7,000 people gathered at an open-air theatre on the country estate of Mr. and Mrs. Ronald Conlin of Long Island. A series of giant tableaux celebrated great historical achievements of the Allied nations: Belgium, Russia, England, France, and other countries affected by the war. The French honorarium told the story of Joan of Arc in three scenes. Jeanne appeared as a supporting character when Joan (Ina Claire) was permitted by King Charles (Guy Faviéres) to lead the French army.

A photograph taken during the week of September 23 at the Hippodrome Theatre shows the cast rehearsing in street clothes. One of the spectators, Clifton Webb, was scheduled to dance the Pavane with Mrs. Ben Ali Haggin, wife of one of the producers. The one-night performance was filmed and shown in movie theaters around the country. Entitled *The National Red Cross Pageant*, the film raised thousands of dollars to send overseas. It is now lost, with only a handful of photographs capturing the spectacle.

"This was perhaps the most attractive episode," *Moving Picture World* commented on the French segment in its October 27 review. "The court group was most picturesque, this scene requiring a group of horses, which gave greater realism to the whole. Here were a larger number of talented people than in any other scene."

On October 31, she signed a contract with World Pictures-Brady to film *The Cross Bearer*. British actor Montagu Love starred in the contemporary tale of Cardinal Mercier, who had protected his church and townspeople when the German army invaded the Belgian city of Louvain (or Leuven). Jeanne played Liane de Merode, the Cardinal's young ward, engaged to Belgian officer Maurice Lambeaux (Anthony Merlo). When the German Governor General tries to steal her away, Maurice breaks through enemy lines in disguise. The Cardinal secretly marries the young couple, and helps them cross the border to France and freedom.

The largest stage at World Pictures accommodated fifteen sets and housed the interiors of the Cardinal's palace and the Vatican. Photographs of the pontiff's residence were obtained, enabling furniture, paintings, and tapestries to be recreated in exact detail. One of the major scenes required an authentic reproduction of the Louvain Cathedral, constructed on the lot next to the studio. A massive outdoor street set that was several blocks long and large enough to allow tanks and other military vehicles to pass through was also created. However, a severe wind storm swept through the night before filming was due to start, destroying the set and upsetting the filming schedule while it was rebuilt.

Before its official release in April 1918, *The Cross Bearer* was given a four-day run at Carnegie Hall to raise funds for the Red Cross. Tickets were priced at 50¢ to $1, with box seats at $10 each. The film was even endorsed by the King of Belgium.

"Miss Eagels has the requisite amount of youth, beauty, and wistfulness" – *Photoplay*

"An altogether exceptional, extraordinary picture ... Jeanne Eagels is charming as Liane de Merode." – *Hattiesburg American*

"The work of Miss Eagels entitles her to rank with the best leading-women of the screen." – *Motion Picture*

"[Eagels] impersonates Liane de Merode . . . with winsome grace and ease." – *Catholic News*

"Charming . . . an ingratiating personality and handles her role expertly." – *Dramatic Mirror*

Top - Eagels as "Rose" in *The Fires of Youth* (1917.) Bottom: With co-stars Frederick Warde (Pemberton) and Helen Badgley (Bill) in a scene from *Fires of Youth*.

Top: Eagels in a group scene from *Under False Colors* (1917.) Bottom: Eagels alone on the same set.

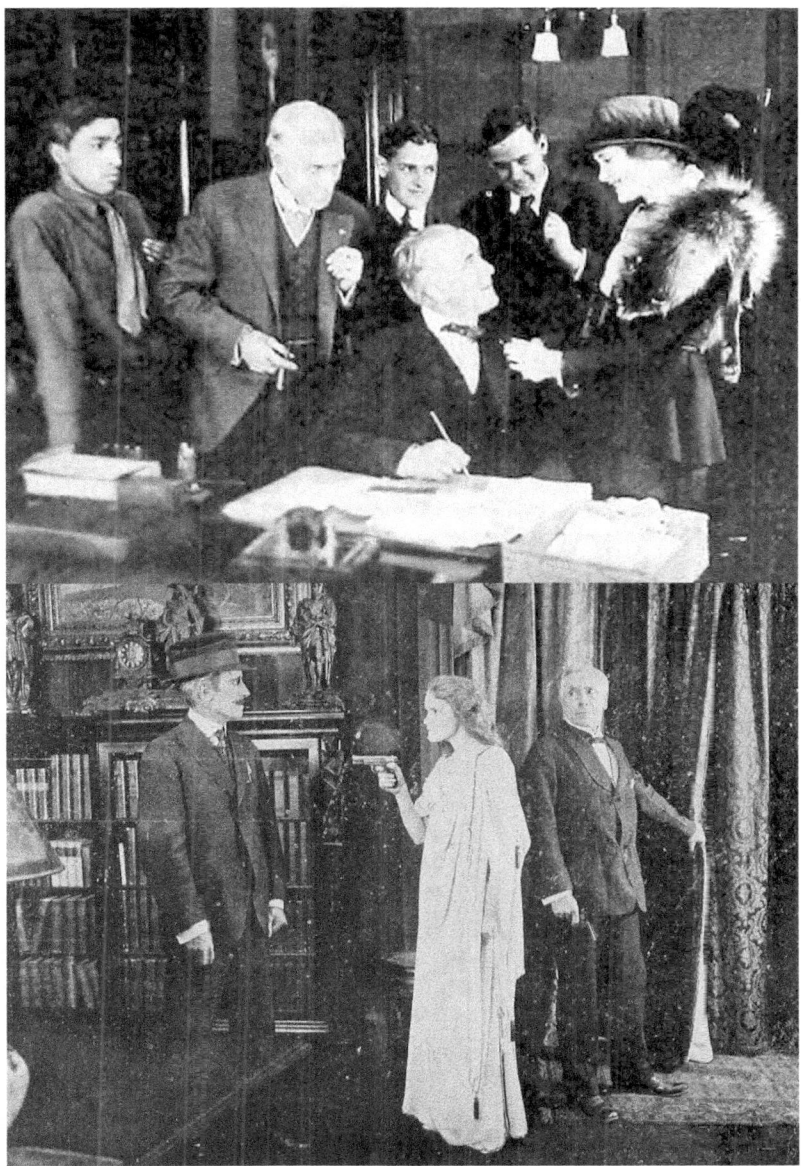

Top - Eagels with (L-R) Ivan Sansonavitch; Frederick Warde; Giuseppe Lena; and director Emile Chautard, in a publicity photo for *Under False Colors*. Bottom: Eagels as "Vera/Countess Olga," protecting Warde as "John Colton."

Top left - George Arliss chose Eagels as his co-star in three plays. Top Right: Jeanne in costume for the Rosemary Pageant (1917). Bottom (L-R): Guy Faviéres, Mrs. Haggin, Ina Claire, Clifton Webb, Ivy Troutman, Eugene O'Brien, Jeanne Eagels, Ben Ali Haggin rehearse for the Rosemary Pageant at New York's Hippodrome Theatre.

Mrs. George Arliss as "Mrs. Hamilton" onstage with Eagels as "Mrs. Maria Reynolds" in *Hamilton* (1917). Insert: Eagels and Arliss during the seduction scene in *Hamilton*.

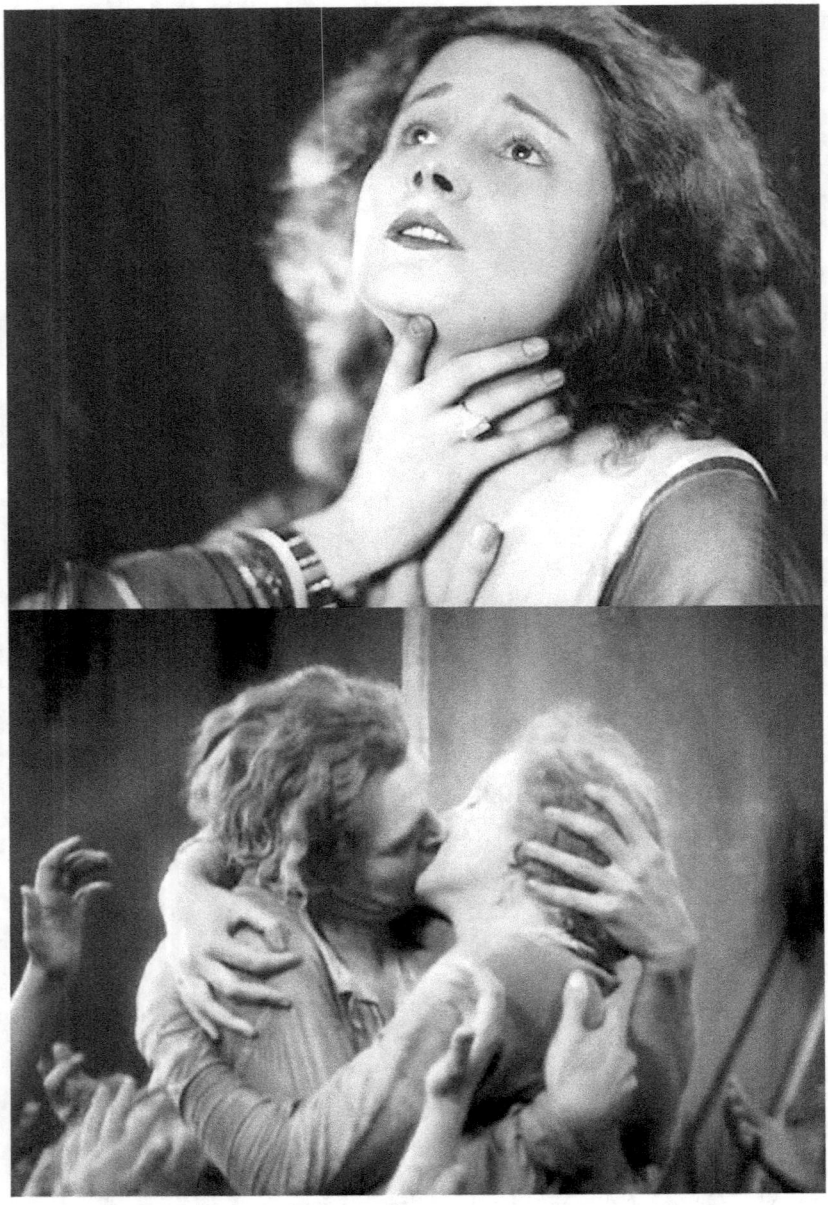

Top - As "Liane de Merode" in *The Cross Bearer* (1918). Bottom: A passionate embrace with co-star Anthony Merlo ("Maurice Lambeaux.")

Top & Bottom – Two scenes with Montagu Love as "Cardinal Mercier."
Bottom - With Love in *The Cross Bearer*.

Chapter 5
Daddies: May 1918–October 1919

On April 25, 1918, Jeanne appeared at the George M. Cohan Theatre in aid of the Duryea War Relief Fund. Following a speech by the charity's founder, there were several patriotic readings, including "The Battle Hymn of the Republic" and "Verdun," and music by the Fifteenth Regiment Band. Jeanne joined the cast of *Her Godson*, a new one-act play.

On May 18 the *New York Tribune* confirmed Jeanne's signing with producer David Belasco and predicted that "her name will burst into electric lights" in *Daddies*, opening at the Belasco Theatre in Washington D.C. on June 10.

"She reminded of nothing in the world but a starved little alley cat," the impresario told Doherty, recalling their first meeting shortly after Jeanne finished her run in *Outcast*. "Beautiful. With wonderful golden hair ... blue angelic eyes ... the tender but firm chin ... but gaunt, starved, sick! ... Her eyes were hard, bitter, and shining with ambition, the eyes of a girl who would do anything to be an actress. Thousands of girls have come to me in my time... but never such a girl as this Jeanne Eagels. She was a contradiction. A girl in shabby clothes, with the air of a Duse, and the voice of an earl's daughter, and the mien of a tired alley cat."

David Belasco—like Charles Frohman—was a Broadway stalwart. After arriving in New York in 1892, Belasco wrote, directed, and produced more than a hundred shows between 1894 and 1930. The theatre he built in 1907—then renamed after himself in 1910—still stands on Forty-Fourth Street in Manhattan.

The successful producer wanted audiences to marvel not only at the talent, but also the sets, costumes, and music presented in his theatre. He believed in spending money to make money. If a play called for a laundry, the set designer was expected to build a real laundry, where clothes could be washed. For one production, an entire restaurant was recreated.

"Belasco seldom left the theatre on Forty-Fourth Street which bore his name," author Allen Churchill revealed. "He worked in an ornate office crammed with memories of production among them an authentic sedan chair. A spotlight shone down on him from above, and some who came to worship at the shrine recall him sitting on a raised dais." The producer's nickname was "The Bishop of Broadway," inspired by his penchant for dark clothing, often worn with a cleric's white collar.

Adopting a fatherly attitude, he greeted his actors with a hearty "Hello children!" At the time Jeanne joined the roster, she was dubbed "the fourth jewel in Belasco's crown" by the press, alongside Ina Claire, Frances Starr, and Lenore Ulric. Fay Bainter and Madge Kennedy became the fifth and sixth, signing with the producer shortly after Jeanne.

However, the theatrical world was one of illusion. At sixty-five, the "Bishop" was a notorious lecher, preying on young actresses. "I have never felt over twenty-five and I shall never see a woman looking older than twenty-one," he is said to have bragged. Many a hopeful ingénue was invited into the boudoir adjoining his office, as detailed by Churchill: "a lavish bedroom dominated by a mighty four-poster. One wall was painted to resemble a bay window, and from the soft depths of the bed, Belasco was able to push buttons which lighted the window, creating sunrise to sunset."

As George Abbott, Jeanne's co-star in *Daddies*, observed in his 1963 memoir, Belasco's greatest successes were with women. "He nearly always fell in love with his protégées and treated them solicitously—and with great jealousy and possessiveness," Abbott claimed. "He never trusted them and constantly called them at odd hours to check on their whereabouts." This controlling nature was unlikely to ensnare the fiercely independent Jeanne.

"Belasco wasn't very attractive as a man," George Abbott recalled. "As a house-painter he wouldn't have appealed to a young woman but to stage-struck actresses, as a great figure in the theatre, he had glamour." His great mistake, Abbott thought, was "to presume Jeanne would fall in love with him."

"There was considerable hypocrisy in Belasco's puritanical stance and clerical garb," Herbert G. Goldman noted in his biography of Fanny Brice, the Broadway actress, Ziegfeld star, and radio comedienne who also worked for the producer. "Belasco had his female stars show their appreciation in two ways: to pull him onstage when they took their bows and to enter a small bedroom in his office. Jeanne Eagels refused to pull him onstage . . . Laurette Taylor refused to enter the bedroom."

Doherty reported that on the opening night of *Daddies*, Belasco stood in the wings, dressed to the nines with even a touch of make-up, waiting for his moment to shine on stage. It was a tradition of any production that bore his name. "It was showmanship . . . a public acknowledgment on the part of the actress of all that she owed to the great master of the drama."

The play ended to thunderous applause. Jeanne took her bows with the cast and then several alone. Glancing over, she couldn't help but notice Belasco preening for his appearance; but rather than come over and take her employer's hand, "she exited the other side of the stage and headed straight for her dressing room." A few moments later, the irate producer barged in. Jeanne stopped him cold by feigning illness, claiming she was about to faint. So often did she use this ploy, that a doctor and nurse were hired to stand by in case of medical emergency.

If Goldman's readers were left wondering whether Jeanne had succumbed to Belasco's offstage advances, Churchill suggested otherwise. By his account, she was invited to his office which conveniently included a small kitchen, for dinner one night. After the meal was over, the producer offered to give her a tour of the other room although he was expecting several business associates shortly. Aside from the forty-year age difference, she was well aware that Belasco "kissed and told," and any actress who returned his affections would soon be the talk of Broadway. She rejected his offer instantly. Nonplussed, he excused himself and went into the bedroom alone, whereupon a suspicious Jeanne "applied eye to keyhole and saw the Master vigorously rumpling his sheets. When the business associates arrived he obviously planned to indicate the bed and claim another conquest." Not about to have her reputation tarnished, she "flung open the door and ordered the Master to straighten the bed. Then the two sat tight-lipped until the guests arrived, at which lovely Jeanne flounced off." Doherty tells a similar story in *The Rain Girl*, but refers to the offender as "a very important man in the Belasco organization."

During a key moment in *Daddies'* first act, a member of the cast was directed to squirt soda into his highball. The ensuing noise drowned out actor John Cope's next laugh line. When Cope complained, Belasco hissed, "This play is about bachelors. I'd rather have the sound of that soda than a dozen laughs."

"In those days," Abbott explained, "the hours of rehearsal were limited only by the producer. David Belasco willed them to continue a very long time; in fact, he had lunch served in the basement of the Theatre so that we wouldn't go out and let our minds wander from the business at hand . . . When there was some particularly difficult problem to be worked out, Belasco would keep us there for dinner, and we would work on into the night." At the opening of the "Belasco Room" at Sardi's Restaurant in 1959, Abbott told the *Boston Herald* how the producer "would have meals sent in for the cast. Once when he had tripe—Jeanne Eagels said 'I'll have some more of that—er—fish.'"

The *Herald* noted that Abbott thought his former employer "a fake and lecherous hypocrite. A Belasco actress who spurned the boss and befriended Abbott was the brilliant, ill-fated Jeanne Eagels."

While Jeanne may have rebuffed his personal advances, her professional regard was unreserved. "Often in the theatre there is a feeling of commercialism in every detail," she admitted. "It may not touch one directly, but it is there, and the consciousness that the financial success of the play is perhaps of first importance is decidedly unpleasant. Now Mr. Belasco puts acting, like every other element of a production, upon an artistic basis. He makes you feel that a thing is important artistically or not at all. Money seems never to be a consideration yet the making of it follows as a result of making the production as nearly as perfect as possible. That point of view on the producer's part means a great deal to the actor; it leaves him free to do so much, and is an incentive to work toward a faithful portrayal of character. To me everything about Mr. Belasco's theatre points toward the one ideal of his—perfection."

Written by John L. Hobble, *Daddies* followed the humorous exploits of three bachelors who wager a $5,000 bet to remain unmarried for life. They each decide to adopt a French war orphan, but complications arise when the children arrive. One expects a boy and gets a girl, while another asks for one child and is landed with triplets. The last of the bachelors, after choosing a six-year-old girl, is confronted by a young lady of seventeen. Jeanne portrayed teenager Ruth Atkins, who persuades her benefactor to use his writing skills to help the orphans' cause, and wins his love.

"Jeanne Eagels' part was really a phony," George Abbott wrote later. "She played an innocent English orphan of sixteen, a synthetic sappy role that was quite unsuited to her, and I think she realized that Belasco had sweet-talked her into a job that was not good for her. Probably she had accepted the assignment in awe of the great maestro's name rather than on judgment; at any rate, she seemed a reluctant and uncooperative actress. Belasco didn't quite dare bawl her out, so he vented his anger on the ingénue, Edith King. This hapless victim had to endure long tirades and generalities which were really directed over her head to our star." Abbott extended a hand of kindness which the actress accepted gratefully.

"Jeanne became friendly to me, and always addressed me as Kid," Abbott recalled in his memoir. "She was a creature of moods, strange and aloof most of the time and with most people. But at other times she would come into the theatre wearing a warm expansive aura and would talk to me with considerable intimacy. She talked about two things; music, which she loved, and men, whom she hated. She gave me the impression that men had wronged her and that her life work was to get even with them." Jeanne might have treated him like a younger brother, but Abbott was already married, and a father. "Obviously she didn't consider me a man," he told the *Milwaukee Sentinel-Journal* in 1963. "I was a sort of sometime pal."

Belasco was renowned for showcasing female beauty, and as such, many expected Jeanne to make a glamorous entrance. The producer realized, however, that public tastes were changing, with audiences favoring credible acting over mere sex appeal. With characteristic showmanship, he enlisted designer Henri Bendel to break with tradition.

Jeanne walked onstage garbed in a pair of dark pants peeking out from under heavy overcoat, her unkempt hair tucked beneath a mannish looking hat and looking, as one critic noted, "as plain as the countrywoman at the zoo." As the play progressed, her costumes became more stylish, culminating in a silk outer-wrap for her final scene. The one area found lacking by the *Millinery Trade Review* was in headwear: "There are a number of smart hats shown, but they are not worn by the leading woman, Jeanne Eagels, whose hats in the play are of negligible style quality."

Belasco directed the pre-Broadway shows in Washington D. C., Stamford, Connecticut, and Asbury Park, New Jersey, before the opening night at the Belasco Theatre, New York, on September 5. Jeanne took a much-needed break on the weekend of July 21, when she visited George and Julia Leary at their cottage in Southampton, Long Island.

Daddies was a hit with theatregoers, and Jeanne's performance attracted critical praise, although Dorothy Parker, a rather less sentimental columnist, voiced her doubts in *Vanity Fair*.

"*Daddies* is one of those things that are simply too sweet for words. It starts right out being sweet the moment rises, and it gets steadily sweeter and sweeter as the evening advances. In fact, when you go to see it, it's just as well to bring the bicarbonate of soda with you ... Jeanne Eagels made a long appeal for war orphans, but, although she recited it very prettily, in her charmingly modulated voice, she didn't take it much to heart. Indeed, she was most impersonal about the whole thing ... not particularly stirring as an appeal for the orphans of war; but, as propaganda for birth control, it was extraordinarily effective."

"Miss Eagels was quite the most surprising part of the performance ... She has a wider range of sympathy, a much better voice and an easy gentleness which has somehow not revealed in other plays." – *New York Herald*

"The acting was so real and convincing, in fact, that one almost had vertigo watching it. Indeed her whole performance was on a very high level and probably marks the advent of an actress of distinguished quality." – *New York Times*

"Jeanne Eagels made Ruth a most delightful young lady, lending her a dainty charm that was irresistible." – *New York Clipper*

"*Daddies* is not a comedy. Farce comedy at its very best ... doesn't run twenty minutes before you know it all. Jeanne Eagels has the chief role among the women ... the seventeen-year-old girl who doesn't look it ... just a little too much of the 'actress' all the way through, though she gave a touch of sincerity to her pleas for orphans." – *Variety*

***

"The critics, as is their custom when dealing with popular stars, gave praise to Miss Eagels," George Abbott remembered. "But realizing her part was phony, she knew she wasn't good in it, even if her critics didn't; and hardly had we opened when she began to make efforts to get out of her contract. Mr. Belasco disappeared; once the show opened we never saw him. I think that he too was disappointed; the play was a potboiler and nothing more."

Nonetheless, the commercial success of *Daddies* and her contract with Belasco enabled Jeanne to lease an apartment at 49 West Fifty-Sixth Street. Julia came from Kansas City to stay while brother Leo arrived from Canada where he'd applied in March to join their military in fighting the Great War. He changed his birth date, surname spelling and previous address, possibly to prevent repercussions for his desertion. But then Leo had been the Eagles' problem child since the death of Edward. After dropping out of school, he had fallen in with the wrong element and began robbing houses until his arrest on March 4, 1914. He was sentenced to two years' detention at Booneville Reformatory outside St. Louis. Founded in 1889 as an alternative to regular child prisons, authorities hoped fresh air, open fields, and hard work would improve the mindset of the juveniles in their care. But by 1914, the place had become "a hell-on-earth," according to one report. The experience seems only to have hastened Leo's descent into criminality, for not five months after his release on March 4, 1916, the now eighteen-year-old stood before Judge Latshaw who sentenced him to two years in the state penitentiary for robbing the homes of J.R. Gentry and R.H. Randall.

When asked if he had anything to say, the young Eagles silently stared out the window as Julia, quietly sobbing tugged at his sleeve, begged him to answer. "Let'er go ma, I'm alright," he replied, as the *Kansas City Star* reported on July 11.

Out on early release and A.W.O.L. from Canada, Leo settled in with his big sister Jeanne, and registered for the U.S. Military on September 10, just under two weeks shy of his twentieth birthday.[9]

Jeanne had grown quite fond of the child actors in the show. She escorted all five with their parents to the September 18 matinee performance of *Everything*, an Irving Berlin musical featuring an appearance by Harry Houdini, at the 5,000-seat Hippodrome Theatre. She would also often leave surprise gifts and candy in their dressing room. Perhaps they reminded her of her younger siblings or the child she might have had and given away.

Like many other young men, George Abbott was preparing for the draft. But to everyone's relief, on November 11, the Allied Powers agreed terms with defeated Germany. "During a matinee, word came backstage . . . that an armistice had been declared; the city was celebrating, and there was dancing in the streets," Abbott wrote. "After the first act I did not need to be onstage for another forty minutes, so I took off my make-up and rushed out of the theatre. The main celebration was on Fifth Avenue, and I pushed my way down there. Indeed there was dancing in the streets, traffic had ceased and delirious people had taken over."

World War One formally ended seven months later with the Treaty of Versailles, and the establishment of a worldwide League of Nations. Although America's involvement in World War One did not officially cease until 1921, and the aftermath would be felt across Europe for years to come, the public mood was celebratory. Author Kevin C. Fitzpatrick has described this period as "the last great era of live theatre in America before radio, talking pictures, and television decimated attendance. In New York, close to eighty theatres were in operation, compared with thirty-five or so left today. Sometimes as many as seven new shows debuted in one night."

"Most of the producers were mining the war effort to fuel their shows," Fitzpatrick noted, adding that critics like Dorothy Parker would typically see three or four new shows each week, often featuring "chorus girls in

---

9   Leo would not have the opportunity to serve as the war ended approximately two months later.

stars and stripes or highbrow dramas set in hospitals and battlefields." A weary Mrs. Parker quipped, "I have been through so many war plays that I feel like a veteran."

"Shows ran for weeks or months to be successful and earn their money back, not years. Modestly priced tickets brought theatregoers into playhouses more often," Fitzpatrick observed, adding that Broadway changed with the seasons: "a tradition that has been completely lost in modern times." Lack of air conditioning meant that many playhouses closed their doors in the summer. Their actors either "rested" or went on the road, although scantily-clad revues such as *The Ziegfeld Follies* stayed open. Dramas, tragedies, and mysteries came in the fall, with the most extravagant shows opening near Christmas. The spring shows, according to Dorothy Parker, were "the rice puddings of the theatrical world; they don't hurt anybody, and they're undeniably filling."

Shortly after New Year, Jeanne posed for the January 20, 1919 issue of the high society magazine, *Town & Country*, modeling "sporting togs" from Abercrombie & Fitch. The Geisler & Andrews photographs were captioned, "Miss Jeanne Eagels illustrating what she would wear in the South if *Daddies* would stop playing long enough to let her go there. . . " She was then playing nine shows a week, with benefits and fundraisers occupying her free time. On some occasions, she was simply unable to honor her commitments.

One of these "no-shows" occurred at the Thirty-Eighth Annual Actors' Fund benefit, held on January 24 at the Century Theatre. Jeanne had been due to perform among the six women and six men of the "Floral Sextet." Her absence was noted, but a special appearance from Houdini amply compensated. Organized by Daniel Frohman with Belasco's assistance, the event raised $15,000 for the Actors' Fund.

Jeanne did appear at the February 23 *Carry On* benefit, presented by Stage Women's War Relief at the Belasco Theatre to raise money for Debarkation Hospital Number 5. Jeanne, Marie Dressler, Fay Bainter, Cecil Cunningham, and Helen Hayes performed in George V. Hobart's

Rough Perfect, which ironically dealt with the obstacles faced during rehearsals for a charitable performance. Two weeks later, Jeanne was found at the Playhouse Theatre, alongside Pearl Gardner and Fransy Shiota in *Cupid's Comeback*, a highlight of the midwinter *Friars' Frolic*.

This much activity in Jeanne's personal life was sure to affect her performance, and eventually it did. "One matinee when she was playing a scene with the leading man, she seemed to grow fainter and fainter," George Abbott recalled. "Finally she stopped in the middle of a line. The actor whispered, 'What's the matter?' Jeanne gasped, 'Water,' and he rushed obediently offstage. But while he was gone, Jeanne suddenly remembered that Winifred Fraser, an English actress, was having her customary cup of tea in the wings, and when the leading man returned with water, she said, 'No, tea.'"

Abbott believed this real-life performance was merely "one of the tactics Jeanne used to persuade the management to cancel her contract." She was gaining a reputation for difficult, inconsiderate behavior. However, another worrying incident suggested that her exhaustion was not just an act.

On May 4, the *Evening Telegram* recounted that Jeanne had fainted onstage during a matinee the week before. Just before her big speech near the end of the second act (an impassioned plea for the war's orphans), she had to cross from one side of the stage to the other. She took two steps and collapsed into a heap upon the floor. Co-star Bruce McRae sprang into action, leading the audience to believe it was part of the story—the result of Ruth's earlier sea sickness—by going to the door and calling out "Mother?" When the actress playing his mother appeared, McRae simply stated, "Poor Ruth is all in." Together, they carried Jeanne to her dressing room, while the curtain was brought down.

The audience was surprised, but not as much as the nameless understudy still in the theatre. She rushed onstage and finished the play in her street clothes and without make-up.

A few weeks later, Jeanne played Ruth for the 300th time. On June

8, the *New York Sun* published a lengthy interview with Jeanne, who explained how she tried to bring a unique quality to every performance.

"Audiences mean as much to an actress as the acoustics of a concert hall mean to a musician. The musician must vary his playing according to his acoustics—according to the sort of room in which his concert is given. It is much the same with my Ruth Atkins. A sort of sixth sense enables me to discern the character of an audience within a few minutes after I have begun to play, and it is only the people for whom I am making this lovable girl live at that one performance that matter. Former audiences are swept from my thought as though they had never been. As far as the audience of the moment is concerned others have never been. What I have done, or have not done, for them doesn't matter to the folk who have come to see the play tonight. I am so very conscious of this that I am able to play to them as though I were creating the part for the first time."

"I do wrong in speaking of playing to an audience however. A true artist never plays to an audience. Rather he or she keeps his/her own vision true and the creation evolves itself. We will take my seasick scene in *Daddies* for instance. It is not the result of something which I have carefully studied out, but rather the outcome of a mental condition. The picture of Ruth Atkins as she is deserted by the author at the end of her voyage from England to America is so vivid a thing in my own mind that her actions are involuntary. I never studied them out and decided that she should do this, that or the other. Rather I became saturated with the sense of the girl in the given circumstances, and the things she does naturally follow. They evolve themselves out of my mental condition at the time, and vary in just so far as my own mental condition varies. Playing is an imaginative art. It is the transmission of the thought of an actress to her people. Therefore this question of keeping fresh in a part after playing it hundreds of times depends upon keeping one's own vision fresh and true . . . A player would go stale in a part very quickly if he or she created that part in the beginning and spent the balance of the time imitating that creation. Such a thing is merely theatrical mechanism and does not deserve the name of art."

"I dare say I give no two audiences exactly the same Ruth Atkins. In her main essentials she is the same, of course, but the lights and shadows of her vary in just the degree that my mental vision of her varies . . . It is for these reasons that I can always answer no to those who ask me if I ever grow tired of a part after I have played it hundreds of times."

***

Nonetheless, *Billboard* confirmed on June 20 that after 350 performances, Jeanne had indeed grown tired, and would be replaced by Madeline Travers.[10] Although it was reported that Jeanne would be sailing for London, she headed home to Kansas City where, on June 29, she told the *Kansas City Star*: "From the time I was a very little girl I had no patience with mediocrity, I think that was why I watched people so closely, and studied them so closely. I had rather not be at all than be mediocre . . . I struck out for myself and endured the wildest, weirdest experiences in barnstorming engagements through the Middle West," she added, recalling her early work with the Dubinskys, before she moved to Chicago, and then New York. "From that it has been easier sailing through a period of all-star productions by Joseph Brooks; with Mr. Arliss in three of his productions; to the present realization of my dreams of all the years, my appearance in a New York theatre under the management of Mr. Belasco." In early July, she headed to White Sulphur Springs, West Virginia, spending two weeks at the Greenbrier Hotel with her friend and *Pink Lady* co-star, Ida M. Adams. The ladies returned just as a long-brewing battle between Actors Equity and the Theatrical Syndicate reached boiling point which could put hundreds, or even thousands, out of work.

The Actors Equity Association (AEA) had been founded six years

---

10   *Daddies* would be filmed by Warner Brothers in 1924 with Mae Marsh in Jeanne's role.

before by 112 professional stage actors, who established the association's constitution and elected officials. In 1919, AEA joined the American Federation of Labor in calling for a strike, demanding recognition as a labor union. Weakened by the deaths of Joseph Brooks and Charles Frohman, the Theatre Syndicate had regained its power that spring, when Klaw & Erlanger and the Shubert Organization formed the Producing Managers Association (PMA). AEA's approximately 2,700 members worried that the merger was designed to court stockholders, prioritizing profit over artistic merit, and they feared that giving that much power to just one individual or a very small group could lead to disaster.

In June, the PMA announced that they would not recognize AEA nor its demands for a four-week limit on unpaid rehearsals; holiday and Sunday pay; eight shows a week rather than the current nine; and a minimum salary of $30 per week for chorus girls (with an additional $5 per week while touring). The July 1 deadline passed with no agreement, and five weeks later, AEA members adopted a contract stating that no member would work for the PMA.

That evening, the casts of twelve shows refused to perform. Having discovered that Florenz Ziegfeld had joined the PMA, former chorus girl Lillian Russell donated $100,000 for the formation of the Chorus Equity, which shut down *The Ziegfeld Follies*. By August 23 all of Chicago's theatres were closed, with twenty-one in New York also dark.

That same week, the Actors Fidelity League (AFL)—an "anti-union union"—was formed, with George M. Cohan contributing $100,000 to finance the organization. Objecting to the tactics of the AEA in the strike, the AFL "pledged not to strike, to secure an equitable contract for the professional, and to work in close harmony with the manager." AEA looked upon the AFL as a mere extension of the PMA, and characterized the AFL as "a managerial-controlled society, formed for the purpose of attempting to injure the morale of the AEA members," adding that "the League's membership is not strictly 'professional.'"

AEA had been seeking Jeanne's address since May 1915, but she remained loyal to Klaw & Erlanger, who had employed her for most of her career thus far. While in retrospect it may seem that she was on the wrong side of history, she was protecting her own interests in not sabotaging her career. On August 22 she joined the AFL, as did fellow actors Jane Cowl, Margaret Lawrence, David Warfield, Fay Bainter, Holbrook Blinn, and Edgar Selwyn, during a meeting at the Biltmore Hotel.

AEA flexed its muscle by closing down the Rodgers and Hart show, *A Lonely Romeo*. By August 29, The Belasco Theatre in Washington D.C. was shuttered, and the Boston chapter of AEA had voted to strike. The PMA had capitulated to all of AEA's demands by September 1.

At 3 a.m. on September 6, after thirty days, thirty-seven closed productions, sixteen prevented openings, and a loss of $3 million, the strike was settled, with the managers signing a five-year contract recognizing AEA as part of the American Federation of Labor, and promising improved conditions. The former dominance of the Theatrical Syndicate was now a thing of the past.

Amid the furor, it was quietly announced on July 25 that Jeanne had left Belasco's management to star in the fall production of *A Young Man's Fancy*. In a 1927 interview with *Collier's*, Jeanne explained her decision: "When I went under Belasco's management—and to him I owe a great deal—friends, and those who pass as such in the profession, were surprised at my steady hunt for new plays. 'Why the restlessness?' they chided me. 'You're featured by Belasco. That's enough for any actress.' 'I'm just beginning,' I told them. 'And this is not enough.'"

A colorized photograph of Jeanne wearing her cap and lace-collared costume from *Daddies* replaced the usual Norman Rockwell illustration on the cover of the *Saturday Evening Post*'s August 16 issue. As photographer James Abbe wrote in a 1960 autobiographical essay for the *Oakland Tribune*, it was a turning point in his fledgling career. "Down in Philadelphia the *Saturday Evening Post* and *Ladies Home Journal* got wind of my success," Abbe recalled, "and perhaps remembering the brief contact I had with them . . . asked me to submit some of my photographs to them. I did. One of those I submitted was of actress Jeanne Eagels, and became a *Post* cover. For that picture I received seventy-five dollars. It was the first time the *Post* had used a photograph on its cover."

A comedy in three acts, *A Young Man's Fancy* told the tale of a wealthy poet, prone to midnight walks about town, who falls in love with a wax dummy displayed in a department-store window. Eagels played both the mannequin and Mary Darling, the flesh-and-blood inspiration for the figure. Her role had first been played during the previous season by Lynn Fontanne, starring opposite husband Alfred Lunt at the National Theatre in Washington D.C. The show's twelve scenes included several intricate fantasy scenarios, from bedroom trysts to garden parties, which showcased the latest fashions. To promote the show, Jeanne appeared in *Town & Country*'s October 1 issue wearing six ensembles available at Bergdorf & Goodman's, designed by leading names including Poiret, Madeline & Madeline, Worth, and Roland. She kept the outfits in lieu of payment, determined to be as stylish in public as she was onstage. Clifton Webb, who had the reputation as the best-dressed entertainer on Broadway, recalled in *Sitting Pretty*, "Jeanne dressed very beautifully, very chic. We had a standing joke: 'Cliffy, let's walk down the Avenue properly dressed.'" The elegant pair were often mistaken for brother and sister, and Jeanne laughed heartily when one critic said she looked like a "glorified Clifton Webb in crinoline."

Webb also remembered attending Thursday matinees of *Redemption*, based on a novel by Leo Tolstoy and starring John Barrymore, at the Plymouth Theatre with Jeanne. They even reserved the same front-row seats each time.

On October 12, Jeanne appeared in *The All-Star Testimonial Performance*, mounted by the Actors Fidelity League at the Century Theatre. The first part of the show included scenes featuring Billie Burke, Fay Bainter, Ina Claire, and Ruth Chatterton. The latter half was an original piece written by League President, George M. Cohan, who also had a guest role. Jeanne performed in a medley of Vaudeville songs between the first and third acts, joined by George White, Irving Berlin, Nora Bayes, and Ann Pennington.

A Young Man's Fancy opened at the Liberty Theatre on October 15. Perhaps someone had whistled in the dressing room, or fallen prey to some other theatrical curse, because on that night, everything that could go wrong, did. Delays were incurred as stagehands struggled with the cumbersome sets. Ropes were left dangling in full view from the flies. Stage braces were visible. Lights flickered on and off throughout the performance.[11]

Unsurprisingly, the first-night reviews for *Fancy* were decidedly mixed.

"Ten long waits, all of them tedious and most of them needless, with the mutilated fragments of a rather pretty little comedy sandwiched between. The comely Jeanne Eagels, who is coming on apace as an actress, moved blameless and cool-headed through a most distressing occasion." – Alexander Woollcott

"Pretty little comedy well worth seeing. Excellent company headed by Jeanne Eagels." – *Brooklyn Standard Union*

"Delightful acting is done by Jeanne Eagels as Mary. Miss Eagels keeps the slightly different characters of sculptor's assistant and mannikin [sic] deftly separate." – *New York Call*

"Empty bit of romance. Miss Eagels manages to differentiate nicely between the girl who, as the wax figure comes to life in the poet's daydreams and the more practical little miss who has come to New York to get away from dull conventional relatives. Her Virginia dialect appears, however, to have had its birth in a desire to imitate the talk of English actresses. She says 'heah' for 'here' and 'figger' for 'figure' and interlards her talk with innumerable other affections. But her lazy voice suits well the

---

11 This first night was only slightly less nerve-wracking than Jeanne's earlier performance as a living work of art in the Dubinskys' presentation of *Pygmalion* which was interrupted by gunfire, as described in Chapter 1.

department store dummy of which the poet becomes enamored in his fancy." – *Brooklyn Daily Eagle*

"In the shop window she was a blond study in pretty attenuation that posed gracefully. In life . . . little more animated and really little more audible, since she talked through her teeth after the prevailing fashion among leading ladies, choked off all nasal resonance in her voice, and was as artificial as only a mannikin [sic] in her off time could be." – *New York Sun*

After only thirteen performances, *A Young Man's Fancy* closed and left Jeanne unemployed as the holiday season loomed. Forgoing the safety and comfort of Belasco's management seemed to have backfired, and it was a sour note to end the first decade of her career in Manhattan. Ten years of hard work had yielded fourteen stage shows and nearly a dozen film roles, but she was still far from where she wanted to be. Little did she know that the New Year would bring a new play, a new confidante, and a broken heart.

David Belasco in his office (circa 1915.)

Posing in her sailor's cap in a promotional photo for *Daddies* (1918).

Top & Bottom - With co-star Bruce McRae as "Robert Audrey" and other cast members in *Daddies*.

Jeanne as "Ruth Atkins" with her fellow orphans in a scene from *Daddies*.

Publicity still featuring a relaxed and casually dressed Jeanne (1918.)

Wearing the latest fashions in *Town and Country Magazine* (January 1919), illustrating what Eagels would wear in the South if *Daddies* would stop playing for long enough to give her a vacation. She hoped to acquire these Abercrombie and Fitch sporting togs for the Spring and Summer. The Oval shows Jeanne in a white cricket cloth sports skirt and sleeveless elastic cloth slip-on, embroidered in brilliant white. The walking suit shown at the left is of natural Rajah. A hand-knitted coat of black vicuna with a white collar and tuxedo is stunning with a black and white plaid skirt (Right).

Wearing the latest fashions in *Town and Country Magazine* (October 1919), to publicize *A Young Man's Fancy*. Left: From ROLAND - Blue and silver brocade. Another ROLAND - Black velvet with chenille sleeve caps, chenille border on overdress, Henna velvet brocade girdle. Right: From POIRET – Silver net foundation; silver tissue overdress with gray fox and silver lace trimming. Hats from Betty and Anne. Left: Poiret model. Blue velvet embroidered in cerise, silver and gold. Seam piping of cerise. Center: Worth. Black velvet embroidered in fluted ribbon. Black lace side drapery. Right: Madelaine & Madelaine. Chiffon velvet with white bead embroidery and low girdle.

Chapter 6
A Wonderful Thing:
November 1919–September 1922

In late 1919, Jeanne began a tumultuous romance with Thomas L. Chadbourne, president and founder of a well-established New York law firm. Nineteen years her senior, Chadbourne was well-known in both political and financial circles and a member of several of New York's most exclusive clubs including the University, Union League, Metropolitan, and the New York Yacht. A prominent Democrat, he had personally corresponded with President Wilson and sat on the War Trade Board. In later years he would advocate collective bargaining rights and profit sharing for workers.

Chadbourne began seeing Jeanne a few months after his second wife, Grace, died from cancer in May 1919. Some had expected him to marry Grace's cousin, actress Maxine Elliott, but it was the younger and prettier Jeanne who caught his eye. She was regularly seen climbing out of Chadbourne's chauffeured limousine—either alone or with its owner—in front of the Playhouse Theatre, where she was rehearsing *The Wonderful Thing*.

The four-act drama, produced by George Broadhurst and based on a Forrest Halsey story, concerns Jacqueline Laurentie (Jeanne Eagels), a wealthy French-Canadian rancher's daughter who falls in love with Donald Mannerby (Gordon Ash), eldest son of an upper-class English family. Mannerby marries Jacqueline to save his family from financial ruin, and rescue his younger sibling from prison. The bride is heartbroken by his deception, but remains faithful, and eventually, Donald realizes his true feelings for Jacqueline.

Written and directed by Mrs. Lillian Trimble Bradley, *The Wonderful Thing* was first staged on January 19, 1920, at the Wieting Opera House in Syracuse. *Variety* raved: "The play threw out tentacles of tantalizing interest, drew in its audience to a state of breathless fascination and then sent it home absorbed in the story, in love with Jeanne Eagels and thoroughly satisfied with an evening that has really become a rarity in local playhouses of late, because interesting plays are so scarce in the sticks."

With many more shows to choose from, critics were less effusive when *Wonderful Thing* opened in New York on February 17. Most considered it little more than a French version of *Peg o' My Heart*, a vehicle for Laurette Taylor several seasons prior. Still, nearly all agreed that the play's bright spot was its lead actress.

"Jeanne Eagels carries the burden of the play upon her shoulders . . . Four acts, and four times does this little blonde actress carry the play to its curtain." – *New York Call*

". . . Nobody in the cast is able to do very much with the play save Jeanne Eagels . . . In her moments of comedy she has ease and grace and lightness, and when the time comes for the display of emotion she meets the test quietly and surely without any emotional monkeyshines." – *Brooklyn Daily Eagle*

A Wonderful Thing: November 1919-September 1922

"Miss Eagels . . . makes even the experienced playgoer forget the weakness of story and characterization so adroitly does she establish interest in herself." – Alexander Woollcott, *Dramatic Mirror*

"In the third act, when a tearful scene was put into her hands . . . she did splendidly. It was a sincere, a skillful and moving piece of work, which was worth twenty times the play itself . . . it may be said that the natural moments were those contributed by Miss Eagels." – *New York Tribune*

"The life of Mrs. Bradley's somewhat shopworn fable. She gave it indeed all the vitality it possessed . . . Miss Eagels is not only most charming, but unusual to contemplate, and her success was never of the ordinary kind." – *New York Herald*

"Animated, merry, generous, expressing the most attractive qualities in a delightfully halting and mal-accented English, she was the life of the whole romantic melodrama. Miss Eagels was able to maintain the sparkle of her performance till the end." – *Evening Post*

"If *The Wonderful Thing* catches on it will be due solely to the altogether delightful, utterly charming work of Jeanne Eagels. . ." – *Billboard*

***

Box office receipts for the first three weeks totaled a paltry $6,000. Press representative Louise Cline began a publicity blitz, feeding news of *The Wonderful Thing* and its leading lady to the press on a daily basis. Cline focused her efforts on female patrons, who would bring their husbands to the theatre. Producer George Broadhurst also took the critics' words to heart, immediately putting Jeanne's name in electric lights on the marquee. Within two weeks, receipts had risen by over 25 percent.

Variety noted that Jeanne's costumes were "delightfully sweet . . . typically French in style but all becoming." Photographs from the production show off her slender figure in a dark demure dress with lace collar, the very image of an ingénue. Her facial expressions range from coy to animated, revealing a seemingly infinite capacity for variation.

Even her hairstyle merited its own publicity campaign, as one *Brooklyn Eagle* reporter learned during an interview published on March 21. "Please don't think this smoke is from a cigarette," Eagels remarked, as the journalist entered her hazy-aired dressing room. "I have been sitting for a photograph. You see, my new coiffure is getting popular and so many people have asked for pictures of it and wanted me to tell how I do my hair to make it resemble a turban that I felt I could save trouble by having my picture taken. The 'Parisienne' women are doing their hair this way now." Articles with detailed instructions on how to achieve the "turban" look—accompanied by large photos of Jeanne—would be published across America. The Garamont Film Company even created a short film of Jeanne styling her hair step-by-step, to be shown at selected theaters in larger cities.

The ingénue denied being "made up" to look like Gaby Deslys, the actress she had met on her first trip to Paris back in 1914. "No, I really do not make up for the part at all," Jeanne insisted. "You see that I have used very little coloring on my face—no grease paint at all. I am myself, in looks at least. But I do look like Gaby Deslys, at any rate people say I do. Once my little brother went to a matinee at a theatre where Gaby was playing and he thought she was I during the whole play. He told my mother that he would have recognized me anywhere, that I looked exactly on the stage as I did off stage, all except my feet. He couldn't quite get it into his head that I would wear such unbecoming boots."

"The success of an actress is measured by intelligence and sincerity," Jeanne believed. "And the degree of success depends on the development of the former and real desire to succeed artificially in the latter. Like any other profession, the stage requires long years of training, with a real desire to reach the top and, usually, if a person has this enthusiasm, coupled with some of the luck that enters into the lives of human beings, it is my belief that any person can become a successful actor or actress, just as writers, provided of course, that they have personality, that most necessary but elusive attribute.

A Wonderful Thing: November 1919–September 1922

"The trouble with most young people of the stage is that they lack stability; they want too much at the beginning. That is where most of them fail," she added. "The public makes the featured and starred players... First, it is necessary that the player work hard, indefatigably and arduously for the opportunity and then work even harder to please the fickle public.

"In fact, it is only by a continual striving to please in the part you are playing, no matter whether you have played it one night or one hundred nights that one succeeds. Try to be always at your best, and the rest is easy."

***

Jeanne admitted devoting many hours of study to perfecting Jacqueline's French accent. "Madame Savage of the Metropolitan Opera House coaches me continuously," she told the *Eagle*. "She comes to every performance to criticize slips I may make. She even makes it a rule that I use my accent at all times, even in my offstage conversation." At the recommendation of her vocal coach, Clara Novello Davies, Jeanne began studying French with Madame Marie Savage, a performer (of mostly walk-on roles) at the Metropolitan Opera for twenty-seven seasons.

As 'Madame' entered the dressing room, Jeanne obediently continued the interview with a French accent. "A Frenchman saw me the other night," she laughed, "and told me to go home to France, that only the French could appreciate the Parisienne accent. He told me said that I spoke English very well for a French girl..."

Marie Savage spoke to *Every Week* magazine in 1935 of her first encounter with Jeanne, on December 26, 1919: "I remember the first day I saw her. We were not wealthy then. We had a tiny, make-believe Christmas tree in the corner. It was a pathetic tree, really. But Jeanne came in and made out it was the most beautiful thing she had ever seen. It was a wonderful piece of acting."

According to Eddie Doherty, Madame Savage's two daughters were eager to show off their new doll's house to Jeanne, who happily played along. She invited them to visit her apartment the next day and opened up her ample closet, allowing the girls to take as many hats as they wanted. Presenting them with a heap of unwanted gowns, she said, "Mama can make them over for you." The children then sat down for a feast of cake, ice cream and boxes of candy, until Jeanne finally revealed a hoard of toys which Santa Claus had left with her by mistake.

"'Mama Froggy' was her pet name for me," Madame recalled. "She would cry like a baby when I scolded her. She would fly into rages and then come back begging forgiveness. Temperamental? Oh. She would spend money so fast, and I would spank her for it."

During one of their quarrels Jeanne stormed out of Madame's apartment, vowing never to return. Half an hour later, Madame heard a knock on her door. Expecting a delivery from the iceman, she was amazed to find a giant cake in the arms of her wayward pupil, whose sheepish grin was just visible as she peered over her delicious peace offering.

Jeanne frequently spent the night (and sometimes several days) at her teacher's apartment. Madame Savage told Eddie Doherty that Jeanne scrubbed the floors, did the shopping, cooking, or washed dishes, telling her teacher, "If I had been your daughter, I would be happy and content today—but I would not be Jeanne Eagels." The pair often strolled down Broadway, through Central Park or onwards to Fifth Avenue, trying on clothes neither could afford. More often than not, curiosity would lure them into an auction house. Madame Savage owned a large, ugly heavy marble-topped table, a gift from her former student. In her eagerness to outdo the other buyers, Jeanne had placed the winning bid. She paid more for transport to Savage's Sixty-Fifth Street home than for the table itself.

On another occasion, Jeanne was repaid an outstanding debt of $100, and set out to "scatter sunshine in the lives of my creditors." Her noble plan was soon forgotten, however, when a sandalwood box caught her eye as she passed by an auctioneer's window. The canny salesman offered to take bids on the spot, but his other customers stayed silent. He then gave a starting price of twenty dollars, and in her haste to beat the non-existent competition, a flustered Jeanne handed him thirty. Only later did she realize that the box was worth very little, and that the auctioneer had duped her.

Jeanne's last movie role for seven years was in *The Madonna of the Slums*, tenth of twelve short films in the Stage Women's War Relief Series. The organization brought stars of the stage to motion pictures, and Jeanne appeared alongside Amelita Galli-Curci, a famous opera singer. The now-lost film was released by Carl Laemmle on March 14, and six days later, the *Dramatic Mirror* noted that "a little dramatic story was carried by the cast to a pleasing finale."

On March 22, the *New York Sun* reported that jewelry worth $6,000 had been stolen from the home of English opera singer Mary Ellis, at West Fifty-Seventh Street. Jeanne, Ellis' neighbor, had also been the victim of a burglary just two months earlier. Although Jeanne refused to reveal the value of her loss, it was estimated to be just over $10,000.

On May 16, Jeanne admitted her health worries in a *New York Tribune* interview. 'I have always been frail and whenever I devote too much attention to ambition, health checks me up and sends signals of warning telling me unless I desist with my ambition, it, health, will cease to be my handmaiden," she confessed. "With health one may obtain everything, without it—nothing. Happiness I get in the theatre and in my home. Health I find outdoors in the glorious sunshine and fresh air. Both are wonderful! Perhaps some time I shall find love . . . but just now the 'wonderful thing' is health!"

She spoke too soon. Just over two weeks later, she and another cast member became so ill that Broadhurst decided to close the show. Touring was delayed until August 29, when *The Wonderful Thing* would re-open at the Princess Theatre in Chicago. On August 21, *Billboard* reported that Jeanne was recuperating at home after undergoing surgery on her appendix a week before, and on August 23, it was announced that the tour had been postponed. When the show finally reached Chicago on September 5, the *Daily Tribune* judged it "a well-intentioned affair, and has its moments . . .

but in somewhat disjointed fashion." However, Jeanne's performance was well-received: "Miss Eagels is a piquant person of airy blondeness and many pretty ways, and, as you may have occasion to observe, she can act."

At least one critic was tiring of Jeanne's "pretty ways", however. While admiring Emily Stevens' vampish performance in *Footloose* that month, Dorothy Parker noted, "There are many who respond too sympathetically to her nervous quickness of speech and gesture, and by the time the first act finished, they are on the verge of complete collapse. Hence, they shun the staccato Miss Stevens, to sit, soothed, before Phoebe Foster or Jeanne Eagels . . . Yet, after long seasons of the humid sweetness and horrific cuteness so sedulously practiced by many of so our most expensive leading ladies, Emily Stevens and her sharp intelligence seem as specially sent from a relenting Heaven."

Complicating Jeanne's recovery was the breakdown of her relationship with Thomas Chadbourne. Many of their friends had thought they would eventually marry, as the lawyer had lavished the actress with gifts of jewelry, and publicly praised her beauty and talent. While Jeanne may have dreamed of summers spent at their Greenwich estate or of being the hostess at parties on Park Avenue, with perhaps an occasional stage appearance, it would seem she was actually little more than a passing fancy for her upper-crust beau. Chadbourne knew that his social standing would suffer greatly if he married an actress. Having adopted the son of his second wife, he still hoped to father his own. Jeanne was certainly fond of children, but unlikely to give up her career to raise a family.

Emotionally and physically drained, Jeanne planned a five-month vacation in England and France, far away from Chadbourne and the stage. A passport application completed on September 30 is filled with the same fabrications about her past that she had previously spun to the press. Perhaps she simply wanted to appear consistent, but by perpetuating these myths in an official document, she risked being charged with perjury. She claimed to have been born in Boston in 1894, and that her father, a native Spaniard, had died in 1906. She even wrote that she had lived in England

and France from June 1913 until July 1914. Perhaps the most truthful part of her application was a request to leave upon "the first steamer available on October 5." With her application approved on October 4, Jeanne made her departure date, but spent a mere three weeks abroad, returning to New York via Southampton on November 13. She had been lured back by a telegram—not a love letter from Chadbourne—but an offer of employment.

***

In the Night Watch was already a success in London under the Shubert mantle. The curtain rises on an August 1914 birthday dance, given on the deck of the *Alma* by the vessel's Captain De Corlaix (Robert Warwick) for his wife Eugenie (Jeanne Eagels). Receiving a message that war has erupted, the Captain is obliged to cancel the celebration and ferry the guests ashore, without explaining why. A furious Eugenie seeks refuge with her lover, Lieutenant Brambourg (Cyril Scott). The *Alma* heads out to sea with Eugenie still on board and is sunk by a German torpedo. Both the Captain and his wife are saved, though he now faces a court-martial. Eugenie's testimony that "he gave the right signals" exonerates the Captain, who forgives her indiscretion with the Lieutenant who was killed trying to save his life.

Rehearsals began during the last week of December in the most unconventional of venues. Broadway was enjoying a post-war resurgence, and space was non-existent. The *New York Tribune* reported that every city theatre was currently occupied, with some adding an extra weekend matinee. Fortunately, locations were found where the separate scenes could be rehearsed, to be sewn together later onstage at the Century Theatre.

Reverend C. N. Moller granted use of the chapel at St. Chrysostom's on Seventh Avenue. "And so it comes about that every day at the chapel the wistful Jeanne Eagels imparts with the otherwise Margaret Dale," the *Tribune* observed. "Cyril Scott with Max Figman, while awaiting their cues, discuss Australia; that handsome Robert Warwick pleads a knowledge of codes and their workings, gained during his service with the AEF [American Expeditionary Forces], to warrant a change in some of their 'business.'"

The cast were welcomed by parishioners. One night, a group of ladies appeared with steaming hot coffee and sandwiches for the tired and hungry actors. The following evening, the actors repaid the kindness with a party for their benefactors. "They were the homiest rehearsals we ever had," Jeanne told the press. "I wish we could always rehearse in a church."

Renovations at the Century Theatre were proceeding smoothly, according to the *Tribune*. Jeanne had convinced the Shuberts to restore what was currently a dressing room to its original purpose as a Green Room similar to a salon, where the cast could relax and entertain friends, reporters, and other guests. She hoped to revive the room's former reputation as a "meeting place for many notable foreign visitors and distinguished guests from all over America visiting New York, the gatherings noted for the wit of their conversation."

On January 4, 1921, the *New York Times* mentioned the upcoming "spectacular production of Michael Morton's melodrama," scheduled to make its American debut on the 24th. Four days later, the *New York Times* announced the engagement of banker Thomas Chadbourne to Miss Marjorie A. Curtis. The wedding, with only relatives invited, would be held at the Park Avenue apartment of the bride's mother. Curtis was the daughter of a well-known throat specialist (who had died the previous May, the same month as Chadbourne's wife Grace), and "a member of the Junior League ... active in war work here and abroad."

The *Baltimore Sun*'s society columnist declared the engagement a total surprise, as "Miss Curtis had long ago ... joined hands with a set that includes such sworn-to-celibacy spinsters..." A list, naming several other unmarried ladies from prominent families, then followed. At thirty-three, Curtis was two years older than Jeanne, and the *Baltimore Sun* politely described her as "exceedingly handsome." It was also mentioned that

Grace's cousin, actress Maxine Elliott, had long been tipped as the next Mrs. Chadbourne, but it was thought Jeanne had eclipsed her. However, Elliott was fifty-two at the time of Chadbourne's nuptials; too old to bear the child he craved.

In *Rain Girl*, it was suggested that Jeanne blamed Elliott for the break-up and "hated her, undeservedly so, for the rest of her life." Doherty wrote that during her relationship with Chadbourne, Jeanne had attended a party given for Maxine. Assuming the other guests would expect her to show up dripping in Chadbourne's jewelry, she arrived wearing a simple white dress "without even a bracelet or ring." Upon returning home to her flat, Jeanne discovered that the property had been broken into, and "every trinket Chadbourne had given her—and they were many and costly—had been taken. Nothing else had been touched." Jeanne informed Chadbourne of the robbery, and while he apologized for not having the items insured, he never replaced them.

While Elliott posed no romantic threat to Jeanne's potential proposal, she was privy to theatrical gossip, and may even have prompted her late cousin's husband to have second thoughts about marrying a flighty young actress. (She may even have tipped Chadbourne off to Jeanne's being out on the night of the robbery.)

In the Night Watch was an expensive production to mount, from cast salaries to costumes. For her grand entrance, Jeanne wore a white silk gown embroidered in silver and crystal beads with a crimson chiffon sash tied tightly about the waist, and hanging below the hem of her skirt. Over the gown a wrap of crimson velvet was worn, minus the usual fur collar.

However, *Night Watch*'s budget was stretched by the cost of special effects, which also caused many problems. During the sinking of the *Alma*, large pieces of machinery were placed backstage to move the set around, while others were kept in the wings to blow smoke onto the stage. Technical challenges led to safety concerns, and the opening date was deferred until January 29. Even then, the premiere was far from glitch-free.

"This long-heralded French melodrama was finally shown to the American public, but even after its several postponements the production was far from ready ... In their haste to pitchfork the thing on the stage, the manager omitted some of the best scenes and committed other blunders that weighed heavily against success ... A large number of stars and prominent actors were associated in the cast. The pity of it is that hardly one of them, with the possible exception of Miss Eagels, is given a chance to do anything worthy their merits." – Arthur Hornblow, *Theatre Magazine*

"Uneven ... due to first night nervousness" – *Dramatic Mirror*

"Moments of great spectacular beauty and effectiveness, but the play did not come up to the spectacle ... *In the Night Watch* must either learn to really to sink its ship and give us a spectacle, or ... give us a story." – *New York Tribune*

"Miss Eagels has two big scenes—one in the second act with Mr. [Edmund] Lowe and the other in the last act. Both were characterized by superior quality of emotionalism, not of the ranting, weepy type, but marked with a sincerity that gets directly over the footlights." – *Variety*

"Miss Eagels went abroad and announced her retirement, but was persuaded to reconsider her intention—happily for playgoers, especially for those who go to the Century, whose vast spaces call for far-reaching voices on the stage. Miss Eagels possesses tones of such resonant and musical timbre that it is a delight to listen to her." – *Munsey's Magazine*

***

Madame Savage had comforted Jeanne during her time of heartbreak, but no one could replace a mother's love. The February 19 issue of *Billboard* announced that Jeanne's mother was visiting the actress in Manhattan. When she arrived, Julia found her daughter in conflict with the landlords of the Fifty-Seventh Street residence where she had lived since October 1919. On May 29 the *San Francisco Tribune* recounted the entire situation:

the building's new owners felt that its location near Fifth Avenue made it a desirable retail spot. They planned to open a shoe store on the first floor and lease out the remaining three apartments.

On February 11 the *New York Tribune's* classified section had included an offer to lease out the second and third floors beneath Jeanne's fourth-floor apartment. Measuring a rather spacious twenty-five by ninety foot, each unit would be "thoroughly remodeled and finely finished," according to the tenant's specifications.

All the tenants had now left, except Jeanne. She had devoted considerable time and money to her home, decorating it with turquoise wallpaper, mauve tapestries, and curtains; furniture upholstered in lavender and robin's-egg blue satin, complemented by a chaise longue in heliotrope; and antique porcelain from the Kand-He Dynasty.

Unsurprisingly, she refused to move for less than $25,000. In an attempt to force her out, the front entrance was blocked with construction materials and the elevator was disabled. Jeanne took the issue to the New York Supreme Court, where Justice Erlanger handed down an order of protection, forcing the owners to cease any operations which threatened the "sanctity, peace and comfort of Miss Eagels' dwelling." This included a stipulation not to touch any part of Jeanne's apartment, and "provide and keep in condition the stairway and self-operating elevator."

On Thursday, March 23, after Julia's departure, the tensions of Jeanne's daily life finally caught up with her. She was too weak to perform in that evening's show and would remain absent until March 26. She was incapacitated again for several days during the week of April 1, with a severe case of *la grippe* (influenza). Illness didn't slow her down for long, however. In addition to *Night Watch*, she also participated in a series of charitable events that would have drained the energies of a healthier actress.

On April 16, a hundred children from the Brooklyn Orphans Home enjoyed the afternoon matinee of *In the Night Watch* before heading to the Biltmore Hotel for a dinner hosted by Jeanne. They were given paper hats, balloons, and toys (boats for the boys, and stuffed animals for the girls), which kept them entertained while the adults made speeches. Jeanne thanked the children for coming, adding that she "hoped to visit them in the near future." From the Biltmore, she rushed to a costume ball for the Chinese politician, Mr. Alfred S. See, at The Ritz-Carlton Hotel. Other celebrities performing at the pre-dance dinner included Marie Dressler, Clifton Webb, and Marilyn Miller.

The next night, Jeanne attended the Actors Fund Annual Benefit at Brooklyn's Montauk Theatre. Beginning at eight o'clock, over fifty entertainers presented six special sketches and a dozen special features. Jeanne and her *Night Watch* co-stars Robert Warwick, Edmund Lowe, and Macklyn Arbuckle starred in *The Man*.

***

After 111 performances, *In the Night Watch* closed, although it would be filmed in 1928. Having weathered heartbreak, illness and an arduous role, Jeanne made plans for a relaxing European vacation. She had received $7,000 from her landlords after agreeing to leave her apartment, and a portion was spent on the trip. On May 12, accompanied by Clifton Webb and his mother, Mabelle, Jeanne set sail aboard *La France*. She hoped to spend time in England, France, and Spain, while Clifton pursued his career in Europe.

Since their first meeting in 1914, Mabelle and Clifton had taken Jeanne under their wing. Over the next seven years, the Webbs had become like a second family to her. She was always welcome at their West Fifty-Eighth Street apartment, mingling with fellow actors, artists, writers, opera singers, and musicians. She was also often spotted with Clifton at the opera, dining in restaurants, or ice-skating in Central Park. If one of the friends had a night off, they were usually found backstage at the other's current show. "We never went anywhere without one another,"

Webb recalled. "People would say 'God damn it—if you aren't married, you should be.'"

Actor Henry Hull told *Picture Play* magazine that Jeanne and Webb had once dropped by his dressing room on the way to an ice-skating party given in his honor by actress Elsie Janis. The trio thought it would be amusing to arrive in evening clothes from the waist up, with corduroy knickers and heavy boots from the belt loops down. Proudly walking down the avenue in their finery, they arrived at the rink to find it closed and locked; after spending so much time getting dressed, they had missed the party. Returning to the theatre, they found it locked, as well, with their street clothes left inside. Hull chauffeured Clifton and Jeanne to their homes just as the milkmen made their deliveries.

Wedding rumors were fueled on May 13, when the *Evening Telegram* published a photograph of Jeanne leaving for Europe with a large orchid pinned to her coat and referring to Clifton as her "fiancé." Until then, her love life had mostly been a private affair, but a syndicated article released after Jeanne's departure, under the headline "How the Young Stage Dancer Won the Leading Lady", changed all that. Its skeptical author asked how a "stage dancer cut through the ring of millionaires, rich professional men, and Apollos of the stage who surrounded Miss Eagels, one of the loveliest and most youthful and successful of leading ladies and won her away from one and all of them." In what may have been a jab at Webb's sexuality, the writer answered his own question with this cryptic statement: "His versatility, say friends, is what enabled the dancer to win the leading lady . . . child actor, fashionable society mingler, painter, singer, comedian, and dancer—these form true versatility." It was even implied that their engagement was more for the groom's benefit than the bride's. "May it not quite possibly be that in marrying Clifton Webb she is also actuated by her earnest devotion to art," the reporter mused. "A devotion so unselfish that she is willing to sacrifice her own best interests in order to link the destiny of a fellow artist to her own success and thus help raise him to the fame she believes his talents deserve?"

Webb's only comment on the subject came nearly thirty years later, in his memoir, *Sitting Pretty*. "Jeanne and I had discussed marriage and were ready to take the step," he wrote.

"I talked it over with Mother. She gave me some advice. If you feel that way, wait a little while. You know what happens to most people when they marry in haste. We had a very romantic affair but marriage would have been fatal—we were very much alike. The moment she knew she had me, she would not have wanted me, and with me the same way. We were very sensible about it." Of course, Webb's homosexuality—an open secret within the entertainment world—meant that theirs would have been a chaste love. His biographer, David L. Smith, suggests that the purpose of Webb's trip was to visit an older male lover. While marriage to her best friend might have seemed like an ideal arrangement, it's possible that neither Jeanne nor Clifton would have been satisfied if it had become permanent.

Other romantic interests named in the article included Chadbourne and Jeanne's *Night Watch* co-stars Robert Warwick and Cyril Scott. The much older Scott seemed to have been included for shock value, and the story had a tragic ending. Two weeks after Jeanne's departure, Scott returned home from buying an evening paper to find his wife of twenty years, the comedic actress Louise Eissing, had committed suicide by hanging herself from the second-floor balcony railing. It was determined that Mrs. Scott had been suffering from depression; not caused by any rumored affair between Cyril and Jeanne, but because of the recent death of her mother, to whom she had been "very close," according to Scott.

The *Lima News* elaborated on Jeanne's turbulent voyage with actress Louise Groody and "millionaire stevedore" Jimmy Auditore, who had paid for the orphans' party at the Biltmore hosted by Jeanne in April, and was apparently smitten with the actress, though he was married with two children. In *The Rain Girl*, Doherty wrote of a romance, but Jeanne's old friend, Cecil Cunningham, didn't believe it. The tale was that Auditore had given Jeanne a diamond necklace which she'd worn on the return cruise the night before docking in New York. It was a "peace offering and a pledge of undying love." The stevedore overheard Eagels badmouthing him and in a fit of rage, grabbed the necklace from around her neck and flung it into the ocean.

Not mentioned in the press at that time was Arthur Fiedler, her Boston beau since early 1919. Perhaps her "engagement" to Clifton Webb was just a red herring, distracting the press from her long-standing romance with Fiedler. Arthur called her "Jeanine," while she nicknamed him "Ruffio." The relationship had survived long separations, as Jeanne's career meant she was usually worked in New York or on tour, while Arthur was mostly based in Boston and the New England area.

"Arthur had never thought of his attachment to Jeanne in terms of marriage, a subject he steadfastly refused to consider with any girl until he was almost forty-seven," his friend Mayo Walder told biographer Robin Moore. "It was not an emotionally overpowering affair, nor as with most of Arthur's passing flirtations, was it entirely casual. He managed to see a lot of Jeanne, mostly in New York." He and Mayo often visited Manhattan to perform with the Boston Symphony Orchestra, and both were invited to all of Jeanne's Broadway show openings.

Unaware of the gossip, Jeanne continued her vacation, and the critic Arthur Hornblow reported in *Theatre Magazine* that he had seen the actress at Le Perroquet, a newly-opened restaurant and cabaret spot above the Casino de Paris. "Jeanne Eagels maintained her reputation for wearing the unusual—a white satin frock strung with ribbons of white crystal," Hornblow noted. "The back was most interesting, with an almost backless bodice of white chiffon and a lattice of crystals."

However, once the rumors of impending nuptials reached her ears, Jeanne sent an urgent telegram to producer Sam Harris, assuring him that reports of her engagement were greatly exaggerated. On July 20 she departed from Southampton, England, aboard the *Adriatic* with Mabelle Webb. Clifton would remain in Europe for almost two years.

***

Upon landing in Manhattan, Jeanne checked into the Great Northern Hotel on 115 West Fifty-First Street. *Billboard* noted on August 6 that this had been her sixth trip abroad, and that she had visited her father's birthplace near the Spanish city of Barcelona. This, of course, was incorrect; her father was a native Kansan, but *Billboard* was merely quoting Jeanne's own words. More accurately, it was also reported that she was to star in a new Sam Harris production, *The New Day* by Leila Burton Wells. Rehearsals were to start that summer under Sam Forrest's direction, to open in New York in the fall.

Sam H. Harris had started his career as a cough drop salesman before finding success as a boxing manager. His first Broadway production was Theodore Kremer's *The Evil That Men Do,* co-produced with A. H. Woods in 1903. A year later, Harris went into partnership with George M. Cohan, producing eighteen Broadway musicals. Separating from Cohan after the 1919 Actors Equity strike, he partnered with Irving Berlin, and in 1921 they built the Music Box Theatre. Harris would eventually produce over 130 shows, including some of the biggest hits of the 1920s and 1930s. He was known for fairness to actors and writers amid the generally harsh treatment prevailing in the industry. At the time of Jeanne's signing, his stable of players included several leading actresses from her own past and future: Francine Larrimore, Mary Ryan, Emily Stevens, and Elsie Ferguson. It has also been suggested that Billie Burke was once on Harris' roster.

Other than a brief report on September 23 stating that William Anthony McGuire was writing *Sunrise* for Jeanne to perform next season, her name remained absent from the newspapers. On December 9, her mother, Julia, unexpectedly announced, "My daughter is not married. She is now in New York, working on a play with Arthur Hopkins which will open on Broadway just after the holidays. I don't know where the report originated. Jeanne was in Europe at the time."

A WONDERFUL THING: NOVEMBER 1919-SEPTEMBER 1922

On January 13, 1922, Jeanne attended a dinner and musical program presented by the opera singer and socialite, 'Madame' Alma Clayburgh, accompanied by pianist Arthur Rubinstein, at Clayburgh's home. Two days later, *The Baltimore Sun* confirmed the title of the upcoming play referred to by Julia two months prior: "Preparations are going on around the offices of Arthur Hopkins for something . . . may be the Hungarian play, *The Ruby Fan*, probably with Jeanne Eagels."

Mentioned in Doherty's *Liberty* serialization was Jeanne committing to, and then suddenly resigning from Harris' production of *My Lady's Lips*, the story of a newspaper reporter sent to investigate a gambling ring which ensnares his editor's madcap daughter, only to fall in love with the gang's female boss. Fellow Missourian William Powell and Martha Hedman were already cast, with Sam Forrest directing. "It's a wonderful part, and I raved about it," Jeanne explained to Harris, "but I find it isn't for me." Rehearsals began March 18 with Gilda Leary in Eagels' role, according to *Variety*. Jeanne's exit may have been wise as the show folded before reaching Broadway, but *My Lady's Lips* would get the Hollywood treatment in 1925, with Powell reprising his role opposite Clara Bow.

Jeanne volunteered for yet another benefit—in aid of the Society for the Prevention and Relief of Tuberculosis, held on February 20. 3,000 women and girls were assembled to manage the Biltmore Hotel for twenty-four hours raising funds for the charity. Jeanne took the lead role in *A Day with a Debutante aka The Adventures of Angela*, a playlet written by George S. Chappell for the Fashion Show portion of the event. The curtain rises on Jeanne (as Angela), following her from day to night, with costume changes for each scene: boudoir clothes into street attire for shopping and luncheon, another for dinner, and then the opera. New York debutantes were recruited to play her friends.

Less than a week later, it was announced that Arthur Hopkins "seemed to have deferred until next season his production of *The Ruby Fan*. A Hungarian romance which will involve Jeanne Eagels, and possibly Roland Young if he is free at the time." But Jeanne didn't let this bit of bad news deter her from helping others. After the news was reported on February 26, she and Laurette Taylor headed a cast of twenty-two in *Evening of Happiness*, a one-off performance for the Second Annual Actors Fund benefit at Brooklyn's Montauk Theatre. Then, from March 12-15, Jeanne joined screenwriter Anita Loos and film stars Mae Murray, William Desmond, and others for the grand opening of Marcus Loew's State Theatre in Boston, Massachusetts.

Social events and benefits kept Jeanne's name in the press, but she had been away from the theatre for a year and was growing restless. The only chance most New Yorkers would get to see her that season was in an advertisement for Best & Company, where she was pictured modeling their exclusive Whitehall Topcoat (available in Misses' sizes on the Second Floor of their Fifth Avenue store).

One night at the Metropolitan Opera with Clifton Webb (who had season tickets), Jeanne was bemoaning her lack of work to box-mates Zoë Akins and her life partner, actress Jobyna Howland. Akins promised her friend that she would author a play especially for the actress but she also had one already written, but promised to *Outcast* actress Elsie Ferguson entitled *The Varying Show*. Zoë gave Eagels a copy of the script "just in case" and it wasn't much later when the writer received an enthusiastic phone call.

"It's beautiful. It's glorious ... I've died and gone to heaven. If I don't get it, I'll be broken hearted."

By then Akins had received a cable from Ferguson accepting the role, and tried to reassure Jeanne: "Don't take it so hard. I'm writing a play for you called *Moonflower*, and I think you'll love it." But Akins went to Europe leaving the play unfinished, and Jeanne still unemployed. It took another two months for Jeanne to find a suitable role.

To keep her face and name in front of her fans, she was photographed wearing headsets while listening to "wireless jazz" at the New York Radio Show, where she had made an appearance. Held during the week of May 22 at the Seventy-first Regiment Armory on Park Avenue, the event exhibited various models of radios with some vendors having complete suites of matching furniture.

On May 26, Sam Harris announced that she would star in *A Gentleman's Mother*, a play by Martin Brown. Forrest's wife, actress Mary Ryan, had received the script and turned it down, as it was too close to a character she had already played. Sending it to her husband, she told him, "There is but one woman who could play this part, Jeanne Eagels."

Forgiving Jeanne for the *My Lady's Lips* debacle, Forrest cast her as Polly Pearl, the owner of a coastal tavern whom as a young woman had been trapped in a loveless marriage, and forced to give up her baby son. But their paths will cross again years later when he is one of two soldiers who arrive at the tavern. During a quarrel between them, one is killed, and the other injured. While nursing the survivor's wounds, Polly discovers a birthmark—that of the son she had lost many years ago. The story hinges on whether or not Polly should reveal her identity and take the blame for his actions.

Rehearsals began on June 12, and *A Gentleman's Mother* premiered a fortnight later at the Apollo Theatre in Atlantic City. Director Sam Forrest told Eddie Doherty that Jeanne had come to him one day "in tears," claiming that she too had given up a son many years ago. Forrest felt the actress was "merely romancing." Actor Ronald Colman was originally cast as her son but was replaced for unknown reasons before New Jersey. Years later, Colman would claim he went into movies because *A Gentleman's Mother* had soured him for the stage.

Billboard's critic implied that Jeanne had worked wonders with inferior material, echoing an all-too-familiar complaint. "Jeanne Eagels, with fine acting and supporting company, lifts *A Gentleman's Mother* from what might easily be mediocrity to a place as a rather excellent play." After Atlantic City, *Mother* moved to Stamford, Connecticut, inaugurating the Stamford Theatre's ninth season on July 9. A large contingency of Manhattan playgoers traveled up especially for the opening; however, the ill-fated production was shelved before New York. Reworked with another leading lady (Mary Nash) and a new name—*The Lady*—Brown's play began a two-month Broadway run in December 1923, and would later become film star Norma Talmadge's greatest success.

With no property forthcoming from Harris, on August 6 the *New York Tribune* confirmed that the PMA-affiliated Selwyn Brothers had cast Jeanne opposite Alan Dinehart in the firm's first production of the season, *The Exciters*. Rehearsals were set to begin the next day, with no opening date specified. Less than a week later, however, the *Boston Sunday Globe* reported that the show was in rehearsal with Tallulah Bankhead in the lead.

Bankhead was twelve years younger than Jeanne. A politician's daughter from Alabama, she moved to New York at fifteen after winning a film magazine contest. Perhaps better-known for her deep voice and flamboyant personality than her considerable talent, Tallulah had appeared in several stage productions and films since her 1918 debut in *The Squab Farm*.

"I was idle until the fall of 1922 when I impersonated 'Rufus Rand' in *The Exciters*, a comedy which belied its title," Bankhead recalled in *Tallulah: My Autobiography*. "It succumbed to popular disapproval after five weeks. I'll capsule the plot. Rufus was nineteen, semi-paralyzed because of a motor accident. In a fit of caprice she marries a burglar. Want to hear more? I didn't think so."

Neither did the audience. Premiering at the Times Square Theatre on September 22, *The Exciters* closed at the end of October after forty-three performances. Bankhead would soon attain great success on the London stage in several Broadway imports.

Jeanne's most recent public appearance had been in an advertisement for the Henning Boot Shop on Fifty-Seventh Street, published in the *New York Times* on September 24. "Youth, vivacity, imagination; restraint, elegance, grace; beauty, flattery, artistry—now you know why Jean [sic] Eagels wears Henning Shoes."

A WONDERFUL THING: NOVEMBER 1919-SEPTEMBER 1922

Jeanne was about to win the part that would finally give her the fame she had dreamed of since she was a little girl in Kansas City.

Top left - Eagels with Madame Marie "Mama Froggy" Savage (1920). Top Right: Mabelle and Clifton Webb (1923). Bottom left: Arthur Fiedler (1930). Bottom Right: Thomas Chadbourne (1924).

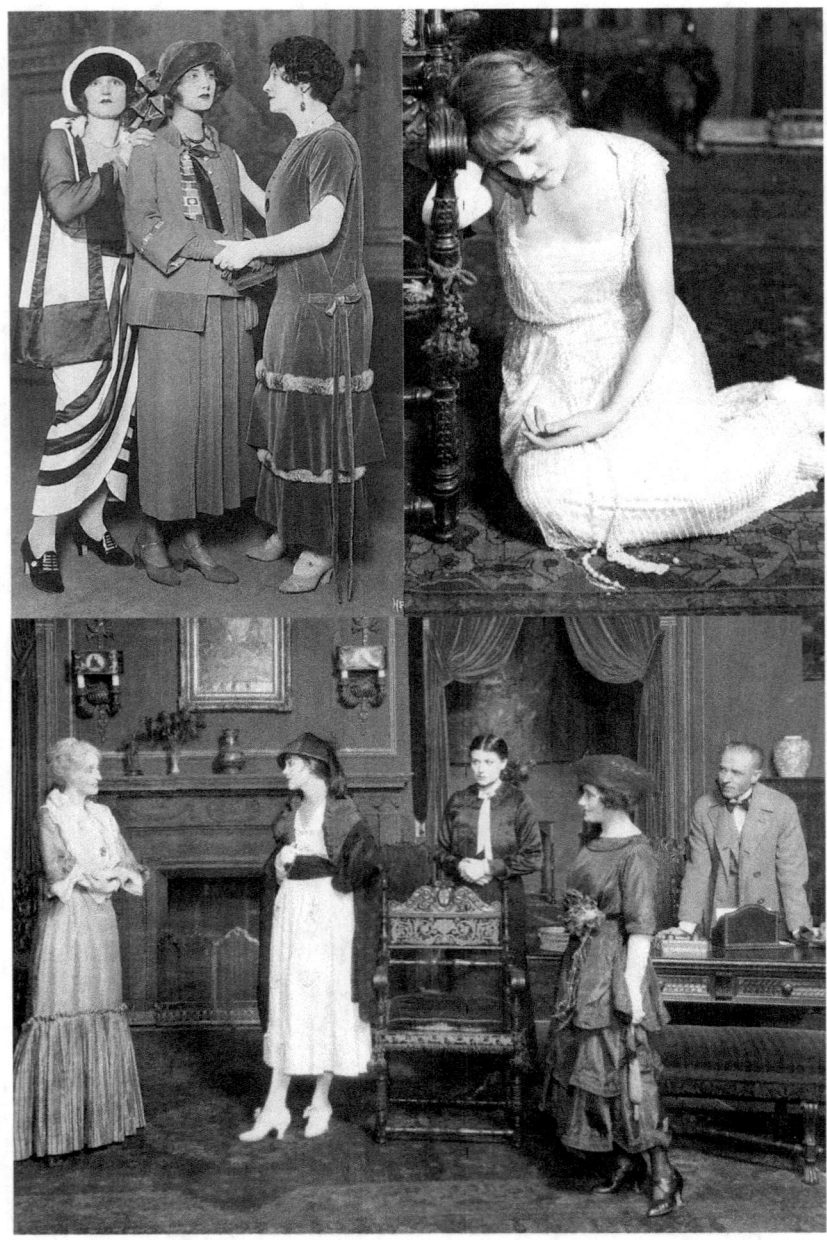

Top Left: Eagels at center. Top Right: Jeanne solo. Bottom (Second from left) As "Jacqueline Laurentie" in *The Wonderful Thing* (1920).

A WONDERFUL THING: NOVEMBER 1919-SEPTEMBER 1922

Top - Photos of Jeanne illustrated a fictional story in the January 1920 issue of *Hearst's Magazine.* Top right - With Holbrook Blinn in *Madonna of the Slums* (1920.) Bottom left - Scene from *In the Night Watch* (1921.)

As "Eugenie de Corlaix" *In the Night Watch* with Robert Warwick as "Captain de Corlaix" (1921.)

Top - Dramatic courtroom finale from *Night Watch*. Bottom - Elaborate promotional material did little to attract audiences or make the show profitable.

Eagels poses aboard *La France* on May 12, 1921.

A Wonderful Thing: November 1919-September 1922

Eagels listens to "wireless jazz" at the May 1922 New York Radio Show.

Chapter 7
Introducing Sadie Thompson: November 1922

For eighteen months, the decade later dubbed the Roaring Twenties limped along like Aesop's lion. The thorn in America's paw was a deep post-war depression, breeding runaway inflation and a 20 per cent unemployment rate. The nation's theatregoers were tired of war, hence the truncated run of *Night Watch* and the outright failure of *Gentleman's Mother*. Soldiers returned to the United States with souvenirs, stories, and even brides, but their eyes had now been opened to Europe's liberal attitudes. Their hard-won "pursuit of happiness" was halted by the passing of the Eighteenth Amendment, deeming the sale, production, and transportation of alcohol illegal. On a more progressive note, the Nineteenth Amendment, passed before 1920's election, granted women in all states the right to vote. The Republican candidate, Warren G. Harding, subsequently became the nation's twenty-ninth President. From national down to local level, lawmakers sought to penalize moral indecency, with mixed results. Vice-

President Calvin Coolidge repeatedly stated "that of the two fundamental motives which inspire motivation, righteousness and gain, the most important is righteousness."

Four months before America's economy rose from the ashes, a woman who would help to turn Coolidge's notion of righteousness on its head made her first appearance in the pages of a literary magazine. Sadie Thompson was a living person, fictionalized in W. Somerset Maugham's short story, "Miss Thompson," which was first published in the April 1921 issue of *The Smart Set*, a literary magazine featuring works by Edna St. Vincent Millay, Sinclair Lewis, Eugene O'Neill, Dashiell Hammett, James Joyce, and F. Scott Fitzgerald.

William Somerset Maugham was born at the British Embassy in Paris in 1874, losing both parents at the age of ten. His shyness and stutter prevented him from taking up the family profession of law, and he instead chose medicine. After working in some of the worst slums of London, Maugham wrote of his experiences and discovered his true talents. By 1914, he was the successful author of ten novels and ten plays. A year later, he wrote *Of Human Bondage*, often cited as his finest novel.

During World War One, Maugham became a volunteer ambulance driver in France. Now quite wealthy, he traveled frequently to Europe, America, the South Seas, the Far East, and India. Wherever he went, he collected stories to work into his fiction. According to Maugham scholar Samuel J. Rogal, "'Miss Thompson' evolved directly from notes that Maugham recorded while he and a number of passengers on their way from Hawaii to Tahiti lodged at a hotel in Pago Pago to await, during the hot and wet season, a quarantine inspection."

Maugham's biographer, Selina Hastings, confirms that the real Sadie Thompson, like her fictional counterpart, was a prostitute from Hawaii's Red Light District of Ilwilei, and she was on the run from the law. Maugham had first encountered her while sailing from Honolulu. "She had a cabin two removed from mine," he recalled, "and she kept that damnable gramophone going all day." Although married, Maugham was secretly homosexual, and his secretary/companion, Gerald Haxton, accompanied him during his stay in Pago Pago. There was nothing furtive about Sadie's sexual adventures, however. "Holed up together in that squalid boarding-house," Hastings writes, "Maugham and his fellow travelers continued to suffer from the brazen behavior of Miss Thompson, or the 'hot lollapalooza from Honolulu,' as one of her boyfriends called her. The missionary was particularly enraged by her, by the ragtime, the drinking, the noise of the rusty bed springs, as she entertained her numerous Samoan clientele..."

The plot of "Miss Thompson" charts the conflict between two missionary couples and a prostitute on the largest island of the West Samoans. The Reverend Alfred Davidson is a narrow-minded, sullen, repressed religious fanatic; and his wife, a sanctimonious prude, idolizes him. By contrast, Doctor McPhail takes a detached, rational view of life, though Mrs. McPhail is impressed by the Davidsons. Traveling on the same boat is a loose woman, Sadie Thompson; loud in voice, vulgar in manner, and on the lam. Horrified, Davidson tries to reform Thompson by shaming her publicly. The missionary convinces the island's Governor to send her back to California, and almost succeeds in his goal when Sadie finally repents, agreeing to return to San Francisco and take her punishment. During one of their nightly talks, however, the Reverend gives into his carnal lust and forces himself on Sadie. The next day, Davidson's lifeless body is discovered on the beach, throat slit, the razor still in his hand. Thompson reverts to her old ways, proclaiming that men are, essentially, little more than dirty pigs.

H. L. Mencken, one of two publishers of *Smart Set*, recalled in his autobiography: "Miss Thompson was meat too strong for the popular magazines, which were the chief American markets, and so Maugham's agent, the American Play Company, was unable to sell it. As a last resort, it was sent to my partner and we published it in the issue for April 1921 and it almost went unnoticed. What we paid for it I do not recall precisely, but I think it was about one-hundred-fifty dollars, Maugham's usual price for a story, of course, was very much more, but, as I have said, his agent could not sell this one anywhere else." Several published reports quoted the figure as $200; but in a discussion with columnist Ward Morehouse, Maugham stated he was paid double that amount.

Exactly how "Miss Thompson" became the great success, *Rain*, has inspired almost as much debate as drops of water have fallen on the shores of Pago Pago. In his unfinished memoir, Mencken offered an explanation. "Soon afterward a woman named Clemence Randolph, one of the girls of the then famous 'Sheriff Bob' Chanler, painter and voluptuary, decided that it would make an effective play and set to work dramatizing it. A friend of mine and one of Sheriff Bob's booze companions, heard through him of La Randolph's project, and after taking a look at her manuscript called in a Broadway jobber named John Colton to give her help."

Born in 1890 (the same year as Jeanne), Clemence Randolph had studied at the American Academy of Dramatic Arts, and founded the Children's Theatre in Woodstock near her family's estate. "Sheriff Bob" was famed painter Robert Winthrop Chanler, close family friend and eventual godfather to Randolph's daughter. John Colton was a prolific American playwright and screenwriter, known for his tales of Americans in far-off lands. He spent the first fourteen years of his life in Japan, where his English father was a diplomat. After returning to the U.S., he worked for a Minneapolis newspaper. Following *Rain*, his 1926 Broadway success, *The Shanghai Gesture*, had Hollywood calling—specifically MGM, who then hired him to write title cards and scenarios for silent films, and later, screenplays for sound pictures.

John D. Williams—a Broadway producer with fifteen shows under his belt before *Rain*— told the *New York Evening Call*, "I read the story 'Miss Thompson' upon which the play *Rain* is founded as it appeared in *Smart Set*. I thought it the greatest example of modern realism I had ever read, but I did not think it contained enough material for a play and I did not buy the story. Some time after, I met John Colton, who explained how he came into possession of the rights."

Introducing Sadie Thompson: November 1922

Colton told the *Brooklyn Daily Eagle* in October 1926 that he had been staying at the same hotel as Maugham, and asked if he had anything for Colton to read. Maugham handed him the galleys of "Miss Thompson," sent for proofing by *Smart Set*. The next morning, Colton asked if Maugham had considered turning his story into a play. As Maugham confirmed to Ward Morehouse in 1965, "I didn't see a play in the story at all, but Colton did. I told him go ahead with it if he so desired." As biographer Selina Hastings has noted, it would prove to be one of the most lucrative deals Maugham ever made.

Colton came East to remold Maugham's story for the stage with Clemence Randolph. Williams' recollection differs slightly from Mencken's. "When Colton [not Randolph] had written half of the first act—on yellow sheets in lead pencil—he showed it to me, and it was then I contracted to buy the play," he told the *New York Evening Telegram* in 1923. "As written by Mr. Colton and Miss Randolph, the magical touch of these two young dramatists had quickened Mr. Maugham's plot and characters into a vivid and dramatic stage representation. The great quest, and the only quest, was for the actress who could play Sadie Thompson. I now owning the play treated with as many managers as had likely young leading actresses under contract."

"During my search, Sam Harris asked to see me, and after the hearing the names of the actresses I had considered, told me that he had Miss Jeanne Eagels under contract. The end of my search was obvious—Mr. Harris could contribute the actress, and I the play. In abidance with a cable arrangement with Maugham, I did have to stipulate that I should cast the play, choose my own scenic artist, and determined in every detail the treatment of the text. This I did down to the smallest detail. *Carte blanche* was given me by Mr. Harris, and his able staff was of great assistance."

At the time, Harris had several prominent actresses under contract including Jeanne, Francine Larrimore, Mary Ryan, and Elsie Ferguson. Some publications proclaimed him the "New Charles Frohman." While Harris did indeed procure Jeanne, she had not been the first or even second choice for the role. Marjorie Rambeau, a leading lady on Broadway and in silent films, had come to Sam Harris' office looking for a new play. The producer took the script off a pile on his desk and asked her to go home and read it, and if she was interested, he'd produce it. It was returned a few days later with a definite "No."

According to Ward Morehouse, when Rambeau later ran into Harris on the street a few weeks after *Rain*'s opening, she confessed that she hadn't read the play, but had given it to her husband, Hugh Dillman, to read—and he thought it would fail. Marjorie later became an esteemed character actress, working steadily in Hollywood until 1957. In the late 1960s, she recalled the incident with magnanimity. "Oh, well. All of that was a long time ago," she told Ward Morehouse. "Maybe it was better that things turned out as they did. I was busy with *The Goldfish* at the time and I doubt if my performance as Sadie Thompson could have touched that of the magnificent Jeanne Eagels."

Actress Alice Brady's father was William Brady, the Broadway producer and head of World Pictures, and on more than one occasion, Jeanne's boss. Brady has stated that she was also considered for the role of Sadie, but her pregnancy at the time makes this claim rather implausible. (Her son was born in August.) Alice Brady did eventually play Sadie Thompson for a season in summer stock. Her greatest success came after moving to Hollywood, where she was nominated for two Academy Awards, before winning as Best Supporting Actress for *In Old Chicago* (1937).

***

Jeanne's earliest account of how she won the coveted role was a typical fabrication, with yet another reference to her imagined Spanish roots, and an idyllic sojourn with her father, (who, in fact, had died in Kansas City several years before). "After reading the story as it appeared in *Smart Set*, I knew the opportunity had arrived for reaching the apex of my stage career. I naturally wanted to make the most of it," Jeanne told the *New*

York Sun, a few months into *Rain*'s Broadway run. "The part of Sadie Thompson had an appeal that to me was irresistible. I read the story over and over again and became enthusiastic over the tremendous possibilities this character presented for stage portrayal, and, realizing it was my 'big chance.' I really could not become interested in any of the parts offered me in other plays. So I packed up and sailed for Spain, to visit my father, who has a snug little home in Castile. I stayed there for one year during which time I studied very hard, and, I might say finished my schooling At last— for it seemed like a very long time—I was cabled that John Colton and Clemence Randolph had completed the stage version of Mr. Maugham's story. On receiving this good news, I was the happiest girl imaginable and lost no time in getting back to America. I never had the slightest doubt about the success of the play. I was so impressed with the story I could not see a failure. If it had not met with heavy approval I should have been terribly disappointed."

However, as John Colton admitted to the *Los Angeles Times* in 1926, "The New York producers were afraid of *Rain*. It was a departure and the box office angle could not be overlooked. One day Jeanne Eagels, under contract to Harris, unearthed the manuscript from a pile on the producer's desk. She read the play and announced that *Rain* was to be her next vehicle. Harris laughed, other producers told her to stick to her own type—the ingénue of the moment. It had been planned that a sort of *Peg o' My Heart* affair should be her next vehicle."

What Jeanne later recalled, in a 1927 *Collier's* interview with John B. Kennedy, seemed closer to Colton's version of events. "The play was shabby from travel," she admitted. "Every office boy in every producing house had tossed it about. Nobody seemed to want it." But Jeanne did, of course. "The instant Sadie Thompson appeared in my reading of *Rain* I recognized her. Dinner-time came and went. I sat in my room, held by the script until the very last word. The next day I hurled myself into Sam Harris' office and demanded the play. Sadie Thompson was mine. I'd lived her in my dreams a thousand times. She was real, somebody I knew. Somebody I could be."

The "somebody I knew" was identified by Jeanne in the same interview. It all started in Mexico City, she explained, where her father was supervising a construction job. On the way to a bullfight, while walking on the Prado, the duo noticed a woman whose heavy make-up and gaudy attire left little to the imagination. Jeanne recalled "her flounced skirt, hunched shoulders, and picture hat. Beneath the hat was a handsome face, but hard, enameled with hues that were not part of nature's gift." The woman whispered something to her father, then upon seeing the child at his side, blushed beneath her rouge. She apologized, adding "I didn't see the little girl."

"That woman lived in my life the moment I saw her," Jeanne told Kennedy. "I thought of her constantly through the years that intervened between my girlhood and my fight for recognition as an actress. I created her origin and filled in her background—a small-town girl ambitious to get on in the city, driven by circumstances to be an outcast, exiled from her own country, a pitiful but kindly wanderer who could ask forgiveness for not having noticed a child." In 1929, she would tell Evelyn Gerstein of *Picture Play* magazine, "I even knew what color Sadie Thompson's panties were when she was a little girl. I knew her so well by the time I had started to play her, and how she swung her books when she went to school."

Though her original story was subsequently relocated South of the border, it is possible that when Jeanne was little Eugenia she first saw a prostitute while out with her father in Kansas City. Each home her family lived in was never more than a mile or two from The Paseo, a long, wide boulevard dotted with parks, and pergolas that ran for nineteen miles through the city. It was named after the Paseo de la Reforma in Mexico City. Ladies seeking to provide paid company would often find their customers in crowded public places, and on walks with her father, it is quite likely that young Eugenia had at least one—if not several—encounters of this kind.

Perhaps Jeanne's embellishments were prompted by something more complex than a simple desire to make her origins seem more grandiose than they really were. The elegance of The Paseo may have impressed Jeanne as a young girl, and inspired the myth of Spanish origins, and the presence of her father in so many of her stories suggests that she had never fully recovered from his sudden death.

***

Six years earlier, Jeanne had played the luckless Miriam in *Outcast* with a deep sense of compassion and inner damaged pride. She understood that these characters weren't morally corrupt, but decent women in difficult circumstances.

While Jeanne may have possessed the talent and sensitivity to play Sadie, there were physical limitations to be overcome. In "Miss Thompson," Sadie was "twenty-seven perhaps, plump, and in a coarse fashion pretty. She wore a white dress and a large white hat. Her fat calves in white cotton stocking bulged over the tops of long white boots in glacé kid." The fine details of Maugham's description worried Jeanne. "This had terrified me on the opening night," she told John B. Kennedy in 1927. "I have spindly legs. One's face can be made older, but one's legs cannot be padded to fleshiness effectively. I've always been grateful to my legs for standing up under the strain."

"Berlin or Russia might have stood for Sadie as Maugham wrote her," Colton later remarked, "but not the United States." In the words of the writers, Sadie became "a slim, blondish young woman, very pretty, very cheery, very rakish. She has a tip-tilted nose and merry eyes. She walks easily, without self-consciousness. She is not more than five feet six, slender and overly rouged, in fact her face, while showing traces of a hard beauty, is a walking advertisement for cosmetics. There is something of the grace of a wild animal in her movements, something primitive perhaps, even as her clothes suggest savage and untutored response to cut and color. She wears a lace coat and a salmon-colored dress which fairly shriek. White-topped high-button shoes, each with a dangling tassel, open-work stockings, a wide-brimmed straw leghorn hat topped by a huge purple plume complete her costume. She carries a not very new parasol which does not match her dress. When she moves, there is a rattling sound, due to the many imitation silver, gold and jade bangles on her wrists. It is undoubtedly her best hat and frock that she has on. It is the sort of hat and frock a lady of her species anxious to taken notice of would wear for an appearance at the race tracks in Honolulu or Yokohama or Shanghai."

Photographs of Jeanne in costume reveal the same attention to detail shown when she had consciously imitated Elsie Ferguson's look during the road tour of *Outcast*. About a month after *Rain* opened, Jeanne described how she perfected Sadie Thompson's flashy style. "This is quite a rig isn't it?" she enthused, in an interview with the *New York Tribune*'s Harold Stark. "I visualized these shoes on Sadie and I went all over New York to find them. They had to be exactly in harmony with the rest of her costume. Pumps wouldn't do, nor ties, nor plain black shoes, nor any other kind that I could imagine. One day, I saw a shop on Sixth Avenue and in the window, just the shoes I wanted. I went in and tried on the sample. I talked to the salesman about the weather, I was so embarrassed for fear he might think I was buying them for myself. I asked him how much they were and he said two dollars, and I thought how much I was saving the management. And then told me there was only one. The other had been lost in transit or perhaps sold to a one-legged woman. But I knew I could never duplicate or better the one I'd seen and finally purchased it for one-dollar fifty cent. It cost me fifteen dollars to have the other made and lasted three months.

"The hat is a triumph, don't you think? And these beads belonged to Geraldine Farrar. She wore them in one of her roles, and then gave them to my singing teacher, who gave them to me. I think it is romantic. I feel the romance of the stage very strongly. Think of this having once been the dressing room of Maxine Elliott! I am even sensitive to what the stage hands think of my work. And I am happy when I know the audience likes me. Of course, applause is applause."

Sewn inside the cheap bag Sadie carried with her onstage was a little "good-luck" trinket she would allude to—but never reveal—in her chats with reporters. The handbag she carried onstage was later used by Tallulah Bankhead in the 1935 Broadway revival. After *Rain* finally closed, Jeanne gave one of her pink dresses to Madame Savage. In 1941, *Life* magazine reported that a pair of her stockings had been donated to the drive for silk to use in the war effort, but were recognized and saved from destruction.

***

In *Method or Madness?*, a collection of lectures on the Method style of acting, published in 1958, Robert Lewis considered how Jeanne accomplished this transformation. "You should look for the essential quality of the part in casting the person to play it. This is aside from physical things. What really is going to tell the story?" Almost thirty years after Jeanne played Sadie Thompson, Lewis and other giants of American theatre, including Lee Strasberg, co-founder of the Actor's Studio, still cited her performance as one of the best of her era. "If any of you are old enough to have seen Jeanne Eagels in *Rain* you will remember that the thing that made it wonderful was that the essential quality of the actress was a certain inner purity," Lewis recollected. "Eagels had pink cheeks, the prettiest face you ever saw, and a desire to be good. No then, with all of that, she dressed up like Sadie Thompson and when she came on you said, 'But that's a basically good girl!' And when she had the scene with the minister who spoke in religious platitudes, you said, 'he shouldn't be talking that way to this lovely fire!' I've seen that play many times since and they have always cast a girl who, when she came out in the beginning, was obviously closer to the cliché of a Sadie Thompson. It then seems like a corny melodrama, but it wasn't with Jeanne Eagels—it was very moving."

"One of the great performances of that time and of my theatre-going experience was that of Jeanne Eagels in *Rain*," Lee Strasberg recalled, more than half a century later. "No one seems to remember the inner, almost mystic flame which engulfed Eagels in the scene with the preacher. It seemed as if she had been brought up to some new dimension of being, so that when she found to her great shock and surprise that he was concerned with what she had left behind—her sense of loss and her disillusion were overwhelming."

Writing for the *San Francisco Chronicle* after *Rain*'s premiere, George C. Warren noted the subtlety of Jeanne's acting. "She neglects nothing that adds a light by which to judge Sadie—that tender little bit on the old sofa that brings back memories of Sadie's home in Kansas, for instance. How lovingly she fingers the woodwork, as she had perhaps done hundreds of times as a child, and all the while she is talking flippantly to a crowd of men around her, trying to make an impression."

***

In Colton and Randolph's *Rain*, Sadie never admits to being a prostitute, despite the missionary's accusations. She expressed her concerns to stage manager Sam Forrest. "I can't feel myself a prostitute. I don't want to be cheap, sordid, vulgar." He suggested she imagine herself "looking for a man with a dollar... a good fellow... no malice... but then, no morals. You'd give your extra shirt if you had one to anyone you liked. You drink when you can. You think Christ is a swear word. You're a lonely soul but don't know it. You're an outcast but don't know it till you fall in love..."

Producer Sam Harris was more worried about the backlash from the ministry, as Reverend Davidson was not a pillar of the island community by any means. "It's not an attack on ministers," Jeanne argued, "but an attack on intolerance." As fate would have it, a sensational crime case would pave the way for *Rain* to proceed with its condemnation of one particular pastor.

Introducing Sadie Thompson: November 1922

On September 14, 1922, the Reverend Edward Hall's body was found next to the body of Mrs. Eleanor Mills under a crab apple tree on a field in Somerset, New Jersey. Both had been shot: Hall once, Mills three times. Love letters between the two were scattered between the bodies. The media circus that followed proved worse for the clergy than *Rain* could ever have been. It would take the Lindbergh baby kidnapping of 1932 to surpass the amount of media devoted to one criminal case.

Miss Thompson is provided with a *bona fide* love interest in a U.S. soldier stationed on the island. Perhaps the dramatists felt that a romance with a fellow American would make Sadie more palatable to audiences than a string of liaisons with island natives. Sergeant O'Hara, not featured in Maugham's story, was played by Robert Elliott, while veteran stage actor Robert Kelly was cast as Reverend Davidson with Catherine Brooks as Mrs. Davidson; John Waller and Shirley King as Dr. and Mrs. McPhail; and Rapley Holmes as Trader Joe. Hawaiian natives filled out minor roles and extras in the cast.

"John Williams did the preliminary directing—set the scene, dictated the tone and pace of the play." according to Burns Mantle in his *Liberty Magazine* column. "He and Mr. Colton were in complete agreement that *Rain* was really psychologically sound and stressfully but not flamboyantly melodramatic."

A week before *Rain* was due to open at Philadelphia's Garrick Theatre, the theatrical section of the *Evening Public Ledger* contained a very small advertisement touting the premiere of Sam Harris' latest production. On October 7, a much larger ad was published that gave the play's title and Eagels' name equal prominence. Also highlighted were the Wednesday and Saturday matinee ticket prices, ranging from 75¢ to $2. Critics were initially unexcited by the production, dismissing it as merely "novel" and complaining about the monotony of the rain that fell throughout the play. Opening night was a low $461.51. Audiences stayed away, resulting in a disappointing first-week gross of just over $6,000.

Patterson James' pre-New York review for *Billboard* was rather blunt: "In the main, Jeanne Eagels gives a fine performance. In spots her hardness seems forced, her laugh too ready and her swagger too stagy, but these deficiencies are more than compensated for by the fierce naturalness of her incentive against Davidson. That is raw, bleeding life without any attempt at restraint and it is Miss Eagels' biggest moment in the play. Incidentally it is the one true touch of the whole mess. That scene might be improved if she did not expend her force in one vitriolic outburst and if the rage were more progressive, leaving the peak of it to the epithet Sadie spits at Davidson as she exits. But it is a piece of real acting as it stands. The intrinsic hollowness of the play is made more apparent by that one bit of sincerity. Neither Miss Eagels nor the piece survive it." Box office for the second week doubled to just over $12,000, but that did not instill confidence in the show's investors.

As H. L. Mencken recalled, "The Philadelphia critics roasted the play and Williams became so dubious of its success in New York that he offered to sell a quarter interest in it for twenty-five hundred dollars." Williams' share of the profits would eventually reach $253,000, but at first, it seemed as if Harris had a flop on his hands. In preparation for the Broadway opening, rewrites were undertaken, involving not only the writer, but also the production's star.

"*Rain* was put on after the usual hectic period when author and star are pitted against those determined to change everything—even the title," John Colton said in 1926. "They wanted to call it 'Red Light Sadie' and when I heard that, I went out and got drunk for three days. Who wouldn't? And they wanted to put in a bedroom scene. But Miss Eagels believed in the play as it was written, and wouldn't permit any changes."

"Actually," Colton told Mantle, "*Rain* has always been Jeanne Eagels' play. She insisted upon its production, fought for it when others were lukewarm and is as directly responsible for the play's success as anyone who has touched it."

"All it needs is a little rewriting," Sam Forrest believed, arguing that Sadie's curtain speech in the second act (when Davidson orders her to return to San Francisco) was "a little flat. Let me see if I can't fix it." As told to Eddie Doherty, the stage manager stayed up until the early hours rewriting the speech, and Jeanne paced moodily in her dressing room while the rest of the company sat around drinking, smoking and chatting.

When Forrest showed her the rewrite, she declared it "Wonderful! Then I go sobbing to my room," she suggested, "and Davidson stands looking at me, his lips moving in prayer, and the curtain falls."

"But it's a *tour de force*," John Colton said doubtfully.

"A tour de force? Sure it's a tour de force," she replied. "But we need a tour de force right there, and this is the tour de force we need."

However, one rewritten speech would not allay the fears of those who thought the play should be dropped. "But Jeanne did more than bring the two factions together," Doherty wrote. "She gave the play all the treasures of her experience, bits of stuff out of her own life, lines that had sung in her brain for years." Certain lines spoken by Sadie seem autobiographical, such as "I came from Kansas once myself—as fast as I could hoof it." Others were lifted from conversations with friends. "A guy out there gave me the dirtiest look!" was a steal from Clifton Webb, much to his amusement.

"It is more trouble to stage a play with Jeanne Eagels than with another star whose disposition is more amenable," John D. Williams divulged. "She is nobody's yes-woman. But she is worth the trouble because the changes she rights for usually make the script into a better play. In story conferences she was never a mere listener. A good example is the second act of *Rain*. As it was written originally, after her great conflict with the missionary, Davidson, he said to her, 'All right, Sadie Thompson, you are doomed.'

"And that was the curtain. It was a negative, but it seemed pretty effective to me. Jeanne wasn't satisfied. We had to worry about it a long time. Then we wrote in her scene where she throws back the challenge to him with her 'All right, Reverend Davidson.' It was one of the most effective scenes in the play, and it made a tremendous curtain for the act.

It was her keen sense of theatre which told her that our original lines were not as good as they could be written. Jeanne Eagels did all sorts of things with Sadie. How she worked that character, twisting it around this way and that!"

A letter to the editor of the *New York Times*, published on May 23, 1926, confirmed Williams' impressions. "I happened to be in the original company of *Rain*. You read in the paper that *Rain* was written by so-and-so and staged by so-and-so. It is my opinion that if *Rain* had been presented in New York the way it was first seen on the road, it would have been a flat failure. Jeanne Eagels' suggestions as to the first act, cordially agreed to by Sam Forrest, and of the second act, gave the play just what it needed, and put it over. Incidentally, Sam H. Harris walked in on several rehearsals and pointed out certain shortcomings in the play which needed rectifying and he did this with a precision and decision that were astonishing." (The mysterious author signed his/her name as 'Young Roscius,' an alias steeped in theatrical tradition.)

Rain opened on November 7 at the 900-seat Maxine Elliott Theatre at 109 West Thirty-Ninth Street, named after the actress who had reportedly opposed Jeanne's engagement to Thomas L. Chadbourne in 1921. Elliott owned a 50% interest in the theatre, in partnership with the Shubert Brothers. Jeanne's entrance line, "So—I'm to be parked here, am I, dearie?" was her cue to winning—and eventually losing—everything she had dreamed of when she was little Eugenia in Kansas City.

One can only image what her thoughts were sitting in her dressing room with its green wicker furniture, yellow hangings and Chinese decorations as it quickly filled up with bouquets from some of Broadway's biggest names—some hoping the flowers were more for sympathy than success.

Kent Thurber, who played Private Griggs, told Eddie Doherty that ten minutes after the show was due to begin, Jeanne was still frantically searching for rosary beads sent by her mother. As Kent headed for the stage, he collided with her, and she angrily called him a "son of a bitch." He confronted her in her dressing room later that night. "Perhaps I shouldn't talk to you now," he said, "but I can't help it . . . what you called me . . . I want you to take back the name you called me."

She was aghast. "I can't believe I called you anything of the kind," she apologized. "I've never said the word until we began rehearsing for this play. I surely didn't mean to. And if I did, I'm sorry, I'm really sorry." She offered her hand and Thurber took it.

Another did not receive such genuine remorse, but revenge. In Doherty's account of that memorable evening, Thomas Chadbourne was seated with his new wife in the front row with Mr. and Mrs. Hebert Bayard Swope. When Sadie delivered her blistering second act speech, not to Davidson, but her former love.

"You! You! I know your kind, you dirty two-faced mutt! I'll bet when you were a kid you caught flies and pulled their wings off! I bet you stuck pins in frogs, just to see 'em wiggle and flap while you read 'em a Sunday school lesson. I know you. You'd tear out the heart of your grandmother if she didn't think your way, and tell her you were saving her soul, you—you—you—you psalm-singing son of a bitch!"

And then, it was over. The applause and demands for another curtain call were still ringing in Jeanne's ears as dozens of people crowded her dressing room congratulating her performance and inviting her to enough parties, nightclubs and dinners to fill the next few weeks. Harris, Forrest and Colton swept in to thank her, as did several of the crew and stage hands.

Eventually, it was just Madame Savage and Jeanne. Changing into her street clothes, she wearily spoke "I've been invited to three parties tonight . . . but I'm so tired." The two left the theatre for a late-night dinner in an uptown diner and then took a ride through Central Park before parting ways.

***

"My father's own favorite play wasn't O'Neill's *Strange Interlude* or *The Iceman Cometh*," Ward Morehouse III wrote in 2015. "It was *Rain*..."

Born in Savannah, Georgia in 1895, Ward Morehouse had arrived in New York in 1919, and would begin writing his "Broadway After Dark" column for the *New York Sun* in 1926. The opening night of *Rain* was an experience he would never forget.

"*Rain* came into the Maxine Elliott Theatre on a November evening in 1922," he recalled, "and the opening brought forth an emotional demonstration never exceeded in the theatre of this country and century. First-nighters stood and screamed when the curtain fell upon Sadie's denunciation of Davidson at the close of the second act; they were as wild as spectators at a football game.

"I occupied a seat in the rear of the balcony on that opening night and experienced one of the most genuinely stirring moments in all my theatre-going years in the final scene of the third act when Sadie's long-silent phonograph broke into the haunting strains of 'Wabash Blues,' her gesture of complete disgust with all mankind. She had learned only too bitterly that the Reverend Mr. Davidson, the foe of all evil, who finally convinced her that she must return to San Francisco and repent her sins, was an idol with feet of clay. Jeanne Eagels had her greatest night and she was acclaimed, and so was the play, the next day, by the enthusiastic critics—Hammond, Broun, Mantle and Woollcott. Miss Eagels achieved a stardom that had been honestly earned..."

***

Writing for the *New York Tribune*, Percy Hammond was rapturous in his praise:

"Miss Eagels was as flawless an example of vivid interpretation as he ever encountered in a New York theatre . . . a marvel of eloquent and explicit reticence; and if you care for illusion in your acting, here it is at its highest point... There is no acting in New York that even approaches in effectiveness Miss Eagels' characterization."

Other critics were equally laudatory, with even the acerbic Dorothy Parker admitting that Jeanne had finally found a role worthy of her talents:

"Another flawless performance... is that of Jeanne Eagels in *Rain*, the merciless tragedy that John Colton and Clemence Randolph have made of Somerset Maugham's masterly story, 'Miss Thompson'... Miss Eagels has been sliding about demurely in such things as *Daddies* and *The Professor's Love Story*, and her startling performance... is the season's greatest surprise. Her voice, her intonations, her bursts of hard laughter and flaming fury—great is the least that you can call them." – Dorothy Parker, *Ainslee's Magazine*

"Miss Jeanne Eagels, whose daring impersonation of the fugitive Cyprian in *Rain* has given her a brilliant place in the stellar map. Her truth to type... touches nearly on greatness." – *Wall Street Journal*

"Seldom have we experienced a more powerful thrill in the theatre..." – *Life*

"In the role of Sadie, the cabaret queen, Miss Eagels offers a study of exceptional emotional variety." – *Variety*

"*Rain* the play is distinguished by the acting of Jeanne Eagels." – *Time*

"The presenting company, headed by Miss Jeanne Eagels, is excellent." – *The Smart Set*

"Miss Eagels is no actress of tricks. She is a demonstration of being." – *Billboard*

***

"Ambition is extraordinary," Jeanne told the *Tribune*'s Harold Stark. "There is a certain kind of awe and fright about being a star. One feels such a responsibility. I've had opportunities to be a star before, but I was always afraid for fear the play wouldn't take. It's better to wait and see how the play goes, and then let the management force your name into headlines. Then it's a trademark."

A week after opening, Harris received a letter from a Mr. Dana Brunette, producer of a May 1922 performance of *Rain*—based on his own short story of the same name, published in 1916 and staged in Ogonoquit, Maine. As Mr. Brunette was quick to point out, he "did have priority of title and production," but he "understood the short notice on securing another name at this point and had no objection offering Mr. Harris the title with no further restrictions."

A generous payoff from Mr. Harris may have helped to ease Mr. Brunette's mind and, of course, the matter would never have arisen if *Rain* had flopped. With an opening week tally of $11,593 and tickets already sold far in advance, Harris knew he had a hit on his hands. "'I always did believe that audiences made stars!' stated Sam Harris," *Billboard* reported, "as he gave instructions for all electric signs, billing and advertising be changed, giving Eagels the full honors of stardom with her name above and before the title in all capital letters."

But even as the box office receipts rolled in, and New York fell under Sadie's spell, the moral clamor surrounding *Rain* gathered pace. In "Too Much Obscenity in Modern Theatre," a *Washington Times* article from November 19, Alan Dale aired his misgivings about *Rain*, arguing, "Regarding the current trend of plays that are nothing more than an adult written version of the child's game 'let's say bad words,' the play at Maxine Elliott's Theatre entitled *Rain* is a game of 'writing bad words' and getting them spoken by an actress who has always been associated with a certain refinement of action. This of course, makes the game all the more thrilling. Such words spoken by those who look as though they would come 'natural' would not be very stimulating. But uttered by a woman who suggest something far different they titillate. Jeanne Eagels, as a lady of speckled virtue, has various scenes with a minister of the gospel and it is he to whom she turns in her moments of indignation with torrents of invective and gutter slang. Words that the critic could merely intimate were hurled at the minister. Expressions that one would hesitate to read aloud were spoken with a vehemence—and this kind of 'sensation' was what *Rain* had to rely upon exclusively."

Top Left: Author Somerset Maugham shipboard (circa 1920.)
Top right - Philadelphia ad for *Rain*. Bottom - Original Inn on Pago Pago (circa 1928-9), where Maugham spent six weeks from mid-December 1916 to the end of January 1917. The author described it described it as a "dilapidated lodging house with a corrugated tin roof", but thought it a perfect setting for his story. The structure still stands to this day.

Eagels as Sadie Thompson - "a wind-blown creature, the victim of her own good humor, fond of life and taking its rebuffs smilingly. She is not more than five feet six, slender and overly rouged . . . She wears a lace coat and a salmon-color dress which fairly shriek. White-topped shoes . . . a wide-brimmed straw hat topped by a huge purple plume complete her engrossing costume. She is ready at all times to be friendly. The only persons she can't understand are those who do not like a wildly good time. . ."

INTRODUCING SADIE THOMPSON: NOVEMBER 1922

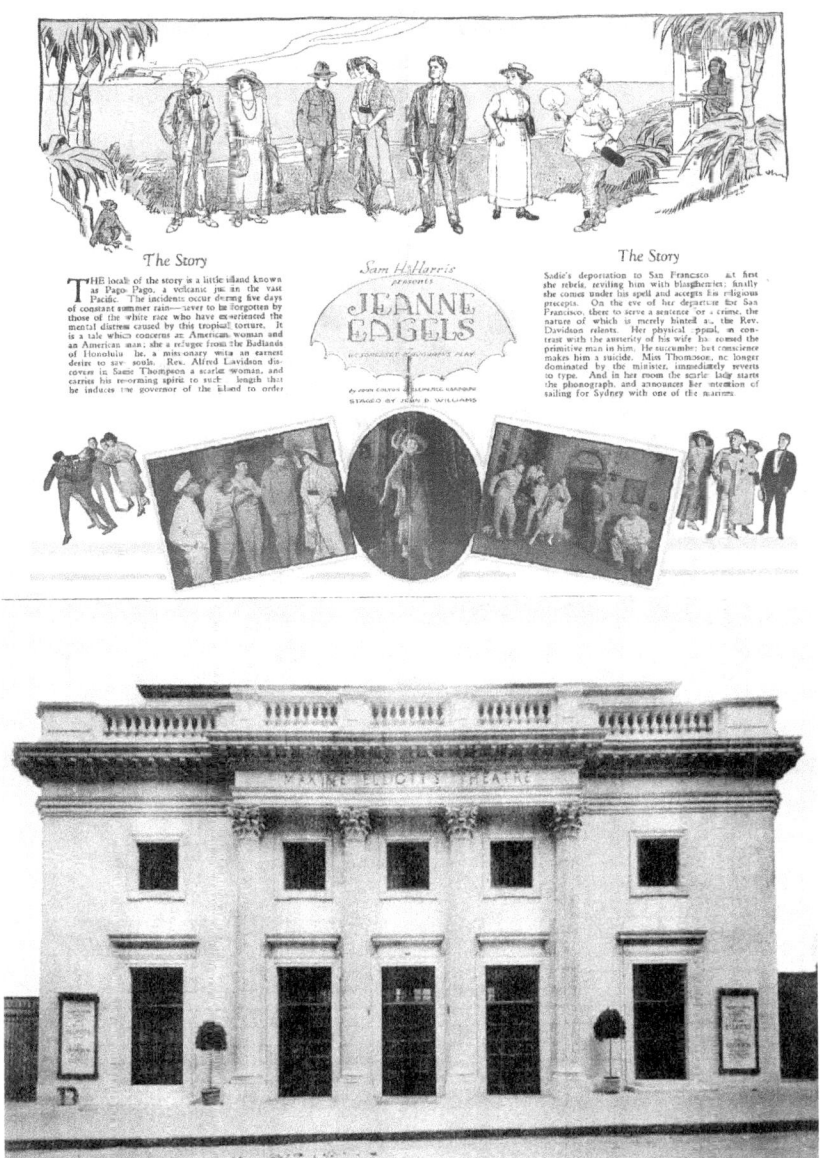

Top - Centerfold spread of the *Rain* program. Bottom – The Maxine Elliott Theatre (1908-1960), 109 West 39th Street.

Top - Sadie meets the sailors (L-R): Harry Quealy, Kent Thurber, Harold Healy, Monkey, Robert Elliott and Eagels. Bottom – "Dr. McPhail is a man of perhaps forty-five, rather gray at the temples, and one whom you would instinctively trust." Mrs. McPhail is a colorless, agreeable little woman of thirty-five. Mrs. Davidson "is a religiously withered creature. Age about forty. Her hair, which is dark, is drawn straight back from her forehead . . . all of which serves to accentuate her sharply determined features . . . Her entire life is devoted to Mr. Davidson's dictates."

INTRODUCING SADIE THOMPSON: NOVEMBER 1922

The majority of the cast on stage.

Chapter 8
High Society:
November 1922–December 1924

On the day after *Rain* conquered Broadway, Madame Savage retrieved Jeanne from her small apartment, and the pair took a taxi to the Maxine Elliott Theatre. Pulling up to the curb, they noticed men on ladders changing the signage. They were rearranging the bulbs to read "Jeanne EAGELS in RAIN." Jeanne wanted to stop and watch, without being recognized. "You go inside and ask for letters," she whispered to her voice coach, "then we can both have an excuse for staying around and watching my name go up." Madame obliged her pupil and milled around inside the lobby, but when she returned the men still hadn't finished their job.

"Go around the block," Jeanne ordered the driver. He did. Once. Twice. By the third attempt, they were crawling past the theatre more slowly than the pedestrians on the sidewalk.

Jeanne was guest of honor at a banquet held in the Hotel Commodore on November 26, 1922, to establish a small theatre and art space on the Upper West Side. On December 2, she joined Norma and Constance Talmadge, former co-star Julian Eltinge, current boss Sam Harris, and film pioneers Joseph Schenck and William Fox at the Plantation Restaurant at Broadway and Fifty-First Street, where the newly re-elected Mayor John F. Hylan stopped by to thank his supporters over a plate of waffles.

The perks of stardom included a larger dressing room, and Jeanne was able to bring her pets with her to the theatre, rather than leave them at home. But only two weeks before Christmas a couple of her dogs somehow managed to escape the confines of the building, and disappeared into the streets of Manhattan. Several December 12 newspapers carried an ad in their classified Lost & Found page inquiring the whereabouts of "Two Pekingese dogs belonging to Miss Jeanne Eagels; male, brown. Female, white with brown spots; answer to names of 'Baby' and 'Rover[12]', both very small, liberal reward: no questions asked. Apply to Thomas Bloom, representative Maxine Elliott Theatre." One hopes the wayward pooches were returned to their owner in time for the holiday.

With the same dedication she had shown while studying French with Madame Savage, she was also taking vocal lessons from Clara Novello Davies, who explained to Eddie Doherty how she prepared Jeanne for the role.

"I want Sadie to have a hoarse whiskey voice," Jeanne told her trusted coach.

"Put your hands on your hips," Davies instructed her. "Draw a deep breath. Lock it up in your chest. Now talk as long as you can. When you run out of breath stop and fill your lungs again."

---

12 Jeanne posed with Rover in several images during a sitting with photographer Arnold Genthe in 1921, now in the Library of Congress.

Under Davies' tutelage, Jeanne learned to sing from the diaphragm, thereby relaxing her throat and strengthening her breathing control. She later credited Davies with saving her voice from the ravages of Sadie Thompson's boisterous warbling.

The older woman, like all her teachers, felt the need to protect Jeanne, who was invited to many engagements at Davies' 15 West Sixty-Seventh Street studio. One on January 8, 1923, when Mrs. Davies welcomed her son, Ivor, home from England. Ivor Novello had composed "Keep the Home Fires Burning," a popular song during World War One. The *New York Times* reported that the "dancing did not begin until nearly midnight, as many of the guests had performances earlier in the evening." Among the guests entertained by Ivor's new compositions—and dances by The Dolly Sisters—were Irving Berlin, Sam Harris, Ina Claire, and Marion Davies. Another, on January 29, was a soiree for actress Gladys Cooper, who would sail for England in two days. Once again, Novello entertained the guests, including Billie Burke, Laurette Taylor, Ethel Barrymore, Dorothy Gish, Lenore Ulric, Leslie Howard, Edmund Goulding, and Clifton Webb.

There were other, more boisterous gatherings. While visiting Ruth Gordon and Gregory Kelly at their West 59th Street apartment late one night after a show, alongside actress Fay Bainter and her husband, plus Zoë Akins and her partner "Joby" Howland, Jeanne presided over a raucous game of forfeits. This culminated in her ordering novelist Joseph Hergesheimer to remove his pants and hang them on the chandelier, which he meekly did, before retrieving them at the end of the evening.

***

After eighteen months in Europe, Clifton Webb had returned to New York on January 17. One of the first things he did was visit the Maxine Elliott Theatre to see his dear friend, whereupon entering "Mrs. Dubinsky's" dressing room, he discovered that Jeanne was not alone. It seems Jeanne had been socializing outside the circle of her theatrical friends in Webb's absence.

"She introduced me to a very handsome, clean cut, and muscular creature in her dressing room named 'Ted Coy'," Webb wrote. "Not being a college man and not being a football player, I did not know him as he was a great gentleman in his field." Jeanne then told him, "You know he wants to marry me." Taken aback, Webb's reply was "That's lovely . . . goody for your side." Jeanne retorted, "But the son of a bitch is married."

Whenever he dropped by to see Jeanne, Webb would find Coy in the orchestra, or backstage. He found Jeanne's infatuation with the ex-athlete rather disconcerting. "[Coy] had never met an actress before in his life," Webb recalled. "He was married. As a matter of fact, we went up to his house one night . . . charming apartment . . . he gave us a party. I thought this was wrong because . . . his wife was away."

Blond, blue-eyed, six feet tall and weighing 195 pounds. Coy was, in the words of Paul Wagner, "powerfully built" and "wholesomely good-looking." A Wall Street Financier, his real claim to fame was as one of the greatest back-fielders and drop-kickers in the history of college football. His wife of nine years, Sophie d'Antigene Meldrim, had borne him two sons, Edward Junior and Peter. Even as it unraveled between the pages of society magazines, the couple's life seemed comfortable, even idyllic; as Paul Wagner observed, "the marriage was considered on all counts a love match of the first order."

According to *Liberty Magazine*, Jeanne first met Ted in a Park Avenue hotel restaurant. He and a brunette she knew slightly were sitting at the next table when Jeanne saw another woman she later found to be Mrs. Coy, enter the establishment and barge up to the couple's table, proceeding to expel a tirade of words to make a sailor blush. After her departure, Jeanne sent a note over to her acquaintance asking if she could be of assistance. The brunette introduced Mr. Coy to Miss Eagels and the three sat together having coffee and discussing what had just transpired.

"It was not long before this young man was calling at the theatre to talk about his domestic affairs —and other things," Eddie Doherty wrote. Over drinks in Jeanne's dressing room, he reminisced about his glory days on the gridiron and she flirted with him, harmlessly at first. "It was all very nice until Jeanne discovered that the window across the street hid a couple of detectives," Doherty added. "She happened to see one of them peering through a spyglass into her room."

Jeanne panicked: this was the kind of scandal that could ruin her career. The press would have a field day and this could quite possibly close down the play. "They will kill Sadie Thompson. They will close the theatre. They'll throw my whole company out of work and cost Sam Harris a million dollars or more. All my fault."

Ted didn't seem to upset by the discovery; possibly the liquor had given him courage. "Let her get the divorce," he said, "then you can marry me." Gathering up his possessions, Eagels quickly tossed Coy from her dressing room. As she closed the door behind him, one wonders if she paid any heed to the nagging feeling that pursuing this romance might not be a good idea.

***

Over fifty performers took part in the Forty-First Annual Actors Benefit, held at the Century Theatre on the afternoon of January 19. Jeanne appeared with her *Mind-the-Paint* co-star Billie Burke, along with pal Ina Claire, Peggy Wood, Florence Nash, and Alan Dinehart in a skit entitled "Nothing But Hits." Along with other playlets, musical numbers, and comic turns, Shakespeare's *Twelfth Night* was condensed into twelve minutes; the balcony scene from *Romeo and Juliet* was staged with Ethel Barrymore; and screen idol Rudolph Valentino danced the tango with his wife, Natacha Rambova. The event was a sell-out, with thousands turned away from the box office. The entire show was repeated at the 5,000-capacity Hippodrome Theatre on January 28, with a society pageant featuring the "Fashions of War" was now included in the 50¢ to $3 ticket price.

Jeanne later explained to the *New York Evening Telegram* why she had not performed in either of the great Bard's works that night. "I haven't the least ambition, and never have had to impersonate any one of the popular heroines of Shakespeare. Early I discovered that those roles were covered, like an ivy tower, with traditions. They are, indeed, edited for the players, and no matter what your ideas may be they are certain to be all wrong from somebody's point of view. Suppose I had a yearning to portray Juliet, for example. Then I'd have to do this thing or that thing, as Julia Marlowe or Jane Cowl did it, or else be scoffed at." Perhaps she also suspected that her lack of formal training would work against her. While her preference for original material is understandable, it's a pity that Jeanne would never play the great heroines of classical drama.

In a syndicated column on February 14, Jeanne described her Latin co-star from the recent benefit as her ideal man. "The hero of my childish Valentino days (not so long ago) was adventuresome and handsome, who did all sorts of daredevil things on account of me," she reminisced. "Yes I do dream, but not so much now of princes and knights. I believe it is a little more practical to have a Valentine ideal in a business suit and an automobile, and just now a cozy sitting room with a Victrola is preferable to leaning out over a balcony to a man all in tin freezing on a chilled horse. My Valentine must be strong, sentimental and human."

With steady employment, Jeanne was able to make good on her debts to friends and businessmen. Recorded as "settled" in *Variety*'s February 15 edition were two such cases—with a Dr. Child claiming over $1,500, and just under $100 owed to H. F. Pierson.

Amazingly, it took five months for Somerset Maugham to see Jeanne play the role he created. As he revealed to Ward Morehouse in 1965, "I was in Bangkok in Thailand when news reached me by cable, of the great New York success of *Rain,* adapted from my short story 'Miss Thompson.' I was astounded and couldn't believe it." On March 23—a day after Maugham boarded the *Aquitania* for London—his first impressions were quoted in the press. "It was with considerable curiosity that I witnessed a performance of Jeanne Eagels in *Rain*," he confessed. "I had heard a great deal of a highly laudatory nature of her performance, and I must submit that I was provided with an amusing surprise. When I first saw Miss Eagels she struck me as being an interesting little English girl, and I could not quite understand how she could possibly represent the original Sadie Thompson of the story." The pair had met at a tea party. After sizing up Jeanne's willowy form, golden hair, and childlike face, Maugham took Sam Harris aside. "Good gracious!" he exclaimed. "This girl is Peter Pan, not Sadie Thompson."

"Judge of my surprise, then when she came on the stage and said 'How's everybody?' with that hoarse, raucous voice," Maugham told reporters. "I wondered where she got the idea. I had never told anybody of the peculiarities of Sadie Thompson's diction, but here was Sadie Thompson to the life. Another curious thing was that Miss Eagels somehow hit upon the same sort of clothes that I saw the original wear; the same sort of coat, the same sort of hat, and the bangles on the wrists exactly as I saw Sadie Thompson in the flesh. Jeanne Eagels is truly an amazing young actress. Little did I ever dream that Sadie Thompson would be played so perfectly."

Jeanne's ingénue days were behind her, and for the rest of the career, her public image would be indelibly connected to Sadie Thompson. But she laughed off the notion of being a 'vamp', leading men to their doom with her siren song. "The professional vamp was only a myth anyway," she had told reporters soon after *Rain*'s Broadway opening. "... If I were going to be a professional vampire, it would be something like this: Dress well. Be as brainy as you can. Be as beautiful as you can. Never, never lose your temper..."

"The season she played *Rain,* Jeanne wore the same dress to every party," her friend Ruth Gordon wrote in her memoir, *Myself Among Others*. "Every night all season at every party there'd be an electric moment and it would be Jeanne in that slim black satin sheath, low-cut neck, low-cut back, pearls, diamonds and a quart of champagne under her bare arm. It was Prohibition and she brought her own special vintage."

The Romanian-born writer Konrad Bercovici recalled a wild party hosted by 'Sheriff' Bob Chanler, the artist and paramour of *Rain*'s co-author, Clemence Randolph. "A backer of *Rain*, the play which elevated Jeanne Eagels to fame, invited me to have dinner with him at Sheriff Bob Chanler's house on East Nineteenth Street," Bercovici wrote. " . . . Bob was as fantastic and exotic as his paintings . . . enormous and woolly, he met me in his slippers and open shirt and put out one paw while he held up his pants with the other."

"I put up some money for *Rain*," Bob told his guest. "Interested in the woman. Ha, ha, ha. Read the play. It doesn't look so good on paper but how it plays!"

"When Jeanne Eagels came in, looking smaller than she really was, and blonder than she was," Bercovici wrote, "Chanler, the millionaire genius and playboy, lifted her high up in the air and shouted at the top of his barrel voice, 'This is the greatest actress of all time. And whoever don't like what I say can get the hell out of here.'"

"Ethel Barrymore applauded," Bercovici remembered. "A colored orchestra appeared, as if from nowhere, and began to play dance music. Bob tore off his coat, threw the slippers off his feet, grabbed Jeanne Eagels and danced with her out of step, out of rhythm, a sort of savage dance, until he collapsed puffing to the carpet. Jeanne Eagels sat down beside him, and the two talked seriously, there on the floor, while the music played and couples danced around them. I had a good look at her. Her face was commonplace, but her eyes weren't; they had fire and strange vacancies. When the music stopped. Bob helped her to her feet, and the two went to a corner of the room and continued their conversation. . ."

***

On June 11, Jeanne and fellow actresses Jane Cowl and Florence Nash were in the audience for *The White Rose*, now in its last week at the Lyric

Theatre. It told the story of a Southern aristocrat who, after graduating from a seminary, falls in love with a young orphaned girl. D. W. Griffith's cinematic adaptation starred Mae Marsh and Ivor Novello. "Everything seemed to be really happening in *The White Rose*, and it was so like life is," Jeanne enthused. "The characters all seemed so right."

Tucked in the back of her current residence at 168 East Sixty-First Street, Jeanne had planted a small garden of geraniums, asters, and pansies, covered by bright red and yellow striped awnings to protect the plants from harsh sun. During a party on June 23, someone flicked a lit cigar onto one of the awnings which then caught fire—going unnoticed due to the fabric's coloring and pattern. After discovering the fire, Jeanne's staff and a next-door neighbor formed a bucket brigade and attempted to put it out. Communication between the Japanese houseman, Spanish maid, and German neighbor proved ineffective, and the flame-engulfed awnings fell onto the wicker furniture, which also caught fire. The entire burning mess was pushed into the flower beds, where it was later extinguished by the fire department.

After the incident was reported in the newspapers, Jeanne began receiving threatening letters regarding the nationality of those involved. One rather bigoted and badly-written postcard—signed "An American"—lambasted her personally: "It is the likes of you that causes us to be bothered with the K.K.K. You, getting your living from the theatre, supported by American citizens, yet you, employ nothing but lazy forigerors [sic]. To [sic] bad you were not under awning when it caught fire. May [it] break your neck next time." Jeanne's response was unequivocal: "I would like to surround myself with a one-hundred per cent American house staff, but no American with bricklaying at seventy-five dollars a week, would shackle his soul to a thirty-five dollar a week job. Hopefully, no one will discover that my house harbors a Venetian dining room, Dutch guest room, a Louis XIV bed chamber and a mess of Chinese and Persian rugs."

One night after the show, Jeanne watched her manager George Holland and a few stage-hands playing a dice game with a wealthy

New York businessman, whose superior capital put him at an unfair advantage. Jeanne asked George, who was holding her salary, to pass her the envelope—and then emptied its contents onto the table. After she challenged the stranger to "shoot a grand," he hurried from the room and never returned.

On another occasion, a cast member came to the theatre in a drunken state, and an imperious Jeanne ordered Sam Forrest to fire him. Forrest advised the actor to behave himself, and he hastily agreed. The wily director then returned to his leading lady, saying, "Well, I gave him the gate." A horrified Jeanne upbraided him, before remembering it was her idea. "Oh, I didn't really want him fired!" she protested. "You knew that Sam, this is terrible. Go back and hire him again ... He's a fine actor when he's sober, and I know he'll be sober from now on."

Jeanne's single-minded dedication was illustrated when the crew noticed a trail of blood on the stage during a performance. She had cut her leg but was determined to go on, even dancing with the Marines to "Wabash Blues" without mishap. When the show ended, she came offstage and almost fainted. The cast physician was waiting in the wings. "A safety pin got loose in my dance girdle and went looking for meat," she explained with a grin. "Can you yank it out, doc?

After more than 300 performances of *Rain*, Sam Harris grudgingly allowed Jeanne a brief respite. On August 30, *Variety* noted Jeanne's original request of three full weeks, and the counter-offer of no shows on Saturday, giving her, and the rest of *Rain*'s cast, a full weekend off. Harris was concerned that if the theatre went dark for an extended period, the box-office might suffer when it re-opened. Jeanne agreed to his suggestion, and receipts averaged $11,000 for six shows per week. Ultimately, though, Jeanne made Harris pay. When she resumed her two Saturday performances, she would be paid $1,000 weekly, increasing her wage by $400; and she would also receive a percentage of the gross. Nobody could dispute that Jeanne had realized her lifelong dream. After more than a decade in the theatre, she had finally reached the top.

Jeanne, however, was already making plans to leave the role that had made her Broadway's most talked-about star, as *Variety* revealed on October 25. Although *Rain* was expected to run for a full two seasons, Jeanne was considering another of Maugham's works, *The Moon and Sixpence*, as her next production, but decided against it. After reading the book, she found the male lead a more interesting character than the female, and she decided that she "doesn't believe the importance of the two characters can be reversed."

***

As Jeanne was still committed to *Rain*'s punishing schedule, and most of her remaining time was taken up with party-going and philanthropy, one might think she had little chance of finding love. Two years had passed since her alleged betrothal to Clifton Webb. In fact, she was highly skilled in the subtle art of concealing her love affairs from the press. Even veteran gossips were caught off-guard on November 2, when newspapers reported that she was engaged, and more surprised as to whom it wasn't. During an intimate dinner party held at Jeanne's townhouse, her mother Julia, let the cat out of the bag that Jeanne was going to marry Whitney Warren, Jr. The couple had planned to make the announcement the following week at a party celebrating Jeanne's one-year anniversary in *Rain*.

The would-be groom's father, Warren Sr., was a successful architect and part of the city's old elite, the Social Four Hundred. He had designed the library at Leuven, the Belgian city that had been the setting of Jeanne's 1918 film, *The Cross Bearer*. The Warrens lived at 230 Park Avenue and Junior was educated in the finest schools. Curtailing his studies to enlist in the military, he served six months with the Ambulance Corps before fighting with the French forces, and was decorated with the Crois de Guerre and Médaille Militaire upon his return. Junior was a member-in-good-standing in several exclusive Manhattan gentlemen's clubs, including the Knickerbocker and Racquet & Tennis. He was handsome and athletic, and the couple had much in common, fulfilling Jeanne's requirements for her "non-Valentino Valentine." They had met when Warren took an office job with Sam Harris, after traveling as an actor with a stock company out west.

A few years earlier, he had been engaged to Miss Geraldine Miller Graham, extolled by the Prince of Wales as "the loveliest girl in America." The Grahams' fortune was in oil, affording them homes in Newport Beach, San Diego, and New York City. Geraldine was beautiful, intelligent, and gifted in the arts and athletics. On paper, this was a match made in heaven. However, Geraldine was first generation *nouveau riche*, her father having made his money from property in Kentucky. Eager to raise her family's social standing, Mrs. Graham was prone to lavish displays of wealth. "Not in our family!" Mrs. Warren might have muttered through clenched teeth, as she greeted the unfortunate young lady. The engagement was called off several months later "by mutual agreement." The threat of losing financial support, and exclusion from the family inheritance, probably hastened Junior's decision.

Now Whitney Warren, Jr. was embroiled with an actress. Of course, Jeanne was one of the most lauded of actresses, although her current role was unlikely to impress her potential in-laws. Regardless of how chastely a young lady of the stage conducted her private affairs, her respectability and virtue would always be in doubt, and "demure" was hardly the most accurate word to describe Jeanne's personal life, which had been making headlines for over a decade. She would not be welcomed into this family.

Their response was swift, with Whitney Warren, Sr.'s office issuing a fierce rebuttal. Although Jeanne refused to discuss the matter, a reporter who obtained her telephone number recounted the maid "laughing heartily." After his absence from Park Avenue was noted, "Sonny". was tracked down in Philadelphia. "I know nothing at all about it," he insisted. "The first intimation I had that such a report was being spread was when a newspaperman called at my office." Hoping that greater distance would quash the romance, "Dad" booked his son on a solo passage to Italy, sailing on November 20. However, newspaper reports indicate that the reservation was canceled by the passenger himself in a handwritten note on Sam Harris' office stationary, delivered to the ship's purser.

As with Thomas L. Chadbourne two years before, Jeanne had been cold-shouldered by high society. But this time, she literally had another beau "waiting in the wings." She might have cooled on Coy when she found out they were being followed, but that didn't stop either of her suitors from appearing at the Maxine Elliott. "Whitney Warren stood in the wings watching Jeanne, and Ted Coy stood in the wings on the other side of the stage, watching Jeanne and Warren," Doherty wrote. "Frequently people backstage worried, fearing that Coy and Warren would get into a fight..."

Despite her romantic woes, the stage still dominated her life. On November 11, she joined stars including Grace Moore, W.C. Fields, Queenie Smith, and Paul Whiteman and his Orchestra in a benefit performance for the American Committee for Hungarian Relief, held at the Manhattan Opera House.

A special cable sent to the *New York Times* on December 19 announced that *Rain* would not be transferring to London's West End for at least three years. "Miss Eagels expressed the wish to play the part in London, and it is only fair that she should do so," Somerset Maugham affirmed. "Though I don't believe there's any part that only one actress can play—if there were it would be a confoundedly bad play—the role of Sadie, the heroine in *Rain*, calls for a certain knowledge of the underworld of Western America. Miss Eagels plays it with a tang racy of the soil which one could hardly expect from an English actress."

Jeanne appeared in another benefit on Friday, December 12, for fellow thespian Cecilia Loftus, who had been forced to cancel her tour due to illness. Ruth Chatterton and Laura Hope Crews were among the celebrities spotted in the audience and onstage. Jeanne performed a scene from *Rain*, and later Miss Loftus entertained her guests and fellow performers with impersonations of themselves and other greats.

***

The New Year started badly for Jeanne. Her romance with Whitney Warren, Jr. had been effectively sabotaged by his family. His father ensured that Junior was among the 1,100 passengers aboard the *Duille*, sailing on January 8, 1924, for a 35,000-mile excursion. He would be gone for nine months, passing through Algeria, Tunisia, Egypt, Palestine, India, Burma, Ceylon, the Dutch West Indies, Australia, New Zealand, the South Sea Islands (where *Rain* was set), China, and Japan.

Already hampered by a severe cold, the break-up left Jeanne emotionally exhausted. She had been absent from the cast since January 4, and the exact date of her return was as yet unknown. *Variety* reported that she was recuperating in Atlantic City, stating that "only two or three patrons have asked for a refund at any performance and the show was reported virtually sold out for the week by Tuesday." A week later, however, *Variety* announced her return, and ticket sales rose to a healthy $13,000.

Perhaps hoping to distract herself, Jeanne increased her social and philanthropic obligations. At the Friar's Club's Frolics on January 27 (entitled *Thrills of 1924*), she entertained the Manhattan Opera House audience with another scene from *Rain*, in which Thompson confronts Davidson—using the strongest language possible. On February 7, the librettist Oscar Hammerstein threw a party at the Casino Theatre, as his musical, *Wildflower*, entered its second year. Joining the show's cast, including Jocko the donkey, were 300 invited guests: including local newspaper critics, theatrical producers, and performers such as Eddie Cantor, Fanny Brice, Gertrude Lawrence, Lionel Barrymore and, of course, Jeanne. She also participated in a March 2 benefit performance at the Music Box Theatre, alongside Mary Pickford, Douglas Fairbanks, Fay Bainter, Alexander Woollcott, W.C. Fields, and Irving Berlin. The glitzy event raised nearly $4,000 for the American Humane Association, who proclaimed it "a brilliant social and theatrical success."

To capture a niche audience and allow actors to let loose after the curtain fell each evening, producers began putting on midnight shows, sometimes running for three hours, which could try the patience of both performers and spectators. The Shuberts introduced their own offering, *Vogues*, on April 10. At the personal invitation of Lee Shubert, Jeanne joined an audience numbering dozens of performers, among them Francine Larrimore, Mary Boland, Walter Huston, and Estelle Winwood. During the show's burlesque version of *Rain*, someone suggested Jeanne come down from her box and join the cast onstage. According to *Variety*, "despite Miss Eagels' protests and the evident displeasure of the audience an impromptu scene dragged along for ten minutes or so. . ."

The long-standing rumor that Lee Shubert was in love with Jeanne, whom he had first seen onstage in *Outcast*, and in every show since, was confirmed by author Foster Hirsch in *The Boys From Syracuse*. "Jeanne Eagels was the love of his life," said playwright Ruth Goetz "Lee once asked me if I had seen *Rain*, in which she played Sadie Thompson, and when I said yes, he asked if I liked the actress who starred in it, and when I said yes, he got very quiet. It was my father [playwright Philip Goodman] who told me how much Lee loved Jeanne Eagels; and when my father asked him why he didn't marry her, he said he was afraid if he married her she would want a child and she would die in childbirth—she had been very much a woman-about-town—and he would kill himself."

On May 15 Jeanne accompanied Kent Thurber, co-star and stage manager of *Rain*, to the Society Circus and Midway Fair, held at the Brooklyn Riding and Driving Club. The three-day event was in aid of the Crippled of Brooklyn Fund, and she was one of several actresses escorted by Thurber to volunteer their services.

The current theatrical season was a success, and highly profitable for producers and investors—but storm clouds were brewing. Actors Equity had been attempting to get the cast of *Rain* to join the organization since the show opened. On June 14, 1923, *Variety* bemoaned the fact that "Miss Eagels is not a member of the organization, with several attempts made during the run of the piece to have her join." Having struck out with her,

Actors Equity's representative approached the supporting cast, but this overture "proved equally unsuccessful." Little progress had been made and the future looked "discouraging."

However, the 1919 contract between Actors Equity and the Managers Protective Association (MPA) was set to expire on June 1, 1924. With a new contract came new demands: namely that 80% of the cast performing in legitimate theatre must be Actors Equity members; and non-members, including anyone who had joined the Actors Fidelity League after September 1, 1923, were obliged to pay an equivalent of dues. Another sticking point involved a two-week salary guarantee to cover every Actors Equity member in a company, which led seven of the larger shows produced by Belasco, Ziegfeld and Sam Harris to close rather than bend to Actors Equity's demands.

May 31 arrived, with no signed agreement between Actors Equity and the MPA. All seven theatres owned by the renegade producers were shut down. Jeanne seized this opportunity for a longer vacation, and set sail for Europe on June 4. According to her passport application of May 26, she planned to visit England, Spain, France, Germany, and Italy.

Jeanne was in good company as the *Berangaria* glided across the Atlantic: her fellow passengers included Jesse L. Lasky, taking a script to *Professor's Love Story* author J.M. Barrie; writers Anita Loos and Edna Ferber; and John Emerson, President of Actors Equity. But she quickly became distressed upon docking in Southampton, when immigration authorities came on board to query passengers. A London source informed *Variety* that she had no labor permit, and she refused to state the purpose of her journey: "Pleasure or work?" Instead, a weeping Jeanne ran to the ship's captain, followed by the ship's doctor, who finally convinced her to provide the desired information.

When she spoke to reporters later, she admitted to "behaving like a baby," and said that she was on holiday. She did have "an offer to play in Paris, but London was out of the question at the moment." Asked when it would be possible, Jeanne "hoped to return next year and remain from spring until end of the summer, under the management of C.B. Cochran." Her last statement implied to the cynical London press that the incident was merely a stunt; their nickname for Cochran was "the Publicity Opportunist."

After this troubling experience, a clearly frazzled Jeanne spent only two weeks in England before departing from Liverpool on June 21 aboard the *Mauretania*, and returning to Manhattan. She had received word by telegram that Sam Harris had settled his issues with Actors Equity, and *Rain* would reopen at the Gaiety Theatre on September 1. Harris assured Jeanne that if she did not want to join Actors Equity, he would assemble a non-union cast; but she expressed her loyalty to those actors who had supported her for almost two years, and reluctantly joined the union.

She did not go quietly into the night, however. She disliked what she saw as Actors Equity's bullying tactics and would always favor the independent producers who had helped to make her a star.

Variety published her full and lengthy letter of August 18 in its August 27 issue: "I now find myself a member of Equity, not, however, with the conviction that my decision is the wise one," she admitted. "No matter how carefully I weigh the pros and the cons I am uncertain about the wisdom, the justice, the fairness of it all. I cannot but feel that even now, in this apparently peaceful hour, clouds are gathering, that a greater storm than we have ever encountered is brewing on the horizon. I hope my fears are groundless and that the sunshine with follow the storm. I cannot, however, join your organization without expressing my honest opinions, not for the purpose of sounding alarms, but to free myself from the bondage of silence."

***

Jeanne returned to Kansas City in July, staying at the Bellerive Hotel. In an interview published in the *Kansas City Star* on August 31, she admitted that her friends could not understand why she had chosen to go "home" that summer, rather than staying in New York or exploring Europe. "Part of my family is there and the rest of my relatives are coming to meet me and we're going to have a good time," she explained. "What if it is hot? I don't have to run races or climb trees or stay in the sun all day long, do I?"

"It is a happy experience to meet Jeanne Eagels," the *Star* reported. "In the first place, she is not affected. She does not try to impress with her importance . . . There are no nervous mannerisms. There is no looking at the watch as a polite hint that time is flying . . . Jeanne Eagels impresses one as a sincere and charming woman."

"The things that one fails to recognize about her appearance are her size, her youth and her general demeanor," the article continued. "You expect a larger person. But she is only of medium height and slender almost to the point of thinness . . . She is dressed all in white, which accentuates the air of coolness about her, and she is not rouged."

When asked if the story that her one ambition was to bring *Rain* to Kansas City was true, Jeanne replied, "That statement is as true as the fact that we are sitting here . . . I do want to act *Rain* here. I worry my managers to death talking about it. Here is the point. I am a Kansas City girl. I started here, and had a hard time starting, too. But it is my home . . . I went out from here and have got along fairly well, and I want to show the home folks what I can do."

Questioned on advising stage-struck girls, Jeanne answered, "Oh, who can tell them what to do? It's the hardest proposition on earth. I can only say what I did. I would be the last one to stand up and lay out a list of rules for a girl to follow to make a success on the stage."

"Personally, the stage has been my life. It is all that I know. It is my work; everything on earth to me. The average girl's life is divided into her babyhood, her childhood, her schooldays, her married life, or her work. I have known nothing like that . . . Every fiber of my being and life has been devoted towards working towards a stage success. If I have made it, who will say I have not earned it?

"The trouble with most of the young girls today is that they see the glamour of stage life and know nothing of the work of it and the toil of it and all we have gone through to get where we are," Jeanne warned. "They do not know or else refuse to think of the trouping through one-night stands, the bad hotels, the muddy little towns, the stranded companies, the flat pocketbooks, the empty stomachs that we all have known."

"*Rain* ran 690 performances and I only missed seven of them, those, unfortunately, in the same week when I was so ill that I could not stand up. The attendance dropped off $4,000 in those seven days and I had to get back and start hitting the ball, as they say in slang, the moment I could to get our crowds back again."

Jeanne then described a typical day in New York: "I have my own home there, at 168 East Sixty-First Street," she revealed. "It is run by three servants, who seem to consider me in the light of a favorite child, or something. I also have what could be described as a second home at the Maxine Elliott Theatre, where *Rain* ran. It consists of a suite of three rooms that are nominally listed under the severe title, 'Dressing Room', but which really are as large as a fair-sized apartment. Passageways give off of it for my own entrances to the stage. My younger sister, Helen, lives with me in my home."

"I rise at ten o'clock in the morning, rain or shine. Then comes the bath, breakfast, my mail, the morning papers, a talk with Helen. Noon and the early afternoon bring dressmakers, photographers, perhaps a girlfriend or so for a call. At four o'clock comes my big meal of the day—and I am willing to confess right out in the open air that it is a big one. Then a bit of rest, and to the theatre early. Eight fifteen to eleven o'clock finds me in *Rain*. Then I go home with one or two of my friends for a supper at my house—this is as invariable as the ten o'clock rising hour and the four o'clock meal. Then bed."

Jeanne confirmed that she would be playing Sadie Thompson for two more years, after which Sam Harris promised her a new play. "Do you know there is just one thing I ask of that new play, and I am going to see that I get my way," she said firmly. "That one thing is that the play must be as dry as the Sahara Desert... Ten thousand gallons of water pours on *Rain* every single performance we appear in, and I'm ready to swear that I believe it almost all hits me. I'm damp all through, damp from a two years' dampness, and I have to guard constantly against colds and rheumatism and neuralgia. The play *Rain* and the character of Sadie Thompson have been wonderful to me, and I love them for all they've done, but if anyone as much as puts a glass of water on a table in my next play I'm going to walk right, straight out of the cast. I mean it."

***

"When Jeanne Eagels was in Kansas City this summer she reckoned to commence playing *Rain* in Chicago September 1, but she reckoned not on the wishes of her New York audiences," the *Kansas City Star* reported on October 26. "Sam Harris called Miss Eagels to New York to appear in *Rain* for a farewell week about Labor Day, and she was received with such fervent enthusiasm that a New York run was started all over again... She personally has wanted to stop *Rain* for some time, but does not appear to have the ghost of an opportunity to achieve her desire for several years."

The article revealed that Jeanne had hoped to perform "special matinees" of Oscar Wilde's *The Picture of Dorian Gray* at Christmas. The titular role of a man who gains eternal youth by selling his soul, while his portrait ages and fades, could not have been more different to Sadie Thompson. However, her ongoing commitment to *Rain* made this intriguing venture impossible.

On September 18, Jeanne brushed shoulders with British royalty. During one of only two excursions into Manhattan, as part of his vacation on Long Island, the Prince of Wales attended his first baseball game, visited Wall Street and the British Ambassador Club, and had lunch and a game of squash before dinner. This was followed by a performance of *Rain*, after which he met Jeanne in her dressing room for about an hour. Her publicist wanted to inform the press of her Royal visit, but she "persuaded" him to keep it a secret. She is said to have cheekily quipped about his Highness, "... it would be kind of cute to hold him in your arms and bite the tip of his ear, wouldn't it?"

Jeanne's three-month run at the Gaiety ended on November 29, with a box office gross of nearly $140,000. Two days later, *Rain* moved to Brooklyn's Werba Theatre for a week. The *Daily Eagle* commented, "Perhaps the most sincere tribute to the complete mastery which Miss Eagels exercises over the part was paid when the curtain went down at the act where Miss Thompson tells the Rev. Davidson that his hard, inflexible God is 'only a cop' and dares the missionary to do his worst. There was no outbreak of applause. For two full minutes the audience sat perfectly quiet . . . then the spell ended and there was conversation." This would be Jeanne's last New York appearance in *Rain*. Following a short break, the company would transfer to Atlantic City immediately after New Year.

On December 7, 1924, it was reported from Paris that Mrs. Ted Coy had filed for divorce on grounds of desertion. Sophie had been in France since the beginning of October, leaving the boys with her mother in Savannah.

"Two years or more ago suggestions of an estrangement were heard," the *New York Times* observed. "And this was not the first time attempted. A year before, Mrs. Coy went to Paris and it was generally understood among her intimate friends that it was her purpose to apply for a divorce at that time, but because of legal complications or for other reason the papers were not filed then and she returned to Savannah for a season of several months." The *Oswego Palladium Times* was one of many newspapers to report that Mrs. Coy had gone to Paris with her children to file for divorce from Ted—who hoped to then marry Jeanne. She was not named in the legal documents, though rumors of her involvement with Coy had been circulating for some time. It seemed likely that their affair would soon go public—or would it?

After discovering Sophie's detectives and her motive, Jeanne had enlisted George Holland to conduct his own investigation. Holland had been a New York reporter before becoming a press agent and he knew something like this would be very difficult to keep from the newspapers. He recounted his conversation with his client. "A million dollars wouldn't do it, no ten million . . . it will be plastered over the front page of every paper in New York—even the *Times*. A famous athlete, his society wife and the greatest actress in the world, all tied up in the scandal—and Whitney Warren in the background. No Jeanne; if that woman names you, it's good night!"

Holland hired his own private investigators, who found that Mrs. Coy had been the mistress of a man for at least a couple of years before Jeanne had met Coy. His name was Frank A. Munsey, a multi-millionaire publisher whose holdings included *The Washington Times*, *The Boston Journal* and numerous New York City publications including *The Daily News*, *The Sun*, *The Press* and *The Globe*.

Perhaps out of professional respect, or because other publishers were just as guilty of philandering as Munsey, the story was not broken by any publication. "The type that might have ruined Jeanne—and others—was to be melted and remade into a type that would ruin somebody else," Doherty noted drily. "The woman so eager for a divorce went to Paris and secured it there on grounds of desertion."

"The Ted Coy-Jeanne Eagels romance began, as far as the public was concerned, with a denial," the scholar Paul Wagner reflected later, describing Jeanne as "a tempestuous genius who could curse like a drover, string along Stage-Door Johnnies and Sugar Daddies, and still appear in her publicity photographs demure, fresh-eyed, and cameo-profiled—just the sort of girl any fellow could take home to mother."

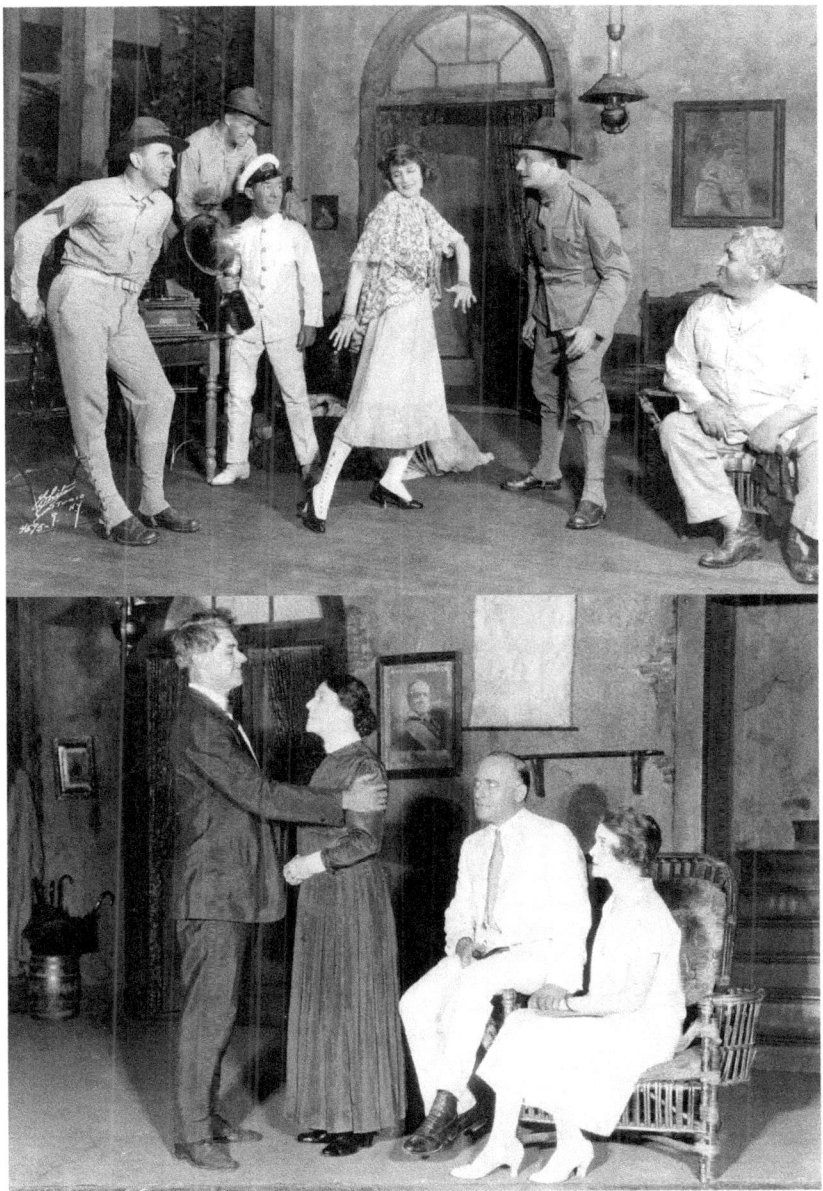

Top - Sadie dances for the sailors and Joe Horn (Rapley Holmes). Bottom - The McPhails and Davidsons (L-R): Robert Kelley, Catherine Brooke, John Waller and Shirley King.

"... if that Davidson gets gay with me again, I'll tell him who his mother is!"

Swathed in white mink (circa 1924.)

Top left - Warren Whitney Junior portrait by Robert Reid (1915.) Bottom - Whitney with film star Audrey Hepburn in his San Francisco residence (1960.)

Ted Coy at Yale (1909.)

Eagels shipboard the *Berengaria*.

Chapter 9
Comfort, Love, Respect:
January–December 1925

Jeanne arrived in Atlantic City on January 2, 1925, and checked into The Ritz-Carlton Hotel. The darling of Broadway was back on the road. *Rain* had broken records when it opened at the National Theatre in Washington D.C., bringing in just under $32,000 in one week. However, Jeanne was frazzled and unable to perform for at least two days. She spent the latter half of February in Pittsburgh at the Nixon Theatre. During a two-week run, the highest day's box office topped $4,400 even though she was absent for three days. It was here that Tallulah Bankhead—still under consideration to play Sadie Thompson in the London production—saw Jeanne's performance twice.

"I had been in London eighteen months when approached by Basil Dean to play Sadie Thompson," Tallulah recalled. On January 4, the *New York Times* noted that *Rain* would soon be produced at St Martin's

Theatre. No actress had been cast, but the move was driven by *Rain*'s remarkable success in the United States. The tour—which Jeanne had begun in Chicago—was planned to last two years. According to Tallulah, producer Basil Dean proposed that the show would open no later than June 30, after she finished her West End run in *The Creaking Chair*, and Maugham returned to England. Dean suggested that Tallulah should sail to New York to see Jeanne in the role.

Tallulah boarded the *Berengaria*, and arrived in Manhattan on February 25, ready to watch Jeanne as Sadie—but she was already in Pittsburgh. After finally seeing *Rain*, Tallulah booked a return journey aboard the *Aquitania*, but Basil Dean and Maugham had also reserved cabins, and the producer thought it best that Tallulah did not meet the author yet. She was forced to find another passage and recounted a terrible journey on "a cattle boat that consumed ten days in crossing. Among the passengers were a corpse and the two daughters of the Governor General of Canada. I locked myself in my cabin and played the jazz records Sadie played in the second act as I acted out my part."

"Maugham sat in the dark auditorium throughout the first rehearsal," Tallulah wrote. "I gave what I'm sure was a brilliant imitation of Jeanne Eagels. I felt my impersonation would electrify Maugham, but if it did he didn't show it and avoided me afterwards." Maugham was unmoved by her performance, and she was replaced by Olga Lindo three days later. Adding insult to injury Tallulah was offered Lindo's role in *Tarnish*, a part she'd turned down to accept *Rain*. "I was inconsolable," Bankhead admitted. "I had hysterics and sobbed as I not sobbed since foiled as a child. That night I gave one of my phoniest performances in my life. Returning to my service flat, I put on Sadie's Pago Pago costume, gulped down twenty aspirin tablets, turned on Sadie's record, then I stretched out on my bed to await the end."

Tallulah scribbled a note: "It ain't gonna Rain no *moh*." She fell asleep "dramatizing every detail of my suicide . . . I was awakened the next morning by the telephone. It was Noel Coward. I felt marvelous." Coward wanted her to star in *Fallen Angels*. After seeing the play, Maugham invited her to lunch, congratulating her on "the most brilliant comedy performance he'd seen."

Meanwhile, Lindo brought Sadie to the London stage—but the production was a failure. Years later, playwright Roland Leigh told Tallulah that during a conversation at his home in the South of France, Maugham confessed his biggest professional mistake had been "not letting Tallulah Bankhead play *Rain*."

***

After two years of performing at the Maxine Elliott Theatre in the evening, and spending time with close friends during the day, the loneliness of touring pushed Jeanne to the brink. *Variety* reported that on the week of March 5, she was taken ill in Cleveland, Ohio, and "rushed to Washington D.C. to undergo an operation." She had been on the verge of collapse throughout the past week, but struggled to perform to the sold-out crowds for as long as possible. Another actress, Georgia Lee Hall, was hired from a company in Racine, Wisconsin, to fill in while she recovered. However, it seemed the new production was cursed. Miss Hall was struck down with pneumonia after her first performance; and a stomach bug felled both the stage manager, and one of the Marines in the cast. Surprisingly, very few refunds were requested.

On February 25, 1925, Jeanne told *Variety* that Ted Coy was a "dear friend," denying their rumored engagement. When she suddenly left *Rain* in Cleveland, many thought she would elope with the former Yale football star. On the same day that she had told the press of her colitis, Jeanne once again denied her engagement to Edward Coy "or anyone else."

Friends like Ruth Gordon and husband Gregory Kelly told a different story. "When Clifton Webb invited us to the Sixty Club," Ruth wrote later, "Gregory couldn't believe he would actually meet the great Ted Coy.

It was a supper party for [playwright] Freddie Lonsdale and his daughter and Jeanne and her fiancé."

On March 1—with Sam Harris' blessing—a second-rate stock company production of *Rain* had opened at Washington's President Theatre. Jeanne was already unhappy with the numerous roadshows currently touring the smaller towns and cities, and D.C. audiences had purchased tickets expecting to see her. Instead, they found Katherine Hayden leading a cast hastily assembled in New York, with none of the original cast.

Jeanne was further aggrieved by the theatre manager, who had been promoting her appearance in a rather lewd manner. "If you get time some evening this week, I wish you would drop in . . . and see Sadie," he wrote, on a postcard sent to patrons. "She gets pretty bad around 10:45 every night, drinking Scotch, playing around with Marines and trying to stand off a missionary who wants to convert her. . ."

Liberty Magazine quotes Jeanne's letter to the editors of several publications. "It is with appalling regret that I find anyone, however benighted, deeming such misrepresentation of *Rain* necessary to attract people to his theatre," she wrote. "Not only is it misrepresentation, but it is also vandalism comparable to the gleeful debauchment of something beautiful by vulgar hands . . . To attempt to draw audiences to *Rain* through the medium of such a postcard is to me rather a terrible act. To suggest the lure of a lecherous exhibit for this play is, to me, little short of criminal. To picture Sadie Thompson, the pathetic protagonist in this study in pity, as a beckoning red light to unclean minds is, to me, a horrific cheapening of one of the great characters in all drama."

"As one cradled in the theatre and consecrated to it, I bitterly protest against this defamation, and will thank you if you will print my protest."

Jeanne's anger at these roadshow productions was based on her belief in *Rain*'s artistic integrity, and a strong feeling that only she could bring Sadie Thompson to life—and this was not an unjustified claim. As both John Colton and John D. Williams had admitted, it was her suggestions which had transformed the play's raw material into an unlikely smash hit; and while many other actresses would take on the role of Sadie Thompson, none had the same impact. "She had made Sadie. Sadie was hers, all hers," Doherty wrote. "Nobody else had a right to play the role. No one else could."

"These companies have caused me no end of trouble," she complained to John Colton. "In a good many instances the censors have forced the players to change the original text, claiming it was immoral. In Newark I was requested to eliminate the most important scene of the play, 'the mountains of Nebraska,' because somewhere in Connecticut the second or third company had been forced to do so. I believe this action was due to the improper interpretation by a mediocre company."[13]

Jeanne returned from Washington to New York, declaring to *Variety* that she had quit the show in Cleveland after an attack of acute colitis, and spent the last month consuming nothing but soup. She would be returning to Washington for further treatment before resuming the tour, with plans to open in St Louis, Missouri at the American Theatre on March 31, before fulfilling her promise and returning home as a star.

"Miss Eagels is easily the leader of Kansas City's contingent of actors and actresses in the stage world today," the *Kansas City Star* declared on April 13. "... She was ill recently, and, for the first time since she began her engagement in *Rain*, took a vacation of some length from the company, desiring, as she told everyone frankly, to be thoroughly rested up for her Kansas City engagement."

"The company that will come here with Miss Eagels in *Rain* is the original New York one—the only change being in three Hawaiians who play minor parts as natives."

Jeanne had returned to her hometown many times over the years, but nearly two decades had gone by since she had performed there with

---

13 "This morning he told me he had been dreaming about the mountains of Nebraska," Mrs. Davidson says of her husband, to which Dr. McPhail replies 'reflectively', "H-m! That's odd" (Act III, Scene I.) Theatre historian Felicia Hardison Londré argues that the mountain dream is indicative of the Reverend's sexual repression.

the Dubinskys. News of the "local girl made good" filled the papers weeks before her sold-out, two-week run at the Shubert Theatre. The *Star* described a line from the box office down Broad Street the first day tickets went on sale. Jeanne arrived at Union Station, and was greeted by a large crowd of dignitaries, friends and fans—but not her mother. Jeanne rushed to the family home at 3021 Harrison Street, where Julia lay in bed, exhausted.

Fortunately, Jeanne's presence soon lifted her mother's spirits. On opening night, Julia and Helen sat in the fourth row on the right aisle—directly behind Georgia Brown, whose former star pupil was now transformed into a reckless harlot, spouting obscenities at a bigoted preacher. "It was the first time Mrs. Eagels or Mrs. Brown had seen *Rain*," the *Kansas City Star* reported, "and Miss Eagels tried to give the performance of her life for them. There were perfectly unprejudiced witnesses in the audience who will say she just about accomplished the feat."

Jeanne visited Brown's dramatic school a day later, carrying a basket of roses taller than herself. On another night, her three unmarried, devoutly religious aunts came to the show. Afterwards, Jeanne took them backstage. She introduced them to the cast and led them to the machinery which produced the constant rain.

When she wasn't busy at the theatre or relaxing with family, Jeanne spent time among girlhood friends, now married with children of their own. Doherty spoke to several of them for his serialization. Ruby Stapp Goins, now widowed, spent an afternoon sifting through old photographs together. One showed a young Eugenia standing across from the Morse School wearing a hat with her ill-fitting coat, arms reaching far beyond the cuffs. "Wasn't I young then?" Jeanne mused, "... and innocent ... and rather sweet. And how poor I was and yet how happy! If I could only go back to those days ... I remember ... I had the picture taken because I loved the coat and realized I couldn't wear it much longer." As Ruby recalled it, Jeanne's bright mood suddenly darkened as she was leaving.

"I envy you," she said wistfully to her old friend. "You've got everything I want—comfort, love, respect." Before Ruby could protest, she cut her off: "Oh, don't say I've got money and fame and Ted. I've got nothing."

Margaret Knowles Lange, who owned a drugstore with her husband, Paul, spoke of Jeanne sitting in a wire-backed chair one afternoon, "as if she were nothing but a high school girl, eating candy and ice-cream . . ." Meanwhile, a steady stream of customers paraded in and out of the store to catch a glimpse of the actress. Margaret's daughter wanted to be a dancer, and Jeanne was happy to watch her perform. She even took some of the candy with her, giving a fistful to 'Handsome' when she appeared onstage that night.

While to some she might still have been little Eugenia, onstage she was Jeanne Eagels and didn't let anyone forget it. Afraid they would distract audiences, she forbade the Shubert's orchestra from performing—although union rules required them to be paid, whether they played or not. With box office receipts of $43,000, a $960 loss was a minor expense to appease *Rain*'s star attraction.

Jeanne's wrath was incurred again during the second act of April 23's afternoon matinee. While making a speech about Sadie's banishment from the island, she noticed that an audience member had propped open a side exit door. Swaggering offstage in character, she briefly returned to the stage before leaving again. The audience overheard her vociferous complaints, and the curtain quickly came down. The *New York Times* detailed how a patron in the rear of the theatre had opened the door to cool himself. An usher had closed it, but the patron re-opened it and told the usher to leave it open. This was not unreasonable, as the Shubert had no air-conditioning. Jeanne refused to go on until the door was again shut, with an usher posted to make sure it remained so.

Another incident involved the removal of Goodman Ace, the *Kansas City Journal-Post*'s dramatic critic, from the theatre. Ace explained this in his column the following week, after Jeanne had left the city. How he had been lurking and talking backstage with the Shubert's manager, when the pair was spotted by Jeanne onstage. Their presence clearly rattled her—and during one of her exits, she ordered the stage manager to have them removed. Told who the duo were she insisted, "Throw them both out."

She also refused to give a curtain speech, despite nightly pleas from the audience. The only interviews she gave during her stay were to Landon Laird of the *Kansas City Star*.

"What am I going to do now?" she pondered, while waiting in her dressing room on the last night of her residency. The interview was published in next morning's *Star*, on April 26. "Well, I play Cincinnati one week and then I go on East and after three weeks in New York, we close for the summer. Then I am going to Switzerland and take all the rest I can get before fall, when we open in Chicago. I need the rest, I think you'll agree. I'm not fit like I was when I was here last summer. But it's because I've had a winter of grueling work—and believe me, it has been grueling."

Asked if she would be glad to leave *Rain* and play a "nicer" role, Jeanne flashed back:

"No I'm not ashamed of my Sadie Thompson role. Far, far from it. I will you tell you one thing, though. I'll be glad to finish playing *Rain* so I can use my own 'speaking' voice on the stage. People hear the hoarse, whiskey husk that I use and think that's my honest speaking voice. They say, 'How can she play the higher type of parts with a voice like that?' That husky voice of mine is all put on, every bit of it. I haven't it now that I'm talking with you, have I?"

"Another thing," Jeanne added, "I don't want Kansas City to think I'm temperamental. I rang down the curtain at Wednesday's matinee, that's true, but I want to tell you that that's the only time I've ever had to do it. I ask you, what would you have done? There was a downstairs exit door open. We tried and tried to get it closed, but the spectator who opened it swore at the attendant who tried to close it, and the door remained open. We heard noise coming from the street from that door, and the rain was on at the same time, and we were just having an awful time up on that stage. I knew if I put down the curtain a minute and got the true word about the matters out to the front of the house, that door would be closed. It was either do that or stumble along in the bad performance we felt we were doing. So I put the curtain down and the door was closed and the curtain went back up and that's all there was to it."

"Listen, I have nothing to be temperamental about. I know that. I'm at the hardest part of my entire career now. I've made good—and I have to keep making good. It's harder work to stay at the top than to get there. I have to show people I can play other starring characters as well as Sadie Thompson."

With the interview at an end, Jeanne made her way back to the stage as Trader Joe Horn called for Sadie. "Goodbye," Jeanne whispered to the *Star* critic. "Tell all my friends and the Kansas City folk goodbye—and that they've been wonderful."

Landon Laird accompanied her to Union Station the next day where she continued the conversation. "I've seen them watching me from all over the audience," she told him. "I've been able to pick out their faces, old friends, old schoolmates, girls I worked with in the department store. I hope I've pleased them all. I tried so hard. But you know how I am. You have no idea how that rain, rain, rain, gets on one's nerves. Part of the time my clothes are dripping; and all the time I am depressed. Did you ever play in the rain night after night after night, year after year after year? I shall be sorry to say goodbye to Sadie Thompson, though some day I must. But it will be nice to play in something where the rain does not fall, and in which I can use my own voice, and not Sadie's." At this point, her composure broke: "It's harder to stay at the top than to get there," she confessed. "I am now at the hardest point of my career. I must show people I can play other characters as well as Sadie Thompson."

Jeanne said her goodbyes to the Langes, who had come to see her off. Looking Margaret directly in the eyes, she warned: "Let your daughter be a dancer if you think her fit for it. But never, never let her be an actress."

After a week in Cincinnati, Jeanne headed back to a three-week return engagement at Brooklyn's Werba Theatre, before moving to Teller's Shubert Theatre for another seven days. Harris then brought the show back to Philadelphia, where *Rain* had premiered over four years before. The seats of the Garrick Theatre remained filled for four weeks, with total receipts approaching $84,000.

"Did I see future greatness in any of the little girls when they were so small?" Georgia Brown repeated a question posed in the *Kansas City Star* on June 14. "Oh, it's hard to tell at that age. A pretty little girl may lose her charm when she grows up. Similarly, a homely youngster may be a radiant debutante and woman. There seems to be no way on earth of telling . . . I knew Jeanne Eagels would make good, of course. Anyone would have done so," she concluded.

Back in New York, *The Garrick Gaieties*—described by author Jon Bradshaw as "the first of the small literate revues"—featured a number by the upcoming songwriting team of Richard Rodgers and Lorenz Hart, satirizing the female stars of the day. Targeting Jeanne Eagels, the Ziegfeld Girl and Mary Pickford, "Ladies of the Box Office" was nicknamed "the aphrodisiac song."

In an interview for *Picture Play* magazine's July issue, actress Dorothy Gish enthused, "I've seen *Rain* nine times. Whenever it comes near New York I see it over and over. Jeanne Eagels grows better every time I see her. She's marvelous, wonderful, superb!"

***

Ossining is one of several small villages and towns scattered across Westchester County, some forty miles North of Manhattan. Home to Sing-Sing Prison, it was also the location of summer and weekend homes of wealthy New Yorkers escaping the city. Large multi-acre estates were nestled among the hilly, forest-filled terrain: with names like The Croft, home of General Electric President Gerard Swope; and ELDA, a stone castle on nearly thirty acres, designed by the wife of department store co-founder David T. Abercrombie. Jeanne had loved the area since her days at Thanhouser Films in nearby New Rochelle.

Jeanne became a neighbor of both men in the middle of June, when she purchased "Kringejan" from N. L. Miller. Located at 1325 Kitchawan Road in Yorktown, about five miles outside of Ossining, its twenty-nine acres harbored a small lake and groves of old maple and pine trees. Uphill, and far from the road, sat two homes—a twelve-room, two-story Georgian Colonial, and a ten-room, stone guest cottage. The property also held a barn, stables, an apple orchard, and kennels for Jeanne's pet dogs: a motley crew of Schnauzers, German Shepherds, and two white English bulls named Rain and Sunshine. And her former police dog Mikka, "so mean," said her cook George, that he "never goes out when there's lightning because God will strike him dead."

Some thought Jeanne had purchased a weekend party house to entertain her many colorful friends, but her inner circle knew the truth. On August 28, every American newspaper devoted its front page to the previous night's wedding of Jeanne Eagels and Edward Harris "Ted" Coy, in Stamford, Connecticut.

The groom was the son of a classical scholar, he was born in Andover Massachusetts, in 1888—a "child of advantage"—including "moderate wealth and the gentle traditions that informed the Eastern upper class." Coy was related to a former president of Yale University, where he studied from 1907-1910. While serving on the college football team, he lost only one game (to Harvard, in 1908).

Ted was also a member of the Skull and Bones secret society, whose members went on to become leading lights in business and politics. In contrast, he was also a member of an acapella vocal choir, The Yale Whiffenpoofs. Coy's membership was kept secret, even within the choir. Coy was described as "a song lover with a good ear and a nice tenor voice." To "cover the heresy" of his joining the Whiffenpoofs, he was given the title of Perpetual Guest.

Named All-American after his three years of varsity came to an end,

Coy returned in the fall of 1910 to coach the team to a record of 6-2-2. During his final season, a Harvard reporter praised "the quiet smiling manner of his leadership." In 1928, the novelist F. Scott Fitzgerald would immortalize him in a short story, "The Freshest Boy," renaming him Ted Fay.

"He found the theatre and entered the lobby with its powdery feminine atmosphere of a matinee. As he took out his ticket, his gaze was caught and held by a sculptured profile a few feet away. It was that of a well-built blond young man of about twenty with a strong chin and direct grey eyes. Basil's brain spun wildly for a moment and then came to rest upon a name—more than a name—upon a legend, a sign in the sky. What a day! He had never seen the young man before, but from a thousand pictures he knew beyond the possibility of a doubt that it was Ted Fay, the Yale football captain, who had almost single-handed beaten Harvard and Princeton last fall. Basil felt a sort of exquisite pain. The profile turned away; the crowd revolved; the hero disappeared. But Basil would know all through the next hours that Ted Fay was here too."

The narrator, Basil Duke Lee, later sees Fay leaving a theatre with Jerry, "a radiant little beauty of nineteen." He follows the couple to a hotel bar and eavesdrops on their conversation. To Basil's astonishment, Jerry rejects Ted—she is promised to another man, who gave her a part in his play.

"Basil got to his feet and hurried down the corridor, through the lobby and out of the hotel," Fitzgerald wrote. "He was in a state of wild emotional confusion. He did not understand all he had heard, but from his clandestine glimpse into the privacy of these two, with all the world that his short experience could conceive of at their feet, he had gathered that life for everybody was a struggle, sometimes magnificent from a distance, but always difficult and surprisingly simple and a little sad."

Coy was also mentioned by name in Fitzgerald's first novel, *This Side of Paradise* (1920). Himself a former college footballer, Fitzgerald acknowledged Ted Coy as one of his sporting idols in an autobiographical piece from 1924. And in "The Bowl," another short story from 1927, Fitzgerald writes about a football game from the fictional perspective of protagonist Jeff Deering, who reflects upon Ted's status as a hero frozen in time, his glory days long past.

***

"Business was in fact to be his future," Paul Wagner wrote of Coy's post-graduate career, as he had proved "an indifferent coach." Using his connections from the Skull and Bones, Coy established himself on Wall Street in finance and insurance, as well as writing sports articles for the *New York World*, the *Boston Globe*, and the *San Francisco Herald*. Coy's earnings were supplemented by a recent inheritance of $300,000 from his mother, and a home at 863 Park Avenue.

By the time of their August 1925 wedding, Coy had been living for several weeks at Mayapple Farm near Stamford, Connecticut in an attempt to elude the press and avoid the five-day waiting period for non-residents in obtaining marriage licenses. A license was granted on Wednesday afternoon, with the groom giving his age as thirty-seven. His bride claimed she was twenty-seven, four years shy of her probable age. The wedding took place that evening at the home of Mr. Reginald Venable. Better known as actress Fay Bainter, Mrs. Venable was Jeanne's close friend, and the couple lived in her guest cottage. The service was performed by the Reverend George Hamilton, Pastor of the North Stamford Congregational Church. Reginald acted as best man for Coy, and his mother, Theresa Venable, was Jeanne's attendant.

On August 27, the *Kansas City Star* quoted Jeanne's brother, Paul, "said the family had heard nothing of the wedding. He said he 'did not remember' whether his sister ever had mentioned Coy in her letters.'"

Julia heard the news by long distance telephone at her 535 Gladstone Boulevard home, the *Star* confirmed on August 28. Daughter Helen, who had lived with Jeanne for nearly a decade, broke the news. "I never have met Mr. Coy but Jeanne has told me much about him and I have no doubt that they will be very happy," Julia remarked. "Her marriage to Mr. Coy at the home of Fay Bainter does not surprise me at all," she added. "Fay and Jeanne have been the closest of friends for years." Julia expected Jeanne to visit her in Kansas City for a day or so before the mid-September opening of *Rain* in Chicago.

The small wedding party drove to Jeanne's Ossining home for a lavish reception. While sitting on the patio with Coy on August 29 (a day later), Jeanne spoke to a reporter from the Associated Press. "Retire from the stage?" she commented. "No—no, not just yet. Mr. Coy does want me to or rather he did. We've talked that over and over and now it's agreed that I shall continue in *Rain* at least for a while. We'll stay here until the show opens in Chicago. No, I don't suppose Mr. Coy will go with me. Wall Street keeps him pretty busy you know." This wasn't entirely true. On November 15, 1924, Coy had left his NYSE position at Davies, Thomas & Co, and accepted the title of vice-chairman of the National Town and Country Club.

The NTCC was an investment group formed by wealthy former college and professional athletes, to build a chain of luxury resort and golf courses in ten major cities across the Eastern United States, exploiting the sport's burgeoning popularity. For a sizable investment, a limited number of lifetime and VIP memberships were available. Alternatively, for an induction fee of $150, and annual dues of $50, middle-class members could "stay and play" at exclusive clubs in Long Island; with Manhattan lodgings in New York, Detroit, Cleveland, Chicago, New England, Florida, and Havana, Cuba. These were upscale venues, with the Lake Wales, Florida resort planned to have two eighteen-hole courses and a luxurious clubhouse. A polo field, bridle path, and yacht club surrounded the twenty-six lakes situated on 420 acres. Coy had been elected onto the board of the New York Chapter of the NTCC, a job that mostly entailed attending meetings at the Harvard or University Clubs, and voting on whether to spend $5 million dollars on a twenty-six-story clubhouse at Lexington Avenue and Forty-Eighth Street.

The bulk of Mr. Coy's money had gone to the first Mrs. Coy, and for better or worse, Jeanne was now the family breadwinner. Ted wanted to be her manager, so that people wouldn't think she was supporting him. She refused, telling him, "It would come to the same thing. Don't kid yourself. Besides, nobody is ever going to manage me but myself."

She kept Coy's financial worries well hidden from the press. At a party thrown by Noel Coward—among guests including Ethel Barrymore and Lynn Fontanne—Jeanne was spotted "wearing a pink chiffon frock with two ropes of exquisite cut crystals—a gift from her husband," the *New York Tribune*'s fashion columnist learned from Jeanne.

***

Kathryne Kennedy, who had played a native girl in the original cast, as well as being Jeanne's understudy, was forced to leave the show due to ongoing issues with tuberculosis. On September 1, Wilma Thompson was hired as the new stand-in. A small-town Iowa girl, Thompson told the *Los Angeles Times* in 1931 that Jeanne had personally coached her to mimic the husky quality of Sadie's voice. "Miss Eagels was always kind and considerate to me," she recalled, "and made it her personal duty to help me become, I hope, proficient in the part. Her fine qualities, to my way of thinking, far overshadow anything which may be said or written against her. She was exceedingly temperamental at times, too much so I suppose for her ultimate good, but the assistance and inspiration she gave those who worked with her will always be a fine memory."

In a 1936 interview with *Silver Screen*'s Elizabeth Wilson, actress Claudette Colbert revealed that Jeanne had given her career a boost in 1925, when Colbert (then twenty-two) was cast in A.H. Woods' *A Kiss in the Taxi*. Jeanne sat beside Woods during the dress rehearsal, and when he told her that he was going to fire Colbert that night, she replied, "Al, don't be a fool, that girl is going to be a hit." Jeanne's prediction came true: after signing to Paramount Pictures in 1928, Colbert went on to enjoy one of the most successful careers in Hollywood history.

Jeanne also advised Ruth Gordon when she and Zoë Akins attended a pre-Broadway try-out of Ruth's new play, *The Fall of Eve*, in Stamford, Connecticut in early August. After the show, Jeanne mentioned a scene with co-star Cora Witherspoon. "Your character can be awfully unsympathetic but she doesn't need to be," Jeanne said. "The key is to listen. Listen to Cora Witherspoon tell you what to do. Listen hard."

"I thought I *did* listen to her," Ruth protested.

"You do, but the way you're doing it, you listen and make it your idea," Jeanne replied. "That makes you as big a cheat as Cora. You do it as if you could have thought of that yourself."

"And how should I?" Ruth asked.

"Well, first thing, do it as though you're pretty," Jeanne told her. "Not a battle-ax like Cora. Act as if you're terribly pretty and trying to remember what homely Cora said. And after she says it, don't be too sure what she meant. The audience will laugh and adore you."

***

Rain opened on October 5 at the Samuel H. Harris Theatre in Chicago, settling in for a four-month run. It was stipulated that there would be no Sunday performances, allowing Jeanne at least one day off. She was beginning to crave distance from her grueling role. Coy accompanied her to Chicago, and *Variety* remarked "that while she loved her art she loved her Ted even more, and that if he hadn't agreed to come to Chicago she would have called it all off."

"This is, at midnight or any other time, no better way to open a report on Miss Jeanne Eagels in *Rain* than to urge attendance thereon," the *Chicago Tribune*'s theatre critic declared. "Most persons who go much to or read much of the theatre know a deal about the play (which is a good play) and about Miss Eagels' acting (which is a matter to see, to laud, and long to remember when you are thinking back over your adventures in the drama) . . . Explicitly and implicitly, Miss Eagels is all there is for Sadie Thompson to be in this capital theatre-piece. I have but woolly remembrance for her previous activities in the drama; and I shall never forget her in this."

Shortly after the opening, Coy returned to the farm and his duties with the NTCC. Less than three months into the marriage, Jeanne realized her mistake. She had hoped that Coy would be able to tame her wild temperament and bring her some much-needed stability. Instead, she found a doting lover who allowed her to dominate the relationship. Nonetheless, Coy did help to keep her personal affairs in order—sorting through her correspondence, making sure bills were paid on time, and collecting monies owed. He also oversaw the daily expenses of the Yorktown estate. Jeanne's brother, George, was now her caretaker; and with a housekeeper, cook, and other staff, monthly expenses were high. Not to mention her life insurance payments, house payments and money to her mother and siblings.

A story told by Mabelle Webb illustrates Jeanne's careless attitude towards her material possessions. Mrs. Webb had found a diamond and emerald necklace belonging to Jeanne, left behind after a visit to the Webbs' Port Washington, Long Island home. Concerned it would be stolen, Mabelle begged her young friend to take it back. 'If you get robbed, that's my tough luck," Jeanne laughed. "I'll just have to buy me another." In fact, the insurance company had already refused to insure her jewels.

Even while on the road, Jeanne didn't forget her charitable duties, both good for the soul and publicity for the play. On November 28, the *Chicago Tribune* featured a photograph of Jeanne holding a *paper-mache* dog named Hokum, to be auctioned that night at a fundraiser for the Red, White, and Blue Club. Several other items would be auctioned off by Jeanne in the ballroom of the new Hotel Sherman. Dancing, mahjong, and bridge would be played amid 3,000 balloons, and other elaborate decorations. Seventeen Chicago-based performers would mingle among the guests.

Jeanne appeared in the *Tribune*'s December 5 issue, a group shot of Jeanne, Grace Moore, Judith Anderson, and several other actresses gathered around a table and looking over the souvenir programs they would sell during the National Horse Show at the Chicago Riding Club. Jeanne also threw a party for the cast of the musical, *Kid Boots*, which was touring concurrently. The party went off with a bang, and the guests made plans to spend Christmas together.

On December 22, Frank A. Munsey—the newspaper baron whose affair with the first Mrs. Coy had been an open secret—died a bachelor, aged seventy-one. "The man she wanted did not marry her," George Holland told Doherty, despite Sophie having recently redecorated Munsey's Long Island mansion in preparation of becoming its mistress. From an estate valued at $66,000,000, he left his lover with just "a few thousand dollars." But the former Mrs. Coy would soon rise from the ashes, marrying New York financier Horatio Shonnard in June 1929. The couple purchased and restored the Harrietta Plantation near Georgetown, South Carolina, and kept another residence on the upper East Side of Manhattan. They would divorce in 1944 with Sophie not contesting Shonnard's charge of "mental cruelty." Shonnard died two years later but Sophie would survive until 1980, finally returning to her hometown of Savannah, Georgia.

"... A moment later the sound of a crashing of furniture is heard; the phonograph...suddenly ceases its strident tune; there is shouting and muffled cursing, above which the Rev. Davidson's voice is heard yelling: "Scarlet woman!" ... the doors are burst open and the missionary is pushed violently into the room and falls in a heap on the floor. "There," shouts O'Hara, towering over him—"if you know what is good for you, get out and stay out."

"Sadie Thompson—you are an evil woman—you have come here only to carry your infamy to other places—you are a harlot out of Iweili!"

O'Hara: "All right; I'll tell the boys to bring your things back. If you and me never see each other again I want to say this: I'll never forget you—ever. Sadie—Good-bye.

Sadie: "I guess I'm sorry for everybody in the world." (O'Hara crosses and stands by Sadie's side. She turns her face toward him.) "Life is a quaint present from somebody—there's no doubt about that. (Little sob works its way into her voice.) It'll be much easier in Sydney."

Mr. and Mrs. Edward Harris Coy meet the press outside Eagels' Ossining home the day after their surprise wedding.

Jeanne poses with bulldog in Chicago (1925.) Top right – Publicizing Coy's golf resort venture, Los Angeles (1926.) Bottom – Aladdin's Birthday Gala advertisement.

Chapter 10
Passion of the Heart:
January–December 1926

In the first month of 1926, Mrs. Coy was hard at work. After a final week at the Harris Theatre, grossing $20,000, *Rain* opened at Boston's New Park Theatre on February 1. "Her portraiture is mastery in every detail, in voice, gesture, bearing, and facial expression, all is absolute realism," the next morning's *Boston Daily Globe* read. "... She reveals splendid emotional powers in the several scenes where Sadie denounces the missionary with impassioned fury, and there is real pathos in the girl's final surrender to his ceaselessly beating arguments. Her ready utterance of racy slang is as natural as it is amusing. It must be recorded that, in respect to the supposed sensibilities of Boston audiences, Sadie's profanity is much less fluent than when the play was given in New York."

***

"I am a book-worm you know," Jeanne revealed, in an interview given at the theatre on February 7. "My hunger for novels that teach you something about life is insatiable, and coupled with my love of reading is a passion for studying the characters of people I meet and analyzing them. I took up psychology seriously some years ago and delved into it. I found it a godsend to me in my work. You get to know why people do things, what motivates them, and without that knowledge you cannot understand character."

"When I began to study Sadie I applied all the psychology I knew to her," she explained. "She is a composite type of a girl of the half-world. I adore Sadie as an acting role, but I revolt against her as a woman. Sadie has nothing in common with me personally, but at the same time I understand her thoroughly. You meet girls of her type in the life of the hotels, the Broadway restaurants, in Europe, on the ocean liners, everywhere these days. But to understand them you have to understand their psychology."

"Was Sadie ever in love?" Jeanne mused. "Of course that depends upon what you call 'love.' Pure love, the love of the idealist and romanticist is absolutely unknown to a woman of Sadie's type. If a woman like Sadie really should love like that the very awakening to it would kill her, I think. She could not stand the shock. I think Sadie has a glimmer of this means in the feeling that the missionary finally awakens within her, but she is too far gone to grasp it fully, to allow it to possess her completely. Sadie's moral sense has been deadened by the life she had led to permit spiritual love to dominate her. She has been too seared by the passion of the heart in the men she has met. Sadie might have loved Sergeant O'Hara truly, and as it is I think she feels a good wholesome affection for him."

***

Jeanne spoke with George Brinton Beal of the *Boston Post*, who described the encounter shortly after her death. "Meeting Miss Eagels for the first time, one noticed her lightning energy," he remembered. "Nothing was placid about her. If she was sitting, she leaned and gestured. If standing, she walked, took dancing steps, whirled around. She talked rapidly, her ideas running ahead faster than her speech. Eyes snapped, voice thrilled, seizing the attention. Her voice had a range as wide as an opera singer's. When slightly excited it went to a high, almost hysterical note. It could descend as deep as a man's voice. It bubbled and rippled."

"Jeanne Eagels' natural speaking voice is anything but heavy, it is an extremely pleasant, well-modulated voice, delightful to hear," a *Boston Globe* reporter noted after a lengthy interview at the Hotel Victoria on March 21. "And Miss Eagels herself, when seen in her own parlor, is an amazingly attractive young woman, younger than most people seem to think she is. She is distinctly pretty, and more than pretty, for there is intelligence, strength of character and kindness in her face. Her eye framed with dark, unusual eyebrows, are of a penetrating dark blue, while her lovely gold hair, which she wears almost literally down her back when at home—just held in place with a pink ribbon—is really beautiful."

Jeanne explained how she made full use of her vocal range. "I've always learned from failures," she said, "and I'll never forget how in a melodrama of the sea, called *The Night Watch*, I learned the full power of my own voice. In a scene of wild confusion on a ship's deck, with dozens of male voices yelling, I had to top the whole scene with words, 'It's a lie!' I did too, over some of the most carrying men's voices on the stage. And I weighed just ninety-six at that time.

"The answer is in the way I breathe, although I don't think I realized that until Caruso, who came behind at a stage reception when I was playing *Daddies*, was introduced to me and told me that he had observed that I breathed in exactly the same way that he did, very deeply, as a singer should."

"Now I can't sing, for I've studied and know I can't, but that habit of deep breathing enables me to place my voice as I wish, to make it tremendously powerful when the need arises, and still not strain the vocal cords at all. In Sadie for instance, I simply use own heavy voice and I can on forever without tiring myself. It's a good trick to know."

Jeanne also revealed that she had been receiving hate mail since her arrival in Boston. These insulting letters hurt and offended her deeply. "I am not Sadie Thompson. I am Jeanne Eagels," she said. "Why do men write me such things . . . and here in Boston, where I thought they would understand, here it has been the worst of all the places I have ever played. I am not Sadie Thompson and they won't believe me. They expect me to drag them into the nearest alley and kill them." When asked why, she replied, "Perhaps I am the resurrection and the life of their eternal fear of the discovery of their own misdeeds. But I am not like that. You can see that can't you?"

"I do love Sadie, and I must say that I consider her a pretty practical little Christian. And what a game little sport, too. Why, there wasn't anything that girl wouldn't do for you. The play itself, to my mind, is a mighty eloquent plea against intolerance in every form—and intolerance to me is always a vicious thing."

No longer content with choosing from the scripts offered to her, Jeanne hoped to play roles of her own choosing in future. "I want to create something new and I have two characters in mind now I am dying to play—if only someone would write a suitable play around them," she explained. "One of these is the immortal Emma, Lady Hamilton, as whom a wonderful portrait of me was painted several years ago."

"The other is—O, a queer little character whom I am almost anxious to portray upon the stage. But so far I haven't succeeded in getting the play I want based upon either. It is a curious thing that no one has ever yet—to my knowledge—written a real play on the love affair of Lady Hamilton and Nelson. I have studied everything I can get hold of regarding Emma Hamilton's life—but the trouble is that I can't write a play!"

"I've decided that I must have a new play next year, for I feel it unwise, much as I still love Sadie, to go on for a fifth season with the same part. I'm going to take her to California when we leave Boston Stopping *en route* at a few cities in the Northwest Butte, Montana, Spokane and places like that. I'm thrilled as a kid at playing on the coast, for I've never been further west than Denver."

Jeanne's former beau, Arthur Fiedler, was now almost as celebrated in

Boston as she was in New York. Their affair had cooled considerably by the time she met Ted, and since then, they had very little contact. Arthur was also troubled by the changes that fame had wrought upon her. "... Eagels had snatched at every opportunity to ascend ... and found the pressures too much to bear with equilibrium," Robin Moore wrote in his biography of Fiedler. "She began to drink immoderately ... became more and more mercurial in behaviour, at times arrogant, capable of towering fury one moment and angelic contrition the next. More and more she isolated herself for days, to emerge either drawn and distant or supercharged and ready for release. Rumors spread that she was resorting to narcotics."

Reluctant to discuss "that lovely, unfortunate girl," Fiedler told Moore about one of their last meetings. "I visited her at her apartment. Everything seemed somber and gloomy. The heavy drapes were drawn. No daylight could penetrate. Her large, oval shaped bed was covered with a black silk spread, almost like a bier. I could tell she had not been out in the fresh air for days. I suggested a walk in Central Park. I noticed a considerable change: it wasn't anything like it once had been: she used to be so gay, so alive. Now she was rather withdrawn, melancholy. There seemed to be an aura of despair about her. I think I managed to cheer her a little that day, but it left me with a strange feeling."

***

In the second week of March, Jeanne was taken ill. Wilma Thompson went on in her place, but by March 15, she was back at work. On April 7, she joined several prominent actors currently performing in the Boston area—including Judith Anderson, Holbrook Blinn, and Peg Entwhistle—at the Theatrical Press Representatives of America fundraiser. Held at the Copley-Plaza Ballroom, proceeds were to be split by the Press Agents' Association Sick Fund, and the Actors Fund. The event lasted from 9 p.m. until 2 a.m., allowing Jeanne's participation after *Rain*'s final curtain.

Eleven days later, the *New York Times* reported that Jeanne's husband had been arrested in Manhattan on April 14. At 5 a.m. Patrolman Nicholas Scolard found Coy at the intersection of Eighty-Seventh Street and Columbus Avenue. An intoxicated Mister Eagels was caught up in a noisy altercation with a taxi cab driver and his passenger. When the former football hero refused to move along, Scolard arrested him.

Coy appeared before Magistrate George W. Simpson the next day. When asked to tell the court his side of the story by his lawyer Morgan J. O'Brien, the defendant answered: "I was standing near the taxi cab when someone I didn't know asked me to get into the back of the cab. Not knowing what motive they had behind the invitation or what lay wait for me once inside, so I struck the man." As to Patrolman Scolard's assertion that he was intoxicated and boisterous, Coy denied being under the influence of alcohol. Furthermore, his client could not have made much noise, O'Brien argued, considering he was suffering from a case of laryngitis. In dismissing the charges, Simpson told Coy he didn't blame him in the least for his actions.

Four days later, extended tour dates for *Rain* were announced. The new schedule would commence on April 26 in Detroit, traveling across the Plains states before reaching Seattle. *Rain* would then journey down the Northwest coast to San Francisco, finishing in Los Angeles. Jeanne would return to New York City before Labor Day, and begin rehearsing her next show, *The Half-Way Girl*. It would be directed by *Rain*'s Sam Forrest, and was set for an out-of-town opening on October 11, reaching Broadway in the late fall. Although *The Half-Way Girl* never made it to Broadway, it had been filmed in 1925, with a storyline rather similar to *Rain*. Doris Kenyon played Poppy LaRue, an actress stranded in Singapore's red-light district who falls in love with an Englishman accused of murder.

During the day while in Detroit, Jeanne visited the courthouse to watch celebrated attorney Clarence Darrow representing Ossian Sweet, an African-American doctor accused of killing a white man during a racist attack on his home by an angry mob. It was one of the most contentious trials of the era, and Jeanne made a powerful statement for civil rights as she sat with Darrow's wife Ruby, and the two women watched the skilled attorney argue and finally win a "not guilty" verdict for Mr. Sweet.[14]

The week of May 3 found Jeanne at the Ford Theatre in Baltimore, Maryland and the following week at Minneapolis' Metropolitan Theatre, where the show grossed $20,000. On May 17 she began a grueling four-day run of one-night stands in Montana, passing through the Babcock Theatre, Billings; Butte; the Marlowe Theatre, Helena; and Missoula. Next came Spokane, Seattle, and Tacoma, Washington; and the company then crossed the Columbia River into Portland, Oregon.

***

In town for her three-day run of *Rain* at the Masonic Temple, Jeanne gave an interview to Ray Budwin of the *Spokane Daily Chronicle* on May 21, while taking a short break in her suite at the Davenport Hotel.

"Life is purpose and the grave is not the goal—for there should be no goal for one who would create rather than repeat the achievements of scores of others. The perfect happiness long sought by the Greeks throughout the ages was never more apparent a part of one's existence than it is today. We were made to be happy and though the future is what we make it, the present is our everything. So it is that I am happy, happy beyond all words."

"Sadie Thompson is a beautiful character. She is not an adventuress, as so many maintain who have seen the presentation. Rather she is one minus the opportunities of learning and a woman strangely misunderstood. Her problems are our problems. Therefore we should not judge, but learn from her the true meaning of intolerance. In her I have found new things of life, a new being, a new creation."

Hundreds were turned away at the box office during a two-week run at San Francisco's Columbia Theatre. Nonetheless, the box office gross exceeded $30,000. Plans for San Diego were quickly canceled, and a

---

14 Ossian Sweet (1895-1960) was born, raised, and eventually buried in Bartow, Florida, the same hometown as *Revealed* author Eric Woodard.

return booking was scheduled to follow the company's three-week stay at Los Angeles' Biltmore Theatre.

Comparing Sadie Thompson to the great courtesans of Europe, Jeanne remarked that such women were celebrated chiefly for their romantic adventures, rather than their strength and intelligence. During *Rain*'s long tour, she had learned that America was still, at heart, a Puritanical nation—as columnist Dorothy Kilgallen would recall while compiling anecdotes about Hollywood's past in 1948. "Jeanne Eagels arrived in California, extended a cool limp hand to the interviewers who had come to write about her 'nimbus of blonde hair' and cried impatiently: 'Sometimes I think Americans are interested in nothing except morals. They don't ask, is she brilliant, charming, clever—but is she respectable? When they think of Madame DuBarry or Pompadour, all they can think of is that they were Kings' mistresses. The fact that they were extraordinary women who practically ruled a country makes no impression on their minds. I tell you I have known several such women. I have found them remarkable. I was at an entertainment not long ago at which one of these women was hostess. She charmed the entire gathering of five hundred people by her wit and graciousness. Respectable! Will Americans ever grow up?'"

The *Kansas City Star*'s Monroe Lathrop reported from Hollywood on June 18: "Motion picture producers are said to be lined up at the little red brick Los Angeles railroad station . . . in the hope that they may ensnare Jeanne Eagels when she arrives for her first visit to the camera coast . . . The movies have already shown a willingness to toy with the dirty Palm Beach suit school of drama which had a recent vogue on the stage," he observed, citing the successful adaptations of plays such as *White Cargo*, *Kongo*, and *Aloma of the South Seas* (starring Gilda Grey) for the silver screen. "This is believed to be the logical time to bring forth a film version of *Rain*, and there is no denying that Miss Eagels' name would be a valuable one to put up in electric lights over the theaters that will show the picture." Lathrop signed off with a note of warning: "It is doubtful if the star will be offered more than a one-picture contract, however, since she is famous for but the one stage interpretation and is not a promising screen type. The camera has its own requirements as has been proved several times. Lenore Ulric, whose *Tiger Rose* was a startling affair on the stage, was [a] worse than indifferent success when she attempted the same role on the screen."

Shortly before the opening, the *Los Angeles Times* secured an interview with Jeanne.

"The play itself is unchanged," she said, reflecting on its long tenure. "Not a line, a situation or a sequence has been altered, but Sadie is surer of herself, physically and spiritually ... There's a fleck of feminine weakness left in the girl, and the saving sense of humor clings to her still, but she is the captain of her soul, the master of her fate, for all that ... We all have to write the last act of our lives or a play. Sadie is outward bound, under sealed orders. Maybe she marries her marine and goes to Australia. If nothing intervenes—but something always seems to intervene in Sadie Thompson's career."

Located on Pershing Square until its demolition in 1964, the Biltmore Theatre stood conveniently next door to the hotel bearing the same name. For a week or so after the June 21 opening, Jeanne stayed there with the company, but by month's end, she had relocated to the secluded Beverly Hills Hotel. *Los Angeles Times* reporter Alma Whitaker spoke with her in one of the hotel's bungalows. She found Jeanne "very slim and youthful looking, very blonde. And wondrous blue eyes that look right into one's own and challenge one."

Jeanne's attention was focused on the Hays Code, which had brought censorship to movies. "Mr. Will Hays is a most incredible person," Jeanne told Alma Whitaker, "because he thinks *Rain* is an immoral play. Ministers, censors, reformers galore have seen the play—coming to censor and to ban and leaving to admire and approve." Hays remained adamant in his refusal to allow a film to be made. Upon asking Jeanne if she would enter a career in the film industry, Whitaker discovered that "she scorns pictures with a frank disgust. She cannot imagine herself ever so 'prostituting' her 'art' as to enter that branch of the profession."

Among other things, Whitaker learned that Jeanne's three brothers—none of whom were employed in the entertainment industry—had been more impressed by Ted Coy's football career than her stage accomplishments.

"Wants to become a great stage director," Whitaker noted. "Has overseen her current production and secured replacement actors for the missionaries and the doctor. Doesn't go to shows, stage or screen very often: 'I don't like seeing other people's work.'"

***

The *Los Angeles Times* review of *Rain* delineated the opening scene: "The set 'alone' is revealed, the lobby for Joe Horn's Hotel and General Store. One side opens up to a wide veranda which in turn brings a vista of waving palms against a tropical sky." Shortly after the curtain rose, a downpour of rain began, persisting through three acts. The *Times* critic marveled at "theatrical effects that would make David Belasco green with envy." The amount of "rain" used for each performance was an astonishing 5,000 gallons, with twice that on matinee days.

The night after *Rain*'s premiere, the newly renovated Hollywood Bowl welcomed an audience of 20,000 guests, some of whom were unable to get tickets to Jeanne's performance at the theatre. "A brilliant opening Monday night at the Biltmore," the *Times* raved. "Jeanne Eagels was given an ovation that must have symbolized today some of the warmth of Southern California sunshine . . . If there was one mistake that Miss Eagels made during the performance, it was not stepping out of the character, even for a moment, during the curtain calls; to give a warm, responsive audience a glimpse of herself. She remained in character, unfortunately to the extent of affectation in making her bows."

In a probable attempt to revive Coy's dwindling golf resort plans, Eagels posed for photographers swinging a golf club in Los Angeles which was later labeled as Del Monte while *Variety* told of her "three-acre purchase at Pebble Beach near Monterey and her announcement to build a pretentious home for her to use between seasons."

The play proved so popular that three weeks turned into five. On July 21, *Variety* reported that in its fourth week at the Biltmore, Rain had accrued $18,000. Plans for San Diego were again canceled so that Jeanne could appear at San Francisco's Columbia Theatre beginning August 16. In mid-July she seized the opportunity to explore California, as she had never visited before. She traveled to Santa Barbara to visit friends, sometimes staying long enough to miss the evening curtain. After the theatre managers were notified of her absence, Wilma Thompson took to the stage. But when the audience saw her replacement, a mass exodus occurred—with 75% of customers asking for a refund. The affair was hushed up by the Los Angeles dailies, probably at the request of the management as *Variety* speculated on July 14.

Unknown to her fans, Jeanne had suffered a personal tragedy—the death of her brother, Leo at the age of twenty-seven. Not much is known about his fortunes in the eight years since the siblings had lived together, but it seems likely he had been drawn back into the criminal underworld. The *Kansas City Star* reported his passing on the evening of July 14 at the family home on 3023 Wayne Avenue, but he had actually died on the afternoon of July 13—at the State Penitentiary in Jefferson City, Missouri. His death certificate listed the cause as kidney failure, with cerebral hemorrhage as a contributory factor.

How mighty the city's respect for Julia Eagles, or its love for a hometown girl must have been for the local press to cover up the true circumstances of Leo's death.[15] The *Star*'s afternoon edition reported on July 15 that funeral services would be held at the family home the next day at 8:30 a.m. with a nine o'clock memorial at St. Vincent's the same church as his father Edward, with the burial at Calvary Cemetery.

***

---

15 The *Kansas City Star* protected the reputation of its favorite hometown girl. One newspaper archive has her name appearing in the *Kansas City Star* nearly 300 times in articles and advertisements from 1913 until her death, and this is surely not a complete list by far.

On July 28, it was announced that Jeanne's next role would be in *The Garden of Eden*. This was confirmed a month later by producer Arch Selwyn, in the hope of a November premiere on Broadway. A risqué comedy set in Paris, *The Garden of Eden* had been a success in London for Tallulah Bankhead. Adapted by Avery Hopwood from a German play, *Eden* opened with Miriam Hopkins taking Jeanne's place at the Savoy Theatre in September 1927, folding after just twenty-three performances.

While Jeanne was appearing onstage in the city by the bay, an advertisement appeared in the August 26th edition of the *San Francisco Chronicle* in which she was listed to appear along several friends and former co-stars in celebrating a birthday party at the Sutter Street Aladdin Studio Tiffin Room. Owned by sisters Harriet and Minnie Mooser, the Chinese restaurant was decorated with paper lanterns, dragon murals and an elaborate pagoda in the lobby. Young girls from nearby Chinatown were hired as servers. Popular with the locals during the day for afternoon tea and cakes, the theatre crowd enjoyed its late-night dinners, which for this special occasion was $2 including cover charge.

Billed as a "Night of Nights of Gaiety", the event's two masters of ceremonies were Julian Eltinge (Jeanne's leading man from *The Crinoline Girl*) and Harold Healy, who played Corporal Hodgeson in *Rain* both on Broadway and the tour. The roster of honored guests included actor William Desmond (then known as the "King of Silent Serials", he would amass more than two hundred film credits in thirty-three years); actor/producer Henry Duffy and his future wife, singer Dale Winter; and most interestingly Isabel Withers, a minor Broadway actress who would in less than three months star to great acclaim as Sadie Thompson in a version of *Rain* to premiere in November at the Orpheum Theatre, where she came closer than most to matching Jeanne's success in the role. In some ways, she had walked the same path as Eagels.

Six years younger than Jeanne, Withers moved to Kansas City as a child where she attended both public and dramatic schools before joining a tent show circuit company. She and Jeanne probably had much to talk about, and Jeanne may even have overcome her possessive attitude towards Sadie to offer advice and encouragement. Withers would later go on to appear in nearly a hundred film and television shows during her 30-year career.

After two weeks in San Francisco, *Rain* moved to Utah for three days. By now, Jeanne was weary of fielding questions about her personal life. "It is a matter of opinion I suppose," she told the *Salt Lake Tribune*, "but I don't think the public cares whether my hair is bobbed or my skirts are short or not, and that seems to be the chief subject of most interviews. If I told you I liked dogs and horses it would sound about as sincere as some of the other things we read about, so I must say I don't care much about them. After all, it is 'Sadie Thompson' folks came to see."

On opening night, the curtain rose an hour late at nine and with no orchestra. Despite these setbacks, the *Desert News* reported, "The play was thoroughly enjoyed by a capacity house which was loath to leave when the final curtain was drawn." As for Jeanne's performance, "No stronger portrayal of an exacting role has been seen in Salt Lake City for many a day." Years later, Alice Pardoe West recalled for the *Ogden Standard Examiner*, "She put so much in the second act that she fainted at the close of the curtain and had to be revived to go on with the third act. We were told that this happened in every performance of the strenuous role."

Rain returned to New York on October 11 for a two-week stay at the Century Theatre. "Miss Eagels is still little short of magnificent as the harassed Sadie Thompson," the *New York Times* noted, adding that the size of the auditorium made the performance a "little diffused and scattered, and some of the lines were inaudible." *Billboard* noticed that audience reactions had changed. "The house, from second gallery to front orchestra stall, broke into guffaws every now and then at moments in the play that were taken most seriously when offered four years ago," the critic commented. "It would seem that the New York public had grown more sophisticated, that it had become more discriminating of its realistic drama."

Jeanne's regular stand-in, Wilma Thompson, was forced to go on the latter half of the second week due to the leading lady being "indisposed." *Variety*'s October 27 issue began the story on their front page and continued it inside of how regarding a party given on Sunday the 17th at her Ossining Estate. "There was no celebration but the star is reported having become highly excited." according to *Variety*, "Miss Eagels is said to have ordered everybody from the house about seven in the morning when it was teeming rain." Coy and a few of her family members refused to obey her orders, so "Miss Eagels jumped into her car and came to New York, repairing to the Algonquin. There Coy later joined her." The trade publication also mentioned how each day, Julia Eagels would call Sam Harris' office insisting that Jeanne would show up at the theatre that night (which, of course, she did not.) Goodman Ace took this opportunity to run a photograph of the *Variety* article in an evening edition of the *Kansas City Post* with the comment, "Surely not our Jeanne." Ace's ego must have still been bruised after the actress had him ejected from the Shubert Theatre during her Kansas City run the previous summer.

Bringing the journey full-circle, *Rain* moved to Philadelphia for a final two weeks on October 25. Jeanne's stand-in, Wilma Thompson wrote home to her parents when she again replaced the star, this time for a few days in the City of Brotherly Love, a fact which her Buffalo City, Iowa hometown newspaper deemed fit to print.

Then, the *Rain* stopped, at least for Jeanne. She had played Sadie for 174 weeks, giving a total of 1,392 performances enjoyed by almost three million people in 164 cities and towns. With gross receipts of $3.23 million, the authors received $323,000 in royalties, with fifty percent going to Maugham, and the remainder divided equally between Colton and Randolph. They went through fourteen live monkeys, fourteen changes of military uniforms, nine green and white parasols, 120 records of "Wabash Blues", 250 palm-leaf hand fans for Rapley Holmes, and enough water to float a battleship or two. Jeanne's starting salary of $350 had risen to $3,500 per week, with an additional percentage of box office profits.

She would now be eternally identified with Sadie Thompson. Amelia Eugenia Eagles from Kansas City, Missouri had realized her dream.

"While you know that the play was my 'thought wish' out of Maugham, not everyone does," John Colton had written to Jeanne during *Rain*'s long tour. "But everyone does know the beautiful and unearthly genius of Jeanne Eagels which gave a thousand new dimensions to a character which a base touch could so easily make half-caste and common-place—perhaps even tawdry. *Camille* was what they called 'actor-proof' until they saw Bernhardt, and *Rain*, to my sorrow and frustration, seems only to be able to tickle the ears of the groundlings unless you play it. It's too bad. You made it too great. It can be no one else's."

***

On November 15, Jeanne rented the 555 Madison Avenue apartment of Raydona Kuba, a Parisian acquaintance, in preparation for her next production with Sam Harris. For a ten-month lease, she was to pay a total of $3,150. She moved in with her husband, their Pekingese, and a parrot she had taught to curse. That night, she and Coy attended the premiere of *A Proud Woman*.

In the November issue of *Picture Play* magazine, Lillian Gish—perhaps the finest screen actress of the silent era—was asked if she had ever considered playing against type as a 'bad girl' like Sadie Thompson in *Rain*. "That is a marvelous character," Lillian replied. "Dorothy [her sister] would just love to play her. But I can't imagine any one playing her better than Jeanne Eagels."

Finally free to enjoy married life, the Coys attended a Thanksgiving dinner and dance on November 26. It was a coming-out ball for debutante Florence Kip Clarke, held at the family home on 998 Fifth Avenue. The *New York Tribune*'s fashion columnist, Betsy Schuyler, noted that Jeanne wore her "golden hair pulled back plainly from her very lovely brow and held in place at the nape of the neck with a jeweled comb of antique gold."

Three nights later, the couple revisited the Maxine Elliott Theatre and watched Jeanne's old friend, Ethel Barrymore, in her first performance as Maugham's *Constant Wife*.

Having repeatedly expressed her desire to escape typecasting, it seems strange that Jeanne would have even considered playing Roxie Hart in *Chicago*, a character who had plenty of moxie but none of Sadie Thompson's genuine warmth. Written by former *Chicago Tribune* court reporter Maurine Watkins, *Chicago* was an inside-out look at a front-page murder trial, from crime to acquittal. Roxie Hart is a hard-boiled Southside Chicago hussy who shoots her lover in the back. With everyone from the district attorney to Roxie's lawyer angling for publicity, her smallest word is reported to the press until she becomes old news, languishing in jail as she awaits trial. Announcing that she's pregnant, Roxie is again the *crime du jour*, and a tear-jerking trial appearance secures her freedom. On her way to a career in Vaudeville, Roxie is photographed next to a woman being escorted into court for a near-identical crime.

On November 30, newspapers reported the addition of Charles Bickford and Edward Ellis to the cast of *Chicago*, currently in rehearsal with Sam Forrest, Jeanne's director from *Rain*. Her former understudy, Wilma Thompson, would play a reporter. As Forrest later told Eddie Doherty, Jeanne insisted on playing Roxie Hart "straight," while he favored "burlesque." The play was scheduled to open in Washington D.C. the following week. By then, however, Forrest had left the project and George Abbott took his place.

Abbott had first worked with Jeanne in 1918, playing bachelor Henry Allen in *Daddies*. Like Jeanne, Abbott had gone on to greater things, establishing himself as a playwright with *The Fall Guy* (1925.) A year later, he scored a smash hit with *Broadway*, a hard-boiled exposé of New York's criminal world under Prohibition, which he also directed. Abbott had acquired a reputation as a "show doctor," with a knack for turning around troubled productions.

"Sam Harris sent for me, and when I arrived at his office I learned that

Jeanne Eagels had asked him to get me as her next director," Abbott wrote in his 1963 memoir. "Mr. Harris told me frankly that another director had at first been assigned by him to do *Chicago* but that Jeanne had asked for me. I was delighted."

"During rehearsals Jeanne was more nervous and high-strung than I had remembered her," Abbott reflected. "She was taut and wary; I felt as though I was dealing with some unpredictable wild animal. But she was a great actress, and in contrast to some of our great actresses who have to mumble their words for a week or so to get the feel of the role, she was able to show her talent on the first day of rehearsal."

However, Abbott was dismayed by Jeanne's chronic tardiness. He broached the subject over lunch one day, and she told him that a man had been following her car that morning, forcing her to walk to the theatre. When Abbott explained that "I can't very well ask the others to come on time if you don't," she looked at him blankly. "Why not?"

"Jeanne had a man-servant called Tony, a big heavy man with a little piping voice who was sort of a bodyguard," Abbott recalled. Tony told him about Jeanne's rambunctious life with Ted Coy. Jeanne, Abbott learned, liked "to see him box with their house guests. She took sadistic pleasure in seeing Ted beat up others. One day she thought she'd like to see Tony given the business; she insisted that he put the gloves on with Ted Coy. Tony didn't want to lose his job, so he played it very cozy and tried to box a defensive game; finally, however, he was stung by a blow which made him lash out, and he knocked Coy to the floor."

Unfortunately, Tony's pugilistic skills were no match for Jeanne. "When I asked Tony if he could help me get Jeanne to work on time, he became evasive," Abbott remembered. "When Monday came we received word that Miss Eagels was sick. She was indeed, and she never returned to the cast."

Chicago was rescheduled to open on December 20 at the Apollo Theatre in Atlantic City, but this didn't appease Jeanne. On December 12, she withdrew from the project and headed for her house in Ossining, refusing all comment. It later emerged that she was dissatisfied with the original cast and had every one of them replaced. She then attempted to do the same thing with the second cast. Sam Harris ended up talking her out of the role and began the search for another actress.

Harris' office was now scrambling to locate an actress to replace Jeanne and settled upon Francine Larrimore. Currently appearing in Noel Coward's *This Was a Man*, Francine had been treading the boards for several years but had yet to find a role that matched her talents. Fortunately for Harris, *This Was a Man* was scheduled to close the Saturday night before the Monday premiere of *Chicago*. For ten days, Francine performed in one role while rehearsing the other. Originally tailored for Jeanne, Roxie was now rewritten for Francine.

Chicago opened on schedule—and to acclaim—in Atlantic City, before moving on to New Haven, Connecticut. The play's foul language aroused indignation and calls for censorship from some patrons. Turning the controversy to his advantage, Harris closed the play in New Haven three days early and moved the play to the Music Box Theatre on December 30. "On the night of the opening, Eagels was in an aisle seat on the second row, attired in a striking white coat," George Brinton Beal wrote in the *Boston Post*. "When Miss Larrimore made her first entrance, Miss Eagels arose, sniffed, and strode up the aisle and out into the theatre lobby. There she upbraided Mr. Harris for half an hour before going home. One can easily imagine her in full flow, berating the captive producer."

Unwanted comparisons between herself and Francine now dogged Jeanne. As one critic remarked, "With only ten days of rehearsals and nine days playing out of town, Francine Larrimore appeared in Jeanne Eagels' shoes before a critical first night audience and did more than make good." Francine had found "her Sadie" in Roxie and would play the part for years to come.

Adding to Jeanne's troubles were backstage rumors circulating within numerous Broadway theatres. It was said that she and Coy were on the verge of separating after only sixteen months of marriage. Gossips predicted that Jeanne was heading to Europe for a divorce, as the first Mrs. Coy had done two years earlier.

The star refused to be drawn on her marital problems, but as December dragged on, the *New York Morning Telegraph* quoted the couple's response: "It is indeed a regrettable fact that fame often breeds publicity that is cruel and sometimes not altogether true."

"Jeanne will get over all this," an unnamed actress friend was quoted in a *Kansas City Star* report on December 22. "Of her troubles with Mr. Coy I know nothing, but the temperamental stories about her are common." An anonymous *Star* writer—probably Landon Laird—countered that he had always found Jeanne "the height of courtesy," adding that on a hot summer morning at the Bellerive Hotel, she had performed *Rain*'s exhausting second act for him, as the play had not yet opened in her hometown and he had never seen it.

"The success of an actress is measured by her intelligence," Jeanne remarked in late 1926. "The stage requires long years of training and self-denial. It always is a question of striving to please. It is fatiguing hard work. The young people who enter the profession in the belief that they are to have one long string of good times are mistaken. Acting is work, and then more work. I revel in contest. But I advise nobody to try my profession because the combination of talent, appearance, opportunity, and sheer luck, plus always the recurrent agony of disappointment and disillusion, is more than I would wish on an enemy, let alone a friend, to bear."

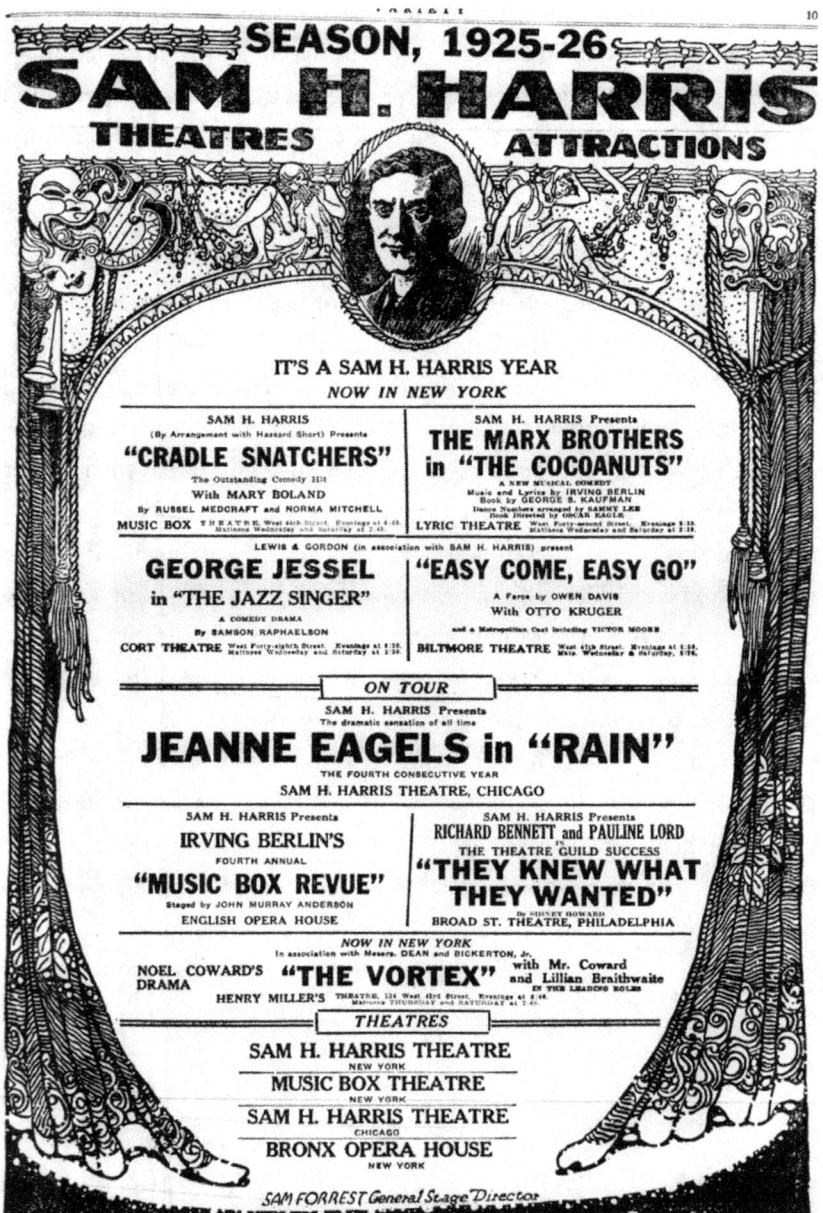

THE SAM H. HARRIS THEATRE — PAGE SEVEN

Sam H. Harris Theatre

A. L. ERLANGER and SAM H. HARRIS, Lessees
Selwyn Theatre Corporation of Illinois, Owners

Sam H. Harris, Manager   William Roche, Business Manager

FIRE NOTICE

Look around now, choose the nearest exit to your seat. In case of fire, WALK (do not run) to that exit.
Do not try to beat your neighbor to the street.

FOURTEENTH WEEK

Beginning Monday Evening, January 4, 1926

Matinees Wednesday and Saturday

SAM H. HARRIS

Presents

JEANNE EAGELS

—in—

"RAIN"

A Play in Three Acts

By John Colton and Clemence Randolph
Founded on W. Somerset Maugham's Story, "Miss Thompson."
Staged by JOHN D. WILLIAMS

PROGRAM CONTINUED ON SECOND PAGE FOLLOWING
PLAN OF EXITS ON PAGE 16

R 453

New Park THEATRE

E. H. & D. Theatre Corporation
Direction of A. L. ERLANGER
T. B. LOTHIAN, Gen'l Manager

This Theatre, under normal conditions, with every seat occupied, can be emptied in three minutes. Look around now, choose the exit nearest to your seat, and in case of disturbance of any kind, to avoid the danger of panic, WALK (do not run) to that exit.

TO LADY PATRONS—The established rule of the New Park Theatre requiring ladies to remove their hats, bonnets or other head-dress while witnessing the performance applies to all parts of the auditorium, including the boxes and loges. It is essential to the comfort and convenience of our patrons in general that this rule be strictly enforced. Ladies who are unwilling or unable to conform to the rule are earnestly requested to leave the theatre without delay, and to receive the price of their tickets at the Box Office.

Week Beginning
Monday, March 15, 1926

SAM H. HARRIS
Presents

JEANNE EAGELS

in

"RAIN"

A Play in Three Acts
By John Colton and Clemence Randolph
Founded on W. Somerset Maugham's Story, "Miss Thompson"

Staged by JOHN D. WILLIAMS

"CHIEF OF THEM ALL"

Samoset CLOTH OF GOLD CHOCOLATES

Always in Good Taste

ERLANGER'S
BILTMORE THEATRE
FIFTH AT GRAND

Direction A. L. ERLANGER

V. E. Kennedy .... Manager
The Los Angeles Biltmore Amusement Corp.

FIRE NOTICE
Look around now, choose the nearest exit to your seat, and in case of disturbance of any kind, to avoid the dangers of panic, WALK (do not run) to that exit.

Fourth Week Beginning Monday, July 12, 1926

SAM H. HARRIS

Presents

JEANNE EAGELS

in

"RAIN"

A Play in Three Acts
By John Colton and Clemence Randolph
Founded on W. Somerset Maugham's Story, "Miss Thompson"

Staged by JOHN D. WILLIAMS

CAST
(In Order of Appearance)

NATIVE GIRL	WILMA THOMPSON
NATIVE POLICEMAN	HOWA OWA
NATIVES	K. A. FERNANDO, LIANO PAULO
AMEENA, wife of Joe Horn	EMMA WILLCOX
PRIVATE GRIGGS, U. S. M. C.	JACK McKEE
CORPORAL HODGESON, U. S. M. C.	HAROLD HEALY
SERGEANT O'HARA, U. S. M. C.	EDWARD KEANE
JOE HORN, Trader of Pago Pago	RAPLEY HOLMES
DR. McPHAIL	ALFRED HICKMAN
MRS. McPHAIL	SHIRLEY KING
MRS. DAVIDSON	BLANCHE FRIDERICI
QUARTERMASTER BATES, of "The Orduna"	JOHN ROGERS
SADIE THOMPSON	JEANNE EAGELS
REV. ALFRED DAVIDSON	ETHELBERT HALES

Time—The Present
The action of the play takes place in the hotel store of Trader Joe Horn on the Island of Tutuila, Port of Pago Pago, South Seas

ACT I—Morning.
ACT II—Late afternoon two days later.
ACT III—Night—Four days later.

(During the third act the curtain will be lowered to indicate the lapse of several hours)

Scenery Designed by Livingston Platt
Painted by W. Oden Waller

STAFF FOR SAM H. HARRIS

Manager	A. L. Rheirstrom
Press Representative	W. E. Gorman
Stage Manager	Harry Hammil
Assistant Stage Manager	Jas. C. Pal

Chapter 11
Her Cardboard Lover: January–July 1927

"From the beginning I have been on the offensive against fate. I've had to fight for what I've got. Women always have to fight harder than men. I've discovered that men always resent a woman's insisting on her rights. She is to be grateful for what is bestowed." – Jeanne Eagels

Walking out of *Chicago* was a bold decision, and, some thought, a foolish one. When Jeanne had appeared in *Professor's Love Story* ten years before, her co-star and mentor, George Arliss, had just finished a six-year run in *Disraeli*. He would later reprise the role to finance his production of *Hamilton*, a modest success only after touring.

Playing Sadie Thompson for so long had taken a physical toll on Jeanne. She was plagued by sinus and respiratory problems, and throughout each performance, her costume was drenched with water. Wilma Thompson had replaced her several times near the end of a two-year tour. To fully recover, she would probably need to take several months off, perhaps until next fall.

Not to mention, the persistent rumors about the Coy marriage contained more than a grain of truth. Ted Coy—athletic legend on the playing field—had become a glorified traveling salesman, hawking golf club memberships to the idle rich. On January 6, 1927 (several months after Coy was relieved of his duties at the board), the Town and Country Club's New York chapter voted to relinquish the charter and liquidate all remaining assets. Membership levels were not high enough to sustain or expand upon their original plans. From then on, Coy's purpose would be to attend pre-arranged events in various cities where Town and Country Club still hoped to establish new chapters.

Of course, it was expected that Jeanne would accompany him on these trips. Maybe she would also pose for photographs and entertain the wives of the bankers, politicians, and potential investors. Wasn't performing in front of a paying audience enough? Jeanne may have protested, and hadn't the many thousands of dollars she'd invested earned her some privacy? Their financial situation left her with little choice but to seek employment rather than rest on her laurels.

"I am always hunting for something better," she told John B. Kennedy of *Collier's Magazine*, reiterating her wish to play Emma Hamilton if the right script came along. "But it will only come after a fight. The authors will want their way and the managers theirs, and they won't listen to me, a woman, until and unless I fight them."

"I married because I fell in love and was fallen in love with," she explained in the same interview. "Let me distinguish between the two careers, matrimony and business. The less fighting in a marriage, the more happiness, and the more fighting in business the greater success." All was not lost, and Ward Morehouse reported the Coys appearance at the February 8 premiere of *Off Key* at the Belmont Theatre, with Jeanne in mink-trimmed ermine. On Valentine's Day, the columnist described Coy "feeding the white leghorns yesterday at Jeanne Eagels' place."

He did, however, omit to mention that on February 11 a lawsuit had been filed by lawyers representing her landlord, Raydona Kuba, for

$2,400—the balance due on her Madison Avenue sub-let. Miss Kuba contended that Jeanne had only paid $750 before vacating the apartment.

When columnist John Mason Brown suggested that Jeanne play Nora in Ibsen's *A Doll's House*, she replied, "I'd never want to play anything that had been played by anyone else." With this in mind, her next choice of a role was unexpected.

Her Cardboard Lover was an English adaptation of Jacques Deval's play about Simone Lagorce, the mistress of a man who will never divorce his wife. Desperate to end the relationship, Simone hires Andre, an impoverished young gambler, to act as a buffer between herself and her former paramour, and finds herself falling in love with him.

Laurette Taylor had been cast as Simone opposite Leslie Howard as Andre. A former bank clerk and soldier, Howard made his debut on the English stage in 1917, crossing the Atlantic in 1920. Howard found fame on both stage and screen, later starring as Ashley Wilkes in *Gone with the Wind* (1939).

Rehearsals for *Her Cardboard Lover* had begun in August 1926 at Taylor's East Hampton home. Valerie Wyngate, who had adapted the play, also directed and was a cast member. Also present was Jacques Deval, who planned on attending the November premiere. In her memoir, Leslie Ruth Howard recalled her father saying he felt Taylor didn't trust the producers, and Deval's hostile attitude toward her hampered her performance. Seemingly miscast, Taylor was ill at ease as the show played in Washington D.C. and Atlantic City. Howard found their intimate scenes "painful to endure."

A. H. Woods, Frohman, and Deval decided to close the show in Baltimore, promising a major rewrite and a swift reopening. Assuming that her run-of-the-play contract was guaranteed, Taylor considered a six-week offer on the Keith-Albee Vaudeville Circuit, but when Jane Cowl was rumored as her replacement, Taylor demanded that *Her Cardboard Lover* open in New York immediately, with herself in the lead. The producers refused, and Taylor filed charges for breach of contract with Actors Equity.

While their dispute with Taylor went into arbitration, Woods and Gilbert Miller gave the script to P. G. Wodehouse for a major rewrite. Author of the popular *Jeeves* novels, Wodehouse was making a name for himself in the US as a musical comedy librettist, who also adapted foreign theatrical farces. Since the Frohman office was controlled by Famous Players-Lasky, and *Her Cardboard Lover* would most certainly become a motion picture, Simone was toned down from a mistress into a divorcee. Wodehouse felt confident enough to purchase a one-third share in the production for $10,000, a move that would bring him a weekly $2,500 profit during the show's run.

On January 15, after several weeks of deliberation, Actors Equity found in favor of Taylor. She relinquished the role, and she was awarded $4,000. Woods and Miller were freed from their obligations, but without a suitable actress to play Simone. Katherine Cornell, then touring in *The Green Hat*, was offered the role, but as rehearsals were due to start just two days after her closing night in Kansas City (of all places), she turned it down.

The script was then sent to Jeanne at her Ossining home, and she accepted the part. It might not have been Lady Hamilton, but it wasn't Sadie either. The most likely reason behind Jeanne's decision was that a major Hollywood studio was wooing her to join their roster of stars. On February 13, *Film Daily* reported, "Jeanne Eagels, of *Rain* fame, is being considered by MGM." An employed actress is a desirable actress and commands a higher salary.

But exactly how serious was Hollywood's premier studio? Two weeks later, more details emerged from the *New York Daily Star*. MGM was having problems with Greta Garbo, who had just finished *Flesh and the Devil* with John Gilbert. Though she was MGM's hottest rising star, studio head Louis B. Mayer decided their Swedish import must be shown a firm hand. Dangling a replacement in front of a "difficult" or "ungrateful" star was a tactic every studio would use to their advantage until the "contract system" died out in the late 1950s. MGM was "going ahead with plans to have Jeanne Eagels play the role of Anna Karenina" in their version of Tolstoy's classic novel, re-titled *Love*. While *Her Cardboard Lover* may not have been Jeanne's most prestigious role, she knew it could lead to greater things.

Rehearsals commenced on February 20, under the direction of George Cukor. Though ten years younger than Jeanne, Cukor's experience in staging Owen Davis' adaptation of *The Great Gatsby* had earned him favorable reviews in New York. He also headed the Cukor-Kondolf Stock Company, whose members included Louis Calhern, Frank Morgan, Ilka Chase, and for one season, Bette Davis.

"All woman stars are likely to be a little high strung," Cukor told columnist Paul Harrison. While this may sound chauvinistic to modern ears, Cukor's description seemed to fit Laurette Taylor and Jeanne, and his courteous approach usually worked, as Cukor later became Hollywood's greatest director of women.

"They have had to fight to get where they are, and they have to fight to stay there," Cukor said of the actresses he coached. "You make some allowances for that. You've got to work on a basis of mutual respect. When an actress knows you have her interests at heart—her interests being the betterment of the play—you can't have much trouble. A director must have a sense of humor and know when to use it, and when to be something of a bully. When a girl gets pompous and grand, a director's cue is to try to kid her out if it. If that doesn't work, he may bully her out of it. I never row with people," Cukor insisted, "but they are a good deal like children pretending to be grand . . . So sometimes, to get along with them, it's necessary to reduce them to what they were. The legends about certain stars don't mean a thing. They may dodge newspaper photographers and otherwise behave in temperamental ways, but they can't dodge their directors, and they must do their best real acting for the stage."

Cukor revisited those days in an interview with freelance writer Mary

Blume during the late 1960s. "What you see when you are impressionable counts for a lot," he reflected. "In my far-off youth there were thirty or forty enormous stars—Ethel Barrymore, Ina Claire, Jeanne Eagels, Elsie Ferguson. If I asked you if there were any great women stars on Broadway now, you would have to say no." Having directed many gifted actresses on both stage and screen (including Joan Crawford, Judy Garland, and Marilyn Monroe), Cukor said, "If I get on with them, it's because I deliver the goods. They know I'm interested in them. Very often you can make people extend themselves, and that's exciting. There's no such thing as a difficult star. To be difficult is to be stupid, and the stupid ones don't last."

Preston Sturges, who went on to direct some of Hollywood's finest screwball comedies, has recalled that during rehearsals for *Her Cardboard Lover*, Jeanne, who was a good friend of his mother, Mary Destl, took him to Tomaso's Speakeasy on Forty-Fifth Street, West of Eighth Avenue. He used the location in *Strictly Dishonorable* (1931). "Happy" Rhones at 143rd Street and Lenox Avenue in Harlem was another favorite haunt of the theatre crowd. It was a "black and tan" or mixed-race club, where America's biggest stars—among them Jeanne, John Barrymore, Ethel Barrymore, and Charlie Chaplin—mingled with black performers, including Ethel Waters, Paul Robeson, and W. C. Handy.

Jeanne's costumes for *Her Cardboard Lover* were a far cry from Sadie Thompson's rags. Reports estimated that her wardrobe cost well over $6,000. A mesh bag carried by the actress was $1,200. Slippers with sparkling brilliants averaged $100 a pair. Gowns, robes, fur coats, a plumed negligee, a fan, and sundry accessories were added to the bill.

Jeanne often changed costumes to sustain her effervescent persona. "As Simone," she told the press, "I feel my purpose is to amuse people, a necessary thing to offset crime news and other serious phases of life. My new part will help answer the many solicitous letters I received while playing in *Rain*, asking what I really was like. On the stage now I am the antithesis of Sadie Thompson and I enjoy the role."

Her Cardboard Lover: January-July 1927

***

When *Her Cardboard Lover* opened in Atlantic City on March 14, Jeanne's name was displayed above the title on the theatre's marquee. However, the Shubert Theatre audience—who had last seen her in *Rain*—failed to recognize the glamorous star until the second act.

Four days before *Her Cardboard Lover* opened in New York, Jeanne had a narrow escape from possible injury or death. While New Yorkers enjoyed the annual St Patrick's Day parade, she was forced out of her third-floor residence at 19 East Sixty-Fourth Street, by a fire that had been caused by a smoldering wooden beam in the upper two floors of the building. This distressing experience cannot have eased her already high anxiety.

On March 21, *Her Cardboard Lover* opened at the Empire Theatre. That night's audience included Peggy Hopkins Joyce, Condé Nast, the Ring Lardners, Jesse Lasky, Adolph Zukor, and of course, Ted Coy. Critics were also in attendance, and Jeanne did her utmost to impress them: flitting from one side of the stage to the other, reciting Wodehouse's lines, and performing bits of physical comedy. In one five-minute scene, Simone mistakes Andre for ex-husband Tony on the telephone. She proceeds to flirt with him, and completely changes from one outfit into another while never letting go of the receiver. Writing for the *Lowell Sun*, James Powers noted that Jeanne's comedic talents were rigorously tested, as she enacted "pajama parties of the first and second parts, subterfuge and fake suicides, broken hearts, and bric-a-brac until the lady knows her mind and the right man."

"There were fears that Miss Jeanne Eagels, having sinned for so long as Sadie Thompson, would find it hard to begin life anew," Percy Hammond remarked in his syndicated March 27 review. "Our tremors, however, were groundless since Miss Eagels, like many of the new girl-stars, proved adept at change. With small trouble she cast the one aside and took the other on . . . Only for a moment at the beginning did Sadie

Thompson's hoarse voice and jazz-swagger intrude upon the pretty ways of Simone Lagorce. Except in that embarrassed moment Miss Eagels took us to a baccarat room in the South of France, then to her ornate nest in Paris and made us feel that we were traveling."

What happened after the curtain came down and the cast assembled for its bows caught Jeanne off-guard, as described by one witness. "After a shaky start, Miss Eagels swept it away magnificently, playing several scenes with an almost fey charm and delicacy and plunging into the romp of the comedy with true comic spirit," Alexander Woollcott observed on March 26, in his "Second Thoughts on First Night" column for the *New York World*. "Only to experience, when she responded to the booming calls at the end of the penultimate act, the pang of hearing that unruly audience yell 'Howard, Howard.' Each time that Miss Eagels led Mr. Howard fondly on to take his bow, the applause would increase from the mannerly patter of routine approval to the cannonade of genuine enthusiasm. Each time she tucked him away somewhere in the wings and came prancing forth alone, all pink and gold pleasure in this touching testimonial from her public, that public would turn and bite her severely, monotonously reiterating, 'Howard, Howard, Howard.' Miss Eagels as star would be expected, (according to contract or custom), to take the final calls alone. I have since been informed by trusty spies, it was the stage manager's ruling that Mr. Howard could not go forth alone on Monday night to take a call, one can hardly blame him, knowing as well he knew, that he was dealing with a star whose contract stipulated that no other player should share with her the distinction of capital letters in the billing."

Percy Hammond viewed the incident rather differently, reporting that "the star, with apparent pleasure at her leading man's popularity, stepped to the footlights and said, 'I thank you on behalf of my cardboard lover.' You never can tell."

Mr. Hammond aside, the press was no kinder than the audience. While some appreciated Jeanne's venture into light comedy, most singled out Howard's performance as the one to watch. After the premiere, Jeanne ran into *New York World* columnist Heywood Broun, who remarked, "It seems to me, Miss Eagels, that you were miscast."

"That's too bad," she replied acidly. "But, Mr. Broun, you have never *seemed* to me."

***

"Looking for a new note in *Her Cardboard Lover* is like looking for a needle in a mound of lingerie . . . Mr. Howard on the other hand has the happiest and rightest role of his days here . . . he keeps the cake of the play in his hands—and the audience rushes to eat it." – Gilbert Gabriel, *New York Sun*

"Eagels lacks the style of scintillating comedy, and her conception of Simone in the current piece must be less than satisfying to herself. On the other hand, Mr. Howard as a blind young fool plays buoyantly with droll flourishes and a sustaining, sardonic intelligence." – J. Brooks Atkinson, *New York Times*

". . . She has her moments when she makes the most of the fun. Mr. Howard is engagingly naive in the name part, a shy lad but honestly determined. The audience liked him so much. . ." – Burns Mantle

"Miss Eagels is not so happily cast as she was in *Rain* . . . Mr. Howard, on the other hand, plays the role of the young man, with fine intelligence and a deft sense of drama." – *Brooklyn Union Standard*

"Miss Eagels is an actress of parts, but this particular part doesn't happens to be one of them. . ." – George Jean Nathan, *Judge Weekly*

On a more flattering note, *Time* discerned a feline quality in Jeanne's performance: ". . . She glides from slouch to crouch as a tawny lioness playing with catnip. . ."

Life chimed in curtly, "Suits Jeanne Eagels only fairly well but Leslie Howard much better."

Her banter with Howard may have seem a little forced from this point on.

While trying to identify a man, Simone asked Andre, *"Did he have a little scar on his temple?" "Aha!"* Andre replied. *"You've been shooting at him."*

"One day he would worship me, adore me, tell me that I was his inspiration, and the only thing that made life worth living for him," Simone said of her married lover, *"and the next day he deserted me for a washerwoman."*

A bemused Andre asked, *"What?"*

"Oh yes," Simone quipped, *"he's very democratic."*

In another, *"I'm beginning to be afraid you don't enjoy seeing me,"* Andre tells her in another scene.

"Indeed?" One can only imagine the venom loaded in that comment.

***

In conversation with the *Morning Telegram*'s Clem Lawrence, Jeanne was unsure whether she preferred Simone over Sadie. "Each is so human and so true." she enthused. "Simone will never have the universal appeal that Sadie had, but women adore the little French monkey. The matinees simply ring with their laughter. They love her. She answers the desire for useless luxury which every one of them has. Probably she will never get the applause that Sadie did. I have two thousand letters from ministers about Sadie."

Away from the theatre, she seemed unfazed by the harsh reviews. The *New York Tribune*'s Ward Morehouse reported on her activities repeated in his column. On March 28, Holbrook Blinn, Jeanne's neighbor and *Madonna of the Slums* co-star,[16] was invited to a late luncheon (5 p.m.) in her Kitchawan Road home. Two days later, her chauffeur, Gustave Flint, was stopped twice for speeding within a ten-minute period and subsequently arrested. Flint was sentenced to eight days in the workhouse, and Jeanne found herself without a driver.

---

16 The pair had remained friends after filming, and in an unpublished manuscript, Blinn's caretaker remembered that Jeanne regularly visited the actor's Croton-on-the-Hudson estate over the years.

On May 2, Jeanne attended the Mayfair Event with close friend Fay Bainter and others. On May 13, Morehouse spotted her driving east on Forty-Fourth Street in her town car. Three days later she was seen again, in the main dining room of the Algonquin Hotel.

Despite her upbeat public demeanor, it must have bruised Jeanne's pride to have not scored the success she did in *Rain*. She had abandoned *Chicago*, only to see Francis Larrimore triumph as Roxie Hart. Rather than use Howard's publicity for the good of the show, perhaps her judgment clouded by her marital problems and burgeoning alcohol intake, Jeanne made possibly the worst mistake of her career—she allowed resentment to supersede her professionalism.

Inside the Empire Theatre, Leslie Howard became the target of her pent-up fury. She ordered the stage manager to move his dressing room as far from hers as possible. When their paths did cross, she ignored him. Even onstage, Howard wasn't safe.

During one mid-run performance, Jeanne suddenly broke character and demanded, "Get me a glass of water." Thinking she had forgotten her lines, Howard continued the play. Jeanne asked, "Didn't you hear me?" Again, she repeated, "Get me a glass of water." At that point, Howard could only stare at her in disbelief. "Well, if you won't," Jeanne decided, "then I will." She then walked offstage, leaving Howard to improvise a line or two about the embarrassment of being alone in a lady's boudoir. A few moments later, Jeanne returned, sipping a glass of water, and finished the scene. From that performance onward, a pitcher and glass of water was kept onstage.

On another occasion, a third actor had exited, leaving the door open. Either Howard didn't notice or didn't move fast enough for Jeanne. Without warning, she rose and closed the door herself, but only after she'd walked through it and retired to her dressing room.

In "One Big Happy Family," a sardonic article about the theatre published in *Vanity Fair*'s July 1930 issue, Howard further exposed his former co-star's attempts at scene-stealing. "Another way [of upstaging] for ladies who may be wearing an evening shawl or wrap, is that practiced so successfully by the late Jeanne Eagels," the actor wrote. "Miss Eagels had a great genius for throwing an evening shawl over her shoulder in a variety of ways without stopping—letting the end of it trail down, picking it up, changing its position, and shrugging her shoulders."

***

On May 29, Jeanne spoke with Samuel Hoffman of the *New York Times*, attributing her success on the stage "to my ability to act and to the astuteness of the managers in noticing it." On what acting can contribute to a play's success, she remarked, "A good play can be read with pleasure. If it is superbly acted, it can also be seen and heard with pleasure. The chances of its being superbly acted are not always bright, as superb actors do not grow on every bush, if I may quote Homer. 'A bad play is improved by good acting'; but as a bad play cannot be particularly well acted, anyhow, there is not much use in producing it at all." And Jeanne knew where to lay the blame: "As for bad acting, you can blame it on not being a good listener. So few people are. For instance, when you and I are talking here and I say 'no' very deeply and quietly, your reply will be 'yes' with something of a rising inflection, a lighter moderation. You have listened to me and have made a correct tonal reply. On the stage, most of the actors and actresses know their cue words and take their cues but they haven't listened to the speech preceding their own. The result is a correct enough answer as to word, but not as to tone. There is not tonal intelligence in the reply. Good listeners ... so rare."

Hoffman asked if she found acting difficult or if she enjoyed it.

"Nobody enjoys anything all the time," she replied. "Sometimes I like it absolutely, sometimes I like it relatively. That is to say, there are times when I dislike it less than anything else I can think of. Sometimes— usually, perhaps—I have no feeling about it whatever. That, I should say, is the habitual human state. The rest is mostly fever and delusion. I do not find acting difficult. If I did, I should find something easier to do, and do it much better. Those who find anything difficult should quit it at once if they can. They will never do it well."

While driving home later that night, according to the June 1 issue of *Variety*, "Jean (sic) Eagels' motor car was side-swiped and shunted into a ditch. The star of *Her Cardboard Lover* escaped with a shaking up but refused to comment when reporters attempted to verify the accident. Her husband, Ted Coy, former Yale football player, who was driving, also escaped injury."

***

Jeanne resumed her charitable work on June 18, at the Army Relief Society Garden Party held on Governors Island, which was a benefit for the Army Relief Fund in aid of the widows and children of casualties. She was one of several film and stage stars in attendance, alongside Natacha Rambova, Jean Gorden, and Mary Eaton. They served as hostesses, selling hot dogs, cigarettes, and homemade candy from brightly-colored booths. Amid the exhibitions of military equipment and displays of fencing and battle maneuvers, a novel event was the Pigeon Derby, using birds trained overseas for war duty. Jeanne released the first of seven batches of birds that raced their way to Fort Monmouth, New Jersey—some twenty-eight miles away—but none of her charges were among the first ten to return.

In her memoir, *Myself Among Others*, Ruth Gordon tells of an ill-fated birthday party that Jeanne planned for herself that month. She invited 150 guests, including Ruth, Ethel Barrymore, Zoë Akins and even Leslie Howard to her estate on Sunday the 26th. Fay Bainter and husband Reginald 'Reg' Venable, who were renting Eagels' stone cottage, offered to provide refreshments, while Ted Coy was charged with finding a band to play in his wife's honor.

The Venables ended up helping with more than punch and cookies. Jeanne asked Fay, who was not currently working in a play, to supervise the delivery of some new bedroom furniture. Once delivered, the impulsive Eagels then decided that the furniture made her curtains look faded, and she and Bainter drove together into Ossining to choose material. After Jeanne cut the curtains incorrectly, she again enlisted Fay's help; and when she bought new porch furniture, Reg agreed to help Ted paint it. But the furniture didn't arrive until the day before the party, and the two men stayed up all night painting. Meanwhile, Fay remained in the guest cottage, boiling hams; decorating six cakes with "Happy Birthday Jeanne," and cutting 350 sandwiches; two apiece for the band and guests, and a few spares.

Before leaving Ossining for the Saturday matinee, Jeanne suggested they light up the grounds with Chinese lanterns. Reg and Ted spent the afternoon on this task, only to have to take down the lanterns when it began to rain. The paint on the porch furniture hadn't yet dried, so they dragged it indoors. Jeanne telephoned, asking to Fay to take all the liquor to her cottage, as Ted was apt to drink too much when tired. Holbrook Blinn (or 'Hal', as his friends called him) hurried home from Broadway's *The Play's The Thing* and brought over a baby's bathtub, filled with his famous potato salad.

When Jeanne returned, the Venables and the Blinns were waiting with Ted on the piazza. Reg opened a bottle of champagne and they raised their glasses, ready to sing "Happy Birthday" to their beloved friend. But as she got out of the car, Jeanne's face turned to thunder. "What the hell is this?" she raged. "I told you not to open the liquor." She ordered her chauffeur to go back and find Leslie Howard, who was following close behind. Approaching Ted, who was finishing his glass of birthday champagne, she tossed her drink in his face and threw him out of the marital home. Jeanne's exhausted husband settled down in a damp hammock, until the Venables took pity and allowed him to stay the night in their cottage.

On Sunday, everyone made their way up the muddy to Jeanne's house, but their sullen hostess refused to come down and join her guests who partied without her. Bainter was not going to allow all her hard work, and all those sandwiches, to go to waste.

Having presumably been forgiven for her birthday tantrum, Jeanne spent Independence Day in Ossining with Fay, playing host to her friend and *National Red Cross Pageant* co-star Josephine Drake, a week later. This may have been an indulgence too far, as she missed that night's performance, citing ptomaine or food poisoning.

About a week later, Jeanne skipped a performance without notifying management, who discovered her absence moments before the curtain went up. When producer Gilbert Miller confronted her in a telegram, she claimed her non-attendance was out of respect for actor John Drew, Jr., who had died in San Francisco on July 9. While her feelings may have been sincere, it did not go unnoticed that Drew's niece, Ethel Barrymore, was performing just around the corner, and hadn't missed a day yet.

Exasperated by Jeanne's antics, on July 18 the producers announced that *Her Cardboard Lover* would close in twelve days and reopen in Chicago in late September.

Jeanne intended to depart immediately for a vacation abroad, lasting four to six weeks. Rumors had been circulating for a month that Howard wanted to quit the show, but management denied this, saying he would join the supporting cast on tour. Burns Mantle's August 7 column suggested that Howard would no longer have to endure the slings and arrows of his former leading lady, as the actor was currently mounting his own production of *Murray Hill* and had plans to open in Galsworthy's *Escape* come November.

Howard had said goodbye to Jeanne but not Andre. *Her Cardboard Lover* moved to London in 1928, according to a *New York Times* review. Tallulah Bankhead, whose career often seemed to shadow Jeanne's, starred opposite Leslie Howard in the successful London production opening at the Lyric Theatre on August 21. After 173 performances, she toured Scotland and later revived the role in the United States.

Once again, Jeanne's planned vacation never materialized. On

August 5, reports circulated that she would star opposite John Gilbert in MGM's *Fires of Youth*. This would not be a remake of Eagels' 1917 Thanhouser film of the same name, but an original story written and directed by Monta Bell, and based on his early experiences as a reporter for the *Washington Herald* during the Taft administration.

Jeanne would play Vera Worth, society columnist for the daily newspaper, where she meets newcomer Al Whitcomb (Gilbert). He falls in love with Vera, who is also the mistress of the paper's owner/publisher. Jeanne left for Washington in the second week of August, joining Gilbert and Bell to film exterior scenes before heading to MGM's Culver City lot for interiors.

Two weeks earlier, Gilbert had completed *Love* in Hollywood (filmed June 22 to July 25 on the MGM lot). Jeanne had already lost out on replacing Garbo as Anna, and would have to satisfy herself with Greta's leading man. Her MGM salary was surely ample, it persuaded her to cancel a relaxing vacation and endure working in a medium she had openly disdained for seven years, but the real motive for returning to the silver screen could be explained in five words: "*Gloria Swanson as Sadie Thompson.*"

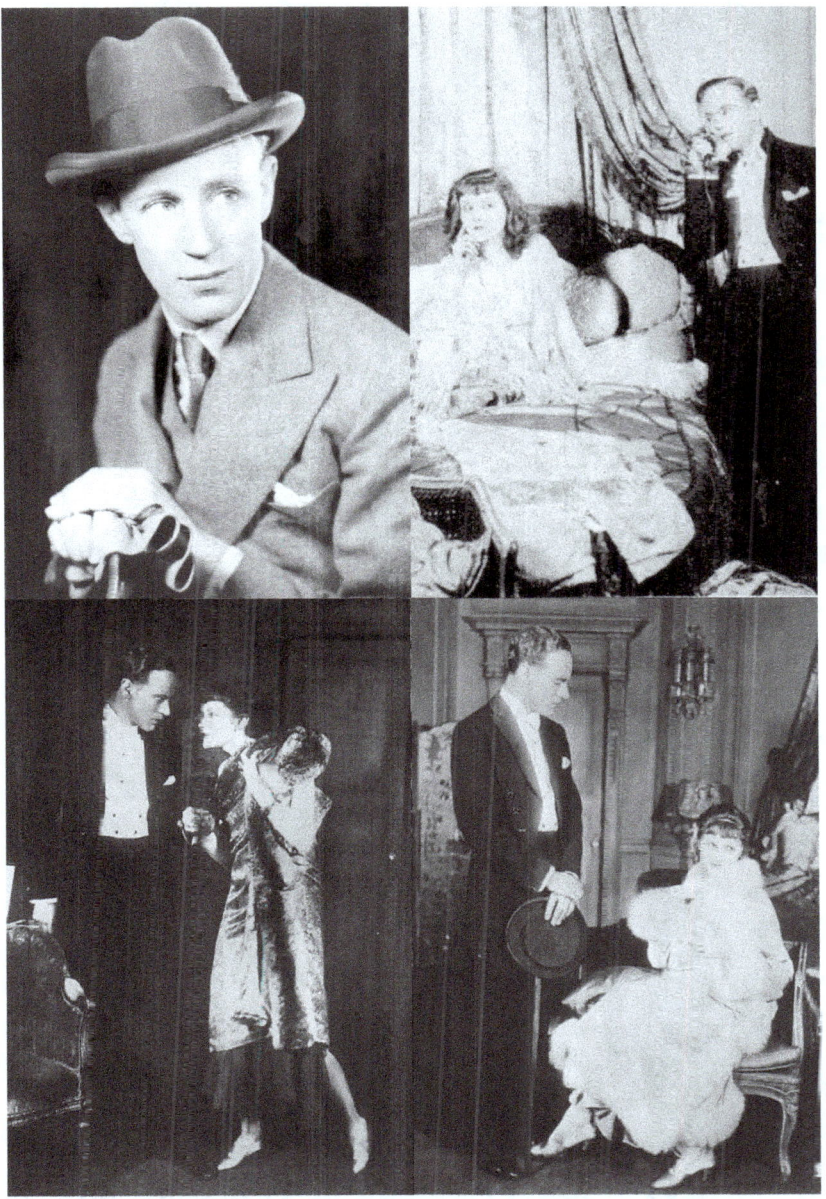

Top left - Leslie Howard. Top right, bottom left and right – Howard and Eagels in scenes from *Her Cardboard Lover* (1927.)

As "Simone Lagorce" in *Her Cardboard Lover* (1927.)

Chapter 12
Man, Woman and Sin:
August–December 1927

Along with most of America, Jeanne read in Louella Parsons' syndicated column on May 27, 1927, that "Gloria Swanson is to film 'Sadie Thompson' as her next part. Gloria was as excited and thrilled as a youngster when she told me that Sadie Thompson will be her next heroine and that Raoul Walsh is to direct her. I think I should make the distinction that Sadie Thompson and *Rain* are not one and the same, although they are both based on Maugham's famous character. *Rain* which Jeanne Eagels made such a hit on the stage is a dramatization of Sadie Thompson, but it is decidedly censurable. Sadie Thompson in the movies will stick closely to the text of the original story."

One can imagine the sound of breaking glass and furniture being tossed around the dressing room of the Empire Theatre that night. How did Gloria Swanson succeed where everyone else had failed? What made Will Hays, who had blacklisted *Rain*, change his mind? Why was Swanson cast as Sadie and not Jeanne?

There had been plans to film *Rain* since 1923, though as Helen Klumph predicted in the *Los Angeles Times*, "It looks as though very little could ever really reach the screen. Of course everyone familiar with this great story of S. Maugham's realized that when the film version came about Sadie Thompson would have been washed white as the driven snow." Klumph even anticipated "the crabby, narrow, domineering Reverend Davison, a sweet old gentleman who spouted sermons in the subtitles."

A Chicago army brat, Gloria Swanson made her film debut in 1914 as an extra at Essanay Studios. She left for California in 1916, appearing in numerous Mack Sennett comedies before signing with Paramount Pictures, where she was groomed for stardom by Cecil B. DeMille. Within two years, Swanson had become one of the screen's most sought-after actresses. And as one of the world's most photographed women, her fashions, hairstyles, and jewels were widely imitated.

Swanson married the Marquis de la Falaise in 1925. After several more pictures at Paramount, she rejected their offer of a million-dollar contract. Instead she joined United Artists, enabling her to produce and distribute her own films.

Her first effort, *The Love of Sunya*, performed badly at the box office.[17] Returning from New York, she wanted to create "my *Gold Rush*," in reference to her U.A. partner Charlie Chaplin's 1925 masterpiece. Swanson met with 20th Century Fox director Raoul Walsh, and the duo came up with the idea of her playing Sadie Thompson. Having seen Jeanne in the role at least twice, Swanson thought it perfect for her next project, but there was one problem—the stage play had been added to the list of "immoral" shows banned from screen adaptation by the Hays Office in 1923.

---

17   According to the November 21 1926 issue of *The Film Daily*, Jeanne's sister Helen Eagles played a bit part in *The Loves of Sunya*, which was filmed at the William Heart's Cosmopolitan Studios.

Swanson and Walsh's solution was to erase all profanity and change Reverend Davidson to Reformer Atkinson to appease the clergy and censors, but the film was still a risky proposition. The pair worked with U.A. partner Joseph Schenck, who purchased the film rights to Colton and Randolph's *Rain* so that no other studio could produce it. Next, the rights for "Miss Thompson"—Maugham's original story—were purchased from his agent. Gloria then invited Will Hays to lunch and briefly outlined her project, framing it as a contemporary moral fable. By glossing over the details, Swanson secured Hays' permission to proceed.

Her production was quietly announced in late May, while America celebrated Charles Lindbergh's unprecedented, non-stop flight from Long Island to Paris on his private aircraft, *The Spirit of St. Louis*. However, a backlash swiftly arose among those who believed the film would irreparably damage American morals. To quell this rising storm, Swanson braved the press, insisting that her motives were honorable.

While many were skeptical, the *Spokane Review* agreed that Hollywood's version of *Rain* would be tamer than its stage incarnation. Observing that Will Hays had denounced the play as "a moral leper that must not invade the movies," the article mentioned Swanson's claim that all religious overtones would be excised from her adaptation, including the character of Reverend Davidson.

"In the play the missionary is quite as important to the plot as a lemon is to a glass of lemonade," the critic wrote. "Without a missionary the play would lose its entire significance ... Consequently, we would not be surprised to see *Sadie* turn out to be anything more than a winter tryst to the South Seas." In the film, Davidson (Lionel Barrymore) is merely a "moralist."

Flouting the unspoken rule that "box office comes before art," the critic failed to see "why the movies should shield the missionary from the light of the screen ... The stage certainly set *Rain* forth before thousands." As for Gloria, she would make a "vivid" Sadie Thompson, though not of

Eagels' calibre: "Miss Swanson, however, isn't a great actress, but she is a good one."

***

Confident that critics and audiences would come around, Swanson forged ahead. Gossip columns and entertainment sections of newspaper across America were filled with stories from the set of the film, which had definitely been titled *Sadie Thompson*. On August 5, the *St. Petersburg Evening Independent* described a lavish luncheon thrown by Swanson one week before. Guests were led into the tropical jungle to Trader Joe's hotel bungalow, as rain drizzled in the background. Island foods and melon-flavored ices were served. Four native Samoan dancers, extras in the film, twirled long heavy-bladed knives over the heads of the nervous diners, and performed war dances and traditional songs.

Anyone who had read Louella Parsons' fateful column back in May would also have seen a smaller item directly beneath the main story, naming Jeanne as the lead in John Gilbert's next film for MGM, *Fires of Youth*. On August 9, Parsons confirmed that "Yesterday Robert Rubin in New York told Irving Thalberg in Culver City, over the telephone, that Miss Eagels had agreed to co-star with Mr. Gilbert." After Jeanne had finished shooting exterior scenes with Gilbert and Monta Bell in Washington, the trio took a train to California.

***

On August 20, Jeanne stepped off the train with John Gilbert and Monta Bell not far behind into the warm Pasadena sunshine to be greeted by several studio executives and a small band. MGM treated its stars like royalty. While Jeanne was undoubtedly a fine addition to their roster, Gilbert had established himself as one of Hollywood's biggest names. Known as "The Great Lover," he found his niche when MGM signed him in 1924. Over the next few years, he played leading roles in some of the most popular films of the day, including *He Who Gets Slapped*, *The Merry Widow*, *The Big Parade*, and *La Bohéme*. In 1926, when Gilbert was cast opposite Greta Garbo in *Flesh and the Devil*, a star-crossed romance had begun both on and off-camera.

The film industry that Jeanne found in Los Angeles was a far cry from the Long Island studios where she had once performed. Hollywood was no longer the sleepy little town where Cecil B. DeMille had made *The Squaw Man* in 1913, and motion pictures were now the city's number one industry. The *Literary Digest*'s October 1927 issue included an article headlined "Movie Industry Created Numerous New Businesses in Hollywood." It was estimated that a single studio "has a thousand acres with 1,500,000 square feet of floor space," while "another company requires twenty-three buildings with several hundred thousand square feet of stage space" and "miles of paved streets."

"It's a big business in which Hollywood is engaged," the article continued, citing Will Hays' description of the area as "primarily a business center." Keeping track of the city's 18,000 listed actors was no mean feat. In 1926, the Central Casting Bureau logged 259,259 placements of extras, entailing 8,000,000 telephone calls.

And the costuming! According to Mr. Hays, "One company has a stock of costumes valued well up in the millions, which it has taken them twelve years to collect. They occupy a modern sky-scraper, from basement to roof, and have over 200,000 square feet of space crammed with every conceivable variety of clothing from the days of our antediluvian ancestors right down to the latest Parisian stuff."

When Jeanne arrived, the "other" Sadie Thompson was filming exterior scenes twenty-six miles away on Catalina Island with a cast and crew numbering over 150. Though most of the action took place on the island's wharf (doubling as Pago Pago), palm trees were scattered across the beach, and a native village, plus military outpost with barracks and out-buildings were constructed. Military personnel who had fought in the South Seas, and dozens of native Samoans were also utilized. Filming proceeded slowly, as Walsh was now co-starring opposite Swanson, as well as directing.

"I know it is an idle dream, but I would be very happy if I could continue playing Sadie Thompson indefinitely," Swanson told reporters, "for she is a character that will live long in the memories of all who become familiar with her story." Though this must have infuriated Jeanne, she could take some satisfaction from the fact that *Sadie Thompson* was now wildly over-budget. Swanson was forced to sell her Croton-on-Hudson country home and was contemplating the same fate for her Manhattan apartment until Schenck stepped in with the needed funds.

Among the umpteen production companies that filled Hollywood, MGM was the Rolls Royce of film studios. Company head Louis B. Mayer expected the best from his crew, staff, and stars. John Gilbert had just completed *Love* with Garbo. After two years as a general assistant, bit-part actor, and story editor at Chaplin's studio, Monta Bell had moved to MGM in 1926 to direct *The Torrent*, Garbo's first Hollywood film.

Asked if she was nervous about returning to the screen, Jeanne replied, "I have no doubt about my acting ability. My success on the stage has given me confidence along that line at least. But the technique of playing before a camera is entirely different from that used on the stage. In the first place," she explained, "one must use entirely different make-up for the kliegs than the footlights. And then there is a difference in the acting itself. On the stage you do the same thing night after night and improve with each performance. But here we go through a scene three or four times then forget it and then on to something else. I really don't get a chance to learn my parts at all, but must act entirely by first reaction."

"Another difference is that on the stage a person's exact position is not vitally important. If you are in approximately the right spot it is all right. But in front of a camera especially for close-ups, you can't be over a fraction of an inch out of position. And you must be far steadier because the camera will detect things an audience won't."

Jeanne's costumes for *Man, Woman and Sin* (as *Fires of Youth* was now re-titled) were as sumptuous as those for *Cardboard Lover*, with one ensemble combining a sumptuous tulle evening wrap with a roundabout collar of full-blown silk roses. A handful of roses and petals were strewn between the layers of tulle that formed the skirt of the frock. A series of regal portraits were shot by Clarence Sinclair Bull of Eagels wearing this costume with ropes of jewels and a tiara. *Variety* gave its readers a descriptive run-down of two more: ". . . a very full skirted taffeta frock which had three bias folds of the silk around the neck, she wore a short cape of crepe with narrow lace edge and soft collar of the velvet, and the felt hat had several roses on the right side. The short chiffon cape with net evening gown had a wide band of roses appliqued for a collar. Her negligee was also chiffon with bands of metallic lace set in to form an odd pattern."

Her elegant wardrobe was recompensed by the frugal set design. Jeanne's apartment in the film was identical to William Haines' in *Telling the World*; even the furniture, knick-knacks, and pictures on the wall were reused. As both films were released just a few weeks apart, the similarities did not go unnoticed by critics.

Difficulties were reported from the set. These ranged from disagreements with MGM executives, to painful sinus infections that kept Jeanne bedridden, and—most worrisome of all—her rumored drinking and drug binges, including a two-week disappearance to Santa Barbara. Eddie Doherty wrote of "the malicious rumors that Jeanne had to be propped up and held while the cameramen were shooting close-ups of her; and that a double was used whenever possible." The Hollywood elite was a members-only club, and this Broadway actress was not welcome.

An article published in *Photoplay* magazine after Jeanne's death recounted how she had arrived late to the set one day for what should have been a simple scene. She was required to sit at a desk, pick up the receiver of the phone, and speak a few words into it. But she was unable to co-ordinate her movements, and the action was rehearsed over and over until Bell was satisfied.

When the cameras rolled, she seemed to lose her nerve. Bell filmed the scene multiple times in an attempt to catch something usable. After nearly thirty takes, Jeanne seemed to be emerging from her fog, but a press-agent approached and her concentration was broken.

"I'm writing your biography for our department," the publicist asked. "Miss Eagels, where were you born?" Her response was later reported by *Photoplay*:

"Her face was enough to tell them all what was about to happen. Worn down by the repetition of the scene, her nerves frayed and jagged, she turned upon the press-agent and shouted at the top of her lungs, 'Where was I born! Good Lord, who cares where I was born? You ask me where I was born! How should I know? Maybe I'm a living ghost. Born, born, born—God in Heaven, where was I born?' Her hysterical shrieks shook the set. She arose from the desk and stumbled away, still shouting, 'He asks me where I was born!' And there was no more work that day."

Jeanne had a reputation for erratic behavior. However, the challenges she faced in making the transition from stage to screen were considerable. Hours were much longer at the studio, often starting before dawn. Rather than flowing continuously, the action was divided into tiny segments, and repeated until the director approved. Scenes were shot out of sequence to save money. This created a start-and-stop mentality which could be frustrating, particularly to an experienced actress of Jeanne's caliber.

Actress Charlotte Greenwood was friendly with Jeanne at the time, according to unpublished notes by her biographer. She taught Jeanne the proper way to apply cosmetics for the camera, and would clean up the volatile star after her infamous "episodes." Greenwood even helped her through the last two days of filming. One anonymous columnist, "Patsy the Hollywood Stenog," suggested the film be re-titled *Man, Woman and G-I-N*. Jeanne was nicknamed "Gin" Eagels for her habit of drinking hot gin, supposedly because it relieved her persistent neuralgia. This unexplainable and sudden nerve pain manifested itself quickly whenever Jeanne was under stress. In addition to her problems at MGM, her marriage was in trouble. Towards the end of September, Coy arrived unexpectedly on the set to escort his wife back to New York.

"I'm feeling pretty cocky today," Jeanne had told a journalist in the spring, when the world was abuzz with the news of Lindbergh's flight to Paris. "Two editorial writers this week said Lindbergh—isn't he a darling?—typified America to the world today, just as two other Americans have done in the past. One of those two, the papers said, was Abraham Lincoln. The other is my husband, Ted Coy."

Buoyed by her movie plans, Jeanne had begun the summer with new optimism. Swanson be damned, she would make the best of her situation. But after a few weeks at MGM, her hopes had evaporated; and by Doherty's account, Coy drank more heavily in Hollywood than ever before. He was afraid that Jeanne was falling in love with her handsome co-star, whom he would rouse from sleep with an early morning phone call to beg, "Jack, are you sure there's nothing between you and Jeanne?" For her part, Jeanne seemed to relish her husband's pain. And if Ted sought reassurance, she would respond with the same line she fed to the press: "My love affairs, my servants and the food I eat are not public property."

Greta Garbo's biographer, Karen Swenson, believes that Gilbert flirted with Jeanne in a futile attempt to make his girlfriend jealous. Shortly after her arrival in Hollywood, he invited Jeanne to a party at his hilltop home. "I was awfully frightened driving up the road to his house," she told the *Los Angeles Times*. "I told Mr. Gilbert he should never be able to get rid of me, because I shall simply never dare to drive down that road again." However, Eve Golden writes in *John Gilbert: Last of the Silent Stars* that "Eagels' timing was off: had it not been for Garbo, Jack would no doubt have taken her up on that."

Interviewed by Doherty, Gilbert recalled that Jeanne had visited with her actress friend, Beatrice Lillie (or Lady Peel, her title by marriage).

Away from the set, and her possessive husband, Jeanne's mask finally slipped, and her deep loneliness was clear to see. "We sat here all evening, and Miss Eagels wasn't drinking anything," Gilbert said. "Then we got to talking of what people wanted out of life, what were the best things to be had of life. And Jeanne said, 'The most perfect gift of God is simplicity of soul.' She sighed a little at that, and then she smiled. 'It doesn't come to many of us though, does it?' she asked. 'And we do not retain it very long.'"

Photoplay noted at least one bright spot in an otherwise miserable period, when Edmund Lowe (Jeanne's co-star from *In the Night Watch*) came by to take her to a party at his home. Arriving at the bungalow court where she was staying, Lowe realized he didn't know her exact address. So he walked down the center court way, singing the male part of the last act duet from the opera *Aida*, which he and Jeanne had sung together between acts of *Night Watch*. Upon hearing his voice, Jeanne came out to greet him. They retold the story over lunch at Ethel Barrymore's home the next day, treating guests to a repeat performance.

According to the *New York Times*, "the report on the Great White Way was that 'the star was released from her film contract owing to 'temperamental differences with the management.'" The *Syracuse Herald* reported on September 22 that "Jeanne Eagels has been let out due to complaints by Montana [sic] Bell the director. Eagels arrived at the studio at any and all times, provoking a scene upon her showing up." The *Oakland Tribune* added that she wouldn't be recalled by MGM any time soon. When she left for the train station, there was no parade and band like the one that met her when she first arrived. Aside from Coy and her maid, she had only "good wishes" from the director, cast, and studio, who were, in truth, all glad to see her go. It was even rumored that they were piecing together Jeanne's remaining scenes from outtakes to avoid having to work with her again.

Man, Woman and Sin was released on November 19. Its final cost was $236,000, and profits would reach $329,000. "It could have been great but it wasn't," Gilbert admitted a year later. "I have my own private reasons for its failure, which I am not permitted at this time to disclose." After Jeanne's death, Gilbert told the *Los Angeles Times* that while he considered Jeanne a great actress, he was shocked by her emotional outbursts during filming. "She seemed to hate the movies for the popularity they could not give her. The blind, unreasoning adulation of the movie fans was a type of popularity she spurned. Fundamentally, Jeanne was much superior to us. Movie actors are crazy to be worshiped. She wanted to be understood and appreciated."

Gilbert saw Jeanne only once more after filming ended, in July of 1929. He was in New York awaiting to sail on his European honeymoon after marrying Ina Claire, Jeanne's friend since their *Jumping Jupiter* days. As the actor later recounted to Doherty, Jeanne arrived at their room at the Ritz Hotel with a bouquet for Claire and congratulations for him. Gilbert described her as "looking like a wraith, thin to almost emaciation. Her smile hadn't dimmed, but her laugh was the ghost of a laugh." He remembered her saying, "I think I'll take the same boat. I need a rest and I'd love to see Europe again, with you two."

Both a 16mm and a 35mm print of *Man, Woman and Sin* exist in the George Eastman Kodak Collection, and a print may be held in the Warner Bros. Archives, but due to legal issues its future release remains in limbo. In a retrospective study of Pre-Code Hollywood, film historian Mick LaSalle thought her work "remarkable." Despite her frustration with movie acting, reviews of Jeanne's performance were glowing.

"Photographs like a million dollars and brings not only loveliness to interpretation but intelligence that is delightful." – *New York Telegraph*

"Jeanne Eagels is splendid. She seems to have established a very definite place for herself in the motion picture world and we are looking forward to seeing her in celluloid soon again." – *New York Journal-American*

". . . She has charm with certain strangeness which makes her as fascinating to us as she was to impetuous boy who loved her." – *New York Herald Tribune*

"The discerning will see a figure of amazing interest . . . quite unlike anyone else on the screen today." – Norbert Lusk, *Los Angeles Times*

"Jeanne Eagels, the stage star of *Rain*, makes her screen debut [sic] as the society editor, and her work is so satisfactory that it is to be hoped she will make more pictures." – Chester Durgin, *Los Angeles Daily Press*

"As to Miss Eagels, nothing could be said that would seem to be extravagant praise for her calculating and altogether superb portrayal." – *Martin Dickstein*

"Jeanne Eagels brings out with utter sincerity the character of the young beauty. . ." – *Schenectady Gazette*

But not all movie critics were ready to toss bouquets at Eagels' feet.

"Jeanne Eagels looks and acts a trifle hard as the society editor, as the part demands. Miss Eagels is not so well-suited to the screen for she doesn't photograph well enough to do herself justice." –*Rochester Democrat*

"Miss Eagels looks haggard in spots. . ." – *Variety*

"Jeanne Eagels is no Garbo." – *Photoplay*

***

Jeanne was expected to return to New York in the last week of September to prepare for a tour of *Her Cardboard Lover*, but as Ward Morehouse revealed on October 1, "Producer A. H. Woods is ready to come cross-country to retrieve his missing star. The last he'd heard from her was by a September 14 telegram, and the show was supposed to open in Pittsburgh on October 10 before moving onto Cleveland." Leslie Howard was now appearing in two other shows, and a new leading man would have to be found and approved by Jeanne. Two days later, she informed Morehouse by telegram from Fort Wayne, Indiana, that she was on her way. She arrived in Manhattan on October 5.

Rehearsals began the next day, for a Syracuse opening on October 20. Jeanne would later claim that Howard's replacement—another Englishman—was suggested to her by the Prince of Wales during a trip abroad in the summer of 1926. But this was nothing more than public relations, as Jeanne had spent the previous summer touring America in *Rain*.

Anthony Bushell was born in Westerham, Kent in 1904. He was educated at Magdalen College School and Hertford College, Oxford. During his first year he was the college's middle-weight boxing champion, and later became stroke of their rowing crew. After Oxford, Bushell studied at the Royal Academy of Dramatic Art, and made his theatrical debut at the Adelphi Theatre in *Diplomacy* (1924), opposite Gladys Cooper and Sir Gerald Du Maurier.

Jeanne's ex-husband was played by Barry O'Neill, also an Englishman, whose commendations for outstanding military service during the First World War included the King George Medal for bravery. Tall, dark and handsome, he had only two Broadway shows under his belt. The first, *Dark Angel* (1925), had lasted a mere forty-nine performances.

The other show was written, directed and produced by its outlandish star, Mae West. *Sex* ran for nearly 400 performances during which the entire cast was arrested, tried, and found guilty of indecency. On the day of the verdict, the *New York Times* reported that O'Neill's face took on "an expression of fear in contrast the display and levity which had characterized his attitude during the trial." Seated beside her leading man, the unsinkable Miss West comforted him: "Don't worry Barry, it'll come out alright."

When the foreman read the jury's decision, O'Neill "leaned over and buried his face in his hands. Mae patted him on the back and spoke more words of consolation, and when he raised his head, tears welled in his eyes." All of those on trial received suspended sentences except for West. Although a romance between Mae and O'Neill remains unconfirmed, she would often date her leading men, who were invariably prime specimens of "beefcake." One such conquest was 1955's Mr. Universe, Mickey Hargitay, who later married another voluptuous blonde, Jayne Mansfield.

While rehearsing for *Her Cardboard Lover*'s upcoming tour, Jeanne found time to socialize with friends and peers. On October 13, she was spotted alongside Katherine Cornell, Basil Rathbone, and Ann Harding in the audience of *Private Slovak* (also known as *Jacob Slovak*, and penned by Jeanne's friend, Mercedes de Acosta) at the Greenwich Village Theatre. On October 26, Jeanne attended the opening of a college co-ed musical, *Good News*, at the Ambassador Theatre. Interestingly, her old adversary, Will Hays, was also there.

Jeanne had recently considered starring in another of Mercedes de Acosta's plays, *The Mother of Christ*. It was an interesting choice, given her Catholic background. She had already played a faith healer to acclaim in 1917's *The World and the Woman*. But Sam Harris advised Jeanne that she was now too identified with Sadie Thompson for the public to accept her as the Virgin Mary. Jeanne then approached Monta Bell, and Paramount Pictures later made Mercedes an offer—which, however, she declined. "She wanted the play produced in the theatre before shown on the silver screen," wrote Mercedes' biographer, Robert A. Schanke. "This decision was probably a major blunder, for it could have paved the way for her introduction to Hollywood. In the 1920s, however, New York theatre folk still snubbed their noses at this new form of entertainment."

As *Her Cardboard Lover* began its tour with stops in Syracuse, Buffalo, and Newark, Jeanne finally won the critical acclaim denied to her during the play's initial run in New York.

". . . Jeanne makes Simone deliciously dumb and 'dumbed' delicious . . . as distinctive and certainly more mirthfully satisfying. Miss Eagels makes you feel a certain innocence that you just know is not in the lines."
– *Syracuse Journal*

"Miss Eagels is radiantly lovely as Simone. One of the charming things about Miss Eagels' performance . . . were her asides . . . These little mannerisms of Miss Eagels endowed the play with individuality and raise it from the class of mediocrity." – *Buffalo Courier-Express*

***

On November 21, Jeanne attended a Pall Mall Supper Club dinner dance at the St. Regis Hotel. She sat with writer Clare Boothe at the Guests of Honor table, staying to enjoy the after-dinner entertainment that began at midnight.

Things were looking up again. Without Leslie Howard to steal her thunder, *Her Cardboard Lover* was running smoothly. Despite its troubled production, *Man, Woman and Sin* was a critical success. The season of goodwill was also just around the corner, putting her in a festive, and forgiving mood. Perhaps that's why Ward Morehouse let it slip that Jeanne, dressed in blue, had caught the November 23 matinee of John Galsworthy's episodic play *Escape*, starring Howard. (Morehouse did not reveal if Jeanne and husband Ted Coy went backstage.) The couple were also seen dancing together at the Embassy Club the following Saturday. On the professional front, Jeanne had spent over two hours in the office of Sam Harris, finally agreeing to reconcile with the producer for a new show. She was also spotted discussing potential projects with Zoë Akins.

Jeanne got an early present from Santa on December 17, when newspapers reported that the release of *Sadie Thompson* had been delayed until the first week of January. By then, she would have resumed her tour of *Her Cardboard Lover*, perhaps hoping to avoid the swarm of publicity surrounding Swanson's latest role.

Sadie Thompson would become one of Gloria Swanson's greatest successes, commercially and critically. But by the 1930s, her popularity had waned and she moved into theatre and television. However, Swanson would have her revenge on Hollywood in *Sunset Boulevard* (1950), in which she played faded movie queen Norma Desmond. It was an Academy Award-nominated performance. As Norma Desmond, Swanson echoed the regrets of many when she declared, "We didn't need dialogue. We had faces!"

Director Monta Bell (L) and co-star John Gilbert (R) present Jeanne with a make-up box on her first day of filming *Man, Woman and Sin* at Metro-Goldwyn-Mayer Studios in Culver City, California (1927.)

Eagels as "Vera Worth" and John Gilbert as "Albert Whitcomb,' sharing a box of popcorn in a scene from *Man, Woman and Sin.*

Top - Eagels selects an outfit in which to seduce Gilbert. Bottom - Seduction in progress during *Man, Woman and Sin*.

Gloria Swanson on Catalina Island, possibly working on script revisions for *Sadie Thompson* (1928.)

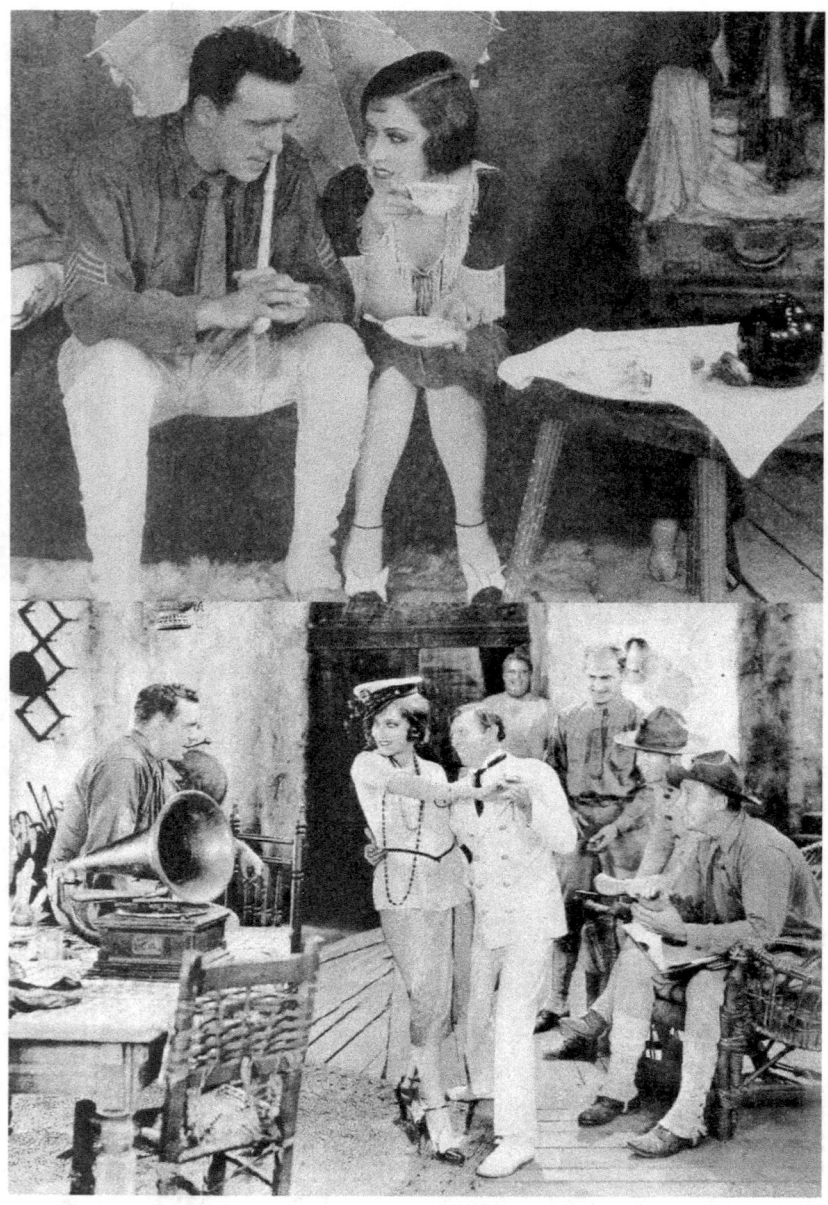

Top - Swanson with co-star and director Raoul Walsh take a break from film *Sadie Thompson*. Bottom – Swanson's version of Sadie's dancing for the sailors.

Chapter 13
The Imp From Hell: January-September 1928

For three days during Christmas week of 1927, *Her Cardboard Lover* played at the Parsons Theatre in Hartford, Connecticut. The New Year's Eve audience was busily chattering when the curtain rose on the second act and a boudoir scene with Jeanne. For several minutes, she tried to speak over the crowd noise. "Finally losing her patience, she looked out across the footlights and asked, 'Well, would you like to have me go on or shall I have the curtain rung down?'" the *Meriden Daily Journal* reported. "The house immediately became quiet and Miss Eagels smiled graciously, picked up the thread where she had been interrupted, and continued to the end when her performance was applauded heartily by what was probably a rather sheepish audience." Sheepish or not, a healthy $9,000 was counted at the box office.

Readers of the *Brooklyn Daily Eagle* opened their New Year's Day, 1928 edition to find a "Day in the Life" article about Jeanne, whose opening performance of *Her Cardboard Lover* would take place at the borough's Majestic Theatre a day later:

"For Miss Eagels there are no sports or any strenuous exercises—the public expects her to be a languid, gentle-looking creature ... Her favorite exercise before every performance—leisurely raising and lowering of the whole body and falling back very gradually—the bear walk."

"Miss Eagels transports in complete comfort as the tonneau of her automobile has seats modeled on the style of easy chairs. A specialty designed table can be adjusted across for a comfortable place for removing her theatrical make-up on the ninety-minute drive to Ossining. Dinner at midnight is taken with her husband or another but not someone else's husband. Then in bed by two a.m. Arising at noon, Eagels would prepare her own breakfast in the small sitting room that adjoined her bedroom—'three slices of toast, coffee and two coddled eggs with lots of butter and baked apple, no cream brought up by the kitchen.' Her only other nourishment until dinner were cups of chicken broth flavored with vegetable stock taken several times daily and especially between the first and third acts of *Cardboard*."

"Her height is five feet six inches, and she weighs 'one hundred fourteen pounds but I should be one hundred twenty pounds.' She revealed that she is unable to wink ever since she was a child. When she tries, she only closes both eyes. Does she get tired easily, especially after two performances in one day? 'Who I? Not a bit. I could be if I thought about it. It's all mental. Let yourself believe you're tired and so you'll be.' Jeanne also recommended: 'Don't worry and don't ever become obsessed with the idea that the whole world is against you because of some idle gossip. If you do, you can waste away faster than through real physical ailments. We overrate ourselves if we think we are consequential to more than a few intimate people. If we could believe that those who go against us are only idlers in search of something to think about we would take ourselves less seriously and stop worrying.'"

***

Patrons of the arts were privy to a self-authored article by Jeanne in the January 1928 issue of *Theatre Magazine*, in which she revealed that—Gloria Swanson's recent coup notwithstanding—she still hoped to bring her Sadie to the big screen. While talking about her recent experiences in the movie industry, she glossed over her early work for Thanhouser and other defunct studios. Clearly, she wanted readers to see her Hollywood debut as an entirely new venture.

"I have completed my first motion picture. That means I shall never again step inside a movie theater, just as I don't go to see plays any more. Watching one actor is bound to affect another's work. I wish to create my own roles and do it without the suggestion from anyone else. Some people might say to me: 'Have you seen so and so? She has a lovely way of closing her eyes when her lover is about to faint—it's so effective.' I don't want to see her close her eyes or open them; it doesn't make any difference to me whether she wiggles her left shoulder before she shoots, or whether the left corner of her right eyelash flutters under the grasp of her father's brawny hand. A few years ago when I was out of an engagement I used to attend first nights, but since then I never go, because I don't wish to imitate other people's work."

"From my own experience in screen acting, I should say that if movie actors were permitted to go through an entire scene, to rehearse it so that they get an idea of the continuity of the story, and know just how to play together, we would have better pictures. I can go over the same scene, or even a bit of business, eight or nine times without tiring. People think I'm impatient; in fact, they think I'm everything that's terrible, but rehearsing never tires me. Is it not natural that a poor performance is inevitable when the players are merely directed business by business? No difference if the camera restricts continued action of an entire scene, it would be more profitable and more satisfying if the director permitted the actors rehearsal of one full sequence."

"Do you know what amused me terribly in pictures? The camera begins to grind. Someone shouts 'Music!' And then the noise of the camera and the voice of the director, his assistants, the electricians, cameramen outsound the music, so that only thing that came to my ear was an occasional wail of the violin. I don't know how anyone else reacts, but it did tickle me."

"When I get too old to act, I'm going to direct—on the stage, of course. I never could do without the theatre. I know it so well; know exactly what an actor should be."

"No actor gets sufficient salary, because if a play is a success it's due to the actor. True, the playwright had a good idea, but if the actor had not been able to put it across, it would have been a failure. I feel that I don't get enough money. Every cent that comes into the box office I bring in. If my performance were not good, the people would not come. And it's not a matter of creating a role once and then repeating it every day thereafter."

"At each performance I re-create the character. No two performances are alike. In *Rain*, for instance, sometimes I had Sadie Thompson sing with the boys or say things that she had not said the night before, but because I give everything I possess at each performance, I just naturally cannot adhere to mechanically set lines, night after night. Once on the stage, I never see or know who is playing with me. The only people I recognize are my audiences. I play to them. Even if I were in love with the man played with me, I would not see him, and he would not know it because I would be giving to the audience all that I would otherwise be giving to him."

"Speaking of *Rain*, I should love to do that on the screen. What a magnificent picture it would make. And how I love the story. Do you know, I wrote the whole first act of that. I always change my stories. Yes, I should love to do it on the screen, but 'The Reverend Dr. Davidson' of Motion Pictures, Mr. Will Hays, thinks it's a 'bad' play. He thinks it is all right for stage audiences, but not for movie audiences—they are too pure!"

"What is a bad girl, anyway? When in *Rain* the Rev. Mrs. Davidson says that she doesn't know a certain girl 'because she is a bad girl,' I say 'let me find out for myself.' Anyway, *Rain* is not a play about religion but intolerance And still I hope to do it on the screen. Even in a modified form it would be interesting."

***

After seeing her latest performance, the *Brooklyn Daily Eagle*'s critic declared, "Jeanne Eagels proved she was at home in light farce in *Her Cardboard Lover*. Miss Eagels is called upon to play a role that is decidedly different from Sadie Thompson. And she does it well. Once the audience had decided to take the play as a bit of nonsense—and it was that—it just settled back to have a good time. The star was ably assisted by Anthony Bushell, a good-looking youngster, who played the part of Andre, and Barry O'Neill as the divorced husband was self-centered enough to be included among the impossible characters of the season. Regardless of a slight cold last night, Miss Eagels seemed to have just as good a time as did her audience. Worth seeing if for no other reason than it is an excellent study of the versatility of Miss Eagels."

However, Jeanne's health was suffering. On January 7, the play's last day at the Majestic Theatre, New York, she missed both the matinee and evening performance. Nearly $4,000 was refunded by the box office to disappointed patrons. Her physician, G. W. Colby, informed the company that she was suffering from a severe attack of tonsillitis, casting doubt on her fitness to open in Boston on January 9 as scheduled. She finally arrived in Boston on January 23, but for only one week instead of the scheduled two: she had personal matters to settle before the Chicago opening on February 1.

Her Cardboard Lover received a mixed review from the *Boston Globe*. "Miss Eagels plays her role with exuberant vivacity and she has some fine moments," the critic acknowledged. "But her manner and gestures are not infrequently more suggestive of Sadie Thompson of the streets than a

French lady of wealth and fashion. She created no end of laughter by her struggles with the intricacies of her flimsy and intimate raiment in the bedroom scenes. Indeed, the audience laughed heartily throughout the evening." And once again, her role was overshadowed: ". . . the best part in the play is that of the young lover. When Leslie Howard acted this role in New York he fairly ran away with the honors of the performance. Here the part is very agreeably played by Anthony Bushell, a personable young English actor." While this might have bothered Jeanne a few months earlier, she now had more pressing matters on her mind.

The reason why she was so insistent on getting to Chicago was made apparent on February 7, when a press statement announced that she was consulting with lawyers to end her marriage. Reporters had gathered at the Adelphi Theatre the night before, to hear it from her own lips, but word came from her dressing room that she had changed her mind. The difficulty with filing in Illinois was that she would either have to become a resident of the state, or else prove that the action on which the divorce was sought had occurred while in Chicago.

Fortunately, audiences and critics of the Windy City loved the show. "The text and business wherewith Miss Eagels gains the public laughter are such as to indicate that she is a valuable collaborator of the adapters," judged the *Chicago Tribune*, adding, "Anthony Bushell is pleasant, engaging and fairly expert."

Theatre manager Ralph Kettering undertook a nightly vigil at the box office, expecting the worst as he waited for his volatile star to appear. And each night Jeanne would enter the foyer humming, doing little dance steps and smiling brightly at Kettering and his staff, and coo sweetly: "Hello, *Bustards*."

Returning her smile with a scowl, Kettering would reply, "Howdy, *Witch*." This became a running joke during Jeanne's Chicago stay, and much to her delight, even hotel clerks would greet her in the same way. She would often inquire about Ethel Barrymore, who was also on tour in Chicago, and laughed uproariously when told the rival show was sold out.

Writing for the *Brooklyn Eagle* on March 1, 1935, journalist Lew Sheaffer remembered another incident during the play's Chicago run. Jeanne had arrived at the theatre and was dressing for that night's performance. She removed her street jewelry and "absent-mindedly dropped the trinkets into a prop jewelry box containing some paste stones." Her maid then took the box and placed it onstage.

When Jeanne realized her own jewelry was missing, "the dressing room was instantly in an uproar. Miss Eagels rushed up and down yelling about robbers and the maid frightenedly [sic] groped about the place as various people ran in."

The curtain time was postponed for fifteen minutes while a frantic search ensued. Jeanne reluctantly agreed to go on with the show, having being persuaded that she must have left her jewelry at the hotel. Sheaffer recalled that "during the act, she so maneuvered her stage business that she was constantly near the wings, and could whisper inquiries to the stage manager or her maid.

"Towards the end of the act," Sheaffer explained, "she opened the prop jewel box and saw her jewelry. Dumbfounded, she stared and remained still until one of the onstage players approached and prodded her back to her wits."

Her Cardboard Lover was originally booked for six weeks and then more performances were added to the nightly sold-out shows. Eagels missed not one night. She showed up on time, sober, looking as young and beautiful as ever.

On February 25, the *Waterloo Evening Courier* reported that after her matinee performance, she had been shaken up and slightly bruised when the taxi cab she was riding in collided with another. After receiving medical treatment, she performed in *Her Cardboard Lover* later that night and was entirely recovered by the next day. Ever the trouper, Jeanne continued on with *Cardboard*'s extended Chicago run before heading North to Wisconsin.

Her hometown of Kansas City had been scheduled in the original line-up but was canceled for unknown reasons, as *Variety* reported on March 3, adding that instead, St. Louis would follow Minneapolis, with a stop in Denver before heading out to the coast.

On March 11, she checked into the Milwaukee Plaza Hotel for a week's run at the Davidson Theatre. However, she was also slated to perform for the Milwaukee Press Club at their annual theatre party. This had been originally scheduled for February, but due to *Her Cardboard Lover's* popularity in Chicago, the Milwaukee start date was pushed back several times. The Press Club lodged a complaint, and a March 12 performance was arranged. Ticket sales promised a full house on opening night, but two hours before the curtain rose, theatre manager Sherman Brown informed critics that Jeanne would not be appearing that night due to severe ptomaine poisoning. Although a notice invited patrons to exchange tickets for another night's performance, they couldn't as the Davidson Theatre remained dark all week. Jeanne was confined to her hotel room, accepting no calls or visitors. Miller and Woods hoped that she would recover in time for the St. Louis opening on March 19, but when the company left, Jeanne stayed on at the Plaza Hotel. According to one of the maids, "The room was stocked with brandy and champagne and a man, supposedly to help her serve."

What had suddenly caused Jeanne to behave so unprofessionally? Throughout her illness, injury, personal crisis, and even after a car accident, a sincere belief that the show must go on had brought her to the stage every night, except when she was at death's door.

John Montague, press-agent for *Her Cardboard Lover*, would later write a play about the debacle. At the time, he told the *New York Sun* that there were several reasons behind Jeanne's meltdown. The split from Coy was a major factor. Additionally, she was angling to star in *Jealousy*, with either John Barrymore or John Gilbert. *Her Cardboard Lover's* producers eventually cast Fay Bainter opposite John Halliday, and *Jealousy* ran for 136 performances from October 1928-February 1929 at the Maxine Elliott Theatre.

On the day Jeanne arrived in Milwaukee, she had read in the *New York Times* that *Her Cardboard Lover* would soon be filmed at MGM with Marion Davies in the lead. Montague believed Jeanne was worried that once the play opened in Los Angeles, Davies would be able to closely observe the characterization that she had perfected over the last year.

But the main reason behind Jeanne's self-imposed seclusion, according to Montague, was love. "Miss Eagels fell in love like she did everything else—tempestuously." Montague didn't name the object of her infatuation, but the most likely candidate was Barry O'Neill. A fourteen-year age gap separated Jeanne and Anthony Bushell, whereas O'Neill was only eight years her junior. At first, there had been no romantic spark between the cast-mates. But Jeanne's impending divorce changed all that. "One night she spoke to him," Eddie Doherty wrote, after interviewing O'Neill. "'Good night,' she said. 'Good night, Miss Eagels.' And they were sweethearts."

Their relationship had blossomed in Chicago, and each night Jeanne would wait in her dressing room for O'Neill to knock on her door and take her to dinner, or maybe an event or party in her honor, before escorting his leading lady back to her hotel. On her closing night, however, Jeanne waited and no knock came. When she inquired as to O'Neill's whereabouts, she was informed that he had left without her.

She had then disappeared entirely, and was finally found alone, and worse for wear, in a room at the Congress Hotel. She had been crying, and a fit of jealousy and rage, hurled a bottle at the luckless Kettering. He sent for Red Gallagher, known to baseball fans as "Red the Bat Boy," mascot of the Chicago Cubs. Gallagher also worked as a stage-hand at the Harris Theatre, and Jeanne had met him there while performing *Rain*. A man's man, he adored Jeanne despite her "nasty temper," and had been aghast at Ted Coy's genteel habit of knocking on her dressing room door. Calling her a "spoiled baby," Gallagher badgered Jeanne to pack up and drive to Milwaukee. Unfortunately, there was no good-natured, fatherly Red to watch over her there.

Not knowing when, or even if their star would be ready to continue with *Her Cardboard Lover,* Woods and Miller canceled the rest of the tour and the cast headed back to New York. An Actors Equity representative was dispatched to Milwaukee, but Jeanne refused to meet him. She left for New York on March 21 and checked into the Hotel Elysée at 60 East Fifty-Fourth Street. The next day, she spent a few hours at her Ossining home before returning to Manhattan. Meanwhile, Actors Equity filed charges against her, with a hearing scheduled for April 3. Alongside the recent incidents at Milwaukee and St. Louis, the committee would also be examining the missed week in Boston, and even the initial postponement of the tour due to her arriving late in New York for rehearsals.

Pearl Gross of the Universal Syndicate was one of many journalists who surrounded the actress outside the Elysée on March 25, as she attempted to walk her dog Moxie to Central Park, five blocks away. Gross thought the actress "looked very wan. Her make-up for the day had apparently been applied hurriedly. It was streaky and unbecoming. Miss Eagels, in fact, looked as gray as her walking costume." She dodged all questions, stating only, "This is terrible! This is terrible!" Pressed further, she continued, "Oh, this is awful. I am being treated shamefully . . . I won't say anything." Another reporter asked if it was really ptomaine poisoning that had closed her show in St. Louis. As Moxie danced around her feet, Jeanne said defiantly, "I can never reconcile myself with such a management. They never gave me an understudy—or anything. I have to take a much-needed rest and I'm going to, whether they decide to punish me or not. Even if nobody pays for that rest but me . . . I'm going to take it. I'm worn out and tired."

Miller and Woods submitted a request to allow her to resume the tour in St Louis. Although the producers would have settled for the two weeks in Wisconsin and Missouri, the charges had been brought by Actors Equity, and even if they withdrew their complaint the case could not be dropped. The committee heard testimony from Jeanne and several members of the cast on April 3, accepting evidence of her illness from several physicians. Among the witnesses for Actors Equity were the representative sent to Milwaukee, the former tour manager, and the Davidson Theatre's Sherman Brown, who referred to Jeanne as "the imp from hell!"

After two days deliberation, Actors Equity made their judgment on April 6: Jeanne was suspended from any union production for eighteen months. This was a retroactive decision, beginning with her first missed performance in Milwaukee, through to September 1, 1929. The union also levied a fine of $3600—two weeks' salary. "Miss Eagels violated some of the most binding and sacred provisions of their agreement with the producers," an Actors Equity statement read, "resulting in serious financial loss not only to the management of the show but to her fellow players, as well. Miss Eagels might appear on Broadway but not with an Equity cast. Either in vaudeville or the movies. Possibly London but no Equity actor would be permitted to be in the cast."

Jeanne responded swiftly. "The suspension is ridiculous and unjust," she said. "Equity had no proof against me. I have the word of twelve physicians in the U.S. that I was really ill when I did not appear and my whole company, and the management appeared on my behalf. My only crime was that I refused to see a deputy of Equity, whom I did not believe to be an Equity Deputy. I'm going to open a new play in the autumn. It might be a one-character drama. There are two such I have in mind." She also mentioned three movie offers, including a version of *Rain* in either Germany or France.

Regarding the accusations that she had been too drunk to perform, Jeanne shot back: "In all my twenty years on the stage—I started at twelve, you know—I have never taken a drink before or during a performance. Whether I drink after one or not I think is my own business. But, as a matter of fact, I do not drink. When I was ill and had lost a great deal of weight, my doctors prescribed a little champagne for me. That is the only thing I ever drink."

According to Clifton Webb, this was not entirely true. "The point is this: Jeanne Eagels never drank a lot," he wrote in his memoir. "She couldn't drink a lot—one drink and she'd be off. It was only when she played in *Rain*, beginning about the second year—and then in the show she would drink champagne. The rain never dried up and everybody felt this constant wet and dank."

Jeanne told the *Brooklyn Eagle* that one man was to blame for her troubles. "Being as important as I am, this attitude of Equity was certainly uncalled for and it is unique in the annals of theatre," she said. "I attribute it entirely to Frank Pearley, a member of my company whom I fired the Saturday night before I went to Milwaukee." While Jeanne claimed many good reasons for her actions, she refused to elaborate. "My entire company appeared in my behalf at the hearing with the single exception of this man Pearley. His was the only affidavit Equity had against me. Unfortunately my cast is English and their word counts for nothing with Equity. No group of actors is going to keep me from earning a living. I shall appear on Broadway next October Equity or no Equity. I was ill and I have the testimony of doctors to prove it. If necessary, I will take the matter to court."

Producer Sam Harris agreed: "I think the order is very drastic. Eighteen months is a long time. I have a contract with Miss Eagels which starts eleven months before the suspension is ended and I expect to work with her under that contract. It is a question of law isn't it?" Harris had plans to cast Jeanne in *Carita*, a love story with a seventeenth century setting.

Pearley's response to Jeanne's latest accusations was published in the *New York Times* on April 11: "I wasn't fired, I resigned. It appears to be a hobby of Miss Eagels to have managers and agents fired for unavoidable things. Her reason for having made the request for a new manager was that I am not enough of a miracle man to control the operating departments of the railroads. Miss Eagels has had more managers and agents during the short period that she has been a star, than all the other stars in the business put together."

Pittsburgh Press columnist Karl B. Krug took Jeanne to task on April 15, commenting, "Miss Eagels has forgotten her duty to the patrons of the playhouses, her employers, and her fellow thespians so many times that one wonders she hasn't had her wings clipped long before this." Krug reminded his readers of her absence when *Rain* opened at the Nixon Theatre, with understudy Wilma Thompson stepping in. On that occasion, Jeanne was supposedly in Washington D.C. "Whispers at the time were Miss Eagels intended to lay off during the entire first week of the engagement here," Krug recalled. After reading favorable reviews for Thompson's performance the next day, Jeanne had been anxious to return, but due to enormous demand for seats, the Nixon's manager had temporarily removed the orchestra pit from the theatre (allowing 111 seats to be placed and filled). An irate Jeanne summoned the manager, insisting that the show would not proceed without an orchestra. He replied that if she didn't perform, "Harris would be refunding the audience's money." Jeanne duly appeared onstage that night, and for the rest of *Rain*'s Pittsburgh run, knowing that if she didn't, Thompson would replace her.

Perhaps Krug regretted his harsh words after reading that Jeanne had accommodated *Her Cardboard Lover*'s fifteen actors at her Ossining home since their return from St. Louis, funding their expenses until the dispute was resolved. She was invited to an AMPA luncheon at the Boulevard Hotel on April 12 along with Eleanor Boardman, Mae West, and Bobby Vernon. Jeanne sent her understudy instead, possibly to avoid any confrontation with Miss West over Barry O'Neill, their shared lover. Prior arrangements for Eagels to sail aboard the *Mauritania* for an extended European vacation, returning sometime in the fall, were canceled at her lawyer's suggestion.

Henry A. Uterhart argued that an appeal was justified because "the appearance of the entire cast of *Her Cardboard Lover* in Miss Eagels' favor had not been considered by the council, which rejected this evidence in its entirety and accepted instead the statements of four persons who, by the nature of their evidence, appeared prejudiced against her." He accused

Actors Equity of "discarding states and laboratory results of prominent physicians attesting to her condition of nervous exhaustion and infection of the throat at the time of the alleged violation of contract." Uterhart also contended that "The whole trouble appears to have been created by Miss Eagels' request for a new manager."

***

As gossip about Jeanne's separation from Ted Coy swirled, the press suggested a possible reconciliation with former fiancé, Whitney Warren Jr. "I'm very fond of her. But we're not engaged," Warren told reporters in San Francisco, as noted by the Associated Press on April 26. "She is married, and I don't believe rumours of an impending divorce."

Ward Morehouse continued to chronicle Jeanne's activities in his column. On May 3, she was spotted in seat CC1 of the Theatre Masque, enjoying Willard Mack's melodrama, *The Scarlet Fox*. According to Eddie Doherty, the Canadian actor, director and playwright had first met Jeanne early in her career while interviewing her for a part, and became a friend and mentor to the future star.

Morehouse also noted that she "was keeping busy by motoring a great deal, walking, working in her garden, and enjoying excellent health. Wants to act again and reading plays. Would like to try directing."

As her suspension didn't include benefit performances, Jeanne appeared at the George M. Cohan Theatre for the Green Room Club's annual revel on May 6. Her twenty-minute performance of scenes from *Rain* and *Her Cardboard Lover* was met with hearty applause.

Actors' Equity may not have considered Vaudeville legitimate theatre, but it offered Jeanne another way to make her living. She quickly assembled a collection of performers, casting herself as the headline act. *The Benefit* featured performances of the telephone sequence and other scenes from *Her Cardboard Lover*, and a modified version of *Rain*'s denouncement scene. Her reported salary was $2,500 per week, which may explain her newly relaxed attitude. "I am not asking for a new trial or anything like that," she told the *New York Sun* on May 25. "My lawyers are doing it of their own accord. If Equity thinks I have done wrong, Equity should stand by the decision it has made. To reverse the decision would be only to reveal its weakness. That suspension makes no difference to me. I can make money—plenty of it—and will continue to do so regardless of any ban put upon me. The suspension will only injure other players who would be working in my companies."

Radio was also permitted, and on May 15, Jeanne appeared on WGBS's *Theatre Period*. Comedienne Fanny Brice, who had known Jeanne since their days under Belasco's management, was also a guest. (In her 1952 memoir, Tallulah Bankhead claimed that—much to the chagrin of others within the theatre world—Jeanne was once paid $10,000 to endorse a particular brand of cigarette. When Brice heard of the outrage she was said to have quipped, "For that kind of money, I'll endorse an opium pipe.")

The Benefit opened at Chicago's Palace Theatre on June 12, when the *Chicago Tribune* reported, "by mid-week indications, is a real box-office draw." In addition to Jeanne's segment, Bert Lahr and Mercedes de Acosta performed 'What's the Idea?' Also in the cast were Jimmy Conlin and Myrtle Glass, a musical duo called Herma and Juan Reyes, and a troupe of European acrobats known as The Florinis.

A June 16 article published in the *Border Cities Star* of Windsor, Ontario, revealed Jeanne's pugnacious attitude towards Actors Equity. "Why, the whole thing is silly," she retorted. "A handful of actors, for whom with a few exceptions, I have no respect, cannot keep me from my public, which I know is a big one. I have never been a full-fledged member of Equity—I joined the organization under protest in 1925, at the insistence of my manager, Sam H. Harris. It's an organization for the rank-and-file, and I don't belong to the rank-and-file. I'm not the kind that stands in line to kick as high as the next. A creative person cannot be bound by labor union rules. It can't stop me."

Jeanne's old friend, Ethel Barrymore, was a member of the ruling committee. Asked about the suspension, she replied, "I have not, will not now, and do not intend ever to have a word to say on that question." However, she did share her thoughts on Actors Equity: "I am Equity. I am its vice-president. Without me it would never have come into being. It is natural, of course, that I support Equity in everything it does and that I have perfect confidence in its officers." Nonetheless, Eddie Doherty contended that it was Barrymore who persuaded the other board members not to ban Jeanne permanently.

"That will only hurt Equity members," fellow council member Ruth Gordon objected. "Jeanne can always be in a show, then actors are employed. She's rich, she doesn't have to work . . . Fine her. If she misses a performance, make her pay a forfeit, she'll think a long time before she pays out money."

"They took the vote and banned her from the stage," Gordon wrote later. "She told Equity to go to hell . . . I got sore at everybody but Frank Gillmore and resigned from the Equity Council."

The following week found Jeanne and company in Cleveland. "One should know a considerable amount about these plays to understand and appreciate Miss Eagels' extracts from them," the *Plain Dealer* observed. On June 24, Jeanne returned to Milwaukee—where her present difficulties had begun—for a week's residency at the Orpheum-Palace Theatre. Perhaps hoping to redeem herself, she confessed to the *Milwaukee Sentinel*, "*Her Cardboard Lover* was too much for me; I couldn't do it. There were many complications. The play is very strenuous. In the second act I am talking continually for more than an hour. I wasn't feeling well. Then I had been loaned out to producers other than Sam Harris, with whom I had worked happily for years and years, and well, the troubles piled up."

"I arrived Sunday. My trunks and wardrobe didn't," she told another reporter. "Therefore it was impossible for me to give a show. The papers will say that I've been on a spree, or that I reeled into the theatre too drunk to play. Well, let them say it. I'm the girl that always gets the swell breaks. I'm the hard-hearted Hannah of the stage."

In between performances and interviews, Jeanne also attended a screening of *If I Were Single*, a comedy with May McAvoy, at the Hennepin Orpheum in Minneapolis. Although the film was silent, McAvoy had recently starred in the first picture with sound: *The Jazz Singer*. As well as providing a much-needed diversion, this exciting development may have helped Jeanne to see the medium in a new light. As Ruth Gordon told Equity, "Famous Players Lasky [were] begging her to give up the stage and do a film in their Long Island studio."

***

Determined to finalize her divorce, Jeanne was traveling back and forth between Milwaukee and Chicago. On June 29, her case was heard by Judge Joseph Sabbath at the Superior Court of Chicago. Jeanne required no alimony, property settlement, or lawyer's fees from Coy, and the divorce was filed on grounds of cruelty. Although Ted had reportedly collected a letter from the Ambassador Hotel on the day of the hearing, he was absent from the courtroom.

"A few months after the marriage he began beating and torturing her," Jeanne's mother, Julia, claimed in court. "Told her that he would ruin her face for the movies."

When Jeanne answered questions in a whisper, Judge Sabbath admonished her: "You must keep your voice up." She replied, "I think I've lost my voice." Perhaps expecting her to be brasher, an incredulous Sabbath responded, "You don't mean to tell me you're nervous?" Whereupon she answered, "I am, honestly—it's my first appearance." She then described repeated altercations that had begun in January 1927—five months after their wedding—when Coy bruised her wrists during a quarrel. Since then, she explained, "... the arguing was non-stop, usually ending up in threats or violence."

While appearing in Chicago during the *Rain* tour, Coy came to her apartment and beat her, pinching her arms so hard she felt the pain for months. The final straw came during a return trip from the West, on the Manhattan-bound train. "Mr. Coy arranged to occupy my maid's berth while she shared my accommodations," Jeanne revealed. "The fighting started again at the station before we boarded the train. When we got aboard he seized my wrist, leaving marks on them. Then he struck me on the face and so disfigured me that I could not appear on the New York stage for weeks."

Ernest Byfield, president of the Hotel Sherman, supported Jeanne's testimony. "Miss Eagels came to the hotel on October 4, 1927 with her eye badly discolored," he told the court. "She said she had quarreled with Ted on the train and that he had struck her." This may explain her hesitation in returning to New York from Los Angeles. Jeanne's high-strung temperament had masked the reality of physical abuse, and although Ted denied being violent towards her, his jealousy and frustration had soured the relationship. Sadly, it seems all too plausible that Coy could have resorted to brute force.

In his interview with Doherty after Jeanne's death, Ted gave his explanation of what caused her black eye in Chicago. By his account, the couple had boarded the train in Los Angeles with half-a-dozen bottles of whiskey in Jeanne's luggage, which she began drinking as soon as the door closed on their compartment. An angry Coy threw all six bottles out the window of the moving train (although it might have been a smarter move to stow one away.) The couple undressed and climbed into their berths, and for a while it seemed that the storm had passed. "I thought she had gone to sleep," Coy said. "But I was wrong. She got up suddenly, saying that her maid, who was sleeping . . . at the other end of the car, had a few bottles. She intended to get them, and defied me to stop her."

According to Coy, Jeanne leapt out of her berth, clad in a flimsy nightgown, and headed for the compartment door. Trying to stop her, he "reached out and tried to grab her arm to hold her. The train was going around a curve at the time . . . She jerked away from me, and slipped and fell, striking a corner of the lower berth. That's how she got the broken jaw and the black eye. I never struck her . . . I never put my hands on her, except in tenderness."

Neither Coy nor Jeanne were in the courtroom on July 11 when Sabbath reached a decision. Jeanne was appearing at the Orpheum in Winnipeg, while Coy was most probably in El Paso. His lawyer informed Sabbath that Coy would not contest the divorce—perhaps because if he did, it might not be granted. It had crushed him to discover that he should have never married Jeanne. He was unable to satisfy her emotional needs, and neither of them could be happy together. Despite everything, Coy still loved Jeanne deeply, but was ready to let her go.

Following the recent divorces of actresses Fanny Brice and Helen Menken, Judge Sabbath questioned Jeanne's legal right to seek a divorce in Illinois. "I don't want to encourage Chicago as a Reno," he told the court, adding, "I want to be sure that the complainant has the legal requirements entitling her to a decree in Illinois." Jeanne's attorney, Orville Taylor, promised to meet the judge's requisites. After submission of evidence, a decree was drafted. Sabbath signed the decree three days later, and the marriage was finally over.

"[Coy] was not cut out for that kind of life," Clifton Webb wrote later. "He was not cut out for the demanding personality she was . . . to be the husband of a star. He had been a great hero in his own name. This [marriage] took something away from him and you could see the deterioration. I think his background impressed her. In the first place he was very handsome. She saw that she could upset his placid life and that intrigued her. One moment a saint, the next a tigress. She could turn at the snap of a finger."

Having interviewed Coy for his *Liberty Magazine* serialization, Doherty drew a similar conclusion. ". . . Ted Coy was as great a legend as Jeanne Eagels was to be. Life sometimes destroys a man by making him a legend." And Coy was no match for Jeanne. "[She] was proud of him—at first. He was so handsome, so willing to be her slave, such a really big man in his own world. Sports writers were always hunting him up and asking his opinion of football stars and football coaches, and now and then they mentioned him in print."

Apart from their fame and physical beauty, the pair had little in common: "Ted lived in the past. Jeanne in the present and future."

It wasn't as if Coy didn't love Jeanne enough; he was deeply besotted, even to the point of self-abasement. "He would rather lose his self-respect and the respect of his friends than lose her . . . he put up with the insults public and private to be with her. He let her humiliate and nag him and never complained . . . He was too much the gentleman. . . ." Almost from the outset, Coy had "no chance of happiness" with Jeanne.

Another breaking point was the couple's mutual tendency towards excess, in the form of alcohol. "Jeanne Eagels never smoked until she began to rehearse for *Rain*. She didn't drink whisky, and she seldom drank heavily of anything until after she married Ted Coy."

Another barrier between them was that Coy had never been exposed to the theatre crowd and didn't know how to act around them. He fell silent, not understanding nor really caring about their gossip or discussion of the latest productions. Given the opportunity to get out of the situation, even running a simple errand for Jeanne, gave him the chance to escape.

"Jeanne dominated him from the start and despised Coy because he let her. She despised him because he couldn't control her increasing alcohol problem. She didn't particularly like to drink. But he begged her not to drink. Therefore she drank to spite him. . . ."

Before their marriage, Jeanne had rarely consumed anything stronger than champagne, although she sometimes took heated gin for her physical issues. "Jeanne wanted to drink only with people she liked, people who knew why she drank, and who would protect her," Doherty wrote. "She had a horror of being watched by strangers. She never wanted to go to night clubs or banquets. Ted who wanted her to shine in public, couldn't understand it." And their quarrels only led to more drinking.

The delicate, reserved manner which older friends like Cecil Cunningham admired in Jeanne changed for the worse when she was "in her cups." While rehearsing for *Chicago*, director George Abbott had heard from Jeanne's man-servant, Tony, about how she had challenged Coy to a boxing match with him.

Clifton Webb also remembered one alcohol-fueled fight with Jeanne as her marriage fell apart. "Jeanne invited me up to Ossining for the weekend," he wrote, "and I when I came downstairs in the morning I found them in the kitchen, both wearing dressing gowns. Eagels jumped up and pointing to Coy told me, 'See that son of a bitch, he's filled with gin, he's hitting the bottle.'" Obviously inebriated herself, she pushed further with Webb. "'Want to know what that son of a bitch tried to do to me on their train ride home?' Before Webb could answer, she continued, 'He tried to break my arm.' Taking great offense at Webb's apparent disinterest, Jeanne threw him out—and when she later telephoned to apologize, Clifton refused to pick up.

Several months after the row, she confronted her friend at Noel Coward's home. "She burst through the door," Webb recalled, yelling, "'You son of a bitch. Why didn't you knock him down? You could have protected me...' We both started laughing and were back again to where we started. She used healthy profanity, but she used it beautifully."

Madame Savage, Jeanne's vocal coach, agreed with Webb. "Her marriage was unhappy, as everyone knows," she told reporters. "Both realized it was a mistake. She wanted him to be her slave. He loved her too much. He let her have her way, always." Many years later, Ruth Gordon would echo their sentiments: "It was awful to see a man so cowed. He was a polite man, and up against Jeanne he didn't stand a chance."

The divorce, as Paul Wagner noted, "added to Jeanne's already gaudy reputation for raising hell." Wagner added that "Coy, who objected to her drinking, drank to excess himself in order to shame her, and she in turn drank still more to punish him for presuming to correct her." The marriage ended, Wagner believed, because "[Ted] and Jeanne were both intensely unhappy, and it was simply easier for him to let her have her own way."

Less than a month after the divorce, Coy married his third wife, Lottie Bruhn, of El Paso. She was twenty-one, nineteen years his junior. The couple had met while Coy was investigating potential franchises for Town and Country. At around this time, a New York City jeweler filed suit against Coy for $700 owed on an emerald and diamond bar pin plus a ring. The newlyweds arrived in Los Angeles for an indefinite honeymoon, as Coy's only job prospect was as Head Coach at El Paso's Texas School of Mines. The couple stayed in Northern California for a couple of years, before returning to New York, where Coy found work as an insurance broker at 56 Williams Street. On March 3, 1933, the former football star and financial investor filed for bankruptcy, owing $14,000 against $700 in assets. Coy died of a heart attack on September 8, 1935.

Several months after his death, *Time* magazine ran a story about Coy's widow pawning his most prized possessions. "Into an Oklahoma City pawnshop stepped a pretty young woman to borrow money on a wedding ring, a gold medal, a gold football, a pin of Yale's famed Skull & Bones Society[18]. Each was engraved: E. H. COY—YALE U. 'Could it be Ted Coy, the Yale athlete?' ventured the pawnbroker. 'Yes,' said the girl, 'I am his wife.' Last week, as the pawnbroker wrote to Skull & Bones in New Haven which immediately bought Coy's relics, news hawks tracked down Lottie Bruhn Coy, now working as a servant. Said she: 'Yes, I'm Mrs. Ted Coy. How on earth did you find me here? I haven't any money . . . Once I went five days in this town without a bite to eat . . . I thank God for a sense of humor. If I didn't have it I'd have been bad off these months since Ted died. . .'"

Another Jazz Age casualty, F. Scott Fitzgerald, paid eloquent tribute. "Ted Coy, if anybody asks you, was one of our greatest athletes," the author told a student. "He's Ted Fay, Basil's godlike football hero in 'The Freshest Boy' and I used him for other characters. He was one of my heroes. Ted

---

18 Coy's personal Skull and Bones 1910 Yearbook was recently offered for sale by a Manhattan rare book dealer.

died a couple of days ago. A heart attack. Forty-seven, bankrupt, and forgotten except by his teammates, sports writers, and fans like me."

***

On August 10, the *Oakland Tribune* confirmed that newly single Jeanne was rekindling a past romance. She had traveled from Seattle to San Francisco aboard the *H.F. Alexander*, and was met at the dock by Whitney Warren, Jr., now studying agriculture at the University of California and living in a small apartment in the Marina district. "They glimpsed each other, shouted first names, and rushed into an embrace," the *Oakland Tribune* gushed. "Thereafter was an uncensored kiss that staggered even the customs inspectors, who see something in everything." Fleeing the press, Junior whisked "the attractive little star away with him in his car."

Jeanne retained her ability to charm, though her latest vehicle was uneven. "That Miss Eagels could portray the two roles in the few minutes allotted her and do them justice is sufficient proof of her artistry to suit the most exacting," the *Oakland Tribune* remarked, warning that "her supporting cast is negligible but sufficient for the purpose of the sketch." By the time *The Benefit* reached Oakland, its few remaining performers included armless golfer Tommy McAuliffe, singing duo the Tiller Sisters, and a bagpiper/comic.

Writing for the *Los Angeles Times*, Philip K. Scheuer thought it offered "the briefest glimpse of this memorable drama by John Colton and Clemence Randolph—merely a pertinent segment of the second act—but it served. It again served to stamp upon the retina the image of one of the greatest of our actresses in the greatest of her roles: there have been other Sadie Thompsons, but there is only one Jeanne Eagels."

"A girl in her early teens leaving the theatre with her companion after the performance, explained, very positively, just what Miss Eagels is like: 'You have to get used to her personality. She stands,' concluded this young lady, 'and squeaks.'"

On September 5, after a week at the Orpheum in Los Angeles, Jeanne returned to Kansas City for the day to visit with her mother, brother George sister Edna, nieces, nephews and aunts before heading off to Chicago and then on to New York. Sitting in her suite at the Hotel Muehlebach, "resplendent in yellow silk pajamas with her hair looking very blond and untrammeled," she commented on a variety of subjects with a *Kansas City Star* reporter during a breakfast interview.

On her homecoming visit: "I would think it would be jinxing my luck if I didn't. I got my start here and all my friends and family live in town, and Kansas City is pretty much the center of things for me."

As for her Equity: "It is going to work out all right, I feel sure. After all, I played five years in *Rain* and missed only eighteen performances and [that] should show I am not such a bad trouper. The case is supposed to be reopened in New York soon and I hope will be adjusted satisfactorily."

On her past experiences in the film industry, and Swanson's *Sadie Thompson*: "The money was both alluring and flattering." But she was in no hurry to recreate her iconic performance for the screen. "I would like to stick very closely to the text if I made *Rain* for the talkies," she said, hinting at the compromises Swanson had made. When asked about the "unbridled moments" in the dialogue, Jeanne "saw no difficulty, 'I slurred them over in the play so no one was offended, and I could do the same thing in the photoplay.'"

Even her romantic relationships were not off-limits, but she was in no hurry to remarry as Coy had done. She laughed at "how the Actor's Colony on the Pacific Coast had speculated on her coming nuptials to no less than four different men. 'And there is safety in numbers,' she quipped, motioning to the man sitting beside her at the table with her mother Julia, and brother George. 'One of the gentlemen is Mr. O'Neill.' The actor smiled in pleasant self-consciousness as she continued. 'Now you can see that he is rapidly demolishing a breakfast consisting of ham and eggs, buttered toast, coffee and a dish of ice cream. Any man who can ham and eggs and ice cream for breakfast should be easy to get along with, at least.'"

Doherty claims O'Neill and Eagels continued their relationship though Jeanne, repeating the pattern of her relationship with Coy, often treated him poorly. At the opening night of a play, she left O'Neill alone while she maneuvered the room, chatting with friends. "Barry would sulk. 'What's the matter with you?' he demanded. 'Why don't you introduce me to your friends? Are you ashamed of me? You needn't be. I'm as big as you are.'" This was wishful thinking, as O'Neill's stage career would subsequently limp along with scattered bit parts, and seasons in summer stock; touring again opposite Mae West in *Sex* for the 1930-31 season; and a final Broadway role in *Shooting Star*, a 1933 play based upon Eagels' life.

Once home, Eagels returned to Ossining, but not to the rambling acreage once shared with Coy. She had purchased a new residence much closer to town, at 145 Cedar Lane. The four-story ten-room Tudor-style home had four bedrooms, each with its own bath, a basement, and a detached two-car garage. Built in 1927, the house hugged the side of Bald Mountain. Jeanne planned to build a wall to keep out noise and uninvited guests. "The kind of house one sees on the sides or the tops of California hills," as Doherty described it. "The land drops away from it in an almost sheer descent...one might roll down but few could walk down that slope...The view from her windows was so lovely that it compensated for the fact."

"You should see my house!" Jeanne enthused, in an interview with *Picture Play*'s Evelyn Gerstein. "It's way up on the top of a cliff...And this time I haven't any farm. It was too much bother. I had hens and cows and a stable and kennels. Now I just have a few fruit trees and Mika, my dog, and my eight Schnauzers, and a box of pansies. That's as rural as I am now. It's really only a town house in the country." Inside, white stucco walls contrasted with dark hardwood floors and matching trim around the windows and door frames. Heavy wood beams crisscrossed the ceilings, with a fireplace against one wall in the living room. "There isn't anything that matches, there's no particular style," she confided. "I just bought things as they appealed to me. I've got Madame Récamier's furniture, the real pieces that are more than two hundred years old.[19] When I bought them they were covered with a worn yellow brocade, so of course I have them recovered. I picked out nice, antique-looking damask, and it looked so lovely and old in the shops. Now that it's on, it's such a bright pink that I guess I'll have to rub cold cream over it to antique it. I've got all sorts of colored pottery, Italian tea sets, red glasses with gold edges—I suppose the reason I'm so crazy about them is because I didn't have them when I was a little girl."

Nonetheless, she still needed to find an apartment in New York and eventually secured one through an old friend. Ward Morehouse was dining at Le Mirliton, on East Fifty-Eighth Street between Fifth and Madison Avenues, when Jeanne arrived and was seated at a nearby table. After exchanging greetings, Jeanne asked if the columnist lived in the area. Pointing at the ceiling, he replied that his home was a third-floor walk-up, directly overhead.

Jeanne admitted that she found the drive to and from Westchester County rather tiring, and was looking for "modest quarters" in a neighborhood like his, "to get away from the crowds." Morehouse showed her his apartment and thought nothing more of the matter. "Two weeks later," he wrote, "there was a circus-like commotion in my block as Miss Eagels, having rented an apartment on the floor just below me, arrived with her entourage—a cook, maid, and chauffeur ... and there were times, I believe, when a butler put in an appearance!"

"Before the coming of the erstwhile Sadie Thompson," Morehouse admitted, "life above the ground-floor Mes Amis restaurant had never been particularly serene, but now, once she had moved in, there was a forever bustle on the stairway..."

According to Morehouse, Jeanne and her entourage stayed for a month in the cramped apartment before heading back to Westchester County. What Morehouse didn't know then was that the actress was secretly preparing for a resurgence in her career.

---

19 Juliette Récamier (1777-1849) was a society hostess and renowned beauty whose salon attracted the leading political and literary figures of early nineteenth century Paris.

Lead actors from the *Her Cardboard Lover* tour: Top left - Anthony Bushell; Top right - Jeanne posing outside her Ossining home; Bottom L-R - Barry O'Neill, George Eagles, Julia Eagles, and Jeanne in Kansas City.

Top - Illustration of Eagels' Cedar Lane home in Ossining, New York. Bottom - Ninety years later, the exterior remains virtually unchanged. *Photo courtesy of John Duel.*

Top - Dining room of Cedar Lane residence. Bottom - Living room.
Photos courtesy and copyright Jean Cameron-Smith/North Country Sotheby's International Realty

Top - Master bedroom Cedar Lane. Bottom - Third floor sitting area.
Photos courtesy and copyright Jean Cameron-Smith/North Country Sotheby's International Realty

Eagels as Sadie Thompson in Seattle Washington during *The Benefit* tour.

Arriving in San Francisco aboard the *H. F. Alexander*, where she would be met by former paramour Warren Whitney Jr.

Ted Coy and his third wife, Charlotte "Lottie" Bruhn. In El Paso Texas, the day of their August 5th marriage.

Chapter 14
Klieg Eyes: January 1928–September 1929

In *The Jazz Singer* (1927), Al Jolson became the first actor to speak (and sing) in a feature-length motion picture, and his audience's thrilled reaction threw the industry into a panic. New stages and equipment were hastily ordered, while even established actors were subjected to stringent vocal tests, which could make or break a career. As 1928 began, Broadway producers including the Shuberts and A. H. Woods toyed with the idea of filming the next season's successes rather than touring, a grave concern for Actors' Equity.

Founded in 1912 by Adolph Zukor and the Frohman Brothers, the Famous Players Film Company became Famous Players Lasky Corporation in 1916. It was renamed Paramount Famous Lasky Corporation in 1927, and finally Paramount Pictures Incorporated in 1936. Paramount's Eastern production manager, Monta Bell (who had directed Jeanne in MGM's *Man, Woman and Sin*) was overseeing the construction of what would soon be referred to as "sound stages," in preparation for the reopening of the old Astoria lot. Paramount had plans to make forty to fifty sound films and "shorts" there, including Erich Von Stroheim's *The Wedding March*; *The Canary Murder Case*, starring William Powell and Louise Brooks; and *Three Weekends*, with Clara Bow. "I don't believe that the amount of talking there will be in films necessitates the importing of new talent," said studio founder Jesse L. Lasky. "We are using the same stars and featured players in our sound films that we used in our silents. Their names are already established—and I believe it is better to use them than to try and build up new players. Even with the new people we are signing, we are stressing acting ability more than vocal quality."

Following Lasky's creed, Paramount's first full-length "talkie" would be *The Letter*. During the same season that Jeanne was starring in *Her Cardboard Lover*, Katherine Cornell had played the lead role in W. Somerset Maugham's stage play. *The Letter* told the story of Leslie Crosbie, the adulterous wife of a Singapore rubber plantation manager. Spurned by her lover, Leslie shoots him and is put on trial for murder. As she lies under oath about why she killed him, her freedom is threatened by an incriminating letter, now in the possession of the dead man's Chinese mistress. A humiliated Leslie is forced to visit a back-alley bordello to collect the evidence. After her subsequent acquittal, she returns home to face her husband, who vows to make the plantation—a place she despises—her prison until death do them part.

"With all my heart," Leslie strikes back, "I still love the man I killed!"

The Letter was inspired by a Malaysian court case from 1911, in which a Mrs. Proudlock, sentenced to hang for murder, was pardoned by the Sultan after a petition was widely circulated among her British colonial friends. Maugham had learned about the case from Mrs. Proudlock's lawyer, who explained that the evidence against her had been non-existent. Leslie Crosbie's guilt, as proven by "the letter," was the novelist's own invention, and the Malaysian press was outraged by his digging up the colony's scandalous past.

Jeanne's much-publicized difficulties during filming of *Man, Woman and Sin* had cost her a long-term contract at MGM. At thirty-eight, she would soon be too old for the youthful parts offered to the studio's leading actresses, Greta Garbo and Joan Crawford. Norma Shearer's recent marriage to Irving Thalberg, who now headed production at MGM, had reduced Jeanne's standing even further. "If you don't want her, I want her," Monta Bell said when she was dropped by MGM. But their decision was final.

More than a year had passed since the troubled shoot, and it seemed Bell was ready to work with Jeanne again. "The popular opinion that Miss Eagels is highly temperamental and is hard to work with has no foundation in fact," he claimed. "I know of no other actress I would rather have working under me than Miss Eagels. Our association together in making *Man, Woman and Sin* was altogether happy. My interest in having Miss Eagels signed for future pictures at the time was prompted by the knowledge that she would be one of the most powerful attractions to the public and would bring a fresh and desirable element to the screen." Jean de Limur—who had worked with Chaplin and DeMille—would be making his directorial debut. As cameraman George Folsey remembered, Bell actually directed most of the picture: "... but he did it kind of in the background. I think he was trying to groom De Limur to be a director."

Jeanne's contract called for her to be paid $25,000 for eight-weeks of production time. Should filming extend past two months, she would receive a prorated salary. On September 28, 1928, the *Exhibitors Daily Review* reported ". . . that exhaustive tests were being made of the star at the Long Island studios." Production began on October 16, with Reginald Owen cast as Mr. Crosbie. Herbert Marshall would play the doomed lover, and Chinese actress Lady Tsen Mei the devious mistress. "Among some of the artists who appear in the courtroom scenes," the *Moberly Monitor-Index and Democrat* would reveal on May 14, 1929, "are Gordon Clifford, brother of Ruth Clifford, picture star; Antrim Short, formerly a star 'boy' actor in Hollywood; Sydney Deane, a veteran of stage and screen. . ."

The Long Island lot's largest stage now held a full-sized bungalow in the heart of a rubber plantation; various homes and offices; an Oriental bordello; and a crowded street-market with stalls, animals, and back alleys. The biggest set by far was the interior of a Singapore courtroom. To ensure authenticity, pre-production research by the studio included court procedures, room interiors, and costume details. A total of 125 extras included over two dozen Chinese, Malays, and Hindus, who arrived in New York during the last week of October. *Photoplay* told its readers that incense was burned on the set daily, and perfumes worn by the Asian actresses—infusions of sandalwood and ylang ylang—were imported from China, as were the tobacco and cigarettes smoked in the film.

It was an unusually cold fall, with snow in mid-October, so visitors to the set wore heavy raccoon coats to protect themselves from the chill. As the *Boston Globe* noted, they "... discarded their wraps while standing near the sets . . . the huge studio, normally quite cold, is heated to the temperature of summer so that the actors and actresses would not acquire pneumonia." The *Boston Globe* also mentioned ". . . the heavy scent of tropical oleanders filling the studio as Jeanne Eagels and other members of the cast lolled about in duck costumes and summer frocks."

"She was a very strange woman I must say," cameraman George Folsey recalled of *The Letter*'s star. "She must have been on some drugs or some other medication or something—I don't know. But she was very weird and strange. She didn't know who I was . . . She was in another world at that time."

Photographs of Jeanne at the time seem to contradict Folsey's words, showing her smiling and healthy on the courtroom set in one picture, and looking over the script with Bell in another. "They say she is the first person in the studio each morning and the last one to leave at night," the *Daily Review Atlas* commented, "and during the making of most of the picture has been far from well but has never complained a minute nor has her famous temperament been in evidence. This, of course, is something to be encouraged about as Miss Eagels did 'her number' on more than one occasion while at the MGM studio last year and the word was passed around that she was impossible to handle." It seems Jeanne was trying hard to prove her reliability. Mark Barrow, a reporter who lived across the hall from Jeanne on East Fifty-Eighth recalled: "She was determined to make a comeback and worked hard for twelve hours every day, twelve hours which were doubly hard because she forcibly suppressed that fiery temperament which kept her in so much trouble."

The studio executives must have disagreed with Folsey, as well, because on November 10, the *Exhibitors' Daily Review* reported that after seeing the rushes, Paramount was offering Jeanne a three-year contract, paying $150,000 a year for two or three films within each twelve-month period. Jeanne only wanted to make two films on that salary, and counter-offered for three films (at an annual wage of $200,000).

Although her reputation preceded her, sound equipment was the foremost challenge to the cast and crew of *The Letter*. Scenes were rehearsed repeatedly, as the actors were learning to move within the microphone's scope The filmmakers were using equipment so sensitive that the gentle pawing of a cat against a door recorded at thunderstorm levels; and they once spent two days figuring a natural-looking method of lighting a cigarette without making it sound like an explosion.

The opening scene culminated with a gun-toting Jeanne crouching over her lover's dead body. As author Scott O'Brien revealed in his biography of Herbert Marshall, while filming this tense moment, a musician dropped his guitar on the set and the sound take was ruined. Jeanne stood by helplessly, until Marshall rolled over and laughed. The scene had to be redone immediately, as Marshall was due to leave for the Fulton Theatre, where he was currently appearing in *The High Road*. "Those new talking pictures, they are like that animal you call the Ass," director Jean de Limur told reporter Rosa Reilly. "Stupid, stubborn ... we don't know what to do with him." As for Jeanne, Reilly thought her "a high-strung, nervous racehorse ... waiting for the webbing to go up."

Also disabling the microphones in this scene was the noise of the pistol Jeanne repeatedly fires. These issues were resolved by putting less powder in the gun's charge and moving the microphone further away. In a 1929 *Photoplay* article, examining the problems incurred by sound technology, it was reported that while Jeanne was filming *The Letter*'s dramatic coda in which Leslie proclaims her undying love, the intensity of her speech "smashed the delicate wiring of the recording instrument."

This was a great deal of effort for a film that would ultimately be shown in very few venues; the *New York Times* observed that work had already begun on a silent version of the film, as only 1,000 of over 25,000 theaters across the USA were currently wired for sound movies.

"*The Letter*, supervised by Monta Bell, is perhaps my favorite picture," legendary producer Walter Wanger told *Silver Screen* magazine in 1933. (At the time of filming, Wanger was overseeing all of Paramount's East Coast productions.) "In fact, I do not believe this has ever been topped in point of dramatic and emotional climaxes," he added. "Jeanne Eagels, what an artist she was! She was ill during the filming of the picture but insisted on keeping on. It was amazing to watch her as the great actress rising to thrilling emotion and power before the cameras, only to droop into a sick little girl the minute they stopped clicking."

Despite all the technical and personal issues that had arisen during production, *The Letter* wrapped two weeks ahead of schedule, in the third week of November. Jeanne was able to enjoy Thanksgiving with her mother who was visiting New York. Their merriment came to an abrupt end on November 23, when Whitney Warren Jr. was involved in a serious car accident in California. Jeanne was advised about the condition of her former fiancé, now hospitalized with a skull fracture. "Of course I'm terribly sorry to hear it," she told the *Brooklyn Standard Union*. "Who wouldn't be? I have a telegram however which says he will undoubtedly recover[20]."

---

20 The seriousness of any physical relationship, dating back to when they first met, is questionable. Junior settled in San Francisco, where he became a patron of the arts and hosted lavish parties for the rich and famous. Warren died in 1986 a lifelong bachelor—or in simpler terms he, like Clifton Webb, was gay.

Two weeks after the accident, columnist Walter Winchell declared, "Whitney Warren Junior isn't Jeanne Eagels 'heart'—it's Gilbert Outhwaite of the social register." With O'Neill currently on Broadway in *A Man With Red Hair*, Eagels needed an escort and Outhwaite fit the bill.

Eddie Doherty described him as a "thin, spruce, aristocratic-looking real estate broker." Partner in Wagstaff and Outhwaite, a firm which dealt in exclusive high-end Park Avenue addresses, "Icky" as Jeanne nicknamed him, lived in the same building and soon became a frequent companion. "She liked him because he was young and wholesome and ... different." He wouldn't drop everything when Eagels summoned him. Like Coy, he didn't know much about the theatre and its crowd, so when Jeanne would get together with friends and Outhwaite grew bored, he would find a comfortable chair and take a nap until the party was over. If she tried to pull a diva act, he cut her down to size and he had no problem telling her that at times, she drank too much. These were qualities she found attractive.

"But it's so refreshing to go anywhere with him,' she told her friends in amazement. "He actually insists on paying the check for my dinner. That hasn't happened to me in years."

Actress Jane Cowl was puzzled the first time she saw Outhwaite and Eagels out together. "Is that another one of Jeanne's lovers?" she was overheard to ask.

"Tragedy!" cried Jeanne, mimicking Cowl in full dramatic flight. "Tragedy, tragedy, tragedy! For God's sake," she admonished, "try to be human once in a while."

***

In the last week of November, both *Moving Picture World* and *Variety* revealed how everyone from studio executives to the property and technical staff have found the actress to be nothing less than a saint. "Not once has her temperamental streak manifested itself, although she has been required to work from early morning to late hours in the evening." On December 10, *Film Review* announced that Jeanne had signed a contract to make two more films for Paramount, though on different terms than either party had initially proposed. The first picture, for which she was to be paid a $60,000 flat fee, would begin shooting in March 1929. The second—to be completed before the August rehearsals of her new stage production—would pay $65,000. Sam Harris was hoping to cast Jeanne in *The Sainted Wench*, penned by *Rain* co-author John Colton.

Jeanne's social activities over the next month were dutifully noted by Ward Morehouse. She was among the guests at Clifton Webb's December 8 party; on December 20, she was helped into her town car by a Japanese chauffeur outside her home. Alongside Claudette Colbert and Charles Ruggles, Jeanne was spotted again on December 28, at the Famous Players Studio in Astoria.

Jeanne started the New Year at an address more suited to her needs. While keeping her small flat on East Fifty-Eighth, she moved to 1143 Park Avenue on January 1, 1929. The residence was sublet from actress, screenwriter, and wife of Basil Rathbone, Ouida Bergére. In *Picture Play*'s July issue, Evelyn Gerstein described the abode as ". . . a dull gold and green and maroon apartment—with Spanish mirrors, Oriental rugs of chaste blues and reds, dull-gold brocade curtains, and a sprawling white-bear rug." Had Gerstein peeked into the upstairs bedroom, she would have found a bed upon a dais, with a pair of giant gold eagles standing guard.

Two days later, Jeanne was back at the Famous Players Studio, joining Richard Dix, Walter Huston, and Monta Bell for lunch in the Dining Room. Walter Winchell's next column delved into her personal life again, revealing she had moved on from Whitney Warren Jr. to former *Her Cardboard Lover* co-star Barry O'Neill, with whom she was now "cooing." (Winchell must have forgotten his previous mention of Gilbert Outhwaite.) Gossips wondered if the couple were resuming their short-lived romance during last year's tour, or if it was merely a rebound fling after a failed attempt on Jeanne's part to seduce her erstwhile leading man, Anthony Bushell.

Paramount announced on February 2 that they had purchased *Jealousy*, the two-character play staged last season with Fay Bainter, for Jeanne's next picture. The storyline focused on Yvonne, newly married to Pierre, a poor and temperamental artist. Envious of Yvonne's warm relationship with former lover Rigaud, Pierre is furious when, in good faith, Rigaud lends Yvonne money to open a dress shop. Discovering Yvonne in Rigaud's apartment, Pierre assumes the worst and kills his supposed rival. When another man is accused of the murder, Pierre does nothing. The truth is finally uncovered in an overwrought courtroom finale, with Pierre confessing his crime and accepting his fate.

The Letter had its premiere on March 7, 1929 at the Criterion Theatre. Jeanne had arranged to bring along twenty guests, including her mother, sister Helen, and escort Barry O'Neill. She didn't stay in her seat for very long, slowly walking up the aisle to the lobby and back, hoping to overhear a positive comment or two. She attended another screening the next day, dressed down to avoid recognition, and quietly observed the audience's reaction. "Jeanne was proud of her work in *The Letter*, and the advertising it was given," Doherty wrote. "She took her mother for a ride up Broadway, that she might see the sign—the biggest sign on Broadway—with Jeanne's name blazoned across it for millions to read. 'I owe that to Equity,' she said with a giggle. 'I hope Frank Gillmore sees it.'"

Although somewhat overshadowed by the 1940 remake starring Bette Davis, *The Letter* remains a lasting testament to Jeanne's extraordinary talent, from the time of its release to the present day.

"None of the cinema's long succession of women testifying in their own defense has told as convincingly as Jeanne Eagels how she fired the shot that saved her virtue. None has begun her testimony with a more positive knowledge of her guilt fixed in the minds of the audience, which has seen her a minute before, transformed with fury, committing the actual murder." – *Time*

"A performance that holds the spectator from first to last with compelling intensity." – *New York Telegram*

"One of the most gorgeous portrayals ever caught upon the silver screen." – *New York Journal-American*

"Jeanne Eagels proves herself as sterling an actress in this talking motion picture as she ever was on the stage. . ." – *Motion Picture News*

"From the expressive acting of Eagels, the audience gets the real character of the woman. She burns with an inner fire. . ." – *Schenectady Gazette*

"A most worthy debut for Jeanne Eagels as a talking actress . . . Miss Eagels does a powerful, we even say magnificent piece of work." – *New York Daily News*

". . . she offers what is assuredly the most moving, honest, and thoroughly exciting portrayal that talking pictures have provided." – *Galveston Daily News*

"Jeanne Eagels, disciplined by Equity, was barred from the stage . . . In spite of an unfortunate temperament and a strong tendency to do what she pleases, she is today highly regarded as a screen actress. The movies certainly came into Miss Eagels' life at the psychological moment, if you will pardon that banality." – Louella Parsons, May 4, 1929

"In a single performance, on the topmost pinnacle of artistic achievement. It gave the motion picture public a kind of acting it had never seen before." – George Brinton Beal, *Boston Post*

Eagels' performance would be lauded as the first to exhibit what would become, decades later, a major acting style still used today, as critics would note when a restored print of *The Letter* was released on DVD in 2011.

"Her ability to seize and stay 'in the moment'—as generations of Method actors would later characterize it—is formidably illustrated in the scene in which she shoots her unfaithful lover Herbert Marshall. Completely unconcerned with her appearance, a wild-eyed Eagels fires again and again, thrusting the gun forward with each shot as if it were a knife. In the climax of the film director Jean de Limur, in what appears to be a continuous take photographed from three angles, builds the scene to an annihilating force as Eagels, slowly realizing that her husband has a dreadful punishment planned for her, strikes back as violently as she knows how. Fixing her husband with a glare of pure hatred, Eagels spits out the famous curtain line—'With all my heart and all my soul, I still love the man I killed!'—and then, clearly carried away by the passion she has summoned, repeats it to even greater effect. It's a moment so sharp and vivid that it doesn't seem like acting at all, but rather an intensified force of being." – Dave Kehr, *New York Times*

"Eagels portrays a woman who spins a fiction under oath like a diva playing the wronged woman, and then loses her composure and social self-control under pressure, her words pouring out as if carried by a flood of unchecked emotions. The unexpected cadences of her line readings turn into spoken arias. It's the first inkling of a modern sound film performance, exciting and unexpected with the feeling of spontaneity, not yet perfected but definitely alive in an otherwise fossilized film." – Sean Axmaker, *Parallax View*

The closing scenes of Billy Wilder's *Sunset Boulevard* (1950), starring Jeanne's old rival Gloria Swanson as forgotten star Norma Desmond, bear a striking resemblance to the plot of *The Letter*. Norma's suicide threat echoes Jeanne's as Leslie Crosbie, and both women are abandoned by their lovers. "You don't think I meant it. You don't think I have the courage...", Leslie accuses Geoffrey Hammond (Herbert Marshall) after he ignores her threat in *The Letter*. The line is repeated almost verbatim in *Sunset Boulevard*, when Norma informs Joe Gillis (William Holden) that she has bought a gun to kill herself, and then runs away and retrieves it. Brandishing it in her hands, she tells him, "See you didn't believe me. Now I suppose you don't think I have the courage..." Hammond chooses his Chinese mistress over Crosbie, and Gillis the copy desk in Dayton, Ohio rather than life as Norma's kept "boy." Shortly thereafter, both women shoot their respective lovers, with Leslie unloading the full six shots while Norma fells Joe with three.

***

Jeanne was looking forward to her role in *Jealousy*, not least because playing a Parisian dress shop owner would allow her to wear the latest French fashions, including original couture by Poiret and Paquin, and a perfume change for each costume. Her clothing may have been new, but Jeanne was surrounded by familiar faces: with de Limur directing, Bell supervising, and Garrett Fort (who had also adapted *The Letter*) renaming the heroine Valerie and adding minor characters only alluded to in the play. Madame Savage's daughter, Nellie, played an unaccredited role as a mannequin. Alfred Gilks, a veteran cinematographer with over forty Paramount films to his credit, was sent from Los Angeles. Rigaud would be played by Halliwell Hobbes, with Jeanne's *Her Cardboard Lover* co-star, Anthony Bushell, cast as Pierre.

After watching Ruth Gordon in a performance of *Serena Blandish* at the Morosco Theatre that spring, Jeanne visited her dressing room. When Ruth asked, "How's the picture?" she replied, "Mad about it. They have to do exactly what I want. You know the chord in my voice? When they do something I don't like, I use it and it breaks the microphone."

Jeanne then asked Ruth about Henry Daniell, an Englishman who had a part in the play. "I'd like to see more of him," she said. As Gordon wrote later, "If she'd like to, she would." Daniell would soon play her lover, Clement, in *Jealousy*, although it is unknown whether Jeanne had any direct influence upon his casting.

With Jeanne among colleagues who knew and respected her, *Jealousy* should have progressed as comfortably as *The Letter*, but a March 24 report in the *New York Times* suggested otherwise.

"Miss Eagels, who takes the part of Valerie [later changed to Yvonne], wearing a tan sports costume with a green bandanna kerchief wound around her hair, slumped into a broad, velvet-backed chair and after folding a handkerchief into a small square she pressed it against her eyes. With her elbows resting on her knees and the handkerchief still pressed against her face, Miss Eagels began to sob. The star had been rehearsing a long, difficult dialogue scene all morning with very little recording done. The glare of the Dietz floodlights perched at all angles around the set along with the ruthless pounding of hammers from other parts of the stage and the difficulty in getting the stage business memorized with the lines, all played havoc with Miss Eagels' nerves."

She and co-star Halliwell Hobbes had spent the morning rehearsing in the library set, surrounded by multiple copies of *Messages and Papers of the Presidents*, and a great number of *The Transactions of the Congress American Physicians and Surgeons*. The pair were going over a pivotal scene between the shop owner and her business partner. So as not to strain their voices, the duo whispered their lines mechanically. At one point, a preoccupied Jeanne bent down to fix her stocking while uttering flatly, "I have come here to be alone with you."

Soon however, the stress became too much. "Miss Eagels stood up ... tears running down her cheeks she swiftly walked from the library into an adjoining set, the foyer of the apartment, and there, as if off-stage she wept again." A crew member came over to see if he could do anything. "But Miss Eagels only flopped into another chair and sobbed, murmuring some words about a 'possible breakdown' and 'strain.'... In a few moments she arose dry-eyed, her makeup partially washed off. With a sigh, she dropped her hands to her sides and slowly walked across the wide stage—to lunch."

***

Rain's director, John D. Williams, was also *Jealousy*'s head of dialogue, and he understood his leading lady's unique talents better than most.

"I have worked with some of the greatest stars of the theatre from

Maude Adams on, and there's not one of them with a keener sense of the thought between the lines than Jeanne Eagels. Many good actors imagine they have done all their duty when they speak their lines perfectly, with studious diction and careful emphasis. It is like putting a record on a phonograph. But Jeanne knows the thoughts and feeling of the character which make her give utterance to those words. She brings that understanding into her expression, and you get the full significance. The lines hit you, the way she speaks them. They are alive. So it happens that an audience at one of her plays or pictures will imagine that the lines she was given to speak were more natural, less banal, than those of other characters. Usually, the difference lies in the way she speaks them—not in the words themselves. But in addition to making the lines sound natural by her manner of speaking, she has a way of taking a script apart and substituting better lines. Phrases that are stilted give way to those which ring true. She has not only an ear for the sound of words but a heart which tells her whether people under such circumstances would feel such sentiments. It is fundamentally, a sense of the theatre, of what is dramatic. I know of no player on the stage whose instinct is more reliable."

Jeanne's illness temporarily halted production on April 3. It was rumored that she had been absent from the set for several days, after a series of rows with De Limur prompted her "retirement" from the studio. Paramount's publicity director, George Brill, denied the actress had walked out, stating, "She's ill. But is anxious to return to work. Hopefully production will resume by April 5 to give the actress the opportunity to travel to London and appear in *Congai* before the next picture in her contract." Based on a novel by Harry Hervey, *Congai* was first staged on Broadway at the Harris Theatre, starring Valerie Bergere as a mixed-race woman in early twentieth century French Indochina.

Variety noted that "leading man Anthony Bushell was also ill and was away two days longer than Miss Eagels." When Jeanne returned, she found herself in the company of a visiting group of Chilean dignitaries. The wives of the Chilean Ambassador and the publisher of its largest newspaper, accompanied by a military attaché, were observing how motion pictures were created. Jeanne was at her most charming that day but must have felt like an animal in the zoo. Production finished without further incident on April 12, and de Limur sailed for Europe eight days later.

After executives saw the finished product, they became concerned with Bushell's performance as Pierre. Published reports implied that his voice hadn't adapted well to the sound equipment, and he was subsequently replaced by Fredric March. But Paramount had just signed Bushell to a long-term contract. An editorial in *Photoplay* may have revealed the truth when posing this cryptic question: "Did you ever hear of a film actress being so tempestuously good that her work dangerously overshadowed that of her leading man?"

Man, Woman and Sin's John Gilbert would endure the same reception when *His Glorious Night* opened later that year. Some claimed his voice was high, thin, and effeminate—thus undermining his image as the screen's reigning male sex symbol, but Gilbert was hampered more by bad dialogue and rumored interference by Louis B. Mayer than any technical issues, and would nonetheless make several more pictures before his death in 1936.

The damage to Anthony Bushell's film career proved not to be fatal. After seeing his performance in Somerset Maugham's *The Sacred Flame*, George Arliss insisted that Bushell play the romantic juvenile in a new screen adaptation of *Disraeli*. The film was released in November 1929, with Joan Bennett in the role formerly played by Jeanne.

***

Another shadow in Jeanne's life was brought to light after the April 22 arrest of Dale Efflund, a thirty-one-year-old homeless man, who had been menacing Jeanne and her sister Helen for the past month. Efflund—in modern terms, a stalker—regularly followed Jeanne wherever she went and telephoned her at all hours to proclaim his love. On separate occasions, he allegedly accosted her on Riverside Drive and in her apartment building hallway. After several complaints to the East Fifty-First Street Police Station, and a personal plea to Police Commissioner Grover Whaler, a three-week surveillance operation was conducted from Jeanne's Park Avenue address. Patrolman Peter Sheehan, who had chased two previous suspects from the building, noticed Efflund leaving early in the morning of April 21 and arrested him on the spot.

A quick search revealed a table knife and fork, a pocket knife, several razor blades, a can opener, a piece of heavy cord, chili peppers, soap, and other articles within Efflund's clothing. Informed of the arrest, Jeanne remarked with some irony, "It's all right to have admirers, but it can be overdone." The prisoner was held without bail until she appeared the next day to press charges. However, Jeanne didn't show at the Sunday hearing at the Yorkville courtroom. If she remained absent the next day Efflund would probably go free, wasting all of Sheehan's hard work. Fearing for her safety, Jeanne went into hiding for the next two days. Fortunately, Efflund confessed to waiting nightly for Jeanne outside her apartment and verbally abusing her. He was sentenced to six months in the workhouse after ten days of observation at Bellevue Hospital.

The premiere of Ronald Colman's first talking picture, *Bulldog Drummond*, was held on May 3 at the Apollo Theatre. Jeanne appeared briefly to support her *Gentleman's Mother* co-star, and was one of many celebrities in the crowd that night which included fighter turned actor Jack Dempsey and Fanny Brice, with a dozen policemen to keep the crowds at bay.

Jeanne's reputation as difficult would be bolstered by sensationalized bits of gossip such as the anecdote published in the *Brooklyn Eagle* during the filming of *Jealousy*: "One day Miss Eagels came upon a stagehand in the act of petting her favorite police dog. The star, somehow, didn't fancy such familiarity on the part of a stranger, even with her dog. Why, they hadn't even been introduced! The following day this notice appeared on the studio bulletin board: 'Notice to all employees—Nobody working in this studio is permitted to speak to Miss Eagels' dog.'"

Actually, her concern was for the crewman's safety. The dog in question was her German Shepard, Mika, who understood three languages, (English, German, French), and was a trained attack dog. During the tour of *Rain*, Mika had stayed in Jeanne's dressing room as he and the show's monkey didn't get along. Had Mika appeared in several scenes of *Jealousy* as planned, he might have given canine superstar Rin-Tin-Tin a run for his money. Instead, because of his temper, he was tied up with a "Beware of the Dog!" sign posted nearby. Misunderstandings like these cemented Jeanne's reputation for grand behavior.

Audience reactions to *The Letter* did not match the rave reviews, as the *St. Petersburg Times* noted on June 9. "One of the surprises of this uncertain film business of ours comes from the meager box office returns of *The Letter*, starring Jeanne Eagels. Miss Eagels is not causing any sensation at the film theaters throughout the country and a Paramount official frankly says *The Letter* would have gone over much better if one of the Paramount movie favorites had played the leading role." Figures from the *Motion Picture News* showed audience ratings decline from 83% in Cleveland, to 75% in Norfolk, Virginia and Winston-Salem, North Carolina; and finally, a dismal 57% in Minneapolis. But they loved her in Houston, Texas, where the Metropolitan Theater recorded a 115% rise in attendance during the seven days it played.

According to Doherty, Jeanne loathed *Jealousy*, believing that when Bushell's scenes were re-shot, some of her best takes were left on the cutting room floor. She also resented the inclusion of a semi-nude bathroom scene featuring a much younger supporting actress, Blanche Le Clair. The day after this racy sequence was shot, Jeanne defiantly appeared on the set in a diaphanous gown that would never have passed the censors. To keep the peace, Le Clair's scene was cut from the final edit.

"I'm going to write Jesse Lasky a letter," she told Gilbert Outhwaite. "I'm going to tell him about the cuts. I'm going to say, 'Dear Mr. Lasky,

After seeing *Jealousy*, might I suggest that you change your motto from "Bigger and Better Pictures" to "Bigger and Better Scissors.""

Outhwaite wisely suggested she hold fire, or Lasky might throw her off the lot. "I hope he does." she replied. "I hate the movies . . . I just want to go back to the stage. Just a little while now and Harris will have a hit for me." Jeanne's Equity suspension was to be lifted on October 7.

The enduring symbol of Jeanne's marriage to Ted Coy was relinquished on May 31, when she sold her thirty acres in Ossining. Julia was there to help her move all remaining possessions into her Cedar Lane home, and visited her at the studio.

"One has to be so exact in the talkies," Jeanne told *Picture Play*'s Evelyn Gerstein. "You can't improvise as you go along the way I always used to on the stage. Why, I never played the same scene twice in the same way. I always made up lines as I went along. But you can't do that in the talkies. I like to play my scenes through, without having them cut up into little parts. You just get all worked up for a big emotional scene, and then someone calls 'cut,' and you have such a ghastly, let-down feeling. And then, of course, you do things backwards. That is, you do your last scene first, and the work back to the beginning. It's much more difficult, because on the stage you begin at the beginning and by the time you've got to the third act, you're worked up for it. Yet I don't feel conscious of the camera at all the way you do if you're not used to it."

Ideally, Jeanne would have liked to make all her pictures at night, when the studio carpenters had gone home and the city was sleeping. After so many years in the theatre with long nights and mornings for sleep, suddenly changing from night to day wasn't easy. "I'd probably have much more sense, in fact, I know I would," she confided to Gerstein. "I could work nights, instead of getting to the studio at six or seven in the morning." She also believed the drastic change in routine had contributed to her six or seven bouts of the flu suffered during her last two films.

"But now I have a few weeks' rest before making my third picture," Jeanne added hopefully. And she made the most of her time off, playfully writing, "You know. You know—I insist on!!!" above her name in 'Cliffy' Webb's guest book after a party. Webb was currently starring in a popular revue, and Jeanne became friendly with his co-star Libby Holman, often watching her sing her big number, "Moanin' Low," in the wings. "If only I'd known Libby and people like her a long time ago," she said wistfully. "How different my life might have been."

Plans were made to attend the Woodstock Summer Festival, a hundred miles from Manhattan. The Maverick Theatre presented *Rain* from July 18-21, and Jeanne was rumored to be in the audience one night. *Rain*'s co-author and a long-term resident, Clemence Randolph, also saw the production. On August 3, Jeanne was the weekend guest of Madame Mary Destl, a Fifth Avenue art gallery owner and mother of director Preston Sturges.

***

Film Daily informed its readers on July 23 that *The Laughing Lady* would be Jeanne's final film for Paramount. Garrett Fort would again adapt the play, which was first staged with Ethel Barrymore in 1923, and had previously been filmed with Gloria Swanson as *The Society Scandal* in 1924. Jeanne's co-star would be Clive Brook, who had just completed *The Return of Sherlock Holmes* and was currently on vacation. *The Letter*'s George Folsey was head cameraman, while Victor Schertzinger would direct, supervised by Monta Bell as Associate Producer.

The Laughing Lady was Marjorie Lee, wife of banker Hector Lee (played by Raymond Walburn.) After a misunderstanding, Marjorie is ejected from a seaside resort where a tabloid reporter is also staying. When the incident makes headlines, Hector, who already has a mistress, opportunistically files for divorce and seizes custody of Marjorie's child. Humiliated in court by her husband's lawyer, Daniel Farr (Brook), Marjorie retaliates. However, her plan backfires and Farr falls in love with her.

According to Eddie Doherty, writer Bartlett Cormack had been brought in to meet Jeanne and discuss the script changes she required. Cormack listened intently and then went home, staying up all night rewriting. When the pair met again the next day in Monta Bell's office, a frazzled Jeanne claimed to have no recollection of their discussion. She was saved from further embarrassment by Bell promising that Cormack would enact the requested changes, which appeased her temporarily.

But Jeanne was dissatisfied with Cormack's revisions. "They take a beautiful English play and vulgarize it," she complained to Outhwaite. "Not only do they use American players, but they stick a life-saver into the cast of characters and some tabloid newspaper reporters. It makes sick to think about it." But she duly deferred to her loyal ally, Monta Bell, and soldiered on as best she could.

Swimming champion Johnny Weissmuller was an early contender for the added role of a lifeguard. After Monta Bell showed Jeanne a photograph of Weissmuller, and she responded enthusiastically: "Ooh! I want him!" Weissmuller failed the audition, but would soon be cast as *Tarzan* in the popular movie series.

Preliminary production began on August 26. After taking time off in Maine, Monta Bell returned on September 3, the day *The Laughing Lady* began shooting. That night, Jeanne went to see friend Helen Morgan, the torch singer and Broadway star, open in *Sweet Adeline* at the Hammerstein Theatre. Pre-production progressed smoothly until September 12, when Jeanne was admitted to St. Luke's Hospital.

She was diagnosed with ulcers of the eyes, caused by a severe sinus infection and compounded by, in Jeanne's own words, a "variation of klieg eyes," or an adverse reaction to the large, harsh studio lights used in filming.

After X-rays determined that surgery was necessary, Jeanne went under the knife on September 14. She left St Luke's Hospital the next day with a positive prognosis from her physician. "Jeanne is recovering nicely," Dr. Sigmund Manheim said from his 865 West End Avenue office, "and with proper rest and no straining her eyes, would be vastly improved within a week or so."

Such was her reputation that many assumed the hospital stay was due to another alcoholic binge, although Sam Harris tried to persuade them otherwise. "If she'd been dying of something," Clifton Webb remembered bitterly, "they'd still have said she was drunk. All this on top of her Equity trouble!"

With her recovery incomplete, Paramount executives were forced to make a decision regarding *The Laughing Lady*. Walter Wanger sent a notice to Jeanne, informing her that production could no longer be delayed, and on September 19, the studio announced that Ruth Chatterton, who had begun her career on Broadway, would replace Jeanne when she returned from vacation. However, Jeanne had already been scheduled for a high-profile appearance on September 22, in the inaugural episode of the Paramount-Publix Radio Famous Theatre Hour, hosted by the WABC network. Jeanne was one of seventeen stage and screen performers including Charles Ruggles, Jack Oakie, Buddy Rogers, Nancy Carroll, Clive Brook, and Fredric March, as well as three orchestras and The Four Merrymakers, in a simultaneous broadcast from New York, Los Angeles, and Chicago. She and Clive Brook were to present a preview from *The Laughing Lady* to promote its November release. On the night of the show, microphones were "switched live" to the Long Island studios, where the filming of a scene was transmitted. Listeners were informed of Jeanne's illness and replacement by Chatterton.

This may have been a wise decision for all concerned, as *Jealousy* was released on September 16 to mediocre reviews. Paramount had heavily promoted the film with full-page advertisements, some in full color, published in fan and industry publications. Jeanne's name was featured among the roster of stage and screen stars in future Paramount productions—alongside Harold Lloyd, William Powell, Clara Bow, Gary Cooper, The Marx Brothers, Jeanette MacDonald, Walter Huston, Helen Morgan, and Claudette Colbert "to name a few."

"Sophisticated story of Paris carries dramatic punch. Jeanne Eagels makes it more important than it really is." – *Film Daily*

"Although Jeanne Eagels plays the girl, Halliwell Hobbes is the best of the cast as the mellow old spider who gets what he wants." – *New Movie Magazine*

"Jeanne Eagels has a decided English accent in this film. The talk becomes a monotone after a while, Fredric March more convincing of the two. It is not the best thing Miss Eagels has done in the talkies." – *Brooklyn Standard Union*

"Miss Eagels gave a clear-cut and finished portrayal of a charming, whimsical woman who is caught in the web of deceit just at the moment when she is absolutely happy." – *Boston Globe*

"Eagels is making pictures that are not along the conventional lines of box-office success ... The Eagels vehicles have strength and bitterness. More than that they are well done. Perhaps a public cloyed by the saccharinities of the usual movie will like quality for a change. Time will tell." – *Montana Standard*

***

Fredric March, Jeanne's co-star in *Jealousy*, put it more succinctly: "Jeanne Eagels was great, but the film we made together was a stinker." Nonetheless, *Motion Picture News* reported a 135% increase in box office returns while *Jealousy* played in Boston, with Portland at 110%, and a 115% rating in San Francisco.

Never a devotee of the movies, Jeanne's feelings towards film-making were now irrevocably soured. She met with Monta Bell and asked to be let out of her contract. "I'm sick Monta." she said. "I'm very sick. My eyes are bad ... the operation may not succeed. Besides, I don't like the picture. The way it's been cheapened and gagged. Can't we come to some agreement? I want to quit the movies forever. I want to go back to the stage—when I'm well."

Bell told her he'd square things with the studio, and Jeanne kissed him on the cheek before walking off the lot and out of the movies for good. Regrettably, her final performance is now believed lost, although stills from *Jealousy* show the actress looking hauntingly lovely, her face having lost none of her expressive powers. Released in December 1929, the recast *Laughing Lady* has survived and can be seen on online. Although primarily a melodrama, *The Laughing Lady* also included some humorous moments, and had Jeanne completed it, today's viewers might have been able to appreciate her comedic talents and versatility. Instead, it is largely remembered as just one more example of how Broadway adaptations often seemed "stagy" to moviegoers, and even as the sound era gained momentum, some notable stage actors preferred to return to the theatre. While some may have been baffled at her decision to relinquish a lucrative contract, intimates like Clifton Webb knew better. "The most awful thing . . . the most tragic thing that happened to her," he believed, "was when Equity kept her from working. It's not pleasant for a person to be kept out of work for a year—it's being sent to Purgatory."

She now had a rare work-free period to fully recover from an extremely strenuous year and she soon got back into the swing of things. Her assistant, Christina Larson—or 'Stina, as she was affectionately known—told Eddie Doherty that she had been helping Jeanne to write her biography. "Maybe I'll write the story myself one day," Jeanne said. "If I do, it will be fearless, sensational and true—and it will make a million dollars for my mother."

She joined Clifton and Mabelle at Broadway shows and read the numerous plays being sent to her by Sam Harris, including *An Affair of State* and *Diana*, based upon the life of dancer Isadora Duncan. Both shows would be staged without Jeanne, making little impact. When she wasn't mulling over her next role, Jeanne bickered with Barry O'Neill and Gilbert Outhwaite, and spent time in Ossining.

But while her long exile from Broadway was now just a painful memory, Jeanne's nagging health worries could not be so easily dismissed.

"If her reputation had frown with the years, her infirmities had kept pace with it," Doherty wrote. Having started smoking during the run of *Rain*, her throat was susceptible to infections and her lungs were at their weakest point yet. She was afraid she might contract consumption. Her neuralgia was acting up, and both her arm and jaw continuously hurt. Jeanne's inventory of her ills was typically blunt: "My body looks like a war map, from all the scars the doctors have made on it."

Australian-born actress Judith Anderson spent some time with Eagels during her last few months. They had first met in Chicago four years earlier, while Anderson was touring in *The Dove*, a Belasco production. Aside from crossing paths at benefits, premieres and other outings, Anderson would be a frequent guest to Ossining.

She recounted for Doherty an afternoon she and Jeanne watched the other guests playing by the river, Eagels ""sitting on the driveway wall, dressed in white, with a blue band around her fine blonde hair, looking like a girl of seventeen." Anderson complimented Jeanne on the diamond ring she was wearing. "It's only a chip," Jeanne joked. "Tomorrow I'll get a real one." She added seriously, "I can say these things to you, and you'll understand. If I said them to other people they wouldn't believe me."

Anderson claimed that Jeanne visited her in Quincy, Massachusetts the end of September, where she was currently starring in Eugene O'Neill's *Strange Interlude*.[21] Judith recounted how during the drive back to Manhattan, Jeanne ruminated about her loneliness, worsening health problems, and a desire to reconnect with her Catholic faith. She talked of writing a play. As they got closer to the city she became more excited. Possibly remembering her times with Madame Novello she exclaimed, "I must have a salon!" she enthused, "a salon where I can have open house, but not too open. Say, on Sunday afternoons, and perhaps one night a week. I'll have artists, writers, musicians, singers, dancers, people of the

---

21 Judith Anderson had replaced Lynne Fontanne during the original Broadway run. According to Doherty, *Strange Interlude* "found refuge in Quincy when Boston banned it." The *New York Times* reported the ban on September 17, 1929, so if Anderson's memory is correct, Jeanne's visit must have occurred not long before her death.

stage, everybody—well, of course, not everybody; only the people I like and revere. I must do that—if I live."

Posing with Anthony Bushell as "Pierre", soon to be replaced by Fredric March. Bushell's voice did not adapt well to early recording equipment. He would go on to have a successful career both before and behind the camera.

Another publicity shot from *Jealousy*.

Top - With Halliwell Hobbes in a scene from *Jealousy*. Bottom - With Fredric March in a scene from *Jealousy*.

Lobby Cards from Eagels' two sound films. *The Letter* (top) and *Jealousy* (bottom).

Top - On the set of *The Letter* with director Monta Bell. Bottom - with co-star co-star O.P. Heggie.

Top left - with co-star Reginald Owen. Top right - Courtroom scene from *The Letter*. Bottom - with Madame Lady Tsen Mei in a scene from *The Letter*.

Chapter 15
October 1929: The Last Act

Recuperating from her recent eye surgery, Jeanne had obediently stayed at home as directed, with only the radio and her records for amusement. Itching to return to her normal routine, she spent the last weekend in September with Judith Anderson. For the first week of October, Jeanne had been seeking daily treatments from her physician, Dr. Spencer Edward Cowles, at his 591 Park Avenue hospital for a 'nervous disorder."

Mabelle Webb recalled how Jeanne had plans to see her friend Beatrice Lillie in a matinee of her show at the Palace Theatre with Mabelle and Clifton, but when the Webbs canceled, she went to visit Cowles with plans afterwards to stop by Lillie's dressing room to wish her a safe voyage. Lady Peel's last show was the next afternoon so that she might sail with Lord Peel to conduct business in London. Although a little tired, Eagels did not want to disappoint her friend and so at around 6 p.m. she began dressing. She slipped into an evening gown complemented by several strands of pearls and a selection of rings acquired over the years. Among these were a 7.5 carat marquis-cut diamond ring in a platinum setting, her seven-diamond wedding band with guard, and her favorite, a "penny-sized" pearl ring. Finally, she wrapped herself in a fur coat to warm herself in the chilly fall air.

However, as Jeanne was getting ready to leave, she suddenly felt quite ill. A little before seven o'clock, she left with her assistant, Christina Larson, and quickly drove some sixty blocks back to where she been that afternoon. Cowles was called from his residence two floors below, while Jeanne was escorted into a fifth-floor examination room by the nurse, Miss Jennie Hoglund. Jeanne removed her coat and was sitting on the bed when she suddenly went into convulsions. Miss Hoglund ran out into the hall calling for Cowles' assistant, Dr. Alfred Pellegrini, but by the time they returned, they were too late to save her.

Jeanne Eagels was dead at thirty-nine.

Dr. Pellegrini called the coroner's office. When the Assistant Chief Medical Officer, Dr. Thomas A. Gonzales, arrived, Dr. Cowles had arrived from downstairs and refused to let him know the patient's time of death, and so Gonzales performed an autopsy at the facility to save time. In his report on October 4, Gonzales stated that a chemical analysis of the internal organs would be performed. "It's the same old story, nothing unusual," he remarked. "Miss Eagels died of alcoholism, not from acute alcoholism but from alcoholic psychosis.[22] She had been acting strangely for three or four days but had not taken a drink in two days."

"Her death came with shock in its suddenness," Ward Morehouse remembered. "I was not at the *New York Sun* office when news of her death was received. But when I reached my typewriter the next morning, there was a memo rolled into it. It read: 'Please call Jeanne Eagels, 3:30 pm.'"

---

22 Mosby's Medical Dictionary defines alcoholic psychosis as "any of a group of severe mental disorders in which the ego's functioning is impaired, including pathologic intoxication, delirium tremens, Korsakoff's psychosis, and acute hallucinosis. It is characterized by brain damage or dysfunction that results from excessive alcohol use."

"I was in my dressing room last night, ready to go on [in *Let Us Be Gay*], when I heard she had died," Barry O'Neill revealed to Doherty. "I had talked to her only that morning, and she said, 'Barry, I love you, I really do.' You know how we quarreled. I loved her, but I couldn't stand much of her. No man could. She was too dynamic, too full of life . . . I thought I would see her after the show. And—and then I heard she was dead. And while I was trying to understand, I heard my cue. I went on singing 'If Love Be All' and felt myself breaking. I couldn't stand it. Then I heard a voice saying to me 'Jeanne wouldn't break. Jeanne would go through with it.'"

"It was a Thursday night: I remember as I had a matinee the next day and was staying in town at the Algonquin Hotel," Clifton Webb recalled. "I was playing in *Little Show* at the Music Box Theatre and was in my dressing room when a stage-hand told me. Said he'd seen it on the Times Square board and called the *New York Times* to confirm it. I called the doctor and got him. He was rather blasé about it: 'Yes, it was an unfortunate accident.' I phoned Mabelle and she was of course speechless. We wanted to talk to somebody about this tragedy and ended up with Tallulah Bankhead and Beatrice Lillie at the Elysée where Tallulah lived and stayed for up for hours. Then next day after my performance we went to see her. . ."

Though barred from appearing on stage by Equity, Jeanne liked tweaking her nose at the Union and visited her friends in their dressing rooms at whichever theatre they were performing. Clifton's quarters at the Music Box were on the first floor above the lobby, near the offices of Sam Harris, Webb's current, and Jeanne's future, producer. Though she liked the space, the location was not ideal, as Webb told her biographer. "But this is inconvenient," she complained. "You've got to walk down all these stairs, and then down an aisle and backstage before you can tread the boards and speak your little piece. When this room is mine—and it will be mine unless you stay here forever, damn you—I'm going to have a chute put in, so that when I'm dressed I can slide right on to the stage." Harris had planned to star Eagels in *Top o' the Hill* when her Equity ban ended on October 7. He had bought and held it for her with hopes of rehearsals beginning in November, and a January opening. Set in a San Francisco hotel, *Top o' the Hill* was staged without Jeanne (or Harris) at the Eltinge 42nd Street Theatre in November 1929, closing after fifteen performances. Among the cast was Jeanne's former stand-in, Georgia Lee Hall.

Jeanne's body was taken to the Frank E. Campbell Funeral Home[23] at 66th Street and Broadway, where she was dressed in a peach-colored evening gown with matching wrap, and placed into a silver and bronze casket. The casket was wheeled into the Louis XIV viewing room, where Valentino's body had been laid almost three years before. The room was filled with large floral tributes from Paramount's Jesse L. Lasky, producers Sam Harris and Walter Wanger, plus co-stars and peers from the theatrical community. Among the many floral tributes were sprays of lilies and roses from Maria and May Saven; roses from Barry O'Neill, inscribed "God bless you, Jeanne, I love you"; and a small bouquet of dahlias (Jeanne's favorite), placed at her feet by the Webbs. A large wreath with ribbon, and a note reading "It will not rain where you are going, darling; it's all sunshine," came from the House of Madame Francis, who had made many gowns for Jeanne.

Webb and his mother arrived early to help with the preparations. Years later, Clifton would remember that when Jeanne was brought out. "There she was lying with a pompadour. So my mother called an attendant and asked for a comb and she took it and dressed her hair. Jeanne wore her hair in ringlets. Mabelle took flowers and put them in her hands. So we did all we could."

At twelve o'clock, the front doors were opened, and a crowd of well-wishers began filing past the casket. In a little over an hour, more than

---

23 The Frank E. Campbell Funeral Chapel was founded in 1898 on 23rd Street. It moved to 66th Street in 1921 and its final Upper East Side 81st St location in 1938. Other entertainment clients have included Enrico Caruso, Rudolph Valentino, Fatty Arbuckle, Montgomery Clift, Judy Garland, Ed Sullivan, Joan Crawford, James Cagney, Greta Garbo, Jackie Onassis, Joan Rivers, and many more.

150 people paid their respects. Jeanne lay in state all Friday afternoon and evening. One newspaper described how Mrs. Webb "tenderly rearranged the draperies and flowers, reluctant to leave their friend of over sixteen years." Across the street, business was quite brisk at the Loew's Lincoln Square Theater, where large posters proclaimed "Jeanne Eagels in *Jealousy*, her latest all-talking motion picture!"

On October 5, Chief Medical Examiner Charles Norris studied a report by Alexander O. Gettler, City Toxicologist, and concluded that Jeanne's death was not caused by alcoholic psychosis as originally stated, but an overdose of chloral hydrate. A strong sedative, taken to induce sleep and escape the hallucinations caused by the psychosis, had fatally depressed her heart. The same day, the papers reported that the rings and pearls worn by Jeanne on the night of her death, previously valued at $350,000, had been examined by an independent jeweler, who found they were mostly paste and worth less than $8,000.

Brief services were held the next day, beginning at eleven o'clock. The small chapel was filled to capacity, with most of the crowd—around 500 people—having to stand in the lobby or on the sidewalk. The officiating priest, James M. Gillis of the Paulist Fathers, led with the reading of prayers, followed by an unnamed quartet singing "Lead Kindly Light" and "Some Blessed Day." Everett Hudson Hall performed Gounod's "Ave Maria" and Massenet's "Elegie" on the organ. The casket was moved back into the Louis XIV room, so that those outside the chapel could pay their respects before Jeanne's body was taken to Pennsylvania Station, and began the homeward journey at 2:45 p.m. aboard the Kansas City-bound *Twentieth Century Limited*. By the time the hearse left for the station, over 3,000 people had passed by Jeanne's bier.

One of those unable to attend was Kathryne Kennedy, who had played a native girl and understudied the part of Sadie for *Rain*'s original and tour runs. She took the opportunity to pay her respects in Chicago—though in unhappy circumstances, as she recalled to Ward Morehouse in 1946.

"I was on my way back to New York because of my father's death," Kennedy said. "A body in a casket rolled past me at the station in Chicago. There was a hush on the platform. I asked who it was and was told it was Jeanne being taken back to Kansas City." Kennedy had fond memories of her friend: "She was a remarkable person. It was a great experience being with her. I only got a chance to play when she got sick and her voice would leave her. Perhaps thirty times total in over two years. I sincerely doubt if Jeanne Eagels really knew, in spite of her pretensions that she was a great actress. She was. Many times backstage I'd be waiting for my entrance cue and suddenly Jeanne would start to build a scene, and (we) would look up from our books at once. Some damn thing—some power, something—would take hold of your heart, your senses, and as you listened to her, and you'd thrill to the sound of her. Jeanne had a fiery temper and she was a long time fighting for everything she got, but beneath it all she was a lovable person. We'd all get mad as hell at her, but we had great affection for her as well."

Helen stepped off the train at Union Station and greeted her waiting brothers Paul and George with a kiss each on the cheek. The trio then went inside to greet Julia, who had arrived an hour earlier with her sons from Los Angeles. The four hugged and wept quietly among themselves for a few minutes before heading off to retrieve their older sibling.

The *Kansas City Star's* October 7 edition detailed how it was Helen who was called to the hospital right after Jeanne's death. She sent her mother, living in Los Angeles with her brothers, a telegram. But it never arrived, so when Helen called to speak to the family, it was a complete shock.

"I suppose you know I have bad news for you dear," Helen told her mother, unaware that the telegram had not arrived.

"Why, no! What is it? Tell me quickly," Julia demanded. "Then came the blow and physicians worked all night with Mrs. Eagles in Los Angeles."

OCTOBER 1929: THE LAST ACT

Jeanne's body was taken to the Mellody & McGilley Funeral Home at the corner of Linwood Boulevard and Euclid Avenue. Hundreds of people came to pay their respects and say goodbye. They stood four across and the line went out the building and around the block. Many in the crowd were women—shop girls, secretaries and clerks who had watched Jeanne on the silver screen or seen her on stage. Others came from her old neighborhood where they had played together as children. Some had probably never known her; but she was their hometown girl, and everyone had heard her rags-to-riches story. Little Eugenia Eagles had earned a grand tribute, and Kansas City gave her just that.

Well-wishers had been passing by the silvered-bronze casket in a slow but steady stream since morning. Jeanne's brother George sat in vigil, and a *Kansas City Star* reporter noted "a look of bewilderment at the persons as they filed in and out." The twenty-six-year-old remained solemn until "the occasional, all-to-infrequent sight of a familiar face [brought] a rare smile across his countenance."

George spoke quietly to the reporter. "I hope all these people are friends . . . They must all be friends. I'd hate to think anyone was here just out of curiosity." Shaking his head back and forth, he continued. "No, they must be all friends. Wouldn't it be terrible if they were not?"

He talked of the last days before Jeanne's death. "It was so unexpected," he said, "and a shock to mother. [Julia] was living with Paul—my twenty-one-year-old brother—and me, out in Los Angeles. Jeanne was in New York of course, but we had often been separated that far before."

"Jeanne would call up by long distance regularly, three or four times a week. Paul or I would get the connection and laugh with her a few minutes and then put mother on the line . . . the last call mother asked anxiously about Jeanne's eyes because they had been troubled by the motion picture glare. 'Don't worry,' Jeanne answered. 'I'm alright, I'll call up again in a day or so.' The next thing we knew, she was gone."

People were still waiting when the funeral director approached Julia at ten o'clock about closing up for the night. She asked if they could remain open. 'Let them all come in. We have no way of knowing who her friends were."

A private service for the family began 9:45 the next morning at funeral home and a gentle rain fell on the 4,000-strong crowd unable to get into St Vincent De Paul Catholic Church for the ten o'clock morning service. The mobs spilled out into the street at the corner of 31st and Flora Avenue. As the flower-draped casket was carried to the hearse, Jeanne's family got into the waiting vehicles that would slowly make their way seven miles to Calvary Cemetery. There, a much smaller crowd watched quietly from a distance as Jeanne was buried on a small knoll near the entrance to the cemetery. Nearby was a gathering of pine trees, "Jeanne's favorite" according to Helen, who had chosen the spot. It isn't known if her paternal uncles (Ernest, Walter, and Frank) traveled from Leavenworth to pay their respects. The day after Jeanne's death, they had been quoted in the *Jefferson City Post-Tribune* as claiming their famous niece was actually born in "the old Latta House" in Leavenworth, and had moved to Missouri when she was just a few years old.

Afterward, the family met at the "little ivy-covered brick cottage at 3023 Wayne Avenue" of Julia's sisters Annie, Nellie, and Sarah. Another sister, Mrs. Johanna Callary, and a fifth, Mrs. Mary Coughlin of Wichita, joined them to continue grieving in private. A few days later, both her father and brother Leo would be relocated from another part of the cemetery to join what was now the family plot. A simple headstone was decorated with a cross that read "Jeanne *Eagles* (her family name)—Died October 3, 1929." Exactly three years after her death, the *Star* reported that an anniversary high mass had been held at St. Vincent's, under the direction of Father J.A. Overberg, and attended by Jeanne's friends and relatives.

Several years later, Clifton Webb was performing in Kansas City and wanted to pay his respects. "I called Jeanne's mother and she took me out to the grave," he wrote. "I saw the birth name on it and I said 'Julia, Jeanne would turn in her grave if she saw her name spelled that way—she'd spit in your eye."

***

Reviewing Eddie Doherty's *The Rain Girl* in 1930, one critic quoted Jeanne: "Hate, and not love makes the world go round. You hate poverty and overcome it. You hate stupidity and ignorance, and rise above it. If you hate people they will let you alone, give you your own way. And you must have your own way or you are only one of the mob. You can't imitate anybody and be anybody." The critic concluded ". . . that Jeanne Eagels lived according to her conviction was abundantly evident by the fact that when she died her intimate friends could be counted on the fingers of two hands—yet she had achieved the goal to which she had, since childhood, aspired, and when, in her own words, Jeanne Eagels referred to herself as the 'Greatest actress in the world' there were few who could truthfully dispute her claim."

Jeanne was extremely demanding at times, expecting a level of professionalism from those around her that sometimes drove them to distraction. She was also quick to anger, but this was certainly no more—and probably much less—than the perfection she demanded of herself.

"When people in the theatre prove difficult, you usually want to get away from them as soon as possible," George Abbott admitted. "But Jeanne Eagels' talent was so great that it was impossible to feel any resentment for her irrational behavior."

She could be maddeningly self-absorbed, focusing solely on what concerned her at any given moment. However, she was essentially kindhearted, and her generosity could be relied upon whenever others within her family, circle of friends, or even strangers were in need. The loyalty, love, and respect they received was worth the difficulties suffered a hundred times over.

"The grand manner came to Jeanne Eagels with the mantle of

success..." Doherty wrote. "But grand and aloof as she might be, she never quite reached the absurdities scaled by some ... she could make herself the pal of stage hands and taxi drivers and bell hops and hotel clerks."

"Her grand manner was not with her when she bought her mother a house in Kansas City. She was then just a daughter who finds she has at last enough money to make her mother happy. She sent her mother to Los Angeles, eventually and bought her a house there too. She brought her to New York whenever she wanted to come, phoned her twice a week no matter where she might be, and established charge accounts for her in many stores. The grand manner was never noticed when Jeanne gave money to those who needed it."

"After all, she was a nervous woman engaged in a profession that was trying on her nerves," a *Kansas City Star* journalist reflected in 1930. "There are times when every person engaged in creative work must have quiet and solitude. Jeanne Eagels was of such a character that when she needed it she asked for it. Her mother recalls that though guests, often uninvited, were sometimes asked to leave, they never were too offended to return a few days later and again partake of Jeanne's hospitality."

In 1930, Jeanne became the first person to be posthumously shortlisted for an Academy Award nomination, for her remarkable performance in *The Letter*. The final nominees included Ruth Chatterton for *Madame X*; Bessie Love for *The Broadway Melody*; Betty Compson for *The Barker*; Corrine Griffith for *The Divine Lady*; and the winner, Mary Pickford in *Coquette*, whose moment of glory was marred by allegations that she had used her influence within the motion picture industry to secure the ultimate accolade. Even today, Jeanne's name is regularly cited in lists of actors who should have won an Oscar.

***

The press whom had praised and punched Jeanne during her lifetime now eulogized her:

October 1929: The Last Act

"Jeanne Eagels burst up her twelve years on Broadway and wound up the customary scorched butterfly. She had lived dangerously by choice and to the end. In the beginning she was a puffball temperament and then she grew brittle. There were few more beautiful or capable actresses than she. In the past two years her piquancy was streaked with a degree of hardness. I saw her two weeks before the end at a theatre—her hair was wild and frowsy, her eyes bright pinpoints and her complexion a deathly oyster pallor. Yet with it all she retained a remarkable beauty and was beloved by many. Broadway!" – O.O. McIntyre, November 3, 1929

James R. Quirk, editor of *Photoplay* magazine, paid morose tribute to a fallen star.

"The show must go on. 'Died from an overdose of chloral hydrate.' 'Alcoholic psychosis kills actress.' Those were the headlines. Her body lay in a Broadway public funeral parlor. A few old friends and five thousand morbid curiosity seekers. Five thousand dollars' worth of 'with sympathy' floral scenery. Across the street the lights of a theatre blazoned 'Jeanne Eagels in her greatest picture.'

"The show was going on.

Star. Success. Fame. Fortune.

Behind the stage front, years of pain and suffering with tuberculosis and neuritis of the optic nerves. Struggle from tent show to Belasco star. Worry. The merciless battle to keep alive and going. Unhappiness. Envy. Gossip.

Pitiless driving of harassed soul and broken, pain-racked body. Making fortunes and giving them away. Hemorrhages. The show must go on. Stimulants to help drive the poor, helpless body. Sedatives to deaden the blind agony.

Temperament, they called it.

Courage, I call it."

Even Jeanne's Kansas City adversary, Goodman Ace, canonized her in verse.

"It rained...

And a slashing, stinging rain beat pitilessly against a frail, fiery body.

Rained...a dull...dead...drip...pounding like a savage tom-tom down upon an oppressed mind."

The poem concluded with these lines:

"The lulling swish...of Rain...lapping gently at gaping wounds...

Weary...rest...In the cool clear Rains to come."

***

Friends and co-workers remembered Jeanne fondly:

"She was a splendid woman and a great actress. It was our difference in temperaments that led to our parting." – Ted Coy

"I probably knew her better than most people here in New York. She had gone through many varied experiences. At the time she first came to my notice we had few managers who would take any chances with new talent. This girl couldn't get any employment, so she was obliged to take a job in the chorus. I remember her coming to me in a very happy frame of mind because a manager had given her several lines to speak. As I remember the girl she was charming, sympathetic, kind and gentle...I'll always remember Jeanne Eagels as a splendid comrade, as a person who was good and generous to her friends, and as one who could not overcome a temperament that was no fault of her own." – David Belasco

"Glad to tell you what I think of Jeanne Eagels. Glad to tell you, or Equity, or anybody. Miss Eagels was the greatest actress in America. She had versatility and that's something our other stars do not have. During all the time she worked for me I never knew her to give anything other than a fine performance. When the curtain rose she was one thousand percent. Two weeks before she died she was right here in this office and said to me: 'Don't ever worry about me, Sam Harris. I'll never do anything to hurt you.' Her death robs me of a friend and the American theatre of one of its most brilliant performers." – Sam Harris

***

Others described her beauty and radiant personality:

"Jeanne Eagels was the most beautiful person I ever saw and if you ever saw her, she was the most beautiful you ever saw." – Ruth Gordon

"Of all the actresses I have ever seen, there was never one quite like Jeanne Eagels. I think she hastened her demise by endless presentations of Sadie Thompson. Playing a role too long is enough to drive anyone mad. It's better, after a time, to let someone else do the parts." – Noel Coward

"I'd like to remember Jeanne the last time she spent time at our Long Island home, a tired little girl in an orchid robe and mules, lying on an orchid chaise lounge..." – Mabelle Webb to Eddie Doherty

John D. Williams, director of *Rain*, spoke in glowing terms of her talent:

"In my score of years in the theatre Miss Eagels was one of the two or three highest types of interpretative acting intelligences I have met... . Acting genius—that is, the power of enhancing a written character to a plane that neither author nor director can lay claim to—Miss Eagels had at her beck and call, whether in tragedy or in comedy... Had she lived, a far greater field was before her in the theatre... There is a dust-laden saying that the career of every fine actress or actor is as fleeting as something written on water. Fine souls, real contributors to truth and beauty, sing on forever."

***

Writers and critics would ponder her legacy for years to come, and while there were a few dissenters, most agreed that her performance as Sadie Thompson in *Rain* would be remembered as one of the defining moments of America's theatrical lore.

"Jeanne Eagels, dead, lives not only as Jeanne Eagels, sincere and gifted actress, but as Sadie Thompson, the *evangel*. How did she scourge bigotry! Unlike the missionary to the ignited, she crossed no ocean; she strode instead a stage and the benefited came to her. And by the bitter, drawing scorn of her role she exorcised the evil spirits of smug sanctimony . . . Speaking the lines of the dramatist whose very art submerged him, she incarnated the play's rich gospel of iconoclasm. American bigotry has never been the same since Jeanne Eagels appeared in *Rain*." – *New York Telegram*, November 11, 1929

"With the death of Jeanne Eagels, America lost one of its most brilliant actresses . . . And to all who knew her and loved her, her passing brings genuine sorrow. Jeanne Eagels loved her art for art's sake alone . . . Let us remember her as a great artist, called too soon from this drab life where she did her bit to make life brighter and gayer for others." – *Rhinebeck Gazette*

"It is stultifying for an actor to follow the vicious old American habit of continuing to play a part indefinitely just because there is a line at the box office waiting to see it. What of it? After five years of imprisonment in the success of *Rain*, the madness of the caged came upon poor Jeanne Eagels, and in a sense she died of that madness. Hers was the desperation and the death of the trapped." – Alexander Woollcott, *Saturday Evening Post*, 1934

Burns Mantle, theatre critic of the *New York Evening Mail* until 1922, and at the *Daily News* until his retirement in 1943, had once included *The Wonderful Thing* in his annual round-up, *Best Plays*. Reflecting on Jeanne's career in 1933, he was more cautious in his praise:

"Jeanne Eagels was the author of her own defeats. She sacrificed her life to her ambitions and to the weakness her ambition fastened upon her. There is nothing in her career to indicate that she burned with the fires of genius. She was an actress of limited range and she knew it."

"It happened that as she was exhausting a line of parts that she could play competently the play *Rain* came her way. Because the Sadie

Thompson of that play fitted perfectly into the narrow range of the Eagels talent, and because Sadie Thompson was a cursing lady who defied all the conventions, the actress shocked a vast public into cheers for her gifts and her daring."

"Success brought her a great deal of money, most of which she wasted and opportunities for further preferment as an actress, of which she was unable to take advantage. In her disappointment she gave was to dissipations. Jeanne Eagels herself asked no favors nor prayed for any public's understanding. She lived defiantly, and, from her standards, courageously."

Still others believed that Jeanne's internal contradictions were the essence of her talent:

"She had beautiful eyes with a lovely fey look in them and tumbling, rich blond hair that, if by any chance its color wasn't nature's, improved upon nature. When she wasn't playing herself and came to opening nights everyone turned to look at her, though she made no attempt to attract attention. She was one of those girls you liked to look at for a long time, a kind of white orchid but real and expressive and very living. At the same time she wasn't just one of the flower women. There was warmth and feeling in everything she did, along with an air of carelessness, almost recklessness." – Arthur Pollock, *Brooklyn Eagle*, 1944

"I am sometimes very annoyed that when some young actress makes a first appearance on the stage, she is touted as a 'young Jeanne Eagels.' Either people making such a claim never saw Jeanne Eagels or don't remember what they saw, because there was no such thing as a 'young Jeanne Eagels.' When she was young no one knew about her. Only when she became older did she become Jeanne Eagels as we think of her. And to throw that albatross around the neck of any young actress gives her an impossible burden to bear; I have seen many flounder under that kind of pressure." – Lee Strasberg, *A Dream of Passion*

***

Twenty years after Jeanne's death, a 1949 *Life* magazine article revealed that during filming of *Mr. Belvedere Goes to College*, Clifton Webb and director Elliott Nugent were discussing a piece of music his eponymous character was to play in a scene. When he finishes, the listener asks, "Beethoven?" Webb then replies, "No, Belvedere." Clifton suggested to Nugent and musical director Alfred Newman that he could use a concerto he'd written as a tribute to Jeanne many years ago. After running through the piece, both men were impressed enough to use it in the film.

Among the next generation of performers influenced by Jeanne was singer and actress Lillian Roth, who had impersonated her as a teenager. "How electric Jeanne Eagels was in *Rain*, how alive—every move, every turn a picture," Roth recalled in her bestselling memoir, *I'll Cry Tomorrow*. "Oh, I thought, to be a dramatic actress! What was vaudeville compared to the legitimate stage—a full three-hour show in which you felt so deeply, in which you reached and touched people's *souls*."

Perhaps the most lasting tribute to Jeanne was immortalized on film in *All About Eve*, Joseph L. Mankiewicz's Oscar-winning 1950 satire of (and homage to) the theatre. In one scene, the acerbic critic Addison DeWitt (played by George Sanders) pays the ultimate compliment to aging star Margo Channing (Bette Davis).

"Margo, as you know, I have lived in the theatre as a Trappist monk lives in his faith. I have no other work, no other life—and once in a great while I experience that moment of revelation for which all true believers wait and pray. You were one. Jeanne Eagels another."

Some final thoughts come from two men who, in different ways, enriched Jeanne's life immeasurably:

"I think the women I have admired have all had great talent. When you get beauty, talent, and a sense of humor in one package, that's a pretty good combination. Jeanne Eagels, the silent film star, had a wonderful sense of humor." – Clifton Webb to actress Arlene Dahl, 1954

"I saw the part of Sadie Thompson played in many cities and in many languages, but no one ever touched Jeanne. Death took a great actress from us. Isn't it strange how short are lives in the theatre? Careers, I mean. People struggle to get to the top. They stay there precariously for a while. And then they're no longer at the top and are forgotten." – W. Somerset Maugham to Ward Morehouse, 1965

***

Jeanne's estate was reportedly valued at $88,974, with a net worth of $58,637 after bills were paid—including $9,500 to Sam Harris for commissions and loans, and $3,069 for both the New York and Kansas City funerals. Her estate was comprised of $29,840 in cash; $37,665 in equity from her Cedar Lane home, which was worth $55,000; $4,900 of furs, including a $2500 ermine coat and a $1,200 Russian sable stole; and a Hispano Suiza automobile, valued at $600. Among her jewelry, which had further depreciated in value since her death, was a 116-pearl necklace, worth $250; three pearl necklaces at $9; the Marquis ring at $4000; the penny-sized pearl ring at $3000; plus a wedding ring set at $150, and a diamond and emerald necklace at $1500.

From the time of her stage debut, it was estimated that she had earned over $2,000,000—and she didn't save any of it. Probably on Coy's advice, Jeanne invested $25,000 in the stock market (and lost it within three days). She considered money something to be enjoyed, not hoarded. One of her Pekingese dogs, Maxine (named after the theatre, not the actress), was given to Zoë Akins by Jeanne's mother. "Jeanne would want you to have her," Julia explained, and Maxine would live with the author and her life partner at their home in the Hollywood Hills.

In death as in life, Jeanne continued to take care of her family. Julia was the sole beneficiary on her life insurance policy, which paid out $110,000.

In 1930, the *Kansas City Star* reported three real estate transactions over the course of several months. The first was a residence for Julia, who had been living at the La Salle Hotel. At the end of April, Julia paid $10,750 for a Dutch Colonial house at 40 West Sixty-Ninth Street, in the Armour Hills district of the city. On June 29 she bought a two-story, "English-type stucco bungalow" at 117 East Sixty-Fifth Street, at a cost of $9,000, for her eldest daughter Edna Ackerley, who was relocating from Needles, California. In November, Julia acquired a large, two-story home with separate garage at 425 West Sixty-Seventh Street Terrace for $21,000. The *Star* revealed that the residence had plenty of room for "antique furniture, at least one piece of museum value, and other personal belongings of the late Jeanne Eagels."

On New Year's Day, 1936, the *Star* reported the donation of an antique couch in "typical Empire design and made about 1820" to the local Nelson Atkins Museum in Jeanne's name. And in 1944, a *Star* classified ad offered this elegant item for sale: "Chair – Antique. Solid oak carved. Brought over from Spain by Jeanne Eagels the actress. Suitable for hall or large room. JA 4715."

Left – Cowles Clinic at 595 Park Avenue. Top right – Doctor Edward Spencer Cowles circa 1919 when he first met Jeanne. Bottom right – Eagels' townhouse rental at 1143 Park Avenue.

Top - Jeanne's casket is removed from Campbell's Funeral Church at 66th and Broadway on October 5, 1929. Bottom - Julia Eagles is escorted from St Vincent De Paul Catholic Church at Flora Avenue and E. 31st Street in Kansas City, Missouri October 8, 1929. Jeanne's brother George is to her left, with sister Helen and brother Paul following behind. As Leo's was before her daughter's, Julia's funeral service would be performed at the same church after her death in 1945.

Photograph courtesy of the Ivan Damiano Collection.

October 1929: The Last Act

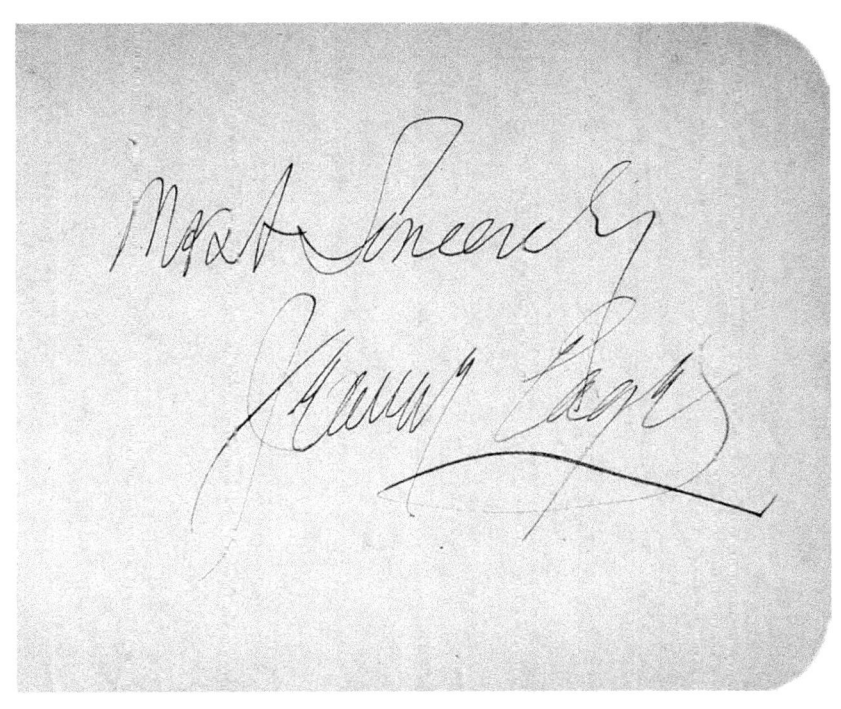

Chronology

Theatre

1901-1907
Pupil at Georgia Brown Dramatic School/Woodward Stock Company
Partial Productions List: *A Midsummer Night's Dream, Uncle Tom's Cabin, Priests of Fallas Parades*

1907-1910
Dubinsky Brothers Stock Company, touring
Partial Production List: *Pickings from Puck, When Women Love, A Slave Girl, The Newsboy, Pygmalion.*

Jumping Jupiter
Joined cast November 1910: touring
New York Theatre: March 1911 (24 performances)
Produced by H.H. Frazee, George W. Lederer
Music by Karl Hoschna; lyrics by Richard Carle, Sydney Rosenfeld. Featuring songs by Irving Berlin and others
Directed by Richard Carle
Cast: Natalie Alt, Burrell Barbaretto, Helen Broderick, Bly Brown, Jessie

Cardownie, Richard Carle, Anna Chandler, Ina Claire, Lester J. Crawford, Blanche Curtis, Naomi Dale, Murray D'Arcy, **Jeanne Eagels (as Miss Renault)**, *John Goldsworthy, Ida Harris, Edna Wallace Hopper, Joseph C. Miron, Beatrice Morton, Will H. Philbrick, Betty Scott, Bessie Skeer, Estelle St. Clair, Margaret Strasselle, Marie Vernon, Isabelle Winlocke*

1912
The Pink Lady
February 18: Colonial Theatre, Chicago — touring
Produced by Klaw & Erlanger
Music by Ivan Caryll, lyrics by C.M.S. McLellan
Cast: Dolly Alwin, Jean Barnette, Clover Briggs, William Clifton, Cecil Cunningham, **Jeanne Eagels (as Gabrielle)**, *Dart Edwards, Elizabeth Finney, Alma Francis, Dorothy Godfrey, Kittie Graham, Jane Grover, Jack Hall, Georgia Harvey, Juliet Lang, Wallace McCutcheon, Jr. Joseph Monahan, Edward, Morris, Louis Pallay, Jed Prouty, Dorothy Quinette, Harold J. Rebill, Eleanor Scott, Edyth Taylor, Harry Wallace, Dottie Wang, Tom Waters, Marguerite Wright, Dan Young*

1913
The Mind-the-Paint Girl
Lyceum Theatre, New York: September 1912-January 1913 (136 performances)
Produced by Charles Frohman
Script by Sir Arthur Wing Pinero
Additional music by Jerome Kern
Cast: Billie Burke, William Raymond, Edith Campbell, E. Douglas, **Jeanne Eagels (as Olga Cook)**, *Arthur Fitzgerald, Marie Fitzgerald, H. E. Herbert, Hazel Leslie, Jeanette Lowrie, Arthur Luzzi, Carroll McComas, Bernard Merefield, John Morley, Barnett Parker, Anna Rose, Morton Selton, Jeanne Shelby*

CHRONOLOGY

1914

The Governor's Boss
February 28, 1914, Washington
Garrick Theatre, New York: April 13 (16 performances)
Written and produced by James S. Barcus
Cast: Frank Andrews, Emory Blunkall, Earle Craddock, Sidney Cushing, **Jeanne Eagels (as the Governor's daughter)**, George Fawcett, D. J. Flanagan, C. W. Goodrich, Richard Gordon, John E. Kellerd, Cecil Kern, Charles Laite, Crosby Maynard, Frances McGrath, Arthur Parmelay, Forrest Seabury, Charles Seiter

The Crinoline Girl
September 1914-May 1915 (touring Atlantic City and New York)
Produced by A.H. Woods, Klaw & Erlanger
Directed by John Emerson
Cast: Herbert Corthell, Edwin Cushman, **Jeanne Eagels (as Dorothy Ainsley)**, Julian Eltinge, Walter Horton, Joseph S. Marba, Herbert McKenzie, Charles P. Morrison, Augusta Scott, James C. Spottswood, Maidel Turner, Edna Whistler

1915

Outcast
October 915-January 1916
Produced by Thomas W. Riley, Klaw & Erlanger
Script by Hubert Henry Davies
Cast: Mildred Cottell, **Jeanne Eagels (as Miriam)**, Stanley Harrison, Vernon E. Kelso, Harold West.

1916

The Great Pursuit
Shubert Theatre, New York: March-April (29 performances)
Produced by Joseph Brooks
Script by C. Haddon Chambers

Cast: Cynthia Brooke, W. Graham Browne, Charles Cherry, **Jeanne Eagels (as Kate Merryweather)**, Dorothea Frisby, Gordon Gunniss, W. S. Helder, Alexandra Herbert, Arthur Holbrook, Nicholas Joy, Edith King, Montagu Love, Bruce McRae, Phyllis Neilson-Terry, Eric Nelson, Marie Tempest

What's Your Husband Doing?
Toledo Ohio, Chicago Illinois (September–October) (canceled)
Produced and directed by Joseph Brooks
Cast: Macklyn Arbuckle, James Brison, **Jeanne Eagels (as Beatrice Ridley)**, Ellen Errol, W. Richard Farrell, Viola Gillette, J.H. Huntley, Mason Jones, Thomas W. Ross, Frances Von Waldron, Harry E. Willard.

1917
The Laughter of Fools
Scheduled for Atlantic City, January 1 (canceled)
Produced by Daniel Frohman
Cast: Edna S. Bruns, Edward Douglas, **Jeanne Eagels**, Eva Le Gallienne, Kate Sergeantson, Hassard Short, Vernon Steel, Frances Wilson.

The Professor's Love Story
Knickerbocker Theatre, February–April (48 performances)
Produced by George C. Tyler, Klaw & Erlanger
Script by J.M. Barrie
Cast: George Arliss, Mrs. George (Florence) Arliss, Ethel Dane, Reginald Denny, **Jeanne Eagels (as Lucy White)**, Arthur Eldred, Violet Kemble-Cooper, Edgar Kent, Malcolm Morley, Molly Pearson, Grant Stewart.

Disraeli
Knickerbocker Theatre, New York: April–May (48 performances)
Produced by Liebler & Co.
Script by Louis N. Parker
Cast: George Arliss, Mrs. George (Florence) Arliss, Langdon Bruce, Lilla

Campbell, Margaret Dale, Dudley Digges, **Jeanne Eagels (as Lady Clarissa Pevensey)**, Arthur Eldred, Helen Erskine, David Glassford, Walter Grey, Edgar Kent Malcolm Morley, Fred Nichols, Leila Repton, Noel Tearle, C.M. Van Clief.

Hamilton
Knickerbocker Theatre, New York: September 17-November (eighty performances)
November 1917-April 1918, touring
Produced by George C. Tyler, Klaw & Erlanger
Script by Mary P. Hamlin, George Arliss
Directed by Dudley Digges
Cast: Carl Anthony, George Arliss, Mrs. George Arliss, Marion Barney, James O. Barrow, Wilson Day, **Jeanne Eagels (as Mrs. Reynolds)**, Guy Favieres, Marion Green, Hardee Kirkland, Harry Maitland, John D. Ravold, Gillian Scaife, Pell Trenton, C.M. Van Clief, George Woodward.

National Red Cross Pageant
October 5, Long Island, New York
Jeanne Eagels appeared in the Joan of Arc segment alongside Ina Claire and Guy Favières. Please see film listing for more extensive cast listing.

1918-1919
Daddies
Lyceum Theatre, New York: November 4-June 1919 (340 Performances)
Produced by David Belasco
Script by John L. Hobble
Cast: George Abbott, Mrs. Armand, Aida Armand, John W. Cope, Edwards Davis, **Jeanne Eagels (as Ruth Atkins)**, Winifred Fraser, George Giddens, Edith King, Bruce McRae, Paulette Noizeux, Mrs. Quinn, The Quinns, Lorna Volare, S. K. Walker.

A Young Man's Fancy
Liberty Theatre, October 15, 1919 (13 performances)
Produced by George C. Tyler
Script by John T. McIntyre
Cast: Frank Allworth, Harry Barfoot, Eugenie Blair, Symona Boniface, Frank Boyd, Jessie Busley, Viola Cain, John Davidson, ***Jeanne Eagels (Mary Darling & Mary's Image)****, Sidney Elliott, Morgan Farley, Alfred Kappeler, Mary Kennedy, J. M. Kerrigan, Howard Lindsay, Philip Merivale, Bessie Owens, Walter C. Percival, John D. Seymour.*

1920
The Wonderful Thing
January 19: Wieting Opera House, Syracuse
Playhouse Theatre, New York: February 17–June (120 performances)
September 25: Princess Theatre, Chicago
Produced by George Broadhurst
Script by Lillian Trimble Bradley, based on a story by Forrest Halsey
Cast: Gordon Ash, Henry Duffey, Philip Dunning, ***Jeanne Eagels (as Jaqueline Laurentie)****. Eva Leonard-Boyne, Edward Lester, Jane Marbury, Gladys Maud, George Schaeffer, Olive Temple, Fred L. Tiden.*

1921
In the Night Watch
Century Theatre, New York: January 29–May (111 performances)
Produced by Lee and J.J. Shubert
Script by Michael Morton; from La Veille D'Armes by Claude Farrere, Lucien Nepoty
Directed by Frederick Stanhope
Cast: Maclyn Arbuckle, Margaret Dale, Harold De Becker, ***Jeanne Eagels (as Eugenie de Corlaix)****, Max Figman, Paget Hunter, B. Huntingdon, Kenneth Lawton, Edmund Lowe, J. Morrison, Jefferson Murray, Knox Orde, Cyril Scott, Robert Thorne, Walter Walker, Robert Warwick, John Webster.*

1922
A Gentleman's Mother
Apollo Theatre, Atlantic City, touring (June-July)
Produced by Samuel L. Harris
Directed by Samuel Forrest
Script by Martin Brown
Cast: Michael Agnus, Eleanor Daniels, Arthur Elliott, **Jeanne Eagels (Polly Pearl)**, *Leon Gordon, Frank Horton, A.P. Kaye, Elizabeth Risdon, Russell Sedgwick, Frank Westerton.*

Rain
October 1922
October: Garrick Theatre, Philadelphia
Maxine Elliott Theatre, New York: November 7, 1922-June 1924 (608 performances)
Produced by Sam H. Harris
Script by John Colton, Clemence Randolph; based on a story by W. Somerset Maugham
Directed by John D. Williams
Cast: Catherine Brooke, Oka Bunda, **Jeanne Eagels (as Sadie Thompson)**, *Robert Elliott, Harold Healy, Rapley Holmes, Robert Kelly, Kathryne Kennedy, Shirley King, Liano Paulo, Harry Quealy, Kent Thurber, John Walter, Bhana Whithawk, Emma Wilcox.*
September 1-December 1924:
Gaiety Theatre, New York; Werba Theatre, Brooklyn (96 performances)

January 1925
Rain – Directed by Sam Forrest
Beginning Cast: Catherine Brooke, Oka Bunda, **Jeanne Eagels (as Sadie Thompson)**, *Robert Elliott, Harold Healy, Rapley Holmes, Robert Kelly, Kathryne Kennedy, Shirley King, Jack McKee, Liano Paulo, John Rogers, Emma Willcox, Fritz Williams.*

*Ending Cast: **Jeanne Eagels (as Sadie Thompson)**, K.A. Fernando, Blanche Friderici, Ethelbert Hales, Harold Healy, Alfred Hickman, Rapley Holmes, Edward Keane, Shirley King, Jack McKee, Howa Owa, Liano Paulo, John Rogers, Wilma Thompson, Emma Willcox.*

1927
Her Cardboard Lover
March 14: Shubert Theatre, Atlantic City
Empire Theatre, New York: March – August (152 performances)
Produced by Gilbert Miller, A.H. Woods
Script by Jacques Deval; adapted by Valerie Wyngate, P.G. Wodehouse
Directed by George Cukor
*Cast: **Jeanne Eagels (as Simone Lagorce)**, Charles Esdale, Leslie Howard, Arthur Lewis, Stanley Logan, Terence Neill, Ernest Stallard, Henry Vincent, Valerie Wyngate.*

Her Cardboard Lover
Touring, October 1927
*Cast: C. Edwin Brandt, Anthony Bushell, Virginia Chauvenet, **Jeanne Eagels (as Simone Lagorce)**, William Eville, Philip Jones, Barry O'Neill, Walter F. Scott, MacKenzie Ward.*

1928
The Benefit
Vaudeville revue, touring
Cast: Bert Lahr, Mercedes Acosta, Jimmy Conlin, Myrtle Glass, Herma & Juan Reyes, The Florinis, The Tiller Sisters, Tommy McAuliffe.

Filmography

1913
The Ace of Hearts (Short)
Produced by Ryno Film Company
Released June 9
Cast: **Jeanne Eagels (as "The Girl")**

The Bride of the Sea (Short)
Released July 28
Produced by Ryno Film Company
Directed by John Noble
Cast: **Jeanne Eagels (as "The Girl")**

1914
A Lesson in Bridge (Short)
Released March 4
Produced by Reliance Motion Picture Corporation
Cast: **Jeanne Eagels (as Mrs. Willis)**, Paul Scardon, George De Carlton, Harry Spingler, George Siegmann.

Judith of Bethulia
Released March 8 (61 minutes)
Produced by Reliance Motion Picture Corporation, D.W. Griffith
Directed by D.W. Griffith
Cast : Blanche Sweet, Henry B. Walthall, Mae Marsh, Robert Harron, Lillian Gish, Dorothy Gish, Kate Bruce, J. Jiquel Lanoe, Harry Carey, W. Chrystie Miller, Gertrude Robinson, Charles Hill Mailes, Edward Dillon, Gertrude Bambrick, Lionel Barrymore, Clara T. Bracy, Kathleen Butler, William J. Butler, Christy Cabanne, William A. Carroll, **Jeanne Eagels (uncredited)**, Frank Evans, Mary Gish, Harry Hyde, Thomas Jefferson, Jennie Lee, Adolph

Lestina, Elmo Lincoln, Antonio Moreno, Frank Opperman, Alfred Paget, W.C. Robinson, Kate Toncray, Louise Emmons.

1915
The House of Fear
Released November
Produced by Pathé Exchange
Directed by John Ince, Ashley Miller
Script by John T. McIntyre
Cast: Arnold Daly, Sheldon Lewis, **Jeanne Eagels (as Grace Cramp)**, *Ina Hammer, Charles Laite, Charles Kraus, William Bechtel, Martin Sabine.*

1916
The World and the Woman
Released November 19 (66 minutes)
Produced by Edwin Thanhouser
Directed by Frank Lloyd, Eugene Moore
Script by Philip Lonergan, William C. DeMille
Cast: **Jeanne Eagels (as Mary)**, *Boyd Marshall, Thomas A. Curran, Grace De Carlton, Wayne Arey, Carey L. Hastings, Ethelmary Oakland.*

1917
The Fires of Youth
Released June 17 (52 minutes; 31 minutes, short version)
Produced by Thanhouser Film Corporation
Script by Agnes Christine Johnston
Directed by Emile Chautard
Cast: Frederick Warde, Helen Badgley, Ernest Howard, **Jeanne Eagels (as Rose)**, *Robert Vaughn, James Ewens, Carey L. Hastings, Grace Stevens.*

Under False Colors
Released September 17 (50 minutes)
Produced by Thanhouser Film Corporation
Directed by Emile Chautard
Script by Lloyd Lonergan
Cast: Frederick Warde, **Jeanne Eagels (as Countess Olga)**, Robert Vaughn, Anne Gregory, Carey Hastings.

National Red Cross Pageant
Released December 1917 (50 minutes)
Produced by National Red Cross Committee
Directed by William Christy Cabanne
Cast: Edith Wynne Matthison, Douglas Wood, Ethel Barrymore, Kitty Gordon, Margaret Moreland, Adelaide Prince, Olive Tell, Irene Fenwick, Montgomery Irving, Annette Kellerman, Josephine Drake, Ethel McDonough, Norman Trevor, George Backus, Marjorie Wood, Macklyn Arbuckle, Lumsden Hare, Frank Keenan, Frederick Truesdell, Mrs. Ben Ali Haggin, Clifton Webb, Ben Ali Haggin, Ina Claire, **Jeanne Eagels**, Eugene O'Brien, Guy Favières, John Barrymore, George F. Smithfield, Alice Fischer, Howard Kyle, Blanche Yurka, Gladys Hanson, Tyrone Power Sr., E.H. Sothern, Rita Jolivet, Richard Bennett, Michio Ito, Marjorie Rambeau, Lionel Barrymore, Mrs. H.P. Davison, Hazel Dawn, William T. Rock, Helen Ware, Frances White.

1918
The Cross Bearer
Released April 1 (50 minutes)
Directed by George Archainbaud
Script by Anne Maxwell
Produced by World Pictures
Cast: Montagu Love, **Jeanne Eagels (as Liane de Merode)**, Tony Merlo, George Morgan, Edward Elkas, Charles Brandt, Eloise Clement, Al Hart, Alec B. Francis, Kate Lester, anny Cogan, Henrietta Simpson.

1920
The Madonna of the Slums (Short)
Released March 14
Produced by the Stage Women's War Relief Fund
Directed by George Terwilliger
Script by Jessie Bonstelle, Calder Johnstone
Cast: Amelita Galli-Curci, Holbrook Blinn, ***Jeanne Eagels****, Helen MacKellar, Luis Alberni, Johnnie Morris, Jessie Ralph.*

Promotional short (Jeanne Eagels demonstrates how to achieve her hairstyle in The Wonderful Thing)
Produced by Garamont Film Company
Released in March 1920

1927
Man, Woman and Sin
Released November 19 (70 minutes)
Produced by Metro-Goldwyn-Mayer
Directed by Monta Bell
Script by Monta Bell, John Colton (titles), Alice D.G. Miller
Cast: John Gilbert, ***Jeanne Eagels (as Vera Worth)****, Gladys Brockwell, Marc McDermott, Philip Anderson, Hayden Stevenson, Charles K. French, Aileen Manning, Margaret Lee.*

1929
The Letter
Released March 17 (65 minutes)
Produced by Paramount Pictures
Directed by Jean de Limur, Monta Bell
Script by Monta Bell, Mort Blumenstock, Garrett Fort, Jean de Limur. Based on a story by W. Somerset Maugham.
Cast: ***Jeanne Eagels (as Leslie Crosbie)****, Reginald Owen, Herbert Marshall,*

Irene Browne, O.P. Heggie, Lady Tsen Mei, Tamaki Yoshiwara, Peter Chong, Fredi Washington, Isabel Washington.

Jealousy
Released September 13 (66 minutes)
Produced by Paramount Pictures
Script by Garrett Fort, Eugene Walter, John D. Williams. Based on the play by Louis Verneuil
Cast: **Jeanne Eagels (as Yvonne)**, Fredric March, Halliwell Hobbes, Blanche Le Clair, Henry Daniell, Hilda Moore, Carlotta Coerr, Granville Bates, Virginia Chauvenet.

Chapter 16
A Cumulative Tragedy

The Roaring Twenties came to an abrupt halt only three weeks after Jeanne's death, when the Wall Street Crash brought America's booming economy to its knees. Over the next three years, the banking system effectively collapsed. The grim period that followed saw millions of ordinary people losing their homes and livelihoods. Even the repeal of Prohibition in 1933 did not alter the fact that for a generation of bright young things, the party had ended just as suddenly as it began.

Given the growing panic seizing the nation, it's perhaps unsurprising that the truth about Jeanne's demise was buried under a slew of lurid tabloid headlines. Almost ninety years later, many of those myths still prevailed. As bigger tragedies were unfolding, the untimely exit of a volatile actress must have seemed trifling, at best. Prodigiously gifted, yet often self-destructive, Jeanne came to embody the dizzying highs and perilous lows of her era.

"Her death was doubly tragic because it was so avoidable," George Abbott wrote years later. "If only she could have achieved a little inner peace and found some philosophy to stabilize her life, or some logic to give her control over that restless demon that drove her to all sorts of silly excesses. Her use of drugs probably accounted for the mood I found so inexplicable—but what accounted for the drug addiction?"

Outlaw Narcotics

On May 30, 1930, newspapers across America revealed the findings of a secret report submitted to the County Medical Examiner's Office by Dr. Gettler two weeks after Jeanne's death, concluding that Jeanne had died from an overdose of heroin. According to the autopsy report, the actress' brain weighed 1,500 grams; 200 grams more than that of an ordinary woman. One-third of the brain contained 0.8 milligram of heroin, indicating the presence in the entire brain structure of 2.4 milligrams. Readers of the *New York Daily Mirror* had already learned this on November 10, 1929, when Gettler told the article's unnamed author (a member of the International Features Syndicate) that he had found "heroin crystals in Miss Eagels' brain."

The June 9 issue of *Time* magazine contended that "The *Daily Mirror*'s article was a piece of journalistic enterprise designed to vex the publishers of the *New York Daily News*, its rival, and of the nickel weekly *Liberty*. For *Liberty* the week before had commenced a vivid, sympathetic biography of Jeanne Eagels. *Liberty*'s article said she died of a dose, not an overdose, of chloral hydrate—not heroin. The distinction: heroin is an outlaw, habit-forming narcotic. Chloral hydrate is a non-habit-forming, much-used hypnotic. Dr. Cowles' response, as quoted by *Time*, was this: "I had treated Miss Eagels for almost ten years and never knew of her taking any drugs. Any story that drugs caused her death or contributed to her death is false."

A semi-synthetic opioid narcotic derived from morphine, heroin's trade name was first coined by a German drug company in 1898, for its "heroic" effect on the user; and it was initially sold over the counter as a non-addictive substitute for morphine. However, subsequent research proved that heroin metabolized into a faster-acting form of morphine than the original.

Widely used as a cough suppressant, heroin wasn't regulated until 1914. However, physicians continued to prescribe the drug until 1924, when it was banned outright. Silent superstar Wallace Reid was first given the drug after a train wreck in 1919, and died four years later, while in withdrawal. Reid's demise was one of several scandals that hastened the formation of the Hays office and the Production Code, in an effort to repair the industry's tarnished reputation. This was a classic case of Hollywood hypocrisy, as the profit-driven studios had often supplied heroin and other drugs to stars like Reid, or simply looked the other way.

Soon after injection (or inhalation), heroin crosses the blood-brain barrier. In the brain, heroin is converted to morphine and binds rapidly to opioid receptors. Abusers typically report feeling a surge of pleasurable sensation, a "rush." The intensity of the rush corresponds with the amount taken, and how rapidly the drug enters the brain and binds to the natural opioid receptors. Heroin is particularly addictive because it enters the brain so quickly. The heroin rush is usually accompanied by a warm flushing of the skin, dry mouth, and a heavy feeling in the extremities, sometimes inducing nausea, vomiting, and severe itching.

After the initial high, abusers usually become drowsy for several hours. Mental function is clouded by heroin's effect on the central nervous system. The heart functions more slowly, and breathing also slackens, sometimes to the point of death. The risk of overdose is heightened when heroin is bought from street dealers, and its volume and purity cannot be ratified.

Physical dependence and the emergence of withdrawal symptoms were once believed to be the key features of heroin addiction. We now know that craving and relapse can occur weeks and months after withdrawal symptoms are long gone. Many patients with chronic pain who need opiates to function (sometimes over extended periods) have few if any problems leaving opiates after their pain is resolved by other means. This may be because the patient is simply seeking relief and not the rush sought by the addict.

It remains unclear if Jeanne was a habitual heroin user. While filmmakers were able to conceal the condition of heroin-addicted stars like Wallace Reid through retakes and careful editing, heroin was unsuited to the demands of stage acting. Drug-taking was not unheard of in the theatre, but actors were more likely to turn to cocaine or amphetamines to boost energy and concentration. Jeanne's schedule was extremely punishing, and it's doubtful that she could have sustained daily performances and lengthy tours under the influence of opiates.

However, it's possible that Jeanne may have used heroin on occasion, to relieve pain. This seems more feasible than recreational use, although over time her tolerance for the drug would have increased, and she would then have needed to take greater quantities for the desired effect. No credible evidence has emerged, anecdotal or otherwise, of tell-tale signs like track-marks on her arms. Was Dr. Cowles so inept as to be unaware of his patient's self-medicating? Or was he condoning, and perhaps even supplying her with an illegal, and highly addictive substance?

Dr. Cowles and the Mysterious Elixir

Aside from various physicians seen for her ills in other cities, when in Manhattan, Jeanne's primary doctor was Dr. Edward Spencer Cowles, psychiatrist, neurologist, and the founder of a private hospital at 591 Park Avenue.

A former minister from an old Virginia family dating back to the 1600s, Cowles attended the College of William and Mary at Williamsburg. He graduated in 1907 from the Medical College of Virginia in Richmond, with post-graduate work at Harvard in 1908. After serving as director of the Psychopathic Hospital at Portsmouth, New Hampshire, from 1910 to 1916, Dr. Cowles came to New York as head of the Department of Psychopathology at Polyclinic Medical School and Hospital. His Park Avenue Hospital opened in 1919, with a principal tenet "that religion and medicine should join in solving both mental and physical ills."

As *Time* noted in June 1930, "Dr. Cowles is not considered 'orthodox.' He is not a member of any local or state medical society, nor of the American Medical Association. Nor does the AMA accept his sanitarium for its register of hospitals. Nevertheless his personality, his shrewdness, his results have won him many a famed and wealthy patient and his little stucco establishment on Upper Park Avenue is both prominent and profitable."

Cowles' methods included the ingestion of a mysterious elixir given patients to relax their nerves, described as "a mixture of three or four ingredients common as household remedies."

Interviewed by Eddie Doherty for *Rain Girl*, Mabelle Webb recalled an incident when Jeanne summoned her to Westchester. Taking a cab which was faster than the train, she was met on the lawn by an agitated Jeanne. The disheveled actress complained of her inability to sleep for days, a dull pain in her arm, and how her nerves were frazzled to a breaking point. Mabelle asked if a doctor had been called. Jeanne reassured her that he was due to arrive shortly. Mabelle remembered Dr. Cowles as "small and dark . . . and his eyes weird and fierce."

"He opened his satchel, took out a bottle, poured a dose, mixed it in a glass. Giving it to Jeanne, 'Drink this,' he said." After ordering Jeanne to lie down on the couch, his next move shocked Mrs. Webb.

"The doctor made mystic passes over her face with his large queer hands and then began to rub her temples. 'Nerves, you are relaxing. Nerves, you will sleep. Nerves, you are asleep. Nerves, you will sleep until morning.'" Mabelle was ordered to undress the patient, put her to bed, and not to disturb her all night.

Was Dr. Cowles' remedy a case of sheer quackery? A combination of Western and Eastern medicine? Perhaps the secret lay in the little bottle brought in his bag—which might have been a strong sedative, or "fix" of morphine for a withdrawing addict.

Whatever his treatment involved, it succeeded. Jeanne awoke the next day "refreshed and sparkling," Mrs. Webb said, as if the previous night's episode was just a bad dream.

It seemed that Cowles' practice and reputation had evaded any negative publicity regarding Jeanne's death at his hospital. Cowles might even have been able to provide a medical explanation for the heroin found in Jeanne's brain, were it not for a suicide on August 16 at his institution. The patient was William E. Swift, of the Chicago and Kansas City meatpacking family, who shot himself on the same floor, just a few doors down from the room where Jeanne had died ten months earlier.

According to a statement issued by Cowles, Swift entered the clinic the previous October and had been improving until he was stricken with pneumonia. Despondent over the setback, Swift attempted to jump out of the fifth floor window of his room, but was restrained by his private nurse, Rudolph Heitmarek. Earlier that day, one of the staff nurses had reported what she thought was a gun. Heitmarek was instructed to locate and remove the weapon. While he was doing so, Swift turned the gun on himself. Police confirmed that Swift was being treated for brain inflammation, alcoholism, and pneumonia.

At the New York State inquest on August 20, Cowles was questioned by Dr. Charles Norris and State Assistant Attorney General Sol Ullman. At one point, Cowles asked if they were "trying to get information or hurt my reputation." After the hearing concluded, Cowles made a statement. "I have welcomed the opportunity of coming to this investigation. I've especially invited the opportunity because there has been in the public press and in the questioning here the impression that drugs are being used in an improper manner in the institution, which I deny and resent . . . I probably use as few narcotics [chloral is not a narcotic] as any man in the profession. . ."

Although Swift's death was ruled a suicide, Ullman's warning that

"We have been watching" should have given Cowles pause. On August 23, the Assistant Attorney General opened an official inquiry into Jeanne's death. As counsel for the State Board of Medical Examiners Grievance Committee, Ullman vowed to conduct a sweeping investigation of the Park Avenue Hospital. As no records can be located, it is possible that the investigation never took place.

However, Cowles would be dogged by negative publicity and further threats of investigation regarding these two high-profile deaths for years to come. On July 20, 1932, a syndicated report published in the *Joplin Globe* revealed that he was being forced to close his Body and Soul Clinic, which for ten years had aided the poor at St Mark's Rectory in the Bowery. "At a protest meeting of his supporters he charged that Bishop William T. Manning 'gave the order to abolish the clinic'," the article stated. "The meeting ended with harsh words . . . [Cowles] impatiently waves aside suggestions, such as cropped up after the death of Jeanne Eagels, the actress, that he employs odd drugs."

His license was revoked in 1942 due to unethical activities, but after it was reinstated in 1944, Cowles resumed his practice for another decade. The Park Avenue Hospital was also home to Cowles and his family. In 1959, five years after the doctor's death, the building was sold and has since been restored to a single private residence.

Her Steady Tipple

The issue isn't whether Jeanne drank alcohol but when she increased her usage to the point of problems and the reasoning behind it. Interviewed for *Rain Girl*, David Belasco remembered that when they first met, Jeanne told him she drank hot gin to alleviate pain. The pattern of her drinking was not unusual during the Prohibition years, when a climate of illicit hedonism was flourishing. Many Americans were making their own beer and gin, and as Eddie Doherty noted, Jeanne "couldn't go anywhere . . . without being flattered and coaxed into a cocktail or two." He also claimed that Jeanne never drank until the final curtain, when she would find a group of friends in their dressing room, and often join them at all-night parties. The purity of bootleg alcohol was frequently debated, and a serious concern as cheap booze was sometimes adulterated with noxious chemicals.

Jeanne's drinking seems to have become problematic during the long, arduous *Rain* tour, as a means of baiting her ineffectual husband Ted Coy. A heavy drinker himself, Coy nonetheless disapproved of his wife's drinking, and so she drank more to spite him. She also drank to calm her nerves at public events with Coy, when she was not among people she knew and trusted.

Charles Collins from Chicago's *Daily Tribune* noted that during *Rain*'s five-year run, Jeanne "missed only eighteen performances because of illness. That record does not suggest alcoholism." While the number of missed shows is greater than Collins' estimate, it still only reached a total of between thirty to sixty out of 1,500 shows. Her formidable work ethic would have been nearly impossible to uphold while under the constant influence of either alcohol or drugs. "Champagne was her steady tipple until she dropped the role of Sadie Thompson," Collins affirmed. "Then she took to brandy and whiskey, in company or alone."

In March 1928, under fire from Actors Equity after failing to complete scheduled tour dates for *Her Cardboard Lover*, Jeanne had indignantly denied drinking alcohol before or during performances. "When I was ill and had lost a great deal of weight, my doctors prescribed a little champagne for me," she insisted, adding, "That is the only thing I ever drink." However, Clifton Webb later recalled that she had begun drinking at work in 1923 during her arduous tour of *Rain*. By the time of her turbulent marriage to Ted Coy, she had taken to drinking heavily at home. Webb observed that her tolerance for alcohol remained poor. "She couldn't drink a lot—one drink and she'd be off."

***

In a 1945 article for the *Milwaukee Sentinel*, Genevieve Parkhurst—a journalist, author and advocate for tee-totalism and spiritual healing—theorized that alcoholism had killed Jeanne Eagels. Her performance in *Rain*, Parkhurst believed, showcased her talents so perfectly that her subsequent roles seemed "flat and inconsequential." This was perhaps not wholly untrue, although Jeanne was justifiably proud of her work in *The Letter*.

After leaving Sadie behind, Parkhurst argued, Jeanne "began to find fault with life," succumbing to "adolescent emotions—a contributing factor to alcoholism. . . " Parkhurst blamed alcohol for "poisoning her mind, her outlook and her personality." In Parkhurst's opinion, it was Jeanne's drinking that led to her being banned from the stage, and a string of failed love affairs, feuds with co-stars, and difficulties on film sets.

This was a rather censorious view, to say the least. Several of Jeanne's contemporaries, such as Tallulah Bankhead, Cecelia Loftus and Laurette Taylor, battled addictions to alcohol, cocaine and morphine throughout their careers, while Emily Stevens died suddenly at forty-five, a year before Jeanne and in chillingly parallel circumstances: while Stevens' death was initially reported as an overdose, it later emerged that her physician had given her a hypodermic injection after finding her in a "nervous state" a week prior. He was called to Stevens' apartment again a day before she died. Her death was ruled to have been caused by pneumonia, which had developed after she fell into a coma. Still more actresses of Eagels' generation were lost in their prime due to entirely natural causes, including the French-born Gaby Deslys who passed away aged thirty-eight in 1920, after contracting the Spanish Influenza a year prior; and Kay Laurell, the thirty-six-year-old former showgirl who died in childbirth in 1927.

In a final flourish, Parkhurst concluded that Jeanne could always have been saved. "Unless a psychosis has taken its victim beyond the realm of reason into the never-never-land of complete delusion," she concluded, "there is always a key to unlock the gates to the road back. If the gates can be found. Unfortunately, there is, as yet, no key to unlock them all."

The Knock-Out Drop

An overdose of Chloral Hydrate, with weakened heart due to alcohol, was *Liberty* magazine's verdict on the cause of Jeanne's passing, an allegation supported by Eddie Doherty in *The Rain Girl*. Chloral Hydrate was regularly used by Dr. Cowles as a sedative for his patients.

First discovered in 1832, Chloral Hydrate became popular during the late nineteenth century, both as a prescribed sedative (to Mary Todd Lincoln, among others) and for recreational purposes. A solution of Chloral Hydrate in alcohol—or "knock-out drops"—was dubbed a "Mickey Finn" after a Chicago saloon owner accused of using the preparation to dope and steal from his customers at the turn of the century.

In the last years of her life, Marilyn Monroe was frequently prescribed Chloral Hydrate along with other sedative drugs to alleviate her chronic insomnia. Although her physician was Dr. Hyman Engelberg, she was also under the daily care of a psychiatrist, Dr. Ralph Greenson. When Monroe was found dead in 1962, aged thirty-six, both Chloral Hydrate and the barbiturate Nembutal were detected in her system.

Today, Chloral Hydrate is a controlled substance in the United States, although it is still used for the short-term treatment of insomnia and as a mild anesthetic. In 2007, the model Anna Nicole Smith died from a combination of Chloral Hydrate and Benzodiazepine. In recent years, Chloral Hydrate has also been associated with date rape.

An Unmentionable Disease

Could Jeanne Eagels have suffered from a life-long illness that contributed to her early demise?

Biographer Doherty mentions that Jeanne's cousin, Kate Callary, who suffered from consumption, went "out West" to seek treatment and never returned. Her death left both young Eugenia and sister Edna with a lingering fear that they, too, would contract tuberculosis. In fact, Edna met her future husband while seeking treatment in Needles, California. Though she returned to Kansas City for a few years after her marriage, she had moved permanently to California by the time of Jeanne's death.

Jeanne's thin, waif-like appearance and constant illnesses would cause many to advise her to seek treatment. She was more susceptible to illness when working too hard or under emotional stress; and in several interviews she spoke of her physicians recommending she drink a small amount of champagne daily.

Jeanne's former *Rain* co-star and stand-in, Kathryne Kennedy, had her own opinions. Having contracted tuberculosis, Kennedy was forced to leave the production shortly after her tour began. She settled in Albuquerque, New Mexico, where she made a full recovery, and went on to run the city's Little Theatre for over twenty years, starring in her own success run of *Rain*.

"Jeanne Eagels had tuberculosis herself," Kennedy claimed, "and she insisted that all I needed was food and rest and that I should keep working, but I knew I was very sick ... In the those days, and in the East, T.B. was something of an unmentionable disease, just like having a venereal disease ... Perhaps she had never quite recovered from the tuberculosis and that play wore her out."

Her Sad Habits

What some saw in Jeanne as artistic temperament, and others as arrogance, would perhaps be diagnosed today as a form of mental illness. Friends and co-workers all agreed that she had a fragile personality, and despite moments of grand-standing, her ego was insecure. Her moods could change dramatically and without warning. Judith Anderson had witnessed Jeanne's abrupt change of mood weeks before her death, while accompanying her on a long drive to New York. She was given to impulsive behavior, and she was unable to sustain a long-term intimate relationship. To the modern reader, it may appear that she possibly suffered from

Bipolar Disorder or "manic depression," in which periods of elation and risk-taking alternate with episodes of deep despair, can lead to incidents of self-harm and even suicide if left untreated. Bipolar Disorder can be managed with therapy and medication, but not all patients respond to treatment.

"If she had not died when she did," Clifton Webb wrote, "I think she could have gained a great deal from psychiatry. She was a definite neurotic." Many creative people—including Zelda Fitzgerald, Ernest Hemingway, Vivien Leigh, Marilyn Monroe, and Kim Novak—have been diagnosed as Bipolar, or were said to have exhibited symptoms of that condition. The singer Amy Winehouse, who died of alcoholic poisoning in 2011, also suffered from manic depression.

During her manic phases, Jeanne's strange behavior was often accompanied by memory loss. On the opening night of *Rain*, she had cursed out a fellow cast member. When the actor confronted her, she could not recall the incident and said she never used foul language. This may have been an extreme example of her acting "in character." On her thirty-seventh birthday, she snubbed her friends who had organized a party, because her husband was drinking. During pre-production of *The Laughing Lady*, she spent an evening discussing script revisions with writer Bartlett Cormack, only to angrily deny that the meeting ever occurred. By then, Doherty believed, Jeanne was so disenchanted with film-making that she would retreat her dressing room to drink in secret. Fay Bainter told Doherty of another curious episode when Jeanne accused her of digging up her finest trees and transplanting them overnight.

Jeanne did not come from an established theatrical family, as her friend Ethel Barrymore did. She had grown up in the loving embrace of a large family, and though she had many devoted friends, her life in New York was lonely by comparison. She had also known poverty and great loss, such as the death of her father when she was still a teenager; and in more recent years, the troubled life and untimely demise of her younger brother, Leo. She had struggled hard to reach the top and was afraid of losing her place. If, with the blessing of a quack doctor, she turned to alcohol and drugs to mask her physical pain, it's likely she also tackled her emotional problems that way. Although her rages seemed to come from nowhere, she knew that anything worth having was worth fighting for. Her combative nature was not the feminine ideal, and the sexual harassment she experienced as a young actress at the hands of lecherous producers like David Belasco, and the lack of understanding or support from Actors Equity at a time when she was over-worked and in emotional distress, made her suspicious of, and increasingly bitter towards the male-dominated Broadway establishment.

"I saw a lot of Jeanne Eagels and always had a battle with her," Mercedes de Acosta wrote in 1960. "I was very fond of her and couldn't bear to see her destroying herself. I spent many weekends at her place in Ossining-on-the-Hudson and there I was able to help her control her sad habits. We used to take long walks in the country and Jeanne would revive and swear she was going to reform. But the city was too much for her. As soon as she returned to New York she would fall back into her old weaknesses."

"Over the six years or so that they remained involved, Papa became aware of the actress's reliance on drugs and alcohol," Johanna Fiedler wrote in a memoir of her father, Arthur Fiedler, who is said to have kept an autographed photo of Jeanne in his study until his death in 1979. "Initially Papa explained away her mood swings as depression or lack of enough exercise and fresh air or the demands of a public life. Eventually, however, he could no longer fool himself about her problems and he began to extricate himself from the relationship. A clue to how difficult this must have been came a few years later, when he singled out Maugham's *Of Human Bondage*, the study of an obsessive relationship, as his favorite book."

"Destruction enchanted her," Ruth Gordon wrote forty years after Jeanne's death. "So beautiful, so gifted, why did she love to destroy?" At the time, Gordon had asked a mutual friend, Katherine "Kit" Cornell, for her thoughts. "Nobody loved her," Cornell replied. "You can't go on living if nobody loves you."

Beauty in Autumn

While Jeanne may have shown an appetite for self-destruction, the roots are hard to track. Perhaps Kathryne Kennedy was right when she said that for all her breezy arrogance, Jeanne was fundamentally insecure. While she remained close to her family in Kansas City, they were ill-equipped to support her in times of need. She had conquered the hearts of Broadway's audiences, but would never truly fit into New York's elite. Her broken engagements to Thomas L. Chadbourne and Whitney Warren Jr. scarred her emotionally. Some of those upon whom she relied most, such as husband Ted Coy, were too troubled to be of help; or, like Dr. Cowles, were financially benefiting from her weaknesses. While Coy had loved Jeanne dearly, their marriage ended in drunkenness and abuse. Barry O'Neill loved her, but like Coy, couldn't control her. (He drifted back into Mae West's professional and personal life, appearing with her in *Sex* for the 1930 touring season.) Although Cowles may have cared for her as a patient, ultimately his irresponsible actions contributed to her demise.

Maybe it was this streak of vulnerability hidden just beneath her bubbly exterior that attracted such fierce loyalty from friends like Clifton Webb, theatrical moguls from the aforementioned David Belasco to Sam Harris, and filmmakers such as Monta Bell. Working with her may have been exhausting, but to bask in the glow of her extraordinary talent and drive was worth the trouble.

Like so many who died young, Jeanne remains frozen in time. Could she have transcended her weaknesses to become a *grande dame* of the stage, or would the fading of her beauty have been too damaging to her fragile ego? More importantly, could she have overcome her demons and regained the high status she had lost at the time of her dispute with Actors Equity?

Actress Helen Hayes, who made her stage debut at Washington's Belasco Theatre when she was just five years old, had left the theatre for Hollywood in 1917, returning in 1935. She would continue working on stage and screen for another fifty years. In a syndicated 1934 interview, Hayes revealed the secret of her longevity. "It all boils down in the final analysis to this: 'Acting is just industry,'" she said. "There is a difference between good acting and great acting. That's a gift from heaven." Citing Jeanne's performance in *Rain* as an example, Hayes added, "Great actors couldn't live through playing a role for two years as sometimes is necessary now."

In his 2004 essay, "When Actors Were Still Players,' Ronald J. Wainscott praises "... Eagels' ability to excel at comedy, even farce, as well as drama. In much of her work in New York, from 1919 until *Rain*, she virtually specialized in French dialect supporting or leading roles in light comedy or farce." But Jeanne, who once admitted that "I wish to create my own roles and do it without the suggestion from anyone else," was not an obvious team player. She demanded script changes and rehearsed at her own pace, maintaining a certain distance from other actors, and even directors. She dismissed more challenging material, like Ibsen's *A Doll's House*, because it wasn't written for her.

It is uncertain whether Jeanne would have been at ease in the collaborative milieu of the Group Theatre, which produced some of the most influential plays of the 1930s, a decade in which social realism became more prized than star allure. Both Robert Lewis and Lee Strasberg, who were prominent members of the Group Theatre (and later the Actor's Studio), had been strongly influenced by Jeanne's performance in *Rain*, and she might have excelled in the grittier roles created by Clifford Odets and other leading playwrights of the new era.

"Eagels ... was always extremely articulate in interviews and in her writings," Wainscott commented. Jeanne spoke of her plans to direct, and perhaps this would have satisfied her independent vision and need for control. On the other hand, her final film roles suggested that for all her misgivings about the new medium, she might yet have made a successful transition from Broadway to Hollywood diva, and the higher salaries she commanded in the movies could have supplemented her stage work. The hard-boiled dames and career girls of the 1930s paved the way for the popularity of "women's pictures" during the early 1940s, and Jeanne perhaps could have become a dramatic star to rival the likes of Bette Davis and Joan Crawford, or even reinvented herself as a sparky comedienne in the tradition of Rosalind Russell or Irene Dunne.

Her fits of temperament and flair for improvisation, however, would not have been so readily tolerated in the studio system, where productivity came first and art second. At thirty-nine, she would not have been able to depend on glamour for much longer.

"Jeanne had never been a popular movie actress," a critic for the *Kansas City Star* remarked in 1930. "There was something in her hard mentality that registered before the camera. She couldn't be all glamorous beauty, all soft curves, all languid elegance. A brain looked out of those brown eyes and challenged a public that wished to surrender itself to a charming personality, but is panic-stricken at the challenge of a magnetic mind."

"The camera recorded everything of that hard, analytical cynicism which appraises the world and men and women. On the stage the barrier of the footlights could efface this when she chose that it be hidden, but the camera was too intimate. It discovered and revealed her secret."

"... Yet though her connections with the movies were turbulent," the article concluded, "it remained for her to be one of the outstanding figures of the talking screen, one of the pioneers who discovered and established a new dramatic medium. It may be that the screen which she despised brought her immortality; it is certain that the movies that sought to snub her, were advanced a tremendous step by this woman's genius."

"Ironically, the anniversary of her death is coincidental with the anniversary of the birth of talking pictures," the *Star*'s critic noted on October 2, 1932. "With almost her last breath before the public, she hailed and revealed the new dramatic medium ... It was because Jeanne

Eagels developed acute spiritual force and emotional observation in her fight to stardom that she was able to supply the great acting that made a great play. Jeanne Eagels is mourned by her profession. The public may well join in that mourning. Talents such as hers are rare in the theatre."

Boston Post reporter George Brinton Beal thought that Sadie Thompson had unleashed Jeanne's inner rage at the men in her life. "So the thing that made her great, that made her in all probability the greatest emotional actress of her day, was her eventual ruin," he reflected However, he added that she never lost her essential sensitivity. "When Sadie let her be, and these periods varied during the run of *Rain*, she was one of the sweetest and most kind-hearted of people. Who worshiped her mother and sent her many gifts, among them an automobile. She did countless acts of kindness wherever she went."

"She was good to children, not nice to them in the usual actress sense with perfunctory mannerisms," the *Kansas City Star* reported. "She really liked to talk to them, to learn their thoughts and to encourage their ambitions. No child was patronized by her."

Lucille Currie, an eight-year-old schoolgirl in New York, was asked by her teacher to write about her vacation. "The most thrilling experience I have ever had was when I visited one of the world's most famous dramatic stars, Jeanne Eagels," Lucille wrote. "On taking our leave Miss Eagels stood before us radiant and happy. Bidding us goodbye, she exclaimed, 'You must come to the studio to see me work.' She seemed so contented in her life and not a bit lonesome. I will never forget how beautiful she looked, with the blue skies and green trees as a background."

Perhaps the final words should go to the younger, more idealistic Jeanne, looking to the future in a 1917 interview with the *New York Sun*.

"Youth and beauty mean absolutely nothing to me on the stage unless they are accompanied by art . . . .and I so desire to become a great artist—many, many years from now, I supposed. Every time a young actress tells me that she dreads the day she will have to cease playing ingénue and straight roles and take to characterization I am surprised anew. Why this fear for characterization? Why do so many actresses fear the loss of their identity with the taking out of a new, strange part? An actress—the true artist—should have no identity. She should be like—well, like the mist, an ever-changing medium of expression . . . But you know, old age has no terrors for me. Age is really the most beautiful thing in the world, and why should women, and especially actresses dread it so? I like to believe that growing old is just a superstition. Just as any other fear which we will readily learn to outgrow someday. Look at [Sarah] Bernhardt and at scores of other beautiful and vital women on our stage who are over forty and fifty. There is as much beauty in autumn as there is in spring, is there not? After all, it's great to be alive and to know that one can work and work at what one likes!"

Chapter 17
'You Can't Slander the Dead'

Yellow Journalism

After her burial, Jeanne's name remained in the press but was no longer headline news, gradually slipping below the front-page fold. Readers had moved on and were gripped by the turmoil on Wall Street, which would soon plunge the country into a ten-year economic Depression. But in late Spring of 1930, the public's attention would once again be brought to Jeanne's life, career and death by way of a fifteen-part serialization in *Liberty Magazine*, written by Edward Doherty.

Jeanne's story was ideal fodder for their readership. Founded in 1924 as a rival to the *Saturday Evening Post*, the popular weekly courted a younger audience with articles about motion picture stars and the entertainment industry. Published until 1950, *Liberty* changed ownership several times and its archives are a treasure trove for historians.

A Chicago-born reporter, as head of the *Tribune*'s Hollywood bureau Doherty had built a reputation for exposing celebrity sleaze – covering scandals such as Wallace Reid's drug-related death and Roscoe "Fatty" Arbuckle's rape trial. After three years in Los Angeles, he moved to New York to write for *Liberty*.

Jeanne's biographer carefully researched his subject, spending several weeks in Kansas City, Los Angeles, and New York, interviewing Jeanne's family, childhood friends, co-workers, and theatrical peers, among others, for an in-depth "warts and all" account of Jeanne's life.

Her family had been forewarned by other interviewees of the content, but they were not prepared when the first installment appeared May 24 advertised with the lurid tag line, "Genius and Drunkard—Artist and Hellion—Poet and Devil—She Battled to the Stars!"

Fearing worse to come, Julia and Helen filed suit on May 20, 1930, in New York Superior Court to literally "stop the presses." A day later, their attorney, Arthur S. Driscoll, explained to Judge Louis A. Valente that they "resented" the imminent publication. "The mother is getting along in life," Driscoll added, "and her life and that of the sister is faced with disgrace if the magazine is permitted to publish the proposed articles."

Liberty's lawyer, MacDonald DeWitt, contested that the first five issues had already been printed, and to destroy them all would cost upwards of $800,000. "While Mrs. Eagles seeks the injunction on the ground that the magazine story is a libel on the memory of her daughter, there is no provision in law to prevent its publication," DeWitt insisted. "We maintain that this story of Miss Eagels' life is not a libel on the plaintiff in the injunction action. Under the laws of New York State there can be no cause for action by surviving relatives for an alleged libel on a deceased person."

Julia and Helen lost their case, and *Liberty* ran all fifteen installments, ending on August 29.

Julia attempted to set the record straight in a *Kansas City Star* interview published June 22. Sitting in her living room, she explained how Doherty had visited her, "seeking information" and promising to write an account of Jeanne's life that she "would be proud of." She accused him of "breaking faith with her and dishonoring the dead. In writing of Jeanne," Julia said, "this man has not only abandoned the principles of charity, generosity and good taste. He has not even been governed by a spirit of fair play."

She gave the example of an adult Jeanne and seven of her friends having a slumber party during one of her daughter's annual visits, where the combined weight of the group broke the slats of the bed. The incident was illustrated with a drawing of shapely young women, clad in silk and satin nighties, tumbling to the floor, limbs askew. Silk and satin? More like "flannel and muslin nightdresses," according to the Eagles' matriarch.

But Julia also knew when to stop fighting. "I shall take no further action," Julia confirmed. "My only desire was to protect Jeanne's name and keep the memory of my child sacred. The courts did not uphold me in this effort."

Doherty's flattering impressions of the Eagles matriarch did nothing to sway Julia from her opinions. Julia was not, he wrote approvingly, "the stage-mother at type at all," and while she had always supported her daughter's chosen career, Jeanne's "comfort and happiness" was Mrs. Eagles' greater concern. Describing the actress as the "shining light" among Julia's eight children, her mother never interfered with her professional life and spent an equal amount of time visiting her other daughters, Helen and Edna.

When a reporter asked Julia about Helen's rumoured engagement to an English aristocrat, she replied, "I don't know anything about it, but it's nothing new to have a nobleman in the family. My daughter Edna is married to a prince." The incredulous reporter asked if she would tell him more. "Of course I will," she said. "His name is Bill Ackerly and he's an engineer on the Santa Fe Railroad."

Jeanne's younger sister Helen also refuted several of the tales in *Liberty*. One occurred a few weeks before Jeanne died. Around midnight, a bird had flown into her apartment's open window, sending Jeanne into hysterics. Telling her secretary, Christina Larson, "It's a sign of death!" Doherty's version led the reader to believe Jeanne was predicting her own demise. Helen, also present that evening but conveniently omitted from Doherty's account, revealed that Jeanne was actually concerned about her mother, who had fallen ill in California. Jeanne instantly placed a long-distance telephone call to Los Angeles, but Julia was unable to speak. According to Helen, Jeanne was in tears.

Helen then relayed how a few weeks later, Jeanne called Julia again, to reassure her that newspaper reports claiming she had lost her sight were exaggerated. She was suffering from 'Klieg Eyes' at the time, and after a minor operation at St. Luke's Hospital, she expected to recover fully and hopefully return to work as soon as possible.

Jeanne's sibling also visited *Liberty*'s New York office shortly after the articles went to print and confronted the writer. "You know," he told her, "everyone who has read my manuscript, has asked me if I was in love with Jeanne Eagels. I had only seen her on the stage and screen, but I was utterly hypnotized by her fascination. They had guessed my secret. I *was* in love with Jeanne Eagels."

"Were Doherty smitten, what a strange way to show it," Helen remarked, "using terms such as 'drunkard', 'hellion' and 'devil' to describe the object of his infatuation."

Others interviewed also questioned the accuracy of Doherty's articles.

"I told Doherty about my brother and Jeanne," Ed Dubinsky insisted, "because it was the truth. I have no sympathy with [*Liberty*] magazine's efforts to blacken Jeanne's reputation or revile her character."

"I have read her life story, and in one sense the author is very unfair to her," Jeanne's friend and *Pink Lady* co-star, Cecil Cunningham, told journalist Elisabeth Goldbeck in an interview for *Photoplay*'s October 1930 issue. "Because Jeanne was, innately and fundamentally, a lady . . . There are many versions of the life and character of Jeanne Eagels," Cunningham admitted. "She invented most of them herself. But the Jeanne I knew had no resemblance to the one who has become notorious and fabled. I don't know what people are talking about when they speak of her hardness, her bad language, her unreliability, her temper."

If Jeanne's friends and relatives were aghast at Doherty's serialization, it was a smash hit with his readership. "Jeanne Eagels' acting has been an inspiration to every student of drama," G.D. Schmaille wrote from Seattle, Washington. "It is wonderful to get the background to that acting, now, in *Liberty*." Another reader from New York City recalled catching a glimpse of Jeanne leaving the theatre after a bravura performance in *Rain*. "She entered her car the same high-strung, nervous woman we had seen on the stage just a short while ago," he wrote. "She was carrying several bouquets of flowers—many having been given to her over the footlights. An old woman beggar shoved her way to Jeanne Eagels' side. Miss Eagels thrust a bouquet into her hands . . . Jeanne Eagels will never be forgotten by us who saw her live."

***

Doherty condensed his story into a 300-page book. *The Rain Girl: The Tragic Story of Jeanne Eagels*, published by McCrea-Smith in March 1931 to scathing reviews.

"One feels this Jeanne Eagels of Mr. Doherty's book is no more the real Jeanne Eagels than was the tawdry, shallow, but enticing figure that walked across the stage as Sadie Thompson from Honolulu. Much of his material appears but the product of an inspired press agent. The story is often disconnected, often confusing." – *Salt Lake Tribune*

"The book sequence is terribly mixed, and the events are related just as they come to the author's mind. It seems that such a spectacular life has caused much fictitious publicity to be written, and it is difficult to really find out the truth.' – *Lawrence Daily Journal-World*, Leavenworth, Kansas

"The author had the tough job to rake up as many scandals about the lady as it was safe to print, and on the other hand to make her out as an important and glamorous person. Whatever else had brought him to

the task, he did not suffer himself to be hampered by careless habits of accuracy... The portrait of Eagels in this book is fantastically distorted."
– *New York Evening Post*

"Another instance of the fair-favored but ill-souled bastard offspring of fiction and biography" – *New York Times*

***

In both versions of his Eagels biography, Doherty quoted several publications within the text, but he compiled no bibliography or list of sources for his book. We do know, however, that he had spent several weeks conducting interviews with sources including the Eagles family, Ted Coy, Madame Savage, Clifton and Mabelle Webb, Ed Dubinsky, Helen Broderick, Ruby Stapp, Margaret Knowles and David Belasco among many others. Several of his anecdotes and quotations attributed to Jeanne herself had first appeared in other publications, and were expanded upon by Doherty. Setting aside minor errors in dates and other small details, a perusal of city directories, census records and local newspapers verifies much of what Doherty wrote, and enables correction for some of his mistakes.

Blocks of first-person dialogue such as that between Jeanne and Maurice Dubinsky, reconstructed by his brother Ed two decades later must be disregarded or given little credibility. While recollections by the likes of Coy, Savage and others may have been colored by their feelings for Jeanne, all give a loving but honest portrayal of their friend.

Though his interpretation of Jeanne's life and character may have been questionable in some aspects, both the magazine series and subsequent book provide much in terms of valuable information to work with.

Eddie Doherty's career continued to prosper, with seven more books and an Academy Award nominated screenplay *The Fighting Sullivans* (1944). His first two wives died prematurely, but by the late 1930s he had found lasting happiness with Catholic social worker Catherine de

Hueck, whom he met at Harlem's racially progressive Friendship House. Together they founded the Madonna House, a mission in Ontario, Canada. In 1969, Doherty was ordained within a division of the Greek Catholic Church which permitted priests to marry. He died in 1975.

The Prodigal Daughter

Long before television made Ed Sullivan one of America's most famous faces, he was a Broadway columnist with a regular show on the Columbia Radio Network. On February 23, 1932, the *Syracuse Journal* noted that the guests for his next broadcast would include actress Peggy Hopkins Joyce, Columbia Records' song-stylist Art Jarrett, and the first public appearance of "Julie Eagels," self-proclaimed "daughter of Jeanne Eagels," who would impersonate the late star in a scene from her life.

The origins of the story were detailed in Gilbert Swan's syndicated column: "Dea Lloyd, an obscure showgirl of seventeen, with raven black hair and moody Gaelic features, walked into the offices of a Broadway theatrical agency looking for a job." According to Swan, that man was agent Chamberlain Brown, and during the interview, Dea looked at a photo of Jeanne displayed in his office and said, "That is my mother."

Sitting in the same office a couple of days later, "Julie" told Swan, "I did not use my mother's name when I first came to New York looking for a stage job . . . You see, I could dance and sing. Mother had attended to that. I had been given very special training while abroad. She encouraged me to go on the stage—taught me little gestures and stage tricks."

"I saw her about once a year. Sometimes she would come to see me; sometimes I would come to New York and stay quite a time with her. I didn't know she was my mother until I grew up. My father took care of me most of the time. Until I found out, I had looked upon Jeanne as an aunt."

"Concerning my claim, I have only this to say: those people to whom it makes any difference have seen the birth certificate. They know I was born in a small Colorado town. They know who my father is . . . I can say also that Jeanne's mother is well-aware of my existence, although I do not know her."

Borrowing liberally from Doherty's account, Dea did her alleged mother no favors by also claiming to have a half-brother. "They also know that there is a son—now about twenty-three," she said. "When he was about nine, it was considered necessary that he seem to disappear. Actually he has been reared by another. I, too, have been shifted about the world and have spent most of my time in Canada."

Side-by-side photographs of Jeanne and Dea failed to show a significant resemblance, but Chamberlain Brown didn't worry too much about the facts—publicity was publicity. Over the next month, syndicated blurbs appeared in newspapers scattered across the country.

On February 29, the *Kansas City Star* published a syndicated report questioning the true identity of Miss Lloyd. She was known as "Claire De Clifford" while living in Detroit, at the Fort Shelby Hotel. She led those around her to believe she was an English aristocrat, Lady Claire De Clifford, without actually saying so. She also admitted "appropriating" the name Dea Lloyd, among others, for her personal use. Upon discovery of her ruse, the "Lady" quietly vanished. The article also stated that she was probably between seventeen and twenty-three years of age, according to those who knew her.

Having returned from New York, Helen (also known as Elaine) was now living with Paul and Julia at the family home 425 West Sixty-Seventh Street Terrace, while George lived nearby at 117 East Sixty-Fifth Street. It had been announced a week previously that an attorney representing "Julie Eagels" was heading to Kansas City with documents proving "Julie's" identity. The attorney never arrived.

Jeanne's family told reporters that the girl who called herself "Julie Eagels" had visited Clifford and Mabelle Webb in Chicago, claiming she was the daughter of Beatrice Lillie. She then changed her mind and told them she was Jeanne's daughter.

"You must very fond of Julia then," Mabelle Webb commented, referring to Jeanne's mother.

"Who is Julia?" the girl replied blankly.

Back in Kansas City, Jeanne's relatives denied that any steps had been taken legally against "Julie Eagels." They regarded the girl as "an imposter, unworthy of serious consideration."

On March 4, it was reported that Dea had declined an offer to appear onstage in *Rain*, planning instead to leave for the coast to "negotiate for picture work." Four days later a photo of the young lady in an evening gown was published, with a caption informing readers she was "making preparations for a film version of *Rain*." Then on March 31, the *Salt Lake Tribune* confirmed that she had turned down the stage offer and would soon move to Los Angeles for "a film version of *Rain*, the play made famous by her mother." Nonetheless, Dea soon vanished from the spotlight, emerging a couple of years later to announce she was expecting twins.

Her Life Onstage

Less than two months after Jeanne's death, Helen Broderick, Jeanne's fellow chorine and roommate from *Jumping Jupiter* days, completed a manuscript entitled *My Memory of Jeanne Eagels*, in the hope of fashioning it into a play. *The Missourian*, as the project was renamed, would focus on "the time Miss Eagels, following the death of her father, a Kansas City policeman[24], began to earn her livelihood on the stage until she entered the motion picture field a full-fledged star." They had drifted apart in recent years, but Broderick remained fond of Jeanne, last meeting her in the lobby of the Morosco Theatre (where Elsie Ferguson was starring in *Scarlet Pages*) shortly before Jeanne's death. Although her project never materialized, Helen's reminiscences were included in Doherty's *The Rain Girl*.

---
24 Edward Eagels was a carpenter, not a policeman.

On May 13, 1930, Edmund Goulding—director of *Love,* the 1927 film adaptation of *Anna Karenina,* a role that Jeanne had lost to Greta Garbo—revealed that he had written a play specifically for Jeanne called *The Woman in the Wheat,* about Hallie—a hardened, gold-digging Midwestern manicurist. After Jeanne's death, the play was rewritten and filmed as *The Devil's Holiday* starring Nancy Carroll.

In his September 30 column, Gilbert Swan had announced that "George Kaufman and Maurine Watkins are collaborating on a drama in which Jeanne would be a central character. And Zoe Akins is another well-known playwright similarly occupied. And you hear along the 'main stems' rumblings to the effect that a biography, written by Eddie Doherty, will provide a third opus."

Maurine Dallas Watkins' *So Help Me God!,* a comedy based on her memories of producing the stage hit *Chicago,* had been due to open on October 28, 1929, after a brief run on the "subway circuit." On October 16, it was announced that another playwright, George S. Kaufman, was revising the script, now retitled *An Old-Fashioned Girl.* Its main character, Lily Darnley, was an "egomaniacal diva" reputedly based on Jeanne, who had walked out on *Chicago* three years earlier. Lily was to be played by Helen McKellar, while Sylvia Sydney was cast as Kerry, the understudy who nearly steals the show.

Four days before the premiere, the stock market crashed and *So Help Me God!* was shelved permanently. However, Jeanne's death on October 3 may have doomed the project, as what promised to be a juicy satire now seemed in questionable taste. Watkins moved to Hollywood, becoming a successful screenwriter at MGM. Devoutly religious, in later life she distanced herself from her early, racier work.

So Help Me God! languished in obscurity for eighty years, until the literary agent for Watkins' estate presented it to the Mint Theatre Company. The play enjoyed a brief, off-Broadway run at the Lucille Lortel Theatre in late 2009, with Kristen Johnston starring as Lily Darnley. *Variety* noted that Watkins' storyline "pre-dated *All About Eve* by twenty years," while theatregoer, author, scriptwriter, and film producer David Stenn instantly recognized sundry references to *Chicago* and the legendary Jeanne Eagels.

Other than *The Rain Girl*, none of those projects came to fruition. In June 1933, two plays based on Jeanne's life briefly reached the stage: *Not a Saint* and *Shooting Star*.

Penned by John Montague, *Not a Saint* was first announced in the *New York Sun* on February 3, 1932 as *America's Greatest Actress*. This epithet came from a promotional tagline that Montague, as Jeanne's press-agent during *Cardboard Lover*'s 1928 tour, had used until other actresses under Woods and Miller's management objected. Montague stated that most of the incidents in the play were drawn from his professional experiences with several unnamed leading ladies. According to the *Boston Globe*, "the dramatic conflict [was] concerned with the battle of two women for the love of one man."

Financed by Montague and Desmond Gallagher, who was also in the cast, the retitled *Not a Saint* opened on Monday, June 19, at Boston's Hollis Theatre, with Queenie Smith in the starring role. It may have closed within a week, or even less, as it was apparently not reviewed in the local or national press. Maybe Montague and Smith admitted defeat after attending the June 13 premiere of *Shooting Star* at New York's Selwyn Theatre.

"Julie Leander, a 'redheaded guttersnipe' runs away from her road show, her husband and child after seeing Duse in Chicago in 1918," *Time* said of Noel Pierce's *Shooting Star*. "In Manhattan she offers herself and her service to a producer in return of a part in a smart comedy. Men she picks up and drops by the hodful until a strapping socialite, not unlike Miss Eagels' husband, Yale Footballer Teddy Coy, does her wrong. A play not unlike *Rain*, called *Port of Call*, furnishes the volatile actress' immense satisfaction. She can tell the men in the play what she thinks of them. But soon physical illness leads her to take narcotics, and narcotics kill her, circumstances similar to those under which Miss Eagels died in 1929."

Shooting Star's temperamental heroine was played by someone who had filled in for Jeanne twice before, and would be described as a "ghost player" for the late actress in an Associated Press report. Francine Larrimore had taken the role of Roxie Hart in *Chicago* when Jeanne walked out on the production in 1926, and had played the role to acclaim for two years. She would do so again shortly after Jeanne's death, perhaps hoping lightning would strike twice.

In his October 22 column, Ward Morehouse recalled that Sam Harris had optioned Sidney R. Buchman's *Storm Song* for Jeanne's stage comeback, a play about the wayward daughter of a ship's captain, who travels the South Seas aboard various freighters filled with sailors. The producer even paid royalties for the property during Jeanne's period of suspension from the "legitimate" stage. When she died shortly after the Actors Equity ban was lifted, Harris relinquished the rights to Robert V. Newman, who wanted either Claudette Colbert or Judith Anderson to star. Larrimore stepped in after both Colbert and Anderson demurred. The production toured before coming to Broadway, with Larrimore's illness closing the show in Washington, D.C. *Storm Song* never reopened, and Francine's next role was a comedy, *Brief Moment*, at the Belasco Theatre. She was also the lead contender for a proposed 1932 revival of *Rain* on Broadway, but those plans were abandoned. Larrimore may have thought this was as close as she would get to Sadie Thompson.

Jeanne's former beau, Barry O'Neill, and her acting coach, Beverly Sitgreaves, also joined the cast of *Shooting Star* as "Tom Blair" and "Miss Frothingham," but bland pseudonyms couldn't hide the play's inspiration, and even casting Jeanne's trusted friends in key roles failed to enhance the play's credibility. *Shooting Star* folded after sixteen performances, despite the *Evening Post*'s prediction that it would "undoubtedly be rewritten with much Hollywood gusto and filmed, probably by Paramount."

"It seems foolish that the producers ... should deny that this drama is based on the rise and fall of the late Jeanne Eagels ... Miss Larrimore did the best she could, but it is doubtful if a constellation of stars could prevent this drama from falling." – Stephen Rathburn, *New York Sun*

"The play isn't a very good play. . . " – Percy Hammond, *Los Angeles Times*

"It is a little less than ghoulish to drag her life back to the stage to create an emotional field day for another actress. It is also a wasted effort. . ." – Burns Mantle

"Whatever their intentions may have been in doing the uncomfortable thing they have chosen to do, the melancholy fact remains that *Shooting Star* is a pretty poor play as Miss Pierce and Mr. Schoenfeld have written it. . ." – John Mason Brown, *New York Evening Post*

Faye Dunaway: 'Nothing Doing'

"FAYE AS JEANNE" read a syndicated blurb in the September 8, 1974 issue of the *Seattle Daily Times*. Faye was, of course, Faye Dunaway; and Jeanne was Eagels, in a remake of the 1957 biopic starring Kim Novak. Born in 1941, Dunaway began her career in the theatre, before starring opposite Warren Beatty in *Bonnie and Clyde* (1967). Further acclaim followed, and by 1974 she was riding high with roles in Roman Polanski's *Chinatown*, and a television adaptation of Arthur Miller's *After the Fall*, playing a thinly-veiled version of his former wife, Marilyn Monroe.

Like many other film projects, the Eagels biopic was teased in the press to gauge interest at an early stage. Nothing more was heard until a curious reader wrote to the *Boston Evening Star* on March 3, 1977, asking why Dunaway, who won the Best Actress Oscar for *Network* (1976.) had relocated to the Boston area with her husband, J. Geils Band singer Peter Wolf. It emerged that she had studied at Boston University in the early 1960s, while Wolf had also spent time in the city. Aside from the rumour that the award-winning actress and her musician spouse wanted to escape the Hollywood rat race, Faye also wanted to be near playwright and Harvard professor William Alfred—who had penned *Hogan's Goat*, a 1965 off-Broadway play, and her first as leading lady. Alfred was reportedly now writing a play about Jeanne Eagels for Faye.

Nearly four years passed before the *New York Times* News Service syndicated a press release giving more details on Alfred's Eagels play. Now titled *Nothing Doing: A Tragic Vaudeville*, with the recently divorced Dunaway not only starring, but co-producing and co-directing with her English boyfriend and future husband, photographer Terry O'Neill. Faye's character, actress Suleika Caswell, was said to be "vaguely based" on Jeanne Eagels. As Alfred told the *Times*, "You follow this actress in and out of her own depression in a world full of depression. It's a complicated play in nine very fast acts. It has been a dream of ours, Faye's and mine, for a long time."

"It's the greatest compliment of career that William Alfred has written this play for me," Dunaway added. When asked about the difficulty of wearing three hats in the production, with this being her first directorial effort, the actress confidently replied, "Bill's plays practically direct themselves."

So what happened? *Mommie Dearest*, the 1981 film adaptation of Christina Crawford's notorious tell-all of her unhappy life as the adopted daughter of Joan Crawford. Dunaway's portrayal of the screen icon was either high drama or high camp, and she found herself being vilified by the Hollywood elite. Convinced that *Mommie Dearest* had irreparably damaged her career, for many years she disowned the overblown biopic (although it has become a cult favorite.) Dunaway's critical mauling scared away any potential backers for the ironically-titled *Nothing Doing*, and she may have worried people would only show up to see how much of Joan was in Jeanne. This was a great pity, as with her combination of aloof beauty and formidable talent, Miss Dunaway could have brought an intensity to Eagels unmatched since Bette Davis.

Which brings us to another, less admired quality that Faye shared with Jeanne: a reputation for being temperamental and high-strung. Even before she was cast as Bette's arch-rival in *Mommie Dearest*, Davis held very little regard for Dunaway, and in 1988, when Johnny Carson asked her, "Who would you not work with again?" on his late-night talk show, the eighty-year-old star immediately shot back, "One million dollars ... Faye Dunaway. Everybody you could put into this chair would tell you the same thing."

Davis went on to share an anecdote about the making of *The Disappearance of Aimee*, a 1976 television movie about the alleged abduction of a flamboyant Californian evangelist fifty years before. Dunaway, who starred as Aimee Semple McPherson, had kept Davis (who played her mother), the entire crew and an auditorium filled with over-heated extras waiting for hours. Ever the trouper, Davis entertained them all by singing "I've Written a Letter to Daddy," from her 1961 shocker, *Whatever Happened to Baby Jane*. "She is totally impossible. Miss Dunaway is for Miss Dunaway," Bette sniffed as Carson's audience roared with laughter. "Seriously, totally unprofessional. A difficult woman."

Eagels in The Big Easy

While a student at Louisana State University, James Roth became fascinated with the life story of Jeanne Eagels, making her the subject of a one-woman play. After working with Roth at a New Orleans script workshop, producer and director Ken Mentel decided to undertake the project for the Artist Company Theatre. Originally conceived as more of "An Evening With...", the production was reworked as an hour-long show divided into three parts. The first has Eagels discussing her early career, followed by a twenty-minute version of *Rain* with two male co-stars, while the final third chronicled her downward spiral after leaving Sadie behind.

In May 1986, an advertisement was placed in the *Times-Picayune* seeking "one woman, age 25 to 35, to portray 1920s actress Jeanne Eagels." Former New Orleans beauty queen and B-movie actress Rhonda Shear, who had moved to Los Angeles eight years earlier to break into films, had come home to promote her latest film, *Basic Training*. Hoping to widen her range from blonde bimbo to serious actress, Shear auditioned for and won the role. "I saw some very strong actresses, and Rhonda was the best," Mentel told the *Times-Picayune*.

As a three-weekend run at the Sheraton Hotel commenced, New Orleans critics savaged the play and its star. "Shear offers only a stiff, uninvolving delivery, a voice lacking in resonance and a pageant-poised manner," Richard Dodds wrote in the *Times-Picayune*, "even when Eagels is suffering from alcoholism, drug addiction and mental disturbance." The final week's "this week" blurb concluded, "Rhonda Shear fails to add any depth of her own to the role." Rhonda Shear would eventually leave the entertainment industry and become the head of her own line of women's wear and undergarments, marketed on cable television's home shopping channels.

Hollywood's Revenge

The gulf between stage and film performers was demonstrated by Hollywood's half-hearted attempt to immortalize Jeanne Eagels, which began on January 30, 1933, with a front-page story in the *Hollywood Reporter* telling of RKO's plans for a biopic. Written by William Rankin, *No Greater Love* would star Irene Dunne, but within a week, it was reported that Constance Bennett would take the lead after her return from a European vacation and upon completing her next film, *Bed of Roses*. Neither project materialized, and "No Greater Love" became the title of a song in Dunne's 1936 film, *Roberta*.

"Bette Davis, whom you'll soon see in the Jeanne Eagels role in *The Letter*, is trying to sell Warners the idea of permitting her to do *The Life of Jeanne Eagels*," columnist Hal Eaton wrote in the *Long Island Daily Press* on July 19, 1940. "But didn't Miss Davis delineate La Eagels' life in *Dangerous*?"

If Francine Larrimore was Jeanne's stage ghost, the young Bette Davis would shadow her on film. Davis won her first Academy Award for her role as troubled actress Joyce Heath in *Dangerous* (1935). She had initially rejected the part, said to be inspired by Jeanne's life story. Like Jeanne, Davis played strong, nervy women, but Joyce Heath was ultimately saved by the love of a good man in a Hollywood-style happy ending, which Jeanne had, of course, been denied.

Herbert Marshall, who had played Jeanne's murdered lover back in 1929, was now cast as the betrayed husband in *The Letter*'s second adaptation, and this wasn't the only parallel between Davis and the actress who preceded her. "Between takes the lady sat in a chair marked 'Bette Davis' and read a book and smoked," the *Chicago Tribune* noted on July 4, 1940. "On her right little finger she wore a square of small diamonds which the late Jeanne Eagels wore when she made the first version of *The Letter*." On November 17, the *Brooklyn Daily Eagle* reported that Davis had returned the ring, loaned to her by Jeanne's devoted friend, Helen Broderick.

By 1940, the Production Code was firmly established, requiring several changes to the original story. Most importantly, murderess Leslie Crosbie could not be allowed to go unpunished. Whereas the 1929 film ends with Leslie proclaiming her love for the slain Hammond, the 1940 version has Davis' character wandering alone outside the gated walls of her compound where she is confronted by Hammond's wife (his mistress in the 1929 version). Aided by a henchman, the angry widow stabs and kills her enemy, and the pair escape as the moon breaks through the clouds, beaming down on Leslie's lifeless body.

Despite these compromises, the William Wyler-directed remake was critically acclaimed, with Davis garnering her first of three consecutive nominations for Best Actress in a lead role—losing out to Ginger Rogers as *Kitty Foyle*. "Never has [*The Letter*] been done with greater production values, a better all-around cast or finer direction," *Variety* opined.[25]

Jeanne's final film, *Jealousy*, was remade as *Deception* in 1946, with

---

25 *The Letter* would be adapted for a third time as *The Unfaithful* (1947), a 'film noir' directed by Vincent Sherman, and starring Ann Sheridan, Lew Ayres and Zachary Scott.

Davis once again taking her place. It was not so well-received, however. "Bette Davis is a competent actress, or so we've been led to believe, but they'd better start giving her good stories—or soon we'll be led to forget," warned *New York Times* critic Bosley Crowther. Another six years would pass before Davis had her turn at playing Jeanne's greatest role, albeit in satirical vein.

Following her trimphant role in *All About Eve,* Davis returned to the stage in 1952's *Two's Company*, a musical revue with a series of show business-themed comedy sketches and song-and-dance routines tailored for her. Choreographed by Jerome Robbins, Davis performed "Roll Along Sadie" at the end of the first act, stoking memories of *Rain*'s anti-heroine in a bright yellow hat and skirt, set off by a black and orange feather boa and a long string of pearls.

The Jeanne Eagels Story

On April 12, 1933, *Film Daily* reported that MGM had purchased the rights to Doherty's *The Rain Girl*. However, many years would pass before the controversial biography was eventually produced by another studio. On January 14, 1956, columnist Hal Eaton revived the subject in gossip shorthand: "*Rain Girl* biog of Jeanne Eagels acquired by Columbia Pic. Queen of B'dway in Roaring '20s reached pinnacle of her career in dramatic version of Somerset Maugham's *Rain*. Studio evidently casting 'against' type. Most glittering star of her era, who created Sadie Thompson, later played by Joan Crawford, Tallulah Bankhead, Gloria Swanson and Rita Hayworth, to be essayed by Eva Marie Saint or Julie Harris, brilliant St. Joan of *The Lark*!"

Five months later, Dorothy Kilgallen reported in her June 5 column, "Part of Rita Hayworth's kiss-and-make-up deal with Columbia is the star role in *The Jeanne Eagels Story*." But Hayworth—who had starred in *Miss Sadie Thompson* three years before—was nearing the end of her reign as the studio's glamour queen, and boss Harry Cohn believed he had found her successor.

Born Marilyn Pauline Novak in Chicago, Illinois, the future actress was a twenty-one-year-old college student and part-time model when she and two girlfriends came to Los Angeles on vacation in 1954. On a lark, the trio stood in line to be cast as extras in a Jane Russell movie. Novak was discovered by an agent and signed to a long-term contract at Columbia. Hollywood already had its Marilyn, and so Marilyn Novak's name was changed to "Kim" Novak. She toiled in unaccredited bit parts before achieving star status in *Picnic* (1955) and *The Man With the Golden Arm* (1956).

The redoubtable Louella Parsons informed her readers that Novak had booked a flight to spend the holidays in Chicago with her family, but Columbia executives insisted she was to "appear the day after Christmas to do her first scene in *Jeanne Eagels*. It will be a hot hoochy-koochy number in the briefest costume Kim ever wore." Parsons also mentioned that Agnes Moorehead had been forced to "cut short her Christmas plans." Moorehead, a versatile character actress best-known years later for her role as Endora in television's *Bewitched*, was signed to play "the dramatic coach, the woman who starts teaching Jeanne Eagels after she leaves Kansas City; in fact, Agnes will be a composite figure of several people." Moorehead's 'Nellie Neilson' combined elements of Georgia Brown, Beverly Sitgreaves, and Madame Savage. Jeff Chandler played Jeanne's first love, Sal Satori, loosely based on Maurice Dubinsky.

Novak bore a slight physical resemblance to Jeanne, though her hair and make-up were more reminiscent of 1930s bombshell Jean Harlow. Costumer Jean Louis created a vast wardrobe for Novak, entailing forty-five costume changes. According to biographer Larry Kleno, Novak "devoted her full energies to the exacting task of presenting Jeanne. She read everything she could find on her, learning, for instance, that 'Eagels was irrational and sensitive and all the things I sort of am, and she used to eat pickles at school like me'... Her dressing room walls were covered with photos of the real Jeanne, and she employed an accordionist for several weeks to play 'Poor Butterfly' during the film's sad scenes."[26]

The American Weekly covered the production in its July 28 issue. "Before each day's shooting, Kim sat with her director, plump, placid, pipe-smoking George Sidney. He would tell her what kind of girl Jeanne Eagels was. He would take a pull on his briar and say: 'You came up out of Kansas City. You're a tough trouper. You've been in carnivals and in stock. You've done all the difficult things in show business. On the outside you're a kind of callous kid. Underneath you're easily hurt.'"

"It's the toughest thing I've ever done," Novak admitted. "It may be the toughest any actress has done. The girl goes through everything, including the bottle and dope." Under Hollywood's modernized production code, Novak would be the first actress allowed to portray a dope addict. Director George Sidney assured the press it would "done in good taste." Sidney's representative, Ted Galanter, told reporters, "Jeanne wasn't the most likable person in the world and we fell we haven't soft-pedaled the more unsavory episodes. It's honest and frank."

However, while *Jeanne Eagels* utilized the basic facts of the star's life story, the end result was distorted beyond recognition. Perhaps the dirtiest trick—as represented in the movie—is the one Jeanne plays on Elsie Desmond, a once-great actress fallen on hard times, who approaches her with a script, *Rain*. Hoping to make a comeback as Sadie Thompson, she prevails upon Jeanne to present it to her producer—but Jeanne demands the role for herself. The rest is consigned to history: she, not Elsie Desmond, scores her great triumph in *Rain*.

In the film, the scorned Elsie commits suicide by jumping from her Bowery hotel window. Having come to make amends, Jeanne discovers a broken window and a shoe caught in the jagged glass. Peering out and down, she sees a crowd gathered around Elsie's body. Wracked with guilt, Jeanne descends into a haze of drugs and liquor.

---

26 As described in Chapter 3, a young Jeanne would often sing *Madame Butterfly* while staying at Helen Broderick's apartment in 1915.

The character's name may have been inspired by Elsie Ferguson, whom young Jeanne had carefully imitated in order to take over her part in *Outcast* for the play's road show tour. However, unlike her fictional counterpart, Ferguson was neither upstaged nor driven to suicide. In fact, she outlived Jeanne by more than thirty years.

This particular scene found its inspiration in the suicide of an actress named Pauline Armitage, who leaped to her death from the window of her fourteenth-floor Hotel Shelton apartment on February 16, 1926. Clad in a pink nightdress, her body landed in front of the service entrance to the building, narrowly missing two workmen unloading supplies. She had been suffering from nervous exhaustion from overwork, appearing in three Broadway shows the previous season. Doherty claims lack of work and a broken romance, but it was also rumored that Armitage was despondent over Jeanne's success as Sadie Thompson. While *Rain* was still in development, John D. Williams and Kent Thurber had reportedly offered the part to Armitage. But when Sam Harris agreed to produce the show, he insisted that his client Jeanne Eagels should be cast. As Doherty commented, Jeanne wouldn't have given up the part even if she had known. Hers was the bigger name, and she also had far greater experience.

Penned by Sonya Levian and John Fante, whose novels would gain him posthumous acclaim, from a story by Daniel Fuchs, *Jeanne Eagels* was intended to showcase Novak's potential as a serious actress, but did the opposite. Released in August 1957, *Jeanne Eagels* did irreparable damage to the legacy of a fine actress, and proved a critical failure. The overblown depiction of Jeanne's struggle with addiction cemented the misunderstandings about her death, and did little to alter the general perception of Novak as a beautiful, but limited actress. Her icy persona—actually a form of shyness—would make Novak an ideal 'Hitchcock blonde" in *Vertigo* (1958), but was wholly unsuited to portray Jeanne's fiery persona. While Novak's efforts were praised by some critics, the film itself was panned.

***

"It is a tiresome and embarrassingly inept film, supposed to be based on the life of a great actress. As a screen biography, it is as absurd as it is inaccurate, and Kim Novak playing the title role is woefully miscast. It was like putting Jayne Mansfield into *Peter Pan*, or like calling Katherine Hepburn to play Alice in Wonderland." – Ward Morehouse

"The kindest way to appraise *Jeanne Eagels* is simply to call it embarrassing ... an incredibly dull, trashy script ... a composite of Little Nell from the country and a woman's *Lost Weekend*, with no soap-opera holds barred." – *New York Times*

"A mixture of fact and fiction which manages to be monotonous. The central character never comes to life and Miss Novak's dramatic inexperience is made extremely obvious by the requirements of the role ... As merely the story of an unhappy, alcoholic egotist it may be possible, but as a portrait of the tragic actress, it's a dismal failure." – *Chicago Tribune*

"Miss Novak will undoubtedly not be satisfactory to every critic and particularly to some who knew Jeanne Eagels ... The fact remains that Miss Novak, undoubtedly aided by [George] Sidney's persistence, gives a remarkable performance ... *Jeanne Eagels* may not be an unqualified success with some critics, but it should be a rousing success with audiences." – James Powers, *Hollywood Reporter*

"The script of the story follows or departs from the basic facts of its subject's life according to the whims of Hollywood showmanship, which often causes historians to mutter derisively in their beards." – Charles Collins, *Chicago Daily Tribune*

"In the title role, Miss Novak turns in a generally fine performance. There are moments when she appears a little unsure of the characterization, but the portrayal is largely sound and penetrating" – *Variety*

"This film will certainly confound the critics who have been complaining that Hollywood is always gilding the lily. In the Eagels case, 'tarring' comes closer to being the right word ... surely the strangest 'tribute' the movies could have paid to one of America's greatest stage actresses, who was also, however briefly, one of their own. Her fans—and I was one—are due for a shock." – Philip K. Scheuer, *Los Angeles Times*

***

Jeanne Eagels was graded B by the Catholic Legion of Decency, who judged that a "low moral undertone which pervades this film is further accentuated by grossly suggestive dancing and costuming. Reflects the acceptability of divorce. Only a biographical background upon which the story elements are based averts a more serious classification."

Relatives of Jeanne Eagels filed suit in the Los Angeles Superior Court, seeking damages of $950,000 from both George Sidney and Columbia Productions for the unauthorized use of the name and likeness of the actress, based on laws in Utah and Virginia that prohibited the exhibition of a film about the life of a deceased person without the written consent of surviving heirs. Jeanne's sister, four nephews, and three nieces stated in the complaint that the film depicted her "as a dissolute and immoral person." In an echo of the *Liberty* lawsuit, Columbia's defense (that you can't defame the dead) was upheld.

Even before the film was released, Jeanne's family were planning to set the record straight with a rival television production. 'Aaron 'Red' Doff, president of Fryman Enterprises, has announced the acquisition of 'all rights to the life story of Jeanne Eagels' from her sister Elaine (Helen) Nicklas, and the commencement of negotiations with CBS-TV Playhouse 90 producer Martin Manulis regarding its production," *Motion Picture Daily* reported on June 7. Doff was a Hollywood publicist, talent agent and producer whose clients included Mickey Rooney, Liberace and Doris Day. Unfortunately, Helen's story never made it to the screen.

The writers of *Jeanne Eagels* had drawn on Eddie Doherty's *The Rain Girl*, expanding its most sensational scenes while largely ignoring more mundane facts. Almost sixty years after its release, *Jeanne Eagels* has reduced its subject to a footnote in theatrical history. By depicting Jeanne as a small-town girl who cheated her way to success, only to lose it all in a haze of drugs and madness, the film sidelines her unique talent and sheer graft, which earned her a place in the highest echelons of early twentieth century American theatre.

Although *The Rain Girl* sometimes reads more like romantic fiction than journalism, it was based on solid research. The producers of *Jeanne Eagels* (1957) could perhaps have paid more attention to the facts Doherty uncovered, rather than invoking 'artistic license' to ramp up the melodrama, and projecting their own hyperbolic fantasies upon a long-lost star.

Julia Sullivan Eagles (1865 – 1945), matriarch of the Eagles clan.
"... a handsome woman with white hair brushed back from a distinguished brow and strong regular features. There is dignity and self-assurance in her manner." (*Kansas City Star* June 1930)
Photograph courtesy of the David Stenn Collection.

Top left – Francine Larrimore in *Shooting Star* (1933.) Bottom left – Bette Davis in *Two's Company* (1952.) Right – Kim Novak in a deleted party scene from *Jeanne Eagels* (1957.)

Postscript
The Ballad of Sadie Thompson

While Somerset Maugham's short story is still considered one of his finest works, *Rain* has been neglected in recent decades. Colton and Randolph's stage adaptation has lost its shock value, although sexual hypocrisy is not yet a thing of the past. In *Art, Glitter and Glitz,* Ronald H. Wainscott compares *Rain*'s fate to Eugene O'Neill's similarly-themed *Anna Christie,* which also features a "compassionate prostitute" as its heroine, but has more successfully endured. Whereas O'Neill's play was an ensemble piece, *Rain* became a star vehicle. Jeanne Eagels was the first and most memorable Sadie Thompson.

"Miss Eagels didn't look like the Sadie in Maugham's story, but forever after the opening of *Rain* Sadie Thompson looked like Jeanne Eagels," Robert E. Sherwood proclaimed in the *New York Evening Post* on February 28, 1931.

From the start of Jeanne's legendary run in *Rain,* her role became one that many other actresses hoped to conquer. Local theatrical and road show companies all had their own Sadies, touring those far corners of the nation untouched by Jeanne. It was Gloria Swanson, not Jeanne, who first played Sadie on film. After Jeanne's death, an eclectic list of recognizable names was considered for or attempted the part. Some rose to the occasion, while others faced ridicule, but none escaped comparison to the original.

Back to Broadway

A decade after being rejected by Somerset Maugham, Tallulah Bankhead was cast by *Rain*'s original producer, Sam Harris, in a Broadway revival, three years after his first failed attempt. "The throaty Tallulah this season made a name for herself along the Gay White Way and now she is to step into the Jeanne Eagels role of Sadie Thompson," the *Spokane Daily Chronicle* reported in January 1935. "Much promise is held for the actress in the forthcoming part, which is believed by many to ideally suit the talents of Miss Bankhead."

Directed by the original stage manager Sam Forrest, *Rain* opened at the Music Box Theatre on February 12. Columnist Paul Harrison noted many celebrities in the audience, including Gary Cooper and his wife Veronica, Beatrice Lillie, Noel Coward, Adolph Zukor, B.P. Schulberg, Francine Larrimore, Ben Lyon, and Bebe Daniels. The revival was not a success, however, and closed after forty-seven performances.

"Miss Eagels played with less effort than Miss Bankhead, sure of herself at all times, hitting the nail accurately on the head the first time where Miss Bankhead has to do a bit more hammering until she achieves the effect she is after. Jeanne Eagels was simple and sure, sharp and crisp. Every word and movement and inflection seemed inevitably right. She never gave the effect that she was acting. Miss Bankhead's performance is an impersonation. The other was Sadie Thompson herself." – Arthur Pollock, *Brooklyn Daily Eagle* (February 13, 1935)

Varied reasons were given for its failure. Aside from Bankhead, the casting was all wrong. Some felt the story should have been modernized to reflect changing attitudes, rather than remaining set in 1920. The loudest complaint was that the revival was "an exact duplicate of the production in which Miss Eagels appeared. The directions are the same."

"Broadway is no longer shocked or enraged to see the collapse of a pious man when tempted by a woman. The stage and screen in the past few years have been too crowded with such incidents." – Mark Barron, syndicated New York columnist (March 16, 1935)

"The revival of the play *Rain* was packed with memories for most of those who saw it. Nobody who saw the late Jeanne Eagels in the role of Sadie Thompson, would forget her strange manic genius ... But it is a strange play to be shown to these times. At points where the audience gasped a short ten years ago, either at profanity or at the presence of a cleric in an unsympathetic role, there are now gales of laughter ... Tallulah, I think played Sadie just about as well as Jeanne Eagels, but Tallulah, whose offstage life is colorful enough, does not bring to the role the obscure chemistry of crazy, don't-care bravado Jeanne brought to it. But Tallulah did immensely well by herself and I see no reason why a younger generation shouldn't get a great kick out of her, despite the fact that they are no longer shocked as ancients of the 1920s were." – Jim Axwell, *Morning Herald* (February 18, 1935)

As always, Tallulah had the last word: "I caught up with the Reverend Davidson ten years too late."

The Fan Dancer

Hattie Helen Gould Beck was born in 1904 in Hickory County, Missouri, moving to Kansas City at around the same time that Jeanne was finishing her stint with the Dubinskys. Appearing older than she was, thirteen-year-old Hattie got her start as a chorus girl at the Empress Theatre, working her way up to nightclubs. Upon her arrival in Los Angeles, Cecil

B. DeMille renamed her Sally Rand after the Rand McNally atlas in his office. She appeared in a number of silent films, and was crowned a WAMPAS Baby Star in 1927, but Rand was most celebrated for her "Fan Dance," in which she maneuvered two seven-foot pink fans made of ostrich feathers to hide what the audience perceived as total nudity. In reality, she was covered in either a flesh-colored body suit, or in full body make-up, exposing nothing.

Rand was arrested four times in one day at the 1933 Century of Progress World's Fair in Chicago Illinois where she was performing her show. At the next year's fair, she danced inside a massive, clear bubble of her own invention. In 1936, Rand appeared at the San Diego Exposition, and opened the Music Box burlesque hall in San Francisco. She would later present "Sally Rand's Nude Ranch" at the Golden Gate International Exposition in San Francisco. For two years in-between, Rand toured summer stock as a legitimate actress. Sadie Thompson was one of two roles she played.

On August 16, 1938, Michel Mok's interview with Rand—then starring in *Rain* at the Westchester Playhouse in Mount Kisco—was published in the *New York Post*. Rand confided to Mok that she felt a mysterious affinity with Jeanne, having "come from the same town—Kansas City. We both started in the same stock company—the Dubinsky Brothers' troupe—though of course, I started later than her. Maybe it's only coincidence, but I think there's something more to it, don't you?"

When Jeanne had brought *Rain* to the Biltmore Theatre in Los Angeles more than a decade before, Rand was in the audience. "I saw Jeanne Eagels playing *Rain* when she revived it in 1925. But I'd dreamed of doing it long before. Ever since I first went on the stage, I knew that I ultimately would play *Rain*. You have to go a long way around sometimes. It took a World's Fair to make an actress out of me."

Two of *Rain*'s original cast, Emma Wilcox (as trader Joe Horn's native wife, Ameena) and John Waller (Doctor McPhail) reprised their roles.

Rand's performance included an exact replica of Eagels' famed costume, down to the armfuls of jangling bracelets.

"She makes a very convincing Sadie Thompson and rises to surprising dramatic heights," the *Norwalk Hour* reported, "although somewhat handicapped by a voice lacking in the resonance and timbre that marks the finished actress. Sally Rand is not, by any means, a Jeanne Eagels."

"She's better with a fan," Michel Mok concurred.

Sadie Thompson: The Musical

"How are they going to turn the tragedy and melodrama of *Rain* into a musical comedy? Even with Ethel Merman playing Sadie Thompson," Jack Gavner pondered in July 1944. "A. P. Waxman the producer says there is no trick at all. In the first place it isn't a musical comedy but a play with music, a distinction that the man in the street doesn't stop to worry about. In the second place, Howard Dietz, who has done the libretto and lyrics in his spare time from being a vice president and publicity director for MGM films, has stuck pretty faithfully to the original. Waxman will call the musical *Sadie Thompson*. It should go into rehearsal in a week or so ... Vernon Duke has done the score."

"The time element has not been tampered with," Gavner noted. "The action occurs back in the early '20s just as it did in the play originally. The author and producer have had sufficient integrity to pass up the easy excuse offered by the present war to jazz up the proceedings with fighting, spies, Japanese, PT boats, WACS, and other headline catchers. Waxman figures that Sadie and sex are still commercial enough."

Paramount Studios invested $50,000 in the musical, which guaranteed them first preference for the film rights if the stage production was a hit.

Cast as Sadie Thompson, Ethel Merman was nicknamed "Old Leather Lungs" for her unparalleled ability to belt out a show tune, and she had starred in a string of Cole Porter musicals over the past decade.

Her greatest successes were still ahead, but this was no small feather in her cap.

Rehearsals began in September, but after five days, Merman withdrew from the production. "We'll never know what Merman as Sadie Thompson would have been like," biographer Caryl Flinn wrote. "Although the role seems an incongruous fit, aspects of the famous temptress lined up with the Merman persona. Who else could expose the pretensions of hypocrites or the upper crust with such gusto?"

Another Merman biographer, Brian Kellow, observed that *Sadie Thompson* ". . . was unlike any musical she had attempted before. It wasn't a girls-and-gags show. The second act featured a big montage sequence involving young Sadie and a chorus of inner voices, and there was a ballet . . . To Ethel it all seemed a little high-toned." According to Kellow, Merman took Dietz's song lyrics and had them altered: "Dietz told her that if she couldn't sing the songs as written, she'd have to go."

June Havoc, the younger sister of Gypsy Rose Lee, replaced Merman, and *Sadie Thompson* opened at the Alvin Theatre (now the Neil Simon Theatre) at East Fifty-Second Street on November 16. Born in 1912, Havoc began performing as a child, and had made her Broadway debut in 1936. She alternated between stage and screen throughout her long career, and published two popular memoirs.

"June Havoc as Sadie brings much more to *Sadie Thompson* than she gets out of it," an early critic opined. "*Sadie Thompson* would be less convincing than it is without Gypsy Rose Lee's little sister June. At first sight, you don't realize how really good Miss Havoc is."

"Candor compels me to say that I was never much of a *Rain* man," Charles P. Driscoll wrote, "but the new version . . . lifts the sordid South Seas drama away out of its original class, and makes it a work of art; one of the few such things in years of theatrical history. I saw Jeanne Eagels do the part of Sadie Thompson during the original two-year run at the Empire Theatre. I saw Tallulah Bankhead in the 1935 revival. June Havoc is in my opinion, a far better Sadie than either of the others."

POSTSCRIPT: THE BALLAD OF SADIE THOMPSON

Despite favorable reviews for Havoc, *Sadie Thompson*'s Broadway run ended in January 1945, after sixty performances. However, June continued to play the role for several years, appearing at the Corning Summer Theatre in July 1952 with an updated version of *Rain*, "in which she has retained the best features of both the original and musical versions."

Sadie Thompson was still in Havoc's repertoire at the turn of the twenty-first century, when at the venerable age of eighty-eight, she "presided over an abbreviated concert version of the show" at the White Barn Theatre in Westport, Connecticut. As Steven Suskin reported for the Playbill website in 2003, "this led arranger/conductor Joshua Pearl to dig out the manuscripts and reconstruct the show, adding back songs lost when Merman departed the project. Pearl had the good sense and good luck to get Melissa Errico to record the show, leading a cast of six. (The original billing sheet for the show boasts 'with a chorus of 70.')"

"Ron Raines sings the role of the zealous Reverend Davidson—who tries to 'save' Sadie but ends up succumbing to her—in a style somewhat too melodramatic for my tastes," Suskin commented on the *Sadie Thompson* soundtrack album, available on CD and for digital download. "Davis Gaines does somewhat better as the compassionate marine O'Hara, who provides the third side of the triangle. But Errico is absolutely marvelous as Sadie..."

According to Louella Parsons, songwriter Jule Styne had planned another musical reworking of *Rain* after his successful adaptation of *Gentlemen Prefer Blondes* in 1949. Barbara Stanwyck would star as Sadie on Broadway, and on the screen for producer Jerry Wald, who had bought the rights to the play.

Stanwyck was born Ruby Alice Stevens in Brooklyn, in 1907. She became a dancer in her teens, spending 1922-1923 with Ziegfeld's *Follies* at the New Amsterdam Theatre. "At this time, Jeanne Eagels was making a huge impact onstage as the prostitute Sadie Thompson in *Rain*, a prototype for many of Stanwyck's later heroines," noted biographer Dan Callahan. "Ruby saw Eagels in *Rain* four times, and this great actress had an effect on the later Stanwyck style ... Stanwyck accessed the same type of seemingly uncontrollable personal emotion, yet somehow managed—through strength, stamina and practice—to build a kind of controlling technique around her displays of feeling, so that she gave us fresh rage and sorrow on command for decades, something the doomed Eagels was only able to do for a few years."

Rain never made it back to Broadway, however, and Jerry Wald's film remake would take five years to reach the screen after two previous incarnations and several never-realized projects.

On October 31, 1950, the *Chicago Tribune* reported that Jane Russell—the busty brunette who had shot to fame in Howard Hughes' *The Outlaw*—would play Sadie in a Hollywood musical, to be produced by Hughes and Eddie Grainger. It never happened, but Russell would play another Honolulu prostitute in *The Revolt of Mamie Stover* (1955), based on a novel by William Bradford Huie.

Crawford's Rain

"It is too late now to cry over spilled milk, but United Artists including Lewis Milestone, are said to be sorry Jean Harlow was passed up for the Jeanne Eagels part in *Rain*," *Variety* announced in an abbreviated report, published on November 15, 1932. "Joan Crawford was loaned from Metro instead. Milestone is said to have advanced as one reason why *Rain* in its talking version isn't an outstanding draw is because the play has been done to death in stock and too many people know the 'hot lines' picture transcription does not have."

Jean Harlow, born Harlean Carpenter, was the daughter of a Kansas City dentist. After her parents divorced, she moved with her mother to Los Angeles. In 1930, the nineteen-year-old was making waves as a gangster's moll in *The Public Enemy*. Dubbed "the blonde bombshell", she was then better-known for her sex appeal than acting. Offscreen, however, she disliked her brazen image, which had been foisted upon her by the studios and her domineering mother (from whom she took her stage name.)

On November 30, the *Kansas City Star* reported that Harlow was promoting Howard Hughes' aviation epic, *Hell's Angels*, in her hometown, and had been introduced to the mother of another local celebrity during an engagement at the Midland Theatre. During their meeting, Julia remarked on "the similarity in appearance between Jeanne Eagels and Jean Harlow."

By 1932, Harlow had joined MGM's roster and was finally proving herself a brilliant comedienne in films such as *Red-Headed Woman* and *Red Dust*. Typecast as a hard-boiled sexpot, she also had a softer side. While she would never play Sadie Thompson, she went on to become one of the most beloved stars in movie history. She died of kidney disease in 1937, at the age of twenty-six.

Another legendary actress of Hollywood's golden age, Joan Crawford was born Lucille LeSueur in San Antonio, Texas, in 1905. In 1916, after two failed marriages, Lucille's mother brought her and brother Hal to Kansas City. With her family now penniless, Lucille received a haphazard education at the various boarding schools where she cooked and cleaned in lieu of tuition fees. While some of her fellow students were sympathetic, others bullied and humiliated her. She briefly attended college in Columbia, Missouri, before dropping out and returning to Kansas City.

Now calling herself Billie Cassin, she joined a chorus line, traveling to Detroit, Oklahoma City, and Chicago on the revue circuit. In 1924, she caught the eye of a producer, who invited her to New York. Her screen test for the newly-formed MGM Studios was promising enough to merit a trip to Hollywood, and she left Kansas City behind a week after Christmas.

Newly-named Joan Crawford as the result of a magazine contest, she busied herself within MGM's Culver City walls and became one of Hollywood's brightest young stars, epitomizing the "shop-girl by day, flapper by night" character in a series of potboilers. She married Douglas Fairbanks, Jr., dubbed the "Prince of Hollywood," in 1929, and unlike many other silent stars, she adapted to sound with ease. In 1932, Crawford held her own opposite Greta Garbo in the all-star *Grand Hotel*, but MGM seemed not to take notice.

With more theaters now equipped for sound, United Artists hoped to repeat the success of their 1927 adaptation of "Miss Thompson," borrowing Crawford from MGM for the lead role. Tongues immediately began wagging. Less than three years had passed since Jeanne's death, and many still associated her with Sadie. Her fellow cast members were plucked from the New York theatre, and remembered Jeanne fondly. "Listen, fishcake," actor Walter Catlett told Crawford, "When Jeanne Eagels died, *Rain* died with her."

Directed by Lewis Milestone, who had won an Oscar for *All Quiet On the Western Front* (1930), *Rain* was filmed on Catalina Island, using sets from Gloria Swanson's silent version. Crawford neglected to build a rapport with her co-stars or the crew, preferring to stay in her bungalow at night and play Bing Crosby records. Her marriage to Douglas Fairbanks Jr. was also in trouble. When she refused to accept his phone calls he showed up unexpectedly, which only made matters worse. Joan was also rumored to have suffered a miscarriage during filming.

When *Rain* was released in October 1932, Crawford's previously loyal fan base railed against her frank portrayal of a "working girl," and for the first time in her career, she began to receive hate mail. Critics were mostly cruel—"the talkie *Rain* has everything but a soul," judged the *Kansas City Star*—but some acknowledged Crawford's bravery in attempting a fresh take on such an iconic character.

"She is excellent though not always consistent," wrote Mollie Merrick in the *Los Angeles Times*. "The role of Sadie Thompson should have died with Jeanne Eagels. But if it must be resuscitated, Joan Crawford gives a brave and artistic concept of a slightly different girl."

POSTSCRIPT: THE BALLAD OF SADIE THOMPSON

"It turns out to be a mistake to have assigned the Sadie Thompson role to Miss Crawford," thought *Variety*'s Abel Green. "It shows her off unfavorably. The dramatic significance of it all is beyond her range ... Crawford's get-up as the light lady is extremely bizarre. Pavement pounders don't quite trick themselves up as fantastically as all that."

In an interview with Sonia Lee of *Movie Classic* magazine, Joan defended her performance. "All I was doing was trying to characterize a role effectively," she explained. "Sadie was a woman whose mouth would be broad and loose, so I smeared my lips."

"Joan's performance was clearly not crafted in the editing room, as she often has long stretches of dialogue in shots that go on for several minutes," Lawrence J. Quirk and William Schoell observed in their biography of Crawford. "Joan was so uncomfortable with the long takes—it was too much like being in a play—and with this kind of filming in general, that she never realized how good her performance was."

"I hope they burn every print of this turkey that's in existence," Crawford remarked, seemingly in agreement with her critics. And her opinion did not change over the years. "Every actress is entitled to a few mistakes, and that was one of mine," she reflected. "I don't care what anybody says, I was rotten."

"Some of the negative critical and fan reaction to *Rain* had more to do with its exposure of religious hypocrisy than it did to how much lipstick Crawford wore as Sadie," Quirk and Schoell reflected in 2002. "While it would certainly be simplistic to suggest that Joan's own conversion to Christian Science late in life was similar to Sadie's conversion in *Rain*, Joan's own animosity to the film may have had something to do with its deliberately one-sided, negative view of religionists."

However, Crawford's *Rain* has aged rather better than predicted. The black-and-white photography convincingly evokes the dismal, claustrophobic atmosphere of besieged Pago Pago, and Joan's hard-edged performance is unexpectedly moving. But as the Great Depression plunged millions of Americans into hardship, moviegoers wanted escapist fun, not grim morality tales. A decade after Jeanne first brought her to life, Sadie Thompson was falling out of fashion.

Eight more years and one failed stage revival would pass before the subject was brought up again.

"Alice Faye is dying to follow Tallulah Bankhead and Joan Crawford as Sadie Thompson," Paul Harrison noted in his syndicated column on December 16, 1939. Faye was then one of Hollywood's top ten box office draws, having starred in two Shirley Temple films and several musicals, including *In Old Chicago* and *Alexander's Ragtime Band.* Perhaps a musical version was being considered by Darryl F. Zanuck, Faye's boss at 20th Century Fox. But Harrison did not mention *Rain* again, and nothing more came of it.

Hopes for a revival were explored in greater depth by Louella Parsons in 1942. "Jerome Kern and Oscar Hammerstein are to put on a musical version of *Rain* if they can get Marlene Dietrich," the columnist told her readers on August 21. Hal Eaton confirmed the casting suggestion. "Dietrich is ready to sign for the Jeanne Eagels characterization in the musical version of *Rain* which is slated to go into rehearsal when La Dietrich returns from a USO Camp shows overseas tour. Paramount and Mary Pickford will be important backers of this A.P. Waxman production which will be directed by Rouben Mamoulian. Howard Dietz wrote the books and lyrics while Vernon Duke composed the music."

While an interesting choice, Dietrich declined the role—a wise decision. Try as she might, Marlene could never pass for American, and to change Sadie's nationality would alter the play. (Besides, "*Towwential* Wain" and *Wevewend* Davison" would have tried *evewyone's* nerves.)

With Dietrich out, in early 1943, a new star was in the running. "Paramount is toying with the idea of a *Rain* remake, with Dorothy Lamour playing the role made famous on the stage by Jeanne Eagels and on the screen by Joan Crawford," Harold Heffernan revealed in the *Long Island Daily Press.* "Lamour goes next into *Road to Utopia.*" Lamour, a sultry beauty most famous as the sarong-clad sidekick of Bob Hope and Bing Crosby, would not make the cut.

Sadie in Harlemwood

Maughams *Rain* and its outcast heroine had gained currency in black popular culture through stage productions by black theatre companies. The New York based Lafayette Players included *Rain* in its 1928 repertoire, playing to sold-out audiences during its successful run at Los Angeles' Lincoln Theatre.

As the white film industry grew, so did the much smaller cluster of independent producers, whose movies played on a circuit of approximately 600 black theaters, mostly in the South. Strangely, about half of the producers and most of the theater owners were white, and the funding came from cities such as Chicago and Dallas rather than Los Angeles or New York. "Harlemwood" was based in Dallas, where in 1946, Sack Amusement Enterprises produced *Dirty Gertie from Harlem U.S.A.*

Director Spencer Williams was an African-American actor and writer who relocated to Dallas in 1940. Williams had begun his career in Hollywood, playing bit parts in mainstream films, and minstrel roles in comedic shorts before turning to screenwriting. In 1948, he would be cast as Andrew Halt Brown on the popular *Amos 'n' Andy* television series.

Though the names, occupations, locations, and even the ending had been changed, *Dirty Gertie*'s inspiration was obvious: Gertie LaRue is a nightclub entertainer from Harlem, nicknamed for the casual nature in which she entices and then humiliates men. She arrives on the Caribbean island of "Rinidad" to perform in a revue at the Paradise Hotel, where she attracts the attention of two US military officers, calling them "Tight Pants" and "High Pockets." The men enjoy sharing Gertie's affections. The hotel's owner also falls for Gertie and showers her with gifts. Amid all the romantic intrigue, Gertie attracts the unwelcome attention of two missionaries.

"Take your hands off me, you dirty psalm-singin' polecat!" Gertie retorts. "If the truth were only known, you want me just like all the rest!" Finally, a jealous boyfriend from Harlem tracks Gertie to the island, with lethal consequences.

Williams hired actress Francine Everett to play Gertie. Everett was born in South Carolina in 1915, but the family relocated to Harlem when she was still a child. By seventeen, she was a chorus girl in the legendary Harlem jazz club, Small's Paradise.

In 1936, Francine became a member of the Federal Theatre Project's "Negro Unit," sponsored by the Works Progress Administration, and played small roles in *Haiti* and *Black Express*. She moved to Hollywood with her second husband, actor Rex Ingram, but rejected offers from MGM and 20th Century Fox to play maids and other stereotypical roles. After divorcing Ingram in 1939, she returned to New York.

Everett filmed between fifty and a hundred "soundies," an early prototype of today's music videos, shown on jukeboxes, including *Toot That Trumpet* and *Ebony Parade*, alongside Dorothy Dandridge, Cab Calloway and the Count Basie Band. Journalist Billy Rowe exalted her as "The most beautiful woman in Harlem."

As with most race films, *Dirty Gertie*'s meager resources could not match Hollywood's slick standard. With an average budget of $20,000 per film, the company drew heavily from local theatre groups and whatever technicians could be found. Unfortunately it showed, with microphones dangling into view from above, and poorly-hidden cables snaking their way across the floor. Prop mishaps, flubbed lines, and missed cues were left uncorrected, as little money was available for retakes. Nonetheless, *Dirty Gertie* has a raw power which the Hollywood adaptations of *Rain* mostly lacked, starkly exposing the ways in which sexually liberated women (and especially women of color) are so often blamed for the transgressions of men.

Williams employed only six chorus girls, and after a short dance number by July Jones and Howard Galloway, Everett removed her over-the-elbow gloves and began a modest striptease. When no suitable actress was found to play the "Voodoo Queen," Williams donned her costume and played the character in his own low voice, still wearing his mustache. Decades later, Everett recalled "only seeing the Voodoo Queen, not Williams, he played the part so well."

Everett's presence raised *Dirty Gertie* above other race films. She was one of the few authentic black movie stars of that period. Despite her glamour, she possessed a warm, earthy appeal that other African-American actresses, such as Lena Horne and Dorothy Dandridge, were forced to tone down in order to attract white audiences.

Award-winning director William Greeves praised Everett as ". . . a true legend of black film and theatre, one of the top stars of the '40s race movies. She would have been a superstar in Hollywood were it not for the apartheid climate in America and the movie industry at the time."

Sadly, *Dirty Gertie* marked the beginning of Everett's decline. She moved back to Hollywood, but her striking beauty worked against her. Like Horne and Dandridge, she struggled to find leading roles. She gave up her career as an entertainer and returned to New York, working as a clerk at the Harlem Hospital for twenty-four years. Everett was largely forgotten until the late 1980s, when race films were rediscovered and discussed on a scholarly level.

A huge hit when released, *Dirty Gertie* continued playing on double bills in small town theaters for several years. It became a fixture on late-night television in the mid-1980s after falling into the public domain, and in 2015, it was fully restored as part of the box-set *Pioneers of African-American Cinema* released by Kino-Lorber Home Video, and finally earning its due with a Film Heritage Award from the National Society of Film Critics.

Miss Sadie Thompson (1953)

Rita Hayworth, who had also begun her career as a dancer, had been dubbed "The Love Goddess" after finding fame in a series of upbeat musicals. In the classic film noir *Gilda* (1946) she played the ultimate glamour girl. Columbia's biggest star, Hayworth had a love-hate relationship with tyrannical boss Harry Cohn, and formed her own production company, Beckworth, to secure better roles.

Miss Sadie Thompson (1953) was one of them, initially filmed in 3-D. To placate the censors, Sadie's "profession" was changed to a nightclub singer. It was partly filmed in Hawaii (ironically, the same island Sadie has sailed from to Pago Pago in Maugham's story). During the May-July shoot, Hayworth began a turbulent affair with bandleader Dick Haymes, who would become her fourth husband. Her own production company, Beckworth, is noted in the credits. Co-star José Ferrer, who played Reverend Davidson, was then co-operating with the House Un-American Activities Committee in their investigation of alleged Communist factions within the entertainment industry.

After the New York premiere in December 1953, the 3-D print was not used again. Hayworth's performance was generally well-received. "She catches the feel of the title character well," *Variety* remarked, "even to braving completely deglamorizing makeup, costuming, and photography to fit her physical appearance to that of the bawdy, shady lady that was Sadie Thompson." However, others shared Bosley Crowther's opinion that ". . . the character of Sadie is drained of considerable point by the prudence of the producers." In retrospect, the island itself, captured in glorious Technicolor, steals the show. One of the film's few truly provocative moments—Hayworth's big dance number, "The Heat is On"—was condemned as "filthy" by Lloyd T. Binford, elderly head of the Memphis Board of Film Censors.

Marilyn and Beyond

"You know, I had a letter from Somerset Maugham the other day, saying how happy he was that I was going to play the part of Sadie, and telling me something about the real woman on whom he based the character. I'm

POSTSCRIPT: THE BALLAD OF SADIE THOMPSON

really excited about doing the part—she's so interesting. She was a girl who knew how to be gay, even when she was sad. And that's important—you know?"

It was March 1961, and Marilyn Monroe was discussing her dream project—a television production of *Rain*—with journalist Margaret Parton. On March 6, Hedda Hopper had noted that Belgian actress Monique Van Vooren would soon bring *Rain* to Milwaukee's Fred Miller Theatre for a three-week stint, before moving to Palm Beach and Chicago. "She's been studying with Stella Adler to lose her French accent," Hopper added. Reviews from Wisconsin cannot be found, but fellow columnist Dorothy Kilgallen noted that Milwaukee reviewers derided Maugham's story but "loved Van Vooren in the lead role."

Born in Belgium, Van Vooren arrived in New York in 1949. She starred opposite Lex Barker in 1953's *Tarzan and the She-Devil* and, some twenty years later, as Baroness Katrin Frankenstein in *Andy Warhol's Frankenstein*, bookmarking a career of mostly uncredited roles and novelty appearances in television and film.

One of television's first female producers, Ann Marlow, had acquired the rights to Maugham's works in 1950. Since then, she had brought fifteen of his stories to the small screen, including *The Moon and Sixpence*, starring Sir Laurence Olivier, in 1959. The full-color, $350,000 production was a success, and Marlow began work on a "South Seas Series." George Roy Hill would direct Marilyn as Sadie, and Fredric March, who had co-starred with Jeanne in her final film, *Jealousy*, would play Reverend Davidson. As a child, Marilyn (then called Norma Jeane) had played on a grand piano previously owned by the actor and purchased by her mother.

Like Jeanne before her, Marilyn was a fragile, mercurial actress. Her marriage to Arthur Miller had recently ended in divorce, and she had narrowly escaped a brief, terrifying stay in the psychiatric ward of New York's Payne Whitney Hospital, after an alleged nervous breakdown. She was also battling addiction to sleeping pills, and her crippling insecurity led to endless delays on film sets.

Initially more celebrated for her sex appeal than her talent, she had been studying with Lee Strasberg at the Actors Studio—home of the Method—and had won critical acclaim for her performances in *Bus Stop* (1956), *The Prince and the Showgirl* (1957), and *The Misfits* (1961). She was also a gifted comedienne, as proven by her roles in *Gentlemen Prefer Blondes* (1953), *The Seven Year Itch* (1955), and *Some Like it Hot* (1959). Apart from occasional interviews, she seldom appeared on television. Casting her as Sadie Thompson was a major coup for Marlow and NBC.

"Marilyn is a much greater actress than anyone gives her credit for," her *Misfits* co-star, Montgomery Clift, told Louella Parsons, as quoted in her syndicated column on April 9. "[Monroe] is in the same class with Jeanne Eagels, John Barrymore, Laurette Taylor, and yes, even Spencer Tracy."

Although the possibility had been mooted for several years, it was Strasberg, who had seen Jeanne in the original stage production, who finally persuaded Marilyn that it would be perfect for her. "I thought that she could have brought it to the same kind of tremulousness which I remember Jeanne Eagels possessing," he told Fred Lawrence Guiles, author of *Norma Jean* (1969). "An inner kind of quality, a sense of something really taking place, a reaching out, a wanting to be different and better, wanting to raise herself out of the kind of morass that she'd gotten into and her terrible disappointment when she (Sadie Thompson) discovers that the preacher is only a man, that all he wants is what every other man wants. It's very vivid in my mind . . . I felt that Marilyn could do that wonderfully and in certain ways, even more so. I hate to say that because maybe it's my memory that's at fault, but I thought she could do that quite superbly. And that's what I saw in the part—a kind of colorfulness, a strange romantic quality, mainly this gauzelike quality, this tremulousness, together with the other things which had that didn't need to be worked on."

Rod Serling, creator of *The Twilight Zone* and screenwriter for *Rain*, agreed. "I went back to the Maugham story, never looked at the play," he explained later. "But, my Sadie Thompson is not exactly Maugham's—she's a beautiful lost woman; she's Monroe." However, Serling was dismayed to learn that Marilyn was still rehearsing scenes from Colton and Randolph's original script with Strasberg. "This whole experience, so help me, has been more twilight-zonish than my own series," he told television presenter Marie Torre. After Fredric March got cold feet, Richard Burton was proposed for the male lead.

For a variety of reasons, including Marilyn's prior obligations at 20th Century Fox, *Rain* was eventually shelved. The decisive factor, however, seems to have been her unshakable loyalty to Lee Strasberg, whom she now wanted to replace Hill as director. "I want to do it because of Lee's concept," she told NBC's executives. "If I can't, then there's no point in going into it. It's not that I have any concern about the director or any criticism of the director, but I don't know what his ideas are or will be. I only know what Lee's ideas are, and those are the ideas I want to put into the thing. I don't again want to go into something and then find myself in something totally different from I expected or what I hoped for."

Marilyn refused to give up on *Rain*, however. In an interview with Alan Levy for *Redbook*, she responded to director Billy Wilder's claim that the character had been played too often: "This 'shopworn' role is lived every day somewhere, somehow. I'd still bring it to life." In July 1962 she told photographer George Barris, "I think it can be an exciting movie for the big screen." When Barris asked who her favorite actresses were, she immediately named Greta Garbo, adding, "I've also heard wonderful things about Laurette Taylor and Jeanne Eagels." Weeks later, Marilyn was found dead of an apparent overdose, in circumstances similar to Jeanne's demise.

On March 30, 1963, the *Chicago Tribune* reported that Eva Marie Saint, who had won an Academy Award for her performance in *On the Waterfront* (1954), would replace the late actress in *Rain*. In September, columnist Hank Grant reported that television star Edie Adams, who was famed for her impersonation of Marilyn Monroe, was hoping to star in

Rod Serling's adaptation, and had even performed a public "audition" for the role by appearing as Sadie onstage at the Packard Music Hall, Warren, Ohio. Frederic March, the original choice as Davidson in Marilyn's version, agreed to star opposite her. Earl Wilson's column for the December 1963 *TV and Radio Mirror* mentioned not only Adams, whom Wilson thought ". . . would probably try playing Sadie in a more comedic manner," but also Carroll Baker, famed for her role in *Baby Doll* (1956). In 1970, Baker would play Sadie Thompson on British television, as part of a BBC drama series, *W. Somerset Maugham*. Seven years later, she starred in a revival of *Rain* on the London stage.

Rain was revived off-Broadway in 1971, with Madeleine Leroux as Sadie. Born in Laramie, Wyoming, Leroux came to New York in 1969, after studying drama at the University of Capetown, South Africa. In 1970, she starred in an "adult musical", *The Dirtiest Show in Town*. She gained a certain notoriety by appearing nude in this topical revue, staged at the Astor Palace Theatre. In October 1971, it was announced that she would perform *Rain* at the same venue. Previews began on December 26, with a scheduled premiere for January 6, 1972. The show would be listed weekly in *New York Magazine* until it finally opened on March 23.

"Pretty Madeleine Leroux, who was a fetching nude in *The Dirtiest Show in Town*, proves she's a talent with her clothes on, too," Earl Wilson commented in his syndicated column. "Miss Leroux is just the one for the job," agreed UPI's drama editor, Jack Daver. "She has looks, a pliable voice, and she knows what to do with Sadie. It is worth seeing just for historic reasons if nothing else."

As a new era of permissiveness dawned, *Rain*'s moral message must have seemed quaint to younger theatregoers. The *New York Times*' Clive Barnes considered it "a gloriously bad play," but admitted to enjoying it. Writing for *Newsday*, George Oppenheimer was less kind: "Miss Leroux, like the character she plays, has gone straight and I regret to say I found her better with her clothes off. Tall as she is, she is hardly up to playing a role made even more difficult by the passing of half a century. The play has dated incredibly and now seems, at frequent times, laughable."

The show closed after just five days, and is now remembered chiefly because it marked the off-Broadway debut of a young John Travolta. After finding fame on television in *Welcome Back Kotter*, he starred in a string of successful movies, including *Saturday Night Fever*, *Grease*, and *Pulp Fiction*.

Gloria Grahame was best-known for her seductive performances in film noir classics such as *In a Lonely Place* (1950) and *The Big Heat* (1954), as well as *The Bad and the Beautiful* (1952), for which she won an Oscar. Long after her glamorous heyday, the actress starred in another English revival of *Rain*, at the Watford Palace Theatre from June 7 to July 1, 1978. Peter Turner, a British actor who befriended Grahame, described the show as "moderately successful, although some people thought she was miscast in the role of Sadie Thompson. She'd been nervous and unsure throughout the rehearsal period, mainly because of her lack of experience of performing in the theatre, and this was apparent on the first night. However, she gained strength through performance and the production was enthusiastically received by each audience." In *Film Stars Don't Die in Liverpool*, the 2017 film based on Turner's memoir, Annette Bening (as Gloria) is briefly shown taking a bow onstage in a 1920s costume fit for Sadie.

In 2016, the Old Globe Theatre in San Diego premiered a new musical adaptation of *Rain* with a score by Michael John LaChiusa and book by Sybille Pearson, starring Eden Espinosa as Sadie and Jared Zirilli as Davidson. Espinosa, who has played Elphaba in *Wicked*, the Broadway musical about the Wicked Witch of the East from Frank L. Baum's *The Wizard of Oz*, recalls Joan Crawford in her flapper heyday with her transformation to Sadie. "She is meaty and complicated," Espinosa said of her *Rain* character in an interview with the *San Diego Union-Tribune*. "There are so many facets to her back story. But ultimately for me it's about not judging her, not judging the character. And just being as honest and truthful as possible, given the circumstances she's gone through."

Performed on a multi-level open set representing Trader Joe's, the latest incarnation of *Rain* received mixed reviews from theatre critics. "The period atmosphere and South Seas ambience have been preserved along with the work's unavoidable mothball aroma," Charles McNulty wrote in the *Los Angeles Times*. "It's not easy to update a stereotype like Sadie," he added, noting that she came off "like an old Hollywood cliché of a working girl . . . Sexual hypocrisy, religious tyranny and imperialist bullying have hardly been eradicated, but they require new guises to speak to us today."

Sadie Thompson no longer haunts the stage, but on the island of Pago Pago in the American Samoa is the Sadie Thompson Inn, reputedly the hotel where Maugham, his muse, and the missionaries stayed during their quarantine. Rumor has it that the original Miss Thompson stayed behind and opened a business of the same name to "entertain" visiting sailors, before being banished to Hawaii for her affair with a Samoan man.

And so the legend lives on.

Top - Filming *Rain* (1932) on Catalina Island. Bottom left - Seductive version of film poster. Bottom right - Crawford with co-star Walter Huston as Reverend Davidson.

Top left - Tallulah Bankhead. (1935.) Top right - Sally Rand (1933.)
Bottom left - Bottom left - June Havoc in *Sadie Thompson* (1944.)
Bottom right - Francine Everett (1944.)

Postscript: The Ballad of Sadie Thompson

Top left - Rita Hayworth in Miss Sadie Thompson (1953.) Top right - Marilyn Monroe photographed in 1961. Bottom left - Monique Van Voren (1961.) Bottom right - Madeline Leroux (1971.)

Bibliography

Archives

Kansas City Library Special Collections
New York Public Library Billy Rose Theatre Collection
Ossining Historical Society

Books

Abbott, George. *Mister Abbott*. Random House, 1963.

Bankhead, Tallulah. *Tallulah: My Autobiography (Southern Icons)*. University Press of Mississippi, 2004.

Barris, George. *Marilyn: Her Life in Her Own Words*. Citadel Press, 2001.

Bercovici, Konrad. *It's The Gypsy In Me: The Autobiography of Konrad Bercovici*. Prentice-Hill, 1941.

Bordman, Gerard. *American Theatre: A Chronicle of Comedy and Drama 1914-1930*. OUP USA, 1995.

Bradshaw, Jon. *Dreams That Money Can Buy: The Tragic Life of Libby Holman*. William Morrow & Co., 1985.

Burke, Billie. *With a Feather in My Nose*. Appleton, 1949.

Callahan, Dan. *Barbara Stanwyck: The Miracle Woman (Hollywood Legends)*. University Press of Mississippi, 2012.

Churchill, Allen. *The Theatrical 20's*. McGraw-Hill, 1975.

Christensen, Lawrence O. *Dictionary of Missouri Biography*. University of Missouri Press, 1999.

Colton, John and Randolph, Clemence. *Rain: a Play in Three Acts*. Samuel French, 1948.

De Acosta, Mercedes. *Here Lies My Heart*. Deutsch, 1960.

Doherty, Edward. *The Rain Girl: The Tragic Story of Jeanne Eagels*. Macrae-Smith Company, 1931.

Dowell, Gary and Jones, Kim. *Heritage Odyssey Music and Hollywood Memorabilia Auction Catalog #616*. Heritage Galleries, 2005.

Eforgan, Estel. *Leslie Howard: The Lost Actor (Second Revised Edition)*. Vallentin Mitchell, 2013.

Ellenberger, Allan R. *Miriam Hopkins: Life and Films of a Hollywood Rebel (Screen Classics)*. University Press of Kentucky, 2017.

Farrell, John A. *Clarence Darrow: Attorney for the Damned*. Random House, 2011.

Fells, Robert M. *George Arliss: The Man Who Played God*. Scarecrow Press, 2004.

Fiedler, Johanna. *Arthur Fiedler: Papa, the Pops and Me*. Bantam Doubleday Dell, 1994.

Fitzgerald, F. Scott. "The Freshest Boy." From *Taps at Reveille*, Scribner's, 1935.

Fitzgerald, F. Scott. "The Bowl." From *The Price Was High: The Last Uncollected Stories of F. Scott Fitzgerald*. (Ed. Matthew J. Bruccoli). Harcourt, Brace, Jovanich, 1979.

Flinn, Caryl. *Brass Diva: The Life and Legends of Ethel Merman*. University of California Press, 2007.

Forrest, Jennifer, and Kous, Leonard R. *Dead Ringers: The Remake in Theory and Practice*. State University of New York Press, 2001.

Golden, Eve. *John Gilbert: The Last of the Silent Film Stars*. University Press of Kentucky, 2013.

Goldman, Herbert G. *Fanny Brice: The Original Funny Girl*. Oxford University Press, 1992.

Gordon, Ruth. *Myself Among Others*. Atheneum, 1971.

Guiles, Fred Lawrence. *Norma Jean*. McGraw-Hill, 1969.

Hamlin, Mary P., and Arliss, George. *Hamilton: A Play in Four Acts*. Baker, 1918.

Hastings, Selina. *The Secret Lives of Somerset Maugham*. John Murray, 2009.

Hayter-Menzies, Grant. *Charlotte Greenwood: The Life and Career of the Comic Star of Vaudeville, Radio and Film*. McFarland, 2007.

Hirsch, Foster. *The Boys from Syracuse: The Shuberts' Theatrical Empire*. Southern Illinois University Press, 1998.

Howard, Leslie Ruth. *A Quite Remarkable Father*. Harcourt, Brace and Company, 1959.

Kaszarski, Richard. *Hollywood on the Hudson: Film and Television in New York from Griffith to Sarnoff*. Rutgers University Press, 2008.

Kleno, Larry. *Kim Novak on Camera*. Gazelle Book Services, 1981.

Kobal, John. *Rita Hayworth: The Time, the Place and the Woman*. Norton, 1978.

LaSalle, Mick. *Dangerous Men: Pre-Code Hollywood and the Birth of the Modern Man*. Thomas Dunne Books, 2002.

Lawrence, A.H. *Duke Ellington and His World*. Routledge, 2001.

Leaming, Barbara. *If This Was Happiness: A Biography of Rita Hayworth*. Viking, 1989.

Leider, Emily Wortis. *Becoming Mae West*. De Capo Press, 2000.

Lentz, Robert J. *Gloria Grahame, Bad Girl of Film Noir: The Complete Career*. McFarland, 2011.

Lewis, Robert. *Method or Madness?* Samuel French, 1958.

Maugham, W. Somerset. *Rain: and Other Stories*. Grosset & Dunlap, 1921.

Mellow, James R. *Walker Evans*. Basic Books, 1999.

Moore, Robin. *Fiedler, the Colorful Mr. Pops: The Man and His Music.* Little, Brown, 1968.

Morehouse, Ward III. *The Bear Who Lived at the Plaza.* BearManor Media, 2015.

O'Brien, Scott. *Herbert Marshall: A Biography.* BearManor Media, 2018.

Parker, Dorothy. *Dorothy Parker: Complete Broadway, 1918-1923.* Ed. Kevin C. Fitzpatrick. iUniverse, 2014.

Quirk, Lawrence J., and Schoell, William. *Joan Crawford: The Essential Biography.* University Press of Kentucky, 2002.

Rogal, Samuel J. *A William Somerset Maugham Encyclopedia.* Greenwood Press, 1997.

Roth, Lillian. *I'll Cry Tomorrow.* Frederick Fell, 1954.

Schanke, Robert A. *That Furious Lesbian: The Story of Mercedes de Acosta.* Southern Illinois University Press, 2003.

Shields, David S. *Still: American Silent Motion Picture Photography.* University of Chicago Press, 2013.

Silverman, Kenneth. *Houdini!!! The Career of Ehrich Weiss.* Perennial, 1997.

Strasberg, Lee. *A Dream of Passion: The Development of the Method.* Little, Brown & Company, 1987.

Sturges, Sandy. *Preston Sturges by Preston Sturges: His Life in his Own Words.* Simon & Schuster, 1990.

Swenson, Karen. *Greta Garbo: A Life Apart.* Scribner, 1997.

Taves, Brian. *P.G. Wodehouse and Hollywood: Screenwriting, Satires and Adaptations.* McFarland, 2006.

Tate, Mary Jo, and Bruccoli, Matthew Joseph. *Critical Companion to F. Scott Fitzgerald: A Literary Reference to His Life and Work.* Facts on File, 2007.

Turner, Peter. *Film Stars Don't Die in Liverpool.* Grove Press, 1987.

Vine, Phyllis. *One Man's Castle: Clarence Darrow in Defense of the Dream.* Harper Collins, 2005.

Vivian, Daniel J. *A New Plantation World: Sporting Estates in the South Carolina Lowcountry 1900-1940.* Cambridge University Press. 2018.

Wagner, Paul. "I Just Can't See Daylight. . . " In Fitzgerald Hemingway Annual 1970, ed. Matthew J. Bruccoli. Bruccoli-Clark Layman, 1970.

Wainscott, Ronald H. "When Actors Were Still Players." In Gerwitz, Arthur and Kolb, James (ed.) *Art, Glitter and Glitz: Mainstream Playwrights and Popular Theatre in 1920s America*. Praeger, 2004.

Warren, Dorothy. *The World of Ruth Draper: Portrait of an Actress*. Southern Illinois University Press, 1999.

Webb, Clifton and Smith, David L. *Sitting Pretty: The Life and Times of Clifton Webb*. University Press of Mississippi, 2011.

Magazines

Ainslee's Magazine, The American Magazine, The American Weekly, Billboard, The Burns Mantle Yearbook, Collier's Weekly, Every Week, Film Daily, Film Review, Green Book, Harper's Weekly, Harper's Bazaar, Hearst Magazine, Judge Weekly, Liberty, Life, The Literary Digest, Look, Motion Picture, Motography, Moving Picture Weekly, Moving Picture World, Munsey's Magazine, New Movie Magazine, Photoplay, Picture Play, Saturday Evening Post, The Smart Set, Theatre Magazine, Time Magazine, Town and Country, Vanity Fair, Variety, Wid's Film and Film Folk

Newspapers

Albany Evening News, Atlanta Constitution, Auburn Citizen, Baltimore Sun, Bemidji Daily Pioneer, Bisbee Daily Review, Border Cities Star, Boston Daily Globe, Boston Globe, Boston Herald, Boston Post, Boston Sunday Globe, Brooklyn Daily Eagle, Brooklyn Standard Union, Buffalo Courier, Buffalo Courier-Express, Catholic News, Chicago Daily News, Chicago Daily Tribune, Chicago Examiner, Chicago Inter-Ocean, Chicago Tribune, Chillicothe Constitution, Cleveland Plain Dealer, Daily Review Atlas, Deseret News, Exhibitors Trade Review, Galveston Daily News, Goodwin's Weekly, Harrisburg Telegraph, Hattiesburg American, Hollywood Reporter, Holt County Sentinel, Iowa Atlantic Evening News,

Indianapolis Star, Ithaca Daily News, Kansas City Journal-Post, Kansas City Star, Kansas City Times, Lawrence Daily Journal-World, Long Island Daily Press, Los Angeles Daily Press, Los Angeles Times, Meriden Daily Journal, Millinery Trade Review, Milwaukee Sentinel, Moberly Monitor-Index and Democrat, Montana Standard, Motion Picture News, New Rochelle Pioneer, New York Call, New York Daily Call, New York Daily News, New York Clipper, New York Daily Mirror, New York Daily Star, New York Dramatic Mirror, New York Evening Post, New York Evening Telegram, New York Evening World, New York Herald, New York Herald Tribune, New York Journal-American, New York Morning Telegraph, New York Press, New York Sun, New York Times, New York Tribune, New York World, Oakland Tribune, Ogden Standard-Examiner, Olean Times-Herald, Oswego Palladium Times, Philadelphia Public Ledger, Pittsburgh Press, Rhinebeck Gazette, Richmond Times-Dispatch, Rochester Democrat, Rochester Post-Express, St Petersburg Times, Saint Petersburg Evening Independent, Salt Lake Tribune, San Diego Union-Tribune, Schenectady Gazette, Spokane Daily Chronicle, Syracuse Daily Journal, Syracuse Herald, Syracuse Post-Standard, Syracuse Journal, Wall Street Journal, Waterloo Evening Courier, Washington Herald, Washington Post, Washington Times, Wichita Daily Times

Websites

Ancestry.com

Archives.com

Archives of American Art. "Summary of the Elizabeth Puitti-Barth Papers, 1893-1954." http://www.aaa.si.edu/collections/elizabeth-puittibarth-papers-7135

Axmaker, Sean, 2011. "The Letter - Stage, Cinema and Jeanne Eagels in 1929." http://parallax-view.org/2011/09/13/the-letter-%E2%80%93-stage-cinema-and-jeanne-eagels-in-1929/

Broadway Photographs: http://broadway.cas.sc.edu/

Eagan, Daniel, 2018. "MoMA's 'To Save and Project' series offers wide-ranging discoveries." http://www.filmjournal.com/momas-save-and-project-series-offers-wide-ranging-discoveries

Fulton History: http://fultonhistory.com/

GenealogyBank.com

Genealogy.com

Hamlin, Mary P., Hoy, Cyrus (ed.) "Mary P. Hamlin: Memoirs and Letters. Volume XXX. Number 1. Autumn 1977." https://www.lib.rochester.edu/index.cfm?PAGE=3570

Internet Broadway Database: IBDB.com

Internet Movie Database: IMDB.com

JeanneEagels.com

Library of Congress: http://chroniclingamerica.loc.gov/

Media History Digital Library: http://mediahistoryproject.org/

Mint Theatre Company: http://minttheater.org

Motion Picture Newspapers.com

Newspapers.com

Playbill.com

Proquest.com

Thanhouser Company Film Preservation: Thanhouser.org.

Turner Classic Movies: TCM.com

Woodard, Eric, 2013. "Marilyn Monroe and Rain: The Project That Never Came to Be." http://www.examiner.com/marilyn-monroe-in-national/elisa-jordan

Index

Numbers in **bold** indicate photographs

Abbe, James 113-114
Abbott, George 101, 102-104, 106, 107, 109, 248-249, 317, 369, 387, 393
Ace of Hearts, The 35, 391
Ace, Goodman 215-216, 246, 371-372
Adams, Edie 459-460
Adams, Ida M. 111
Adams, Maude 43, 56, 344
Adventures of Angela, The 143
Akins, Zoë 144, 183, 224, 269, 291, 377, 424
Alfred, William 427-428
All About Eve 376, 424 432
All-Star Testimonial Performance, The 114-115
Amazons, The 34
Anderson, Judith 226, 237, 354, 361, 407, 426
Anna Christie 65, 441
Arbuckle, Macklyn 61, 62, 138, 386, 388, 393
Arey, Wayne **72**, 392
Arliss, Florence 74, 82, **95**, 386, 387
Arliss, George 73-75, 76-77, 82-83, 86, 87, **94, 95**, 111, 257, 345, 386, 387
Armitage, Pauline 435
Atkinson, J. Brooks 265
Auditore, Jimmy 140-141
Axmaker, Sean 341
Axwell, Jim 443

475

Badgley, Helen 77, **91**, 392
Bainter, Fay 100, 108, 113, 114, 183, 194, 221, **222**, 267, 269-270, 271, 304, 339, 408
Baker, Carroll 460
Bankhead, Tallulah 146, 165, 209-211, 244, 271, 311, 363, 405, 432, 442-443, 446, 452, **464**
Barcus, James S. 38, 385
Barnes, Clive 460
Barney, Marion 85, 387
Barrie, J. M. 73, 75, 196, 386
Barris, George 459
Barron, Mark 335, 443
Barrymore, Ethel 43, 76, 80, 183, 185, 188, 223, 248, 262, 269, 271, 286, 302, 312, 349, 393, 408
Barrymore, John 114, 262, 304, 393, 458
Barrymore, Lionel 37, 194, 279, 391, 393
Bates, Helen 13
Beal, George Brinton 234-235, 250, 340, 413
Belasco, David 30, 59, 87-88, 99-104, 106, 108, 111, 113, 116, **117**, 196, 242, 311, 354, 371, 372, 387, 403-404, 409, 410, 420
Bell, Monta 272, 280, 282, 284, 286, 290, **292**, 331, 333, 334, 336, 338, 342, 349, 350, 352-353, **359**, 394, 410
Bendel, Henri 104
Bening, Annette 461
Bennett, Constance 430
Bercovici, Konrad 188
Bergére, Ouida 338
Berlin, Irving 107, 115, 142, 183, 194, 383
Bickford, Charles 248
Binford, Lloyd T. 456
Blinn, Holbrook 113, **149**, 237, 266, 270, 394
Bloom, Thomas 182
Blume, Mary 262
Boothe, Clare 291
"Bowl, The" 221
Boys from Syracuse, The 195
Bradley, Lillian Trimble 126, 127, 388
Bradshaw, Jon 218
Brady, Alice 160
Brady, William 160
Brice, Fanny 43, **49**, 101, 194, 311, 315, 346
Bride of the Sea, The 35-37, **48**, 391
Brill, George 344
Broadhurst, George 126, 127, 131, 388
Broderick, Helen 28-29, 51-52, 383, 420, 423, 431, 434
Brook, Clive 349, 351
Brooke, Catherine 167, **203**, 389
Brooke, Cynthia 57, 386
Brooks, Joseph 57, 58, 61-62, 67, 111, 112, 385, 386
Broun, Heywood 172, 265
Brown, Chamberlain 421, 422
Brown, Georgia 6-7, 9, 10, 11, 20, **21**, **24**, 27, 29, 44, 59, 214, 218, 383, 433
Brown, John Mason 259, 427

Brown, Martin 145-146, 389
Brown, Sherman 304, 307
Brown, W. Graham **72**, 386
Bruhn, Lottie 318, **329**
Brunette, Dana 174
Buchman, Sidney R. 426
Budwin, Ray 239
Burke, Billie 33, 34, 35, 53, 79, 114, 142, 183, 185, 384
Burton, Richard 459
Bushell, Anthony 289, 301, 302, 305, **323**, 339, 342, 344, 345, 347, **355**, 390
Byfield, Ernest 314

Callahan, Dan 447-448
Callary, Kate 406
Carita 308
Carle, Richard 19-20, **45**, 383, 384
Carson, Johnny 428-429
Caruso, Enrico 235, 364
Catlett, Walter 450
Cecile, Sister Alma 5
Chadbourne, Thomas L. 125-126, 132-133, 134-135, 140, **147**, 170, 171, 193, 410
Chambers, C. Haddon 57, 385
Chandler, Jeff 433
Chanler, Bob 158, 188
Chaplin, Charlie 262, 278, 282, 333
Chappell, George S. 143
Chatterton, Ruth 114, 193, 351, 370
Chautard, Emile 77, 78, 80, **93**, 392, 393
Chicago 248-250, 257, 267, 317, 424, 425, 426
Churchill, Allen 100-101, 102
Claire, Ina 17, 28, 29, 88, **94**, 100, 114, 183, 185, 262, 287, 384, 387, 393
Clift, Montgomery 364-458
Cline, Louise 127
Coburn, Grace 40-41
Cochran, C.B. 197
Cohan, George M. 67, 99, 112, 114, 142, 310
Cohen, Alma 8
Cohn, Harry 433, 456
Colbert, Claudette 223-224, 338, 351, 426
Collins, Charles 404, 436
Colman, Ronald 145, 346
Colton, John 158-159, 161, 163, 166, 167, 168, 169, 171, 173, 212, 213, 246, 247, 279, 319, 338, 389, 394, 441, 459
Congai 344
Constant Wife 248
Cooper, Gladys 183, 289
Cope, John 102, 387
Cormack, Bartlett 350, 408
Cornell, Katherine 260, 290, 332, 409-410
Coward, Noel 210-211, 223, 250, 317, 373, 442
Cowl, Jane 113, 186, 188, 259, 337
Cowles, Dr Edward Spencer 361, 362, **379**, 398, 400-403, 406, 410

Coy, Edward "Ted" 184-185, 193, 201-202, **207**, 211, 215, 219-223, 224, 225, 226, **231**, **232**, 237, 238, 242, 246, 247, 249, 250-251, 258, 263, 269, 270, 285, 286, 291, 304, 305, 310, 313-319, 320, 321, **329**, 337, 348, 372, 377, 404, 410, 420, 425
Coy, Sophie 184, 201, 226
Crawford, Joan x, 262, 333, 364, 412, 428, 432, 448-452, 461, **463**
Crawford, Lester 29, 51, 384
Crinoline Girl, The 40-41, 42, 43, **47**, 244, 385
Crosby, Edward Harold 42
Cross Bearer, The 89-90, **96**, **97**, 191, 393
Crowther, Bosley 432, 456
Cukor, George 261-262, 390
Cunningham, Cecil 17-18, 32-33, 108, 140-141, 317, 384, 418-419
Currie, Lucille 413
Curtis, Marjorie A. 134

Daddies 99-106, 108, 110, 111, 113, **118**, **119**, **120**, **122**, 173, 235, 248, 387
Dahl, Arlene 376
Dale, Alan 174
Daly, Arnold 52, **70**, 392
Dangerous 431-432
Daniell, Henry 342, 395
Darrow, Clarence 238-239
Darrow, Ruby 239
Daver, Jack 460
Davies, Clara Novello 129, 182-183
Davies, Hubert Henry 54, 385
Davies, Marion 183, 305
Davis, Bette x, 261, 339, 376, 412, 428-429, 430-432, **440**
Dawn, Hazel 32, 86-87, 393
De Acosta, Mercedes 290, 311, 390, 409
De Limur, Jean 333, 335, 341, 342, 344, 345, 394
Dean, Basil 209-210
Deception 431-432
Deslys, Gaby 39, 128, 405
Destl, Mary 262, 349
Deval, Jacques 259, 390
Devil's Holiday, The 424
DeWitt, MacDonald 416
Dey, Harriet Hold 66
Dickstein, Martin 288
Dietrich, Marlene 452
Dietz, Howard 445, 446, 452
Dillman, Hugh 160
Dinehart, Alan 146, 185
Dirty Gertie from Harlem U.S.A. 453-455
Disappearance of Aimee, The 429
Disraeli 73, 76-77, 87, 257, 345, 386-387
Dodds, Richard 430
Doff, Aaron "Red" 437

Doherty, Edward xi, 3, 5, 7, 15, 17, 41, 51, 76, 99, 101, 102, 129, 130, 135, 140, 143, 145, 169, 170, 171, 182, 185, 193, 202, 213, 214, 226, 248, 283, 285, 287, 305, 310, 312, 314, 315, 316, 321, 337, 339, 347, 350, 353, 354, 363, 369, 370, 373, 401, 403-404, 406, 408, 415, 416-417-421, 422, 423, 424, 432, 435, 437-438
Doll's House, A 259, 411
Drake, Josephine 271, 393
Draper, Muriel 39
Draper, Paul 39
Dressler, Marie 60, 108, 138
Drew, Jr., John 43, 271
Driscoll, Arthur S. 416
Driscoll, Charles P. 446
Dubinsky, Ben 11, 12, 13, 14, 15, 16, 18, **25**, 27, 28, 59, 111, 115, 214, 383, 443, 444
Dubinsky, Ed 11, 12, 13-14, 16, 17, 18, **25**, 27, 28, 59, 111, 115, 214, 383, 418, 420, 443, 444
Dubinsky, Maurice 11, 12, 13, 14, 15, 16, 17, 18, **25**, 27, 28, 31, 59, 111, 115, 214, 383, 418, 433, 443, 444
Duke, Vernon 445, 452
Dunaway, Faye 427-429
Dunne, Irene 412, 430
Durgin, Chester 288
Duse, Eleonora 44, 100, 425

Eagan, Daniel 67
Eagels, Julie see Lloyd, Dea
Eagles, Daniel Paul 11, 43, 221, 366, 367, **380**, 422
Eagles, Edna 2, 3, 18, 59, 320, 378, 406-407, 417
Eagles, Edward 2, 3
Eagles, Edward W. 2, 4, 9, 18-19, 106, 243, 423
Eagles, George 7, 9, 225, 320, **323**, 366, 367, **380**, 422
Eagles, Helen 4, 7, 11, 199, 214, 221-222, 278, 339, 345, 366, 368, **380**, 416, 417, 418, 422
Eagles, Julia 2, 3, 4, 15, 16, 18, 29, 106, 136, 137, 142, 143, 191, 214, 221-222, 243, 246, 313, 320, **323**, 348, 366, 367, 368, 377-378, **380**, 416-418, 422, 423, **439**, 449
Eagles, Leo 4, **21**, 106-107, 243, 368, 380, 408
Eagles, Tessie Marshall 7
Eaton, Hal 430, 432, 452
Efflund, Dale 345-346
Eissing, Louise 140
Elliott, Maxine 60, 125, 135, 164, 170, 172, 174, **177**, 181, 182, 183, 193, 199, 211, 248, 304, 389
Elliott, Robert 167, **178**, 389
Ellis, Edward 248
Ellis, Mary 131
Eltinge, Julian 40-42, 43, **49**, 182, 244, 385
Emerson, John 196, 385
Erlanger, A. L. 30, 32, 43, 52, 53, 55, 57, 74, 77, 86, 112, 113, 384, 385, 386, 387
Errico, Melissa 447
Escape 271, 291
Espinosa, Eden 461
Evening of Happiness 144
Everett, Francine 454-455, **464**
Everything 107

Fall of Eve, The 224
Fallen Angels 211
Fante, John 435
Farrar, Geraldine 164
Faviéres, Guy 88, **94**, 387, 393
Faye, Alice 452
Ferguson, Elsie 52, 53, 55, 56, **71**, 142, 144, 159, 164, 262, 423, 435
Ferrer, José 456
Fiedler, Arthur 85, 141, **147**, 236-237, 409
Fiedler, Johanna 409
Film Stars Don't Die in Liverpool 461
Fires of Youth, The 77-80, **91**, 272, 392
Fitzgerald, F. Scott 156, 220-221, 318-319
Fitzpatrick, Kevin C. 107-108
Flinn, Caryl 446
Flint, Gustave 266
Folsey, George 333, 334, 335, 349
Fontanne, Lynn 114, 223, 354
Footloose 132
Forrest, Sam 17, 142, 143, 145, 166, 168-169, 170, 171, 190, 238, 248, 389, 442
Fort, Garrett 342, 349, 394, 395
Fraser, Winifred 109, 387
"Freshest Boy, The" 220, 318
Frohman, Charles 30, 33, 34, 43, 68, 100, 112, 159, 331, 384
Frohman, Daniel 67, 68, 108, 259, 260, 331, 386
Fuchs, Daniel 435

Gabriel, Gilbert 265
Gaines, Davis 447
Galanter, Ted 434
Gallagher, Desmond 425
Gallagher, Red 305
Galli-Curci, Amelita 131, 394
Garbo, Greta 65, 260-261, 272, 281, 282, 285, 288, 333, 364, 424, 450, 459
Garden of Eden, The 244
Garrick Gaieties, The 218
Gavner, Jack 445
Gentleman's Mother, A 17, 145-146, 155, 346, 389
Gerstein, Evelyn 162, 321, 338, 348
Gettler, Dr. Alexander O. 365, 398
Gilbert, John 260, 272, 280-281, 282, 285-287, **292, 293, 294**, 304, 345, 394
Gilks, Alfred 342
Gillis, James M. 365
Gillmore, Frank 312, 339
Gish, Dorothy 37, 183, 218, 247, 391
Gish, Lillian 37, 247, 391
Goetz, Ruth 195
Goldbeck, Elisabeth 17, 418
Golden, Eve 285
Goldman, Herbert G. 101, 102
Gonzales, Dr. Thomas A. 362
Goodman, Philip 195

INDEX

Gordon, Douglas 55
Gordon, Richard 38, 385
Gordon, Ruth 86-87, 133, 187-188, 211, 224, 269, 312, 313, 317, 342, 373, 409
Goulding, Edmund 183, 424
Governor's Boss, The 38, 41, 385
Graham, Geraldine Miller 192
Grahame, Gloria 461
Grant, Hank 459
Great Pursuit, The 57-58, **72**, 87, 385-386
Green, Abel 451
Greenson, Dr. Ralph 406
Greenwood, Charlotte 284
Greeves, William 455
Griffith, D.W. 37, 189, 391
Groody, Louise 140
Gross, Pearl 306
Guiles, Fred Lawrence 458

Haggin, Ben Ali 88, **94**, 393
Haines, William 283
Half-Way Girl, The 238
Hall, Everett Hudson 355
Hall, Georgia Lee 211, 364
Hall, Reverend Edward 167
Hamilton 82-84, 85, 86, 87, **95**, 257, 387
Hamlet 7, 44
Hamlin, Mary P. 87, 387
Hammond, Percy 172-173, 263-264, 427
Harlow, Jean x, 433, 443-449
Harris, Julie 432
Harris, Sam 141, 142, 143, 145, 146, 159-160, 161, 166, 167, 168, 170, 171, 174, 182, 183, 185, 187, 190, 192, 193, 196, 197, 199, 200, 212, 218, 224, 246, 247, 248-249, 250, 290, 291, 308, 309, 311, 312, 338, 348, 351, 353, 363-364, 372-373, 377, 389, 410, 425, 435, 442
Harrison, Paul 261, 442, 452
Hart, Lorenz 113, 218
Hastings, Selina 156-157, 159
Havoc, June 446-447, **464**
Haxton, Gerald 157
Hayden, Katherine 212
Hayes, Helen 108-109, 411
Hayman, Al 30
Hays, Will 241, 278, 279, 281, 290, 300, 399
Hayworth, Rita 432-433, 455-456, **465**
Healy, Harold **178**, 244, 389, 390
Heffernan, Harold 452
Heggie, O.P. **359**, 395
Heitmarek, Rudolph 402
Hepburn, Audrey **206**
Her Cardboard Lover 259-266, 269, 271, **273**, **274**, 283, 288-291, 297-306, 309, 310, 312, **323**, 332, 338, 342, 390, 404, 425
Her Godson 99
Hergesheimer, Joseph 183

481

Hervey, Harry 344
Hill, George Roy 457
Hirsch, Foster 195
Hobbes, Halliwell 342, 343, 352, **357**, 395
Hobble, John L. 103, 387
Hoffman, Samuel 268
Hoglund, Jennie 362
Holland, George 189-190, 202, 226
Holman, Libby 349
Holmes, Rapley 43, **49**, 167, **203**, 246, 389, 390
Holstein, Harold 87
Hopkins, Arthur 142, 143
Hopkins, Miriam 244
Hopper, Edna Wallace 41-42, 384
Hopper, Hedda 457
Hopwood, Avery 244
Hornblow, Arthur 84, 136, 141
Houdini, Harry 107, 108
House of Fear, The 52-53, **70**, 392
Howard, Leslie 183, 259, 264, 265, 267-268, 269, 270, 271, **273**, 288, 291, 302, 390
Howard, Leslie Ruth 259
Howland, Jobyna 144, 183
Hudson, Teddy 33
Huie, William Bradford 448
Hull, Henry 139
Huston, Walter 195, 338, 351, **463**

I'll Cry Tomorrow 376
In the Night Watch 133-136, 137, 138, 140, **149, 150, 151**, 155, 235, 286, 388

James, Patterson 167-168
Jazz Singer, The 313, 331
Jealousy 304, 339, 342-353, **356, 357, 358**, 365, 395, 431, 457
Jeanne Eagels 433-438, **440**
John Gilbert: Last of the Silent Stars 285
Johnson, Carl 13
Johnston, Agnes Christine 77, 392
Johnston, Kristen 424
Judith of Bethulia 37, 391-392
Jumping Jupiter 19-20, 28-30, **45, 46**, 51, 287, 383-384, 423

Kaufman, George S. 424
Kehr, Dave 341
Kellow, Brian 446
Kelly, Gregory 87, 211
Kelly, Robert 167, 183, **203**, 389
Kennedy, John B. 10, 161, 162, 163, 258
Kennedy, Kathryne 223, 365-366, 389, 407, 410
Kenyon, Doris 238
Kettering, Ralph 302, 305
Kid Boots 226
Kilgallen, Dorothy 240, 432, 457

King, Edith 104, 386, 387
King, Shirley 167, **203**, 389, 390
Kiss in the Taxi, A 223-224
Klaw, Marcus 30, 32, 40, 52, 53, 55, 57, 67, 74, 77, 86, 112, 113, 384, 385, 386, 387
Kleno, Larry 433
Klumph, Helen 278
Knowles, Margaret 8, 9, 215, 217, 420
Krug, Karl E. 309
Kuba, Raydona 247, 258-259

"Ladies of the Box Office" 218
Lady, The see *Gentleman's Mother, A*
Laemmle, Carl 131
Lahr, Bert 311, 390
Laird, Landon 216, 217, 251
Lamour, Dorothy 452-453
Lange, Paul 215, 217
Larrimore, Francine 142, 159, 195, 250, 267, 426, 430, **440**, 442
Larson, Christina 353, 362, 418
LaSalle, Mick 287
Lasky, Jesse L. 196, 260, 263, 313, 331, 332, 347-348, 364
Lathrop, Monroe 240-241
Laughing Lady, The 349-351, 353, 408
Laughter of Fools 68, 386
Laurell, Kay 76, 405
Lawrence, Clem 266
Le Clair, Blanche 347, 355
Leary, George and Julia 105
Leary, Gilda 143
Lee, Sonia 451
Leigh, Roland 211
Lena, Giuseppe **93**
Leroux, Madeleine 460-461, **465**
Lesson in Bridge, A 37, 41, 43, **48**, 391
Letter, The 332-336, 339-342, 347, 349, **358**, **359**, **360**, 370, 394-395, 405, 430-431
Levian, Sonya 435
Levy, Alan 459
Lewis, Robert 165, 411
Lewis, Sheldon 52, 392
Lillie, Beatrice 44, 285, 361, 363, 422, 442
Lind, Jenny 27
Lindbergh, Charles 167, 279, 285
Lindo, Olga 210, 211
Lloyd, Dea 421-423
Loftus, Cecilia 193, 405
Londré, Felicia Hardison 213
Lonergan, Philip 62, 63, 392
Love 261, 272, 282, 424
Love, Montagu 57, 89, **97**, 386, 393
Loves of Sunya, The 278
Lowe, Edmund 136, 138, 286, 388
Lusk, Norbert 288

Luttrell, Helen 40, 41

Mack, Willard 310
Mackensen, Al 11
Mackey, Eunice 32
Madonna of the Slums, The 131, **149**, 266, 394
Mall, Anna Belle 8, 19
Malone, Ruth M. 8, 19
Maloney, Joseph 9
Mamoulian, Rouben 452
Man, Woman and Sin 280, 283-288, 291, **292, 293, 294**, 331, 333, 345, 394
Manning, Bishop William T. 403
Mantle, Burns 167, 168, 172, 265, 271, 374, 427
Manulis, Martin 437
March, Fredric 345, 351, 352, **357**, 395, 457, 459, 460
Marlow, Ann 457, 458
Marlowe, Julia 186
Marsh, Mae 111, 189, 391
Marshall, Herbert 333, 335, 340, 341, 394, 431
Maude, Margery 74, 76, 87
Maugham, W. Somerset 156-158, 159, 161, 163, 167, 173, **175**, 186-187, 191, 193, 210-211, 246, 247, 248, 277, 278, 279, 332, 345, 376-377, 389, 394, 409, 432, 441, 442, 453, 456, 457, 458-459, 460, 462
Mayer, Louis B. 260, 282, 345
McAvoy, May 313
McGuire, William Anthony 142
McIntyre, O.O. 371
McKellar, Helen 424
McNulty, Charles 462
McRae, Bruce 57, 87, 109, **119**, 386, 387
Mei, Lady Tsen 333, **360**, 395
Mencken, H. L. 157-158, 159, 168
Menken, Helen 315
Mentel, Ken 429-430
Merlo, Anthony 89, **96**, 393
Merman, Ethel 445-446, 447
Merrick, Mollie 450
Milestone, Lewis 448, 450
Miller, Gilbert 260, 271, 390
Mills, Eleanor 167
Mind-the-Paint Girl, The 33-34, **47**, 384
Miss Sadie Thompson 432, 455-456, **465**
"Miss Thompson" 156-159, 163, 173, 186, 279, 450
Mok, Michel 444, 445
Monroe, Marilyn x, xi, 262, 406, 408, 427, 433, 456-459, 460, **465**
Montague, John 304, 425
Moon and Sixpence, The 191, 457
Moonflower 144
Moore, Robin 85, 141, 237
Moore, W. Eugene 62, 64, 392
Moorehead, Agnes 433
Mooser, Harriet and Minnie 244

Morehouse, Ward 158, 159, 160, 172, 186, 258, 266, 267, 288, 291, 310, 322, 338, 362, 365, 376-377, 426, 435
Morgan, Helen 350, 351
Morton, Michael 134, 388
Mother of Christ, The 290
Mr. Belvedere Goes to College 376
Munsey, Frank A. 43, 136, 202, 226
Murdock, Ann 68
Murray Hill 271
My Lady's Lips 143, 145
My Memory of Jeanne Eagels 423
Myself Among Others 187-188, 269

Nash, Florence 185, 188
Nash, Mary 146
National Red Cross Pageant, The 88-89, 271, 387, 393
New Day, The 142
New York Radio Show, The 144-145, **153**
Newman, Alfred 376
Newman, Robert V. 426
Newsboy, The 18, 383
Nirdlinger, Samuel F. 30
No Greater Love 430
Noble, John 35, 36, 391
Norris, Dr. Charles 365, 402
Not a Saint 425
"Nothing But Hits" 185
Nothing Doing: A Tragic Vaudeville 427-429
Novak, Kim 408, 427, 433-438, **440**
Novello, Ivor 183, 189
Nugent, Elliott 376

O'Brien, Eugene **94**, 393
O'Brien, Scott 335
O'Neill, Barry 289, 301, 305, 309, 320, 321, **323**, 337, 338, 339, 353, 363, 364, 390, 410, 426
O'Neill, Eugene 65, 156, 172, 354, 441
O'Neill, Terry 428
Odets, Clifford 411
Of Human Bondage 156, 409
Old-Fashioned Girl, An 424
Oppenheimer, George 460-461
Outcast 52-57, 58, 59, 60, 62, 65, **69, 70, 71**, 75, 87, 99, 144, 163, 164, 195, 385, 435
Outhwaite, Gilbert 337, 338-339, 347, 348, 350, 353
Overberg, Father J.A. 368
Owen, Reginald 333, **360**, 394

Parker, Dorothy 105, 107-108, 132, 173
Parkhurst, Genevieve 405
Parsons, Louella 277, 280, 340, 433, 447, 452, 458
Parton, Margaret 457
Patterson, Ada 4, 16
Pearl, Joshua 447

485

Pearley, Frank 308
Pellegrini, Dr. Alfred 362
Pickford, Mary 194, 218, 370, 452
Pickings from Puck 12, 15, 18, **25**, 383
Picture of Dorian Gray, The 200
Pierce, Noel 425, 427
Pinero, Sir Arthur Wing 33, 384
Pink Lady, The 17, 32-33, **47**, 86, 111, 384, 418
Pollock, Arthur 375, 442
Powell, William x, 143, 332, 351
Powers, James 263, 436
Prince of Wales 192, 200, 288-289
Professor's Love Story 73-75, 76, 87, 173, 196, 257, 386
Puitti-Barth, Elizabeth 85
Pygmalion 13, 115, 383

Quirk, James R. 371
Quirk, Lawrence J. 451

Rain x, 10, 17, 41, 43, 58-175, **175-179**, 181, 186-188, 190-191, 193, 194, 195, 197, 198, 199-200, 201, **203**, 209-213, 215-218, 222, 224-225, **228**, 233, 234, 236, 237, 238, 239-240, 241, 242-243, 244, 245-247, 248, 251, 260, 262, 263, 265, 267, 277-278, 279, 288, 289, 300-301, 305, 307, 308, 309, 310, 314, 316, 320, **327**, 338, 343, 347, 349, 354, 365, 373, 374-375, 376, 389-390, 404, 405, 407, 408, 411, 413, 419, 423, 425, 426, 429, 432, 434, 435, 441-462, **463**
Rain (1932) 448-451, **463**
Rain Girl, The xi, 102, 135, 140, 369-370, 401, 403, 406, 419-420, 423, 425, 432, 437, 438
Raines, Ron 447
Rambeau, Marjorie 160, 393
Rand, Sally 444-445, **464**
Randolph, Clemence 158, 159, 161, 166, 173, 188, 246, 279, 319, 349, 389, 441, 459
Rankin, William 430
Rathbone, Basil 290, 338
Rathburn, Stephen 426
Redemption 114
Reid, Wallace 399, 400, 416
Reilly, Rosa 335
Revolt of Mamie Stover, The 448
Riley, Thomas W. 54, 385
Rodgers, Richard 113, 218
Rogal, Samuel J. 156
Rosemary Pageant 88-89, **94**
Ross, Thomas 61, 62, 386
Roth, James 429
Roth, Lillian 376
Rough Perfect 109
Rowe, Billy 454
Rubinstein, Arthur 143
Ruby Fan, The 143
Russell, Jane 433, 488
Russell, Lillian 112
Ryan, Mary 142, 145, 159

Sadie Thompson 272, 277-280, 281-282, 285, 291, **295**, **296**, 299, 320, 432, 442, 450
Sadie Thompson (Broadway) 445-447, **464**
Saint, Eva Marie 432, 459
Sainted Wench, The 338
Sanders, Muriel G. see Draper, Muriel
Sansonavitch, Ivan **93**
Savage, Madame Marie 129, 130, 136, **147**, 165, 171, 181, 182, 317, 342, 420, 433
Schanke, Robert A. 290
Schenck, Joseph 182, 279, 282
Schertzinger, Victor 349
Scheuer, Philip K. 319, 437
Schmaille, G.D. 419
Schoell, William 451
Schuyler, Betsy 247
Scott, Cyril 133, 140, 338
See, Alfred S. 138
Selwyn, Arch 146, 244
Selwyn, Edgar 113, 146
Serling, Rod 458-459, 460
Sex 289, 321, 410
Sheaffer, Lew 303
Shear, Rhonda 429-430
Shearer, Norma 333
Sheehan, Peter 346
Sherman, Vincent 431
Sherwood, Robert E. 441
Shields, David 53-54
Shonnard, Horatio 226
Shooting Star 321, 425-427, **440**
Shubert, Lee 195
Sidney, George 434, 436, 437
Sitgreaves, Beverly 43-44, 426, 433
Sitting Pretty 15, 39, 134, 140
Slave Girl, A 18, 383
Smith, Agnes 66
Smith, Anna Nicole 406
Smith, David L. 140
Smith, Queenie 193, 425
So Help Me God! 424-425
Somebody's Luggage 59
Stanwyck, Barbara x, 447-448
Stapp, Ruby 4-5, 7, 214-215, 420
Stark, Harold 164, 173-174
Stenn, David 425
Stevens, Emily 132, 142, 405
Storm Song 426
Strange Interlude 172, 354
Strasberg, Lee 165, 166, 375, 411, 458, 459
Strictly Dishonorable 262
Sturges, Preston 262, 349
Styne, Jule 447
Sullivan, Ed 364, 421

Sullivan, Eugene 3
Sulzer, William 38
Sunrise 142
Sunset Boulevard 291, 341-342
Suskin, Steven 447
Swan, Gilbert 421, 424
Swanson, Gloria 272, 277-280, 282, 285, 291, **295, 296**, 299, 320, 341, 349, 432, 450
Sweet, Blanche 37, 65, 391
Sweet, Ossian 238-239
Swenson, Karen 285
Swift, William E. 402-403

Tallulah: My Autobiography 146
Talmadge, Constance 182
Talmadge, Norma 146, 182
Tanguay, Eva 14
Tarkington, Booth 33, 87
Tarnish 210
Taylor, Laurette 101, 126, 144, 183, 259-260, 261, 405, 458, 459
Taylor, Orville 315
Telling the World 283
Tempelman, Thecla 8, 19
Tempest, Marie 43, 57, 60, 386
Terry, Phyllis Neilson 57, 386
Thanhouser, Edward 62, 392
This Side of Paradise 220-221
Thompson, Wilma 223, 237, 243, 246, 248, 257, 309, 390
Thurber, Kent 170-171, **178**, 195, 389, 435
Tolstoy, Leo 114, 261
Top o' the Hill 364
Tracy, Spencer 458
Travers, Madeline 111
Troutman, Ivy **94**
Turner, Peter 461
Tyler, George C. 74, 75-76, 386, 387, 388
Ullman, Sol 402-403
Ulric, Lenore 100, 183, 241
Uncle Tom's Cabin 7, 383
Under False Colors 80-82, **92, 93**, 393
Unfaithful, The 431
Uterhart, Henry A. 309-310

Valente, Judge Louis A. 416
Valentino, Rudolph 185, 186, 192, 363, 364
Van Vooren, Monique 457, **465**
Varying Show, The 144
Venable, Reginald 221, 269, 270

Wagner, Paul 184, 202, 221, 317-318
Wainscott, Ronald J. 411, 441
Wald, Jerry 447, 448
Walder, Mayo 85-86, 141

Waller, John 167, **203**, 389, 444
Walsh, Raoul 277, 278, 279, 282, **296**
Wanger, Walter 336, 351, 364
Warde, Frederick 76, 77, 80, 81, **91**, **93**, 392, 393
Warren, George C. 166
Warren, Jr., Whitney 191-193, 194, 202, **206**, 310, 319, 336, 337, 338, 410
Warren, Sr., Whitney 191, 192, 194
Warwick, Robert 133, 134, 138, 140, **150**, 388
Watkins, Maurine 248, 424
Waxman, A.P. 445, 452
Webb, Clifton 15-16, 38-39, 88, **94**, 114, 138, 139, 140, 141, 144, **147**, 169, 183, 191, 211, 307-308, 315, 317, 336, 338, 351, 353, 361, 363, 364, 368-369, 376, 393, 404, 408, 410, 420
Webb, Mabelle 38, 39, 138, 141, **147**, 225, 353, 361, 363, 364, 373, 401, 420, 422-423
Weissmuller, Johnny 350
Weitzel, Edward 79
Wells, Leila Burton 142
West, Alice Pardoe 245
West, Mae x, 289, 309, 321, 410
What's Your Husband Doing? 61, 386
When Women Love 18, 383
Whitaker, Alma 241-242
White Rose, The 188-189
White, Glen **48**
Wilcox, Emma 389, 390, 444
Wilde, Oscar 200
Wilder, Billy 341, 459
Wildflower 194
Williams, John D. 158, 159, 167, 168, 169, 170, 212, 343-344, 373, 389, 395, 435
Williams, Spencer 453, 454, 455
Wilson, Earl 460
Wilson, Elizabeth 223
Wilson, Francis 68, 386
Winchell, Walter 337, 338
With a Feather in My Nose 34
Withers, Isabel 224, 244-245
Witherspoon, Cora 224
Wodehouse, P. G. 260, 263, 390
Wolf, Peter 427
Woman in the Wheat, The 424
Wonderful Thing, The 126-129, 131-132, **148**, 374, 388, 394
Woods, A.H. 41, 142, 223-224, 259-260, 288, 304, 306, 331, 385, 390, 425
Woollcott, Alexander 115, 127, 172, 194, 264, 374
World and the Woman, The 62, 63-67, **72**, 78, 290, 392
Wyler, William 431
Wyngate, Valerie 259, 390

Young Man's Fancy, A 113-114, 115-116, **123**, 388
Young, Roland 143

Ziegfeld Follies 28, 29, 34, 108, 112, 447
Ziegfeld, Florenz 34, 76, 101, 112, 196, 218
Zimmerman, Frederick 30

Zirilli, Jared 461
Zukor, Adolph 263, 331, 442

www.ingramcontent.com/pod-product-compliance
Lightning Source LLC
Chambersburg PA
CBHW070159240426

43671CB00007B/490